"A LIVELY PORTRAIT . . . TERRIFICALLY ENTERTAINING."
—*Los Angeles Times*

"Read the book for Noonan's sense of what went on around Reagan . . . how things operate behind the closed doors you and I never enter. And delight in her command of words. She writes like an angel. . . . Beyond the sound bites stands an impressive talent. . . . An often funny, engaging story."

—*Houston Chronicle*

"A literate, sometimes hilarious, occasionally scary account of what went on behind the scenes—of who manipulated, who backstabbed, who were the good guys and bad guys."

—*Chicago Tribune*

"Fresh and funny . . . The most piercing—and damning—insights yet offered about those who made the key decisions and filled the key posts in the Reagan years."

—*The San Diego Union*

"There's no doubt that this lady can write and write well. . . . More than once you find yourself nodding in agreement at the expert way in which she sums up her feelings, no matter your political persuasion. . . . By the time you've finished the book you know her as a person and want her as a best friend."

—*The West Coast Review of Books*

"An engaging book, now funny, now poignant."

—*USA Today*

"A welcome oasis in the desert of political memoirs . . . *What I Saw at the Revolution* is likely to be the most honest, lucid and enjoyable look at the Reagan White House that we'll get."

—*The Dallas Morning News*

PEGGY NOONAN

WHAT I SAW AT THE REVOLUTION

A Political Life in the Reagan Era

Fawcett Columbine • New York

A Fawcett Columbine Book
Published by Ballantine Books

Copyright © 1990 by Peggy Noonan

All rights reserved under International and Pan-American Copyright Conventions. Published in the United States by Ballantine Books, a division of Random House, Inc., New York, and simultaneously in Canada by Random House of Canada Limited, Toronto.

Grateful acknowledgment is made to the following for permission to reprint previously published material:

CPP/BELWIN, INC.: Excerpt from the song lyrics "Blue Moon" by Lorenz Hart and Richard Rodgers. Copyright 1934 by Metro-Goldwyn-Mayer, Inc. Copyright renewed 1961, 1962, by Metro-Goldwyn-Mayer, Inc. Rights throughout the world controlled by Robbins Music Corporation. All rights assigned to EMI Catalogue Partnership. All rights controlled and administered by EMI Robbins Catalog, Inc. International copyright secured. Made in USA. All rights reserved. Reprinted by permission of CPP/Belwin, Inc. Excerpt from lyrics "When Your Old Wedding Ring Was New" by Charles McCarthy, Joe Solieri, and Bert Douglas. Copyright 1935 by Mills Music, Inc. Copyright renewed. All rights reserved. Reprinted by permission.

HARCOURT BRACE & COMPANY, AND FABER AND FABER PUBLISHERS: Excerpt from "The Love Song of J. Alfred Prufrock" from Collected Poems, 1909-1962 by T. S. Eliot. Copyright 1936 by Harcourt Brace & Company. Copyright renewed 1964, 1963, by T. S. Eliot. Rights throughout Canada and the Open Market administered by Faber and Faber Publishers. Reprinted by permission of Harcourt Brace & Company, and Faber and Faber Publishers.

SIMON AND SCHUSTER: Excerpt from "Second Coming" from The Poems of William Butler Yeats: A New Edition edited by Richard J. Finneran. Copyright 1924 by Macmillan Publishing Company. Copyright renewed 1952 by Bertha Georgie Yeats. Reprinted by permission of Simon and Schuster. Excerpt from "Bryan, Bryan, Bryan" from Collected Poems of Vachel Lindsay. Copyright 1920 by Macmillan Publishing Company. Copyright renewed 1948 by Elizabeth C. Lindsay. Reprinted by permission of Simon and Schuster.

NEW DIRECTIONS PUBLISHING CORPORATION: Excerpt from "Danse Russe" from William Carlos Williams: Collected Poems, Volume I, 1909-1939. Copyright 1938 by New Directions Publishing Corporation. Reprinted by permission of New Directions Publishing Corporation.

http://www.randomhouse.com

Library of Congress Catalog Card Number: 97-90335

ISBN: 0-449-00100-8

This edition published by arrangement with Random House, Inc.

Manufactured in the United States of America

First Ballantine Books Mass Market Edition: March 1991
First Ballantine Books Trade Edition: July 1997

10 9 8 7 6 5 4 3 2 1

To the Noonans—
Mary Jane, Jim, Barbara, Cookie,
Kathy, Jimmy, Patty, Dorian—and Will

ACKNOWLEDGMENTS

Many people in Washington talked to me about the meaning of the Reagan era and helped while I was researching and thinking out this book. Some gave me interviews that stretched over weeks, some talked for an hour, all gave me great and generous assistance. Among them: Dick Armey, Gary Bauer, William Bennett, Pat Buchanan, George Bush, Dick Darman, Ben Elliott, Craig Fuller, Michael Horowitz, Marlin Fitzwater, Newt Gingrich, Fred Khedouri, Mari Maseng, Nancy Reynolds, Joe Sobran, Lesley Stahl, Alessandra Stanley, Paul Weyrich.

Some people spoke to me privately. Sometimes they're quoted without attribution; sometimes they're not quoted but gave me thoughts and ideas I happily appropriated. To all, my thanks.

A first book is an exciting trauma. I thank my mother and father, who came down to Washington to help me in the final stages. I thank the friends and family without whom—Christie Beck of Mansfield, Ohio, Terri Belli, Emily Byrne, Pat Byrne, Peggy Byrne, Mary Cole, Joe Condo, Jack Edwards, Margaret Edwards, Rosemary Edwards, Ramona Dunn, Patty Egan, Ken Gellman, Janis Kinzie, Patty Lewis, Barbara Noonan, Cookie Noonan, Dorian Noonan, Jim Noonan, Judy

Fertig Panneton, Dan Rather, Amy Roberts, Joe Scarpelli, Kathy Scarpelli, Carol Schneider, Lisa Schwarzbaum, Lesley Stahl, Kathy Van Winkle.

I thank Anne Edwards and Tom Skrabak Edwards. At the end, near deadline, Tom took three weeks off from his life to print out, collate, and make coherent this manuscript. Anne gave me, gratis, the summer of 1989, during which every day she came to my house, talked politics with the baby and made sure I ate my dinner.

Carlos Bonilla left work in Washington and drove through the Virginia countryside the day after a blizzard to retrieve two chapters my computer and I had erased. It had been a difficult section to write, and I sat, pale with panic, as he said cheerful things such as, "Computers don't really erase. They just take the label off and throw the file away, and if we try we'll probably retrieve large portions, which is how, by the way, they got Ollie." He succeeded.

Great thanks go to my editor, Peter Osnos, who helped find the book within the manuscript, and to Miss Esther Newberg, who when she is on your side is on your side.

CONTENTS

Introduction   xi
1 I Am Often Booed Because of Who My Friends Are   3
2 CBS   17
3 The President's House Is Many Mansions   39
4 I First Saw Him as a Foot   49
5 "Speech! Speech!"   68
6 I Am a Camera   93
7 Knee Deep in the Hoopla   120
8 Who Was That Masked Man?   149
9 New Terms   186
10 George Raft   201
11 *Ich Bin ein* Pain in the Neck   215
12 "That's Not off My Disk"   234
13 *Challenger*   252
14 Come Walk with Me   263
15 Summits   272
16 Leaving   280
17 A Thousand Points of Light   298
18 Hydroplaning   318
19 Hail and Farewell   325
Epilogue   339
Another Epilogue   343
Index   347

INTRODUCTION

Every now and then when I worked in the Reagan White House, I would look up from my notes at a meeting and look at the faces around the table or, walking the halls, look into the offices and see the young men and women with their heads bent over a report, and think, We are the ones who will walk behind the caisson. Someday when we're older he will die, and there will be a great funeral with a flag-draped coffin and a riderless horse with the boots turned backward, and behind that the family and friends, and behind them—us. The television cameras high up near the plywood anchor booths hastily assembled on Pennsylvania Avenue will go to a wide shot, and Dan Rather will say, "And there, the men and women who were the special assistants and the undersecretaries and perhaps a regular secretary or two, I hope. When you say Reagan administration, you're talking about them."

It wouldn't be sad. I could even imagine it as jolly. He would die with his boots on, "having known not . . . bitterness nor defeat." He would have just turned one hundred the day he was thrown from the horse that was bit by the snake as they paused in a gallop through the brush to watch the sun disappear behind the hills. He would have lived to see the Communist world break up, and seen us build the manned space station. An old man exhausted in a great struggle, one of the leaders of the eighties we now, in the year 2011, acknowledge to have been great—Reagan, Thatcher, John Paul II, perhaps Gorbachev—dead now, and here we are gathered once again, like the end of *Chariots of Fire*, where one of the old running stars, bent and gray, turns to a friend at Harold Abraham's funeral and says, "We did it, didn't we?," as the stern chords of "Jerusalem" boom from the cathedral.

When I left the White House I decided to write this book. In the past such things were expected of a few top aides and a speechwriter or two. John Kennedy would call out to Arthur Schlesinger, Jr., "Don't forget this for your book," and William Safire tells how Nixon used to introduce him, saying, "This is Safire. He's a fine fellow, but he's a writer, of course." Meaning: He's taking notes.

Most White House books have been written by men and have an unspoken subtitle: What I Did with Power. Many have another: If Only They'd Listened to Me, the Fools! But I didn't have much power, and sometimes if they'd listened to me they would have been wrong.

I grew up in the great days of White House memoirs—*A Thousand Days* by Schlesinger, *Kennedy* by Ted Sorensen, Safire's *Before the Fall*. For those who loved the genre, there were Judge Samuel Rosenman's memoirs of the New Deal, and Robert E. Sherwood's. It is that book that made me think of writing this one. I read it when I was new in the White House and looking for the flavor of things. Sherwood, of course, was a wonderful dramatist, author of *The Petrified Forest*, screenwriter of *The Best Years of Our Lives*, and I knew he had written the White House book I wanted to read, the human one, the one that tells you what it's like to be there and lean against the pillars. But he had not. What I found was a weighty, fact-filled tome that was without the sparkle I had expected. I was surprised. How could such a colorful dramatist write such a dull book? Then I thought, He did it on purpose, he thought if it was dull it would show he was serious, not just Broadway Bob but a man equal to the history he'd seen. I decided that if I ever wrote a White House book I would try to write the one I wished Sherwood had written.

At the heart of it, as of the era, is Reagan.

Every generation gets a president. My grandmother's was FDR. Long after the National Recovery Act was killed by the courts, Mary

Byrne kept a banner on the front-door window that said NRA—WE DO OUR PART. For my parents, it was JFK. "Ask not . . ." was real to them, and they were never the same and never felt the same about politics after he died. For me and for the young people I worked with in the White House, it was Reagan. We came to Washington because of him. He moved us. We loved him.

I used to see him walking through the halls, putting his hands together in the fighter's victory clasp, waving up at us on the old Executive Office Building balcony, nodding as he left the reception. I would wonder, What does he feel? This man of awesome cool warmth, so friendly and so remote, who in his eighth decade still roused himself each morning for the role and all its rigors—who was he?

I would see him in the last weeks of his presidency, after Iran-*contra*, at big Washington dinners: He sits far away on a long white dais; I watch him chat. He wears a tuxedo. I think, It's not easy for him anymore. I imagine him turning to us, surprised, as a thousand forks touch a thousand plates, and speaking for once his anguish:

"Eight years!" he would say. "And why do you think I did it? Eight years of dull, dead meetings and bureaucrats with big faces, eight years of late nights, long speeches, and sitting next to somebody's wife on the dais trying to pull some kind of life and spontaneity out of her flat little eyes. I was old! I wanted to take a nap and ride a horse. I think I'd earned a rest, if I do say so.

"But I loved America and I knew I'd give her the right leadership. I'm no intellectual or big theorist, but I know the few big things that if you get them right everything else falls into place. And look around— was there anyone better? I'm sorry to be such an egotist, but was there? And don't forget it worked! It pretty much worked."

Which is, in fact, correct.

This book is an attempt to catch and freeze an era before it fully recedes. It's about politics in its most essential sense: who "the people" are and what they want. Because I come from people who were part of the fruits of the FDR realignment—the Catholics of the big cities who fully adhered to the Democratic party in the thirties and forties and never meant to let go—and became myself part of the quiet realignment of the eighties, in which what had seemed in my youth the party of rich dullards became, almost in spite of itself, the party of the people—it is about me, and what led me to be the first of my family to become that dread thing, a Republican. It is about CBS, where I worked, about the media in general and their dance with politics. It is also about speechwriting, what it's like to be a writer in politics, a woman in politics, and a visitor for five years to its capital. From 1984 to 1986 I worked for Reagan; off and on in 1987 and then steadily through 1988 I worked for George Bush; it's about that too. But most of all, I suppose, it's about Reagan, the man at the center of the big turn, and what his presidency meant, and what I saw at the revolution.

This book has its own shape. It doesn't start in the usual way, with a moment of high drama—"I heard the shots, turned to the president, and saw a look of pain cross his usually amiable features as an agent forced him into the back of the car." I didn't see high drama, and I'm impatient with the formula even if I couldn't think of a better one. I just start at the beginning and end at the end. There are times when I express myself in a manner that might fairly be called idiosyncratic. Sometimes I experimented with writing speeches in free verse, which may give you an idea of what you're occasionally in for.

WHAT I SAW AT THE REVOLUTION

I Am Often Booed Because of Who My Friends Are

A few years ago I was in Tallahassee with the man I'd recently married, who was making a speech to a group of businessmen. When I was introduced from the dais, the speaker said, "Now Miss Noonan here worked for Dan Rather and then went on to work for Ronald Reagan, and not too many-people can say that!" When he said the word Rather a boo began to build, softly at first, then rising and spreading. But when they heard Reagan they became confused—He's my president, and, dammit, I like the old guy!—and the "oooooooohhhh" turned into an "eeeeehhh"—"Booooeeeeeeee!"— which finally made everyone laugh. "Well, you've certainly changed your mahnd, haven't you, sugar?" said a lady in a large hat. "Not really," I said, though I did not explain.

This is the nice part of who I like: Back a Christmas or two ago I received a letter from Dan Rather telling me he would not, as he had in years past, be sending me a Christmas present. Instead, he would make a donation in my name to my favorite charity, and did I have one? Indeed I did. I called his office and told his secretary I would like my gift to go to the William J. Casey Fund to help the Nicaraguan *contras*. There was a pause on the end of the line. And it would be good if you could remember to say it's in my name. Peggy, came the reply, don't worry: It will definitely be under your name. Later I heard Dan laughed and said, "She never gives up," which if true makes me proud. I got a nice mass card from Mrs. Casey, with a copy of Jeane Kirkpatrick's eulogy.

I have spent my professional life as a writer of speeches and broadcast news, and so I am perhaps abnormally attuned to the way people talk and the things they say. A drawback is that sometimes the voice of the person I'm writing for comes, unbidden, to the forefront and dominates my speech. When I worked for Rather I'd find myself saying, "You look like you been rode hard and put to bed wet," and "He's got a lot of off-road miles on him." When I worked for Reagan, I found myself going, "Well . . ."

Speechwriting is an odd profession, part policy-explainer, part hack, part . . . what? Innocent in a way, for speechwriters, no matter how long in the game, have to continue being moved as if for the first time by things like democracy; and speechwriters are, somehow, the kids of politics, itself in some ways a kid's game. Prohibited from policy, temperamentally unsuited, many of them, to political leadership, and consigned to a city that both esteems and dislikes writers, a city of powerful men on the Hill, in the agencies, who are often inarticulate and who dislike being reminded of their condition by the presence of a pale and nervous wordsmith—that's what they call them, word-smiths, as in "Get that wordsmith in here, I've got a great idea, but I don't have time to put it into words, flesh it out, find the music"— with a pad on his lap and watchful eyes and all these . . . unspoken yearnings. They are such lonely souls. They're mostly boys.

But what they do is important. I don't mean to make too much of it—rhetoric is only a small stream off the river of American prose—but in terms of politics it is the ocean you sail on or sink in. Ask Joe Biden. Or Ronald Reagan.

Think of the people who work in government. I come from where they don't come from. I'm going to ask you to sit back for a while as I tell you about it.

I was born smack-dab in the middle of the century, in Brooklyn, New York, in 1950, the third in an Irish-Catholic family of seven children.

After two girls my parents hoped for a boy, and my mother got the news as the doctor handed me to a nurse. "At least this is one child who won't have to go to war," he said. A week later MacArthur landed at Inchon.

We lived in Brooklyn and my father was a merchant seaman. When I was five, we joined the migration from the cities and moved to Massapequa, Long Island. My parents, like all of their friends, left the city to get a lawn and let the kids ride their bikes in the streets. Everybody had a tree, and all the neighbors got to know each other. My father became an appliance salesman at Friendly Frost and then E. J. Korvettes, which people at the time thought stood for Eight Jewish Korean War Veterans.

It was a world of different rules and different facts, a world of people getting by, a world that carried within it an immutable fact: Not everything is possible, you can't have everything, and that's not bad, that's life.

Like most baby boomers, I live this paradox: Nothing really memorable happened in my childhood, yet I think about it all the time. No blitz, no holocaust, no depression, just us and the childhoods we cannot leave behind. We'll be watching TV, and a black-and-white movie from the thirties will come on with an old lush score, and there will be a shot of a woman's hand opening a picture album with the credits on each page—and suddenly we are overwhelmed. Such longing, such nostalgia and remorse, such sadness about . . . something or other. We surrender to reverie and tumble back in time.

I think of the old ones we grew up with, the immigrants of Europe who were our grandparents and great-uncles, who taught us to go to church and pray to God and if you work hard you could become somebody. Show respect, love your country, stop complaining!

Here is my great-aunt Jane Jane, my grandfather's sister and my parents' friend, Jane Jane who received her nickname from a stuttering child and who worked as a domestic in the great houses of New York and Connecticut. She came over from Ireland in 1912. She was smart and funny, and when she visited us, she would walk through the house reciting poetry—"Oh London is a man's town, there's power in the air / and Paris is a woman's town with flowers in her hair. . . ."

She never married, but not for lack of suitors. "A man once told me I have ears like seashells," she would say, and "Once after a great dinner one of the gentlemen came to the kitchen to compliment us, and he told me, 'And you, young lady, are a beauty.' That was Black Jack Bouvier, who looked like Clark Gable."

She knew things before being told. It ran in the family. Her brother Jimbo was still in Ireland, but they didn't need the mails. Jane Jane learned things in her dreams. So-and-so is going to die, this one is sick. She knew my grandfather was dead the morning he died, and told everyone before the call came. (When my sister Cookie wanted to scare me, she'd say, "Yeah? Well, I was talking to Jane Jane, and she had a *dream* about you. I asked her what, and she wouldn't tell me. And then she started to *cry.*") Jimbo used to tell people there was no point going to mass anymore, a revolution was coming and they'd stop saying the mass in Latin and go to playing banjos and clapping.

Jane Jane told us of how everyone on the Belfast docks knew the *Titanic* would go down. "The workers at night heard the wailing of the banshee!" And then she foretold the strangest story of all. An Irish Catholic with blue eyes and red hair would be elected president of the United States but it didn't matter because they'd shoot him. I cannot tell you how startling this was to hear in the fifties.

We were in love with the Kennedys. They were Irish Catholic just like us, and they were smart and glamorous with their tuxedos and silk dresses, and they always said the right thing and had a wonderful humor—and with a little time and money and education we could be just like them. They opened the doors of American glamour to the working class.

I bought two goldfish at Woolworth's and called them Jack and Jackie. I cleaned out the chicken coop at Aunt Etta's, out in Suffolk County where the potato fields were, and made it into the John F. Kennedy Fan Club. I called it the Pro-K's. I made speeches to the chickens. One day my mother, who had joined the Massapequa Democratic Club, came home with a handful of Kennedy-Johnson bumper stickers and a black hat with sparkly little rhinestones and the name "Kennedy" spelled out with little black donkeys. She wore it to upset Mrs. McCormack down the block, who was Irish but for Nixon. I plastered every car within a mile with bumper stickers and handed out campaign literature door-to-door. I was so swept away that when my fifth-grade teacher, Miss Scott, told my mother I didn't do my homework, I explained, seriously, that I was too busy with the campaign.

It is the Saturday before the election on Long Island, in New York, in the autumn of 1960, the autumn of a world that does not know that it is leaving.

It is crisp and fall and a yellow plastic Philco plays "Tequila" in the sun. It is crisp and fall and mothers burn leaves on the street. They stand like soldiers, rakes held high, poking the fires in the big metal cans, shooing the children away.

The mothers poked the fires and the children gathered leaves, and above them the air of the Eastern Seaboard was awash in the thick sweet acrid smell of a million burning leaves.

Late in the morning I got on my bike and met my friend Tommy, and we went campaigning. We tied kitchen pots to the handlebars and got some big spoons and rode along the streets beating the pots and chanting, "Vote Row C and you will see / What the Democrats do for you and me." This is what we pedaled past:

We rode by the little Cape Cod houses and split-levels of Massapequa, Long Island, in 1960, and it was a different time, a different place. Life was lived somehow more obviously. You could go by the front of a house and hear the sounds within, the sounds of a family, living: shouts and laughs and the TV and loud words and a door slammed.

Through the thin trees of a suburb newly settled you could see the houses and in the houses were people who had moved here from the cities—first-generation Americans!—and they brought with them the rhythms of the people of Brooklyn and Queens and Germantown. The immigrants of Europe were their parents, who were getting old and dying; the children and grandchildren would come in from the Island to the city for the funeral. But even as the old ones were dying they set a tone, an Old World tone, an emotional tone where people yelled and threw their hands out and beseeched and pointed—

People yelled then!

You could pedal by the houses, the Capes and track houses and split-levels, and hear the tones of domestic drama. You could see a family drama acted out on the lawn in front of the house: a teenage daughter runs out, followed by a father running and screaming and a mother running and screaming and a hurled bowl of spaghetti and the mother catches the child and pulls her head back and the child yells, "I hate you!," and the mother yells, "You do that for everyone to see in fronna the whole naybuhhood—" and the lady next door yells over the hedge, "Are you people crazy for Chrissake!" And we'd stop and watch and move on and chant our chant.

This is what we pedaled past:

The flat beige newly built school and the empty parks and the little houses and the potsy line so deeply chalked that no rain could erase it, and the baseball diamond painted in the street by somebody's dutiful dad, past the hoods hanging out in front of the deli with their DAs and heavy jeans and leather jackets, over Sunrise Highway and through the parking lots of the big stores.

And the commonest sight in the suburbs, the emblem of the age, was a hefty woman heaving down the street, four children straggling behind her as she pulls roughly on the arm of the youngest, whose mouth is ringed like a clown's by a cherry ice; she is huge and old and tired, she is carrying her fifth child, and she is huge and old. She is thirty-two.

The fathers with a precious day off are painting and hammering in the garage. They are not wearing their uniforms—for this one is a conductor on the Long Island Rail Road and that one is a cop in the city and this one is a foreman at Grumman—but are dressed in stiff khaki slacks and a zippered jacket from when they were in Korea. Their skin is blue-white. They look soft and lost without their uniforms.

And people had Irish names and Italian and German and Polish names and they were mostly Catholic and Jewish, and they had city accents and said yiz, whatta yiz gonna do? I gave it to yiz and ya lost it.

It was the last age of big families. Every block had at least one family with seven or ten kids spilling out of the house onto the lawn and catching fireflies, playing catch.

And everyone had *Reader's Digest* Condensed Books and read them and the women had coffee klatches late in the morning and there was a round swirl of Entenmann's coffee cake and they would leave deep red lipstick marks on the coffee cups and they wore pedal pushers and bounced babies on their freckled knees and gossiped about . . . what? For no one had affairs, there was no intrigue, mothers were home, and fathers came home and no one knew the private lives of the famous.

There were songs that everyone knew and when they had the yearly party at the fire department, the volunteers and their wives sat at tables with plastic cloths and drank beer and sang "Toot, Toot, Tootsie,

Good-bye" and "Five Foot Two, Eyes of Blue." Everyone knew when the Second World War was, and some had lost a brother.

And the sound of the suburbs was the bell of the Good Humor and the soft cry of a child, and the theme song of the suburbs was heard through the screen door, "Roll along, wagon train . . ."

And no one wore seat belts and the cars were big and had colors like peach with big white fins and cream-colored real leather seats and families went to church and the fathers knew which priest gave the quickest mass and at Easter you got new black shiny shoes and a hat—you didn't get dressed up for work in those days, you got dressed up for church—and on Friday you had fish sticks and went to Carvel in the flat little shopping center sitting in the sun.

And grown-ups lowered their voices when the children walked into the room, so children walked quietly and made believe they weren't listening as the parents said in hushed tones, ". . . had a nervous breakdown." There was a neighborhood woman who was our celebrity because she tried to commit suicide. On the next block there was a boy who was the celebrity because he was going to go to college.

And that was the world we pedaled past. A different time, a different place, and it couldn't be so long ago because it was my life—but you don't have to be old in America to say of a world you lived in, That world is gone.

We swam in a neighbor's three-foot pool, holding our breath underwater to build up our endurance for when we'd be in the Peace Corps and natives would chase us. We wrote away for autographed pictures of the members of John F. Kennedy's Cabinet, and I papered my walls with pictures of Dean Rusk and Bobby. We played astronaut, taking the kitchen chairs out into the backyard, lying down, looking up at the clouds, and saying, "Ignition—lift-off—we have lift-off at T minus twenty and counting." Once in school, the day John Glenn went up, they rolled in a television, and it was exciting to be watching TV in class and seeing such a great thing, a man going into space. We read a poem called "High Flight" by an airman who was killed during World War II. "O I have slipped the surly bonds of Earth," it went, ". . . and touched the face of God."

We didn't have much money, and for a while my parents had little luck. My father worked hard, but wages were low, and making the situation worse was the fact that when you lived in the suburbs you had to have a car. In the city you took the subway for a quarter, but now my father spent his time worrying about tolls and gas. I can remember him saying at the gas station, "Gimme a dollar's worth," and the guy wouldn't blink. (Now my father is a star salesman at a big furniture outlet, and he wears a ring full of diamonds for every time he was Salesman of the Month. Now he says, 'Fill 'er up—and check the oil.")

Sometimes they turned off the electricity and sometimes they turned off the phone, which we kept proudly displayed in the kitchen nonetheless. That was a poorism. Poorisms are the habits and perceptions developed by people who are temporarily or permanently in financial distress. A poorism: For years I thought everyone in America bought their Christmas presents and the tree on Christmas Eve, I didn't know it was people looking for half price. A poorism: There are lamps and clocks in all the right places, but none of them work. Fix them? That costs money. Throw them away? Hey, it's a clock! (In the eighties when a TV news show would have a call-in thing where you get to register your opinion on an issue, the day after the results came in the young people at the networks would say, "But it's skewed in favor of the affluent, the poor didn't vote because they don't have the fifty cents." But of course the poor voted. They didn't think for a second about the fifty cents because for people just getting by a pleasure deferred is a pleasure denied. They'll worry about the bill another time.)

It couldn't have been so unusual to be a family with no money in that time and place, but there was no acknowledgment of it as a human problem. It was just assumed that people had enough to pay the mortgage and the bills and buy food, and if they didn't—well, the polite thing is not to notice. Back then it was shameful, and I felt the bite. (A few years later the Democratic party made us more aware of how it is for people who don't have much, and that was good. But the culture of resentment the Democrats churned up in an effort to create consensus helped build a burgeoning underclass with a bitter sense of entitlement—which wasn't good at all. Still, it's hard not to like the party that at least noticed.)

We wound up finally in a little apartment over a candy store in Rutherford, New Jersey. My father sold furniture in Passaic, my mother coped, we went to school, I read. It was great to live over a candy store, because the newspapers, stacks of them, were all there in the morning—the *Daily News*, the *Post*, the *Mirror*, the *World Journal*

Tribune, and the Jersey papers, the *Newark Star Ledger* and the *Bergen Record* and the *Herald News.*

I fell in love with reading in that apartment. There were biographies of the great, American poetry, Leon Uris novels like *Battle Cry* and *Exodus.* But it was the newspapers that really gave me the world outside my room above the store. Dorothy Kilgallen and her gossip column, Jimmy Cannon, Jimmy Breslin, Pete Hamill, Gay Talese, and a young guy named Tom Wolfe. They were doing the new journalism—"Frank Sinatra Has a Cold," "Breslin and the Burtons Hoist a Few," "The Bridge." It was wonderful, the first journalism I ever knew, and still the most striking.

We moved to various houses, and I was a bad student. I cut high school a lot. My mother was often sick and my father left the house early, and I'd stay up all night reading Scott Fitzgerald and Hemingway and the *Ladies' Home Journal* and "Can This Marriage Be Saved?" I would go to bed at 5:00 or 6:00 A.M., after a final cup of tea and a last cigarette, and sleep until two in the afternoon. Then I'd quietly dress and sneak downstairs to the front door, go out on the porch, turn around, bound back up the stairs, and throw my books down hard on the table, saying, "Mom, I'm home!" in a breathless I-just-walked-home-fast sort of way—and my mother would say hi. This worked for a year. Then they sent the school psychologist to the house and the jig was up.

We were in love with the Kennedys but they died. I was a child when JFK was assassinated, but in the spring of 1968 I was a senior in high school. One night I fell into a restless sleep; in a dream I saw Abraham Lincoln in Ford's Theatre. He was sitting in a box and suddenly a shadow came from behind and Lincoln turned to look and there was a sharp retort and he slumped in his chair. But the moment before he was shot, I saw his face, and he was black. The next morning I went into school and told my friends, and we laughed at the oddness of it. That night my friend Judy called to tell me Martin Luther King had been shot. "The dream!" she said, "the dream!"

One night soon after, just as I was falling asleep and my mind was swimming with the images one has before one enters a dream, I thought I heard a voice. It said, "Forty-four days." That's all, just those words. I didn't sleep all night, and the next day I told my friends, and this time I didn't laugh. Forty-three days later I walked into school, and my friends crowded around me and said, "Did you hear? Robert Kennedy was shot last night." The next day he died. I have never since had such an experience. In some ways I'm disappointed, in many ways relieved. Jane Jane died soon thereafter, and her death seemed to separate me from my childhood and lay down a demarcation point into adulthood. She would not have understood the world she left.

It is hard to communicate to people who weren't there what those days were like, but I tell young people now that there was a time in the sixties where when the words "Special Report" were flashed on the TV, your heart would pound in your chest and you'd get up and leave the room. My generation never had it hard, but after the sixties a lot of us had bad nerves.

I was a waitress. I liked serving truck drivers coffee at dawn, liked the personalness of it and the smells from the kitchen and the eggs crackling. I worked at a little restaurant in Rutherford and at the lunch counter at Rutherford Drug and at the Holiday Inn on Route 3.

I didn't go to college after high school. I went to Newark, to work as a clerk at the Aetna Insurance Company. It was the summer after the riots and no one was insuring plate glass but I think they had to go through the motions, so I'd sit with a little book and figure the size of the glass by the thickness, factor in the location, and calculate the premium, which was, I believe, usually a lot more than the plate glass cost. It was my first business office. There were all these adults bent over their desks talking quietly on the phone. It was so soul-deadening. (Years later, after I had worked on an inaugural address, an aging English journalist sniffed that no one who had worked in an insurance company belonged in such a rarefied atmosphere. But then he is a Brit.)

I went to college at night at Fairleigh Dickinson University, ten blocks from my house. After two years I was accepted as a full-time student.

Fairleigh was another world. There were people there my age who did nothing but go to class and read, and they seemed so adult and experienced. I started school in the fall of 1970, six months after Kent State, and for the first time in my life I determined to do well and did. I became the editor of the undergraduate newspaper. It was a hot, hot time and I would like to tell you that I wrote angry editorials and we took over the school, held the dean captive, and issued nonnegotiable demands, but the fact is we didn't. It was New Jersey, and we were first-in-our-family college students, and we were working a job and studying and partying, and only rich kids wanted to occupy a dean's office, normal kids just wanted to not get called on the carpet there.

I don't mean we didn't care about Vietnam. We did. I can't get over it to this day, nor I suppose can anyone in my generation. I would say it gave shape to an era, but perhaps it only guaranteed that the era would be shapeless, that our politics would lack symmetry, perhaps for the rest of our lives.

The war didn't affect me in a direct and personal way. I lost no one. My brother was too young. My best friend, Kathy, lost a boyfriend she loved, and every Thursday night a local TV station showed pictures of the kids who died that week. But mostly the war was something we talked about in school, where the discourse was polite. We all knew some of us were for it and some against, but there was a calmness to the debate, an assumption that we are all citizens together. I find New Jersey to be like this: Conflict is presumed.

I fought the war inside myself, like everyone else. I hated it because innocent children died in it and young boys got crippled in it and it seemed so uncompassionate to support it. So much pain for so many innocents, and all to achieve . . . what? Our objectives kept shifting, the government didn't seem to know what it wanted. And yet: If the Communists were on the other side, then we just couldn't leave, could we? I mean, Communists are bad, intend to do bad, right? They're the declared enemy of the democracies—Khrushchev said right there at the UN in New York, "We will bury you!" I know, I saw it on TV. It was the Kennedy years that taught me what to think about communism, Kennedy himself and his speeches about communism and Castro. During the Cuban Missile Crisis we actually thought the world might end, that the Russians might bomb us all to smithereens—and nonbelligerent countries don't do things like that, people with innocent intent don't aim missiles at you from ninety miles off your shore.

My college boyfriend had big bushy hair and wore workshirts and jeans because that was how he expressed his egalitarianism (in those days the rich kids dressed poor, the not-rich kids wore carefully pressed denims and blouses from Mandee and Mays). Ed was a humorous and happy young man and he was against the war because it seemed so cruel, because it was such a mess, because he didn't want to go. We would talk.

—But if the North is Communists and they want to take over the South, and the South is people who want democracy and not a dictatorship and we're their only chance at pushing back the North—then isn't it morally right for us to be there?"

—Well . . .

—I mean, you want democracy here, right?

—Of course.

—And you'd fight if someone wanted to take it away, right?

—Yes.

—Well, the Vietnamese are as good as we are, right, and have as much right to the things we want as we do, right? Unless you think they're less than we are.

—No. I don't know. Do we have to settle this tonight?

—Yes.

He would sigh.

—The people who rule South Vietnam aren't exactly passionate about democracy to begin with, and they're pretty corrupt.

—Yeah.

—It's not really good versus bad, it's bad versus bad.

—But the Communists, once they're in you can't get them out. You can't ever make an improvement, that's it, a dictatorship.

—Well . . .

—Well . . .

My friend Kathy's mother was sick with heart disease, and when I used to go over to her house, I'd hear her mother yelling at the TV upstairs, "You tell 'em, Bill! Tell that big jerk!" She was watching William F. Buckley, Jr.

"Facile jackass!" She was warming up on John Kenneth Galbraith.

"Poseur!" That must have been Jerry Rubin. "Boob!"

Every few weeks she received a magazine called *National Review*. Kathy told me, "You should read it. You don't know it, but you think like my mother." I started reading *NR*, and it sang to me. They saw it the way I was seeing it: America is essentially good, the war is being fought for serious and valid reasons, the answer to every social ill is not necessarily a social program, when you let a government get too big you threaten your own liberties—and God is real as a rock. I was moved, and more. It assuaged a kind of loneliness. Later I found that half the people in the Reagan administration had as their first conservative friend that little magazine.

People always ask me how I came from my generation and became a conservative. It's hard to pinpoint where the rebellion began, but I can tell you the moment I knew I wasn't of the left.

I was going to a big antiwar demonstration in Washington. I think it was the spring of '71, and I think we were going to shut the government down. Early that evening, before we got in the buses that would take us down the Jersey Turnpike, we went to a rally in the student union and a guy got up and made a speech. I think he was high. I think we were high. He said words to the effect of, Let's face it, man, this is a country thats greatest contribution to humanity is Coca-Cola, which we make in a lab, sell on TV, and force down the bloated throats of Third World children who are dying of malnutrition.

Hooray, everyone said.

I listened to the kids on the bus. They were very earnest. I listened to the grown-ups, women with intense faces and men who were starting to wear beads and medallions. Everybody's liberal parents, hurtling down the turnpike toward mayhem.

I couldn't get in the spirit, into the swing. I kept observing. There was contempt for the nineteen-year-old boys who were carrying guns in the war or in the Guard. It was understood that they were uneducated, and somewhat crude. There was contempt for America:

—What can you expect of a culture that raises John Wayne to the status of hero?

—We were founded on violence and will meet our undoing in violence.

—We're at the collective mercy of a bunch of insecure males who have a phallic fascination with guns.

—We're a racist, genocidal nation with an imperialistic lust for land that isn't ours, and . . . and . . .

And get me off this bus! I looked around, and I saw those mouths moving and shrank in my seat. What am I doing with these people? What am I doing with these intellectuals or whatever they are, what am I doing with this—this contemptuous elite?

As far as I was concerned they were encouraging the real bastards of the world. As far as I was concerned from here on in I would use my McGovern button as a roach clip. *And what was the Democratic party doing on the side of these people?*

That was the moment it changed for me, that was the day I got skeptical. I never again assumed the young had pure motives, never again thought intellectuals had the answers, never again thought the people who write for the papers and talk on TV knew more than the rest of us, never again assumed that just because people talk loud they care.

I always come back to the war as the formative political experience of my life because it involved one of the most painful political injustices of our time. I still think that America's attempt to help another people in a country far away resist a Communist takeover was not proof of America's cynicism but an illustration of that peculiar American mix, one part idealism and one part strategic calculation, which may have been wrong but at least had a point.

The grunt work of the war was fought by the grunts of American society; and while they were fighting, their more advantaged brothers and sisters were back home giving interviews to Eric Sevareid on the Concord Bridge. When the veterans returned, they were sometimes patronized by the privileged—and I mean privileged not only in money but in gifts, in standing, in background—who, as the vets were going back to pumping gas on Route 80, went on to become the professionals and news producers and opinion leaders of the baby-boom generation, where they have, some of them, devoted a considerable amount of time to talking about the lessons of Vietnam, which is to say: the lessons we taught you by not going, the painful lessons you learned because you did.

But I'm not sure the gifted lucky ones got a clean getaway. The characters they invent on *thirtysomething* and *L.A. Law* will probably never say, "You know, that war, I look at what happened after we left and we were wrong, we should have stayed," and they are probably not going to write columns saying, "What the Communists did was terrible, and we should have known what they were going to do." But I think I perceive an unease, the chronic unease of the person whose instinct it is to be honest but who has trouble acknowledging a painful fact: that our protests and the politicians' withdrawal from the war and the manner in which they withdrew helped produce the boat people, the Cambodian holocaust, a gulag called Vietnam, and an untold increase in horror for the people of that part of the planet. That chronic unease: That's the real big chill.

TWO

* * * * * * * * * * *

CBS

I left Fairleigh with a degree in English lit, a journalism minor, and a desire to expose injustice like Ida M. Tarbell and Lincoln Steffens. I tried to get a job in New York. Get outta town, they told me, start out on a weekly somewhere. I tried radio and TV. Get outta town, try a smaller market. My friend Lisa wrote from Boston saying her roommate was getting married and why didn't I come north and make my fortune?

So I did. I went to CBS's all-news radio station in Boston, got an interview with the general manager and took a writing audition. While I was in the newsroom typing in panic—I had no idea how to write for radio—a newswriter was in the news director's office handing in her resignation. She was leaving the next morning. The news director came in and looked over my copy. He grunted. "When can you start?"

"You're hiring me?"

"Don't you want to be hired?"

"But I'm not very good, am I?"

"No, but then we don't pay very well."

"Oh. I'll start now."

He laughed. "Tomorrow at five A.M."

To this day, I don't know why they call it the lobster shift. They ought to call it the mental-illness shift, because when you work over-night long enough and sleep all day long enough, your skin gets bad and you're always pale and you find you have only two modes, depression and anxiety. But I was so happy to get a job in journalism that all I felt was joy. I had a job and an apartment with Lisa Schwarzbaum in Cambridge, and it was a wonderful place to be young.

I began my career writing for the ear. I learned how to write for broadcast, how to be conversational and catch the listener's attention, how to try to sum up a situation with a good, true line. WEEI's stars sat down with me and helped: Jim Pansullo and Norm Nathan and Les Woodruff, and a talented young writer named Dick Spencer. I started to listen to the network hourly reports and hear the work of the great CBS writers, Eric Sevareid and Winston Burdett. I listened closely to how they talked on the air, what they said and how they said it. I listened to headlines. It was a CBS writer who, an hour after the story of Rose Mary Woods and the eighteen-minute gap broke, headlined it, "Rose Mary's booboo!" When there was heavy flooding in Missouri, the network headlined, "Everything's up to here in Kansas City." I listened to Charles Osgood, the most gifted of the radio network stars, and how he said profound things in a deceptively simple way.

I started to produce news blocks, telling the writer what to lead with and what stories to include. I learned the rules of broadcast journalism, the first of which is that you don't have time for extended debates when a story moves on the wires, so you'd better know your profession before you sit at that desk.

Most of us were in our twenties when we wrote and produced the news at EEI, and we were all learning together. At the end of the day we'd debate. What kind of story merits a Special Report? A president is shot, sure. But what about . . . Johnny Carson dies? All right, what about Donny Osmond? What if it's Donny *and* Marie? What if it's a Donny-Marie murder/suicide? What about the radio network anchor who went on the air with a special report that Tito was dead, and it turned out one of the wires had just accidentally run Tito's obit? (When the mistake became clear she wondered what to say in the retraction. A reporter leaned over and offered helpfully, "Why don't you just say, 'Regarding our previous bulletin, please change "dead" to "sleeping"?' ")

It was the winter of 1974, and Boston was convulsed by the school-busing crisis. Sometimes I'd walk the streets of Southie, where the working-class Irish lived in rows of neat houses. Southie was the epicenter of the earthquake, where black kids were bused in and the local kids bused out. On the first day of school at South Boston High in the fall of 1975, there was a phalanx of what seemed like hundreds of policemen dressed in dark uniforms on big black motorcycles, escorting a long line of buses as they made their way through the streets. It looked like an invasion.

Antibusing groups with names like ROAR, liberal pressure groups, academics who were running around sticking their fingers in the wound—everyone was using everyone, I thought, and few seemed to care about the kids. The working-class whites were derided by their betters in the media, the working-class blacks were ignored, the intemperate got attention and went into politics, the judge blithely tore up a world and retired to Wellesley, we in the media made our bones and moved on. At the end I thought busing in Boston was an urban Vietnam. They made a desert and called it peace indeed.

One day Lynn Vaughan, an intense young black woman who was one of the station's best reporters, came in from a day of watching the fighting on the streets to go to a meeting the news director had called to discuss the fairness of our coverage. I was ready to say I thought our coverage reflected a kind of high-handed corporate liberalism in which the proper view, parroted consciously or unconsciously by all of us, was that the whites of Southie are racist and wrong and the school committee is racist and wrong and the judge is clean and good, and busing, though uncomfortable for all of us is, essentially, good.

I was winding up to throw this ball when Lynn spoke up. She'd just been through the usual day in Southie, she said. She had been taunted and harassed by both adults and children who thought because of her size that she was a student, she had been addressed as "nigger" and told to get out before she got it good but apart from that she'd had a good day, and perhaps if we were here to say that Southie's real views hadn't been adequately covered, she was certainly willing to go on the air and talk about what she had experienced firsthand of its opinions. Her eyes welled up.

Everything I meant to say was true, everything she said was true, and one of the tragedies of busing was that some good people acted like less than they were. But then the Irish can be fractious even in the most concordant eras—I was recently told by an elderly lady from Brooklyn that a well-balanced Irishman is a guy with a chip on both shoulders.

I became the editorial director at EEI, writing and taping the station's editorials. I deplored and voiced reservations and spoke always in a cool, calm, above-the-fray voice. It often occurred to me that I was only twenty-five, which might be young to be passing judgments on the actions of your elders, but—somebody had to do it.

When I walked the halls of Boston City Hall, some of the city counselors saw me as the enemy because I was The Media, but they talked to me anyway because if their voices were on the radio they would seem like leaders. These were good old-line Boston Democrats who supported the welfare state but who didn't support busing. They had wonderful names out of *The Last Hurrah*, like Dapper O'Neill, no relation to Tip, and Pixie Pallodino, and Louise Day Hicks, called Louise by everyone in town. It was *The Last Hurrah* meets modern technology: Every pol had a little cassette in his neck, and when you asked a question, he pushed a button and the answer came out. "The judge is once again proving that he doesn't understand the most basic facts of the school system." "The school committee is once again proving it is blind to our pleas for justice." It was my introduction to soundbiteology. The pols knew it before everyone else, they just didn't know the name.

A moment when I saw hope for Boston:

One summer night WEEI had a softball game and invited all the local politicians. There was a good turnout, and after the game we went to a bar and went upstairs to a private room where we drank beer and got to know each other. Suddenly there were sharp words between one of the politicians and one of our reporters, a young man named Chip Whitmore. I don't remember what it was about, but it revolved around our busing coverage, and it got tense. I looked at the politician next to me. He was generally considered another mug from Southie who's fighting the busing. He'd been singing old songs, leaning back in his chair with his long basketball player's legs stretched out before him, but he was watching everything.

"It's nice to sing, isn't it?" he said to me.

"Yeah," I said, as I leaned to hear what the guys who were fighting were saying.

"A peaceful activity." He smiled.

"Do you know an old song my mother used to sing, 'When Your Old Wedding Ring Was New'?"

"I think I can sing it," he said. "Will you sing too?" We started to croon.

"When your old wedding ring was new / And the dreams that you dreamed came true. . . ."

A few pols joined in.

"I remember with pride / As you stood by my side. . . ."

Now a few reporters.

"What a beautiful picture / You made as my bride. . . ."

He was a great guy, Ray Flynn. He's now mayor of Boston, where he croons on a broader level.

A job opened up at CBS network radio in New York in 1977, and I took it. They put me up in the Essex House on Central Park South while I looked for an apartment, and I reported to work as a writer/editor at CBS News on September 7, 1977, my twenty-seventh birthday. I was assigned to . . . the lobster shift, this time midnight to 8:00 A.M. It was my job to cut soundbites (in radio those five-to-twenty-second bursts of an interviewed person speaking were called actualities) for the *CBS World News Roundup*. I also wrote the hourly news reports that I used to listen to in Boston.

It was exciting. I stood in the newsroom that first day, and everywhere I turned I saw: greatness. Across the room Walter Cronkite stood with a cup of coffee reading the cable traffic. I passed a man with white hair yelling into a phone, 'Hello, Mogadishu, Allah ba salaam!' It was the veteran correspondent Richard C. Hottelet. Across the room a group erupted in laughter, and Charles Osgood walked away grinning at his joke.

CBS in those days had style. There was an esprit, a sense of being a veteran of something; people acted as if they were members of a winning team or pioneers who'd made it through the snows. Everyone had stories about covering civil rights and the moon landing and the assassinations and the war. I was working with people who'd succeeded during the most intense and triumphant age in journalism since the rise of the muckrakers eighty years before. The first desk editor I worked with was the woman who answered the phone when Dan Rather called from Parkland Memorial and said, "He's dead." That makeup woman used to do Ike. The guy in the edit room is the one who told Nixon to wear makeup in the debate. There was an air; the people who worked there thought they were important; their stride was sure.

The newsroom itself was a big, brightly lit room in the middle of what used to be a barn on the West Side of Manhattan. It looked like the newsroom of a great network. In the middle were the wire machines, the old heavy metal ones with metal plates that said Associated Press and United Press International and Reuters News Service, proud old machines that shook and made noise, not the soft, insistent computer buzz they make now but big noise—they sounded like *news*. Half of the room was for those who worked in TV; beyond their desks was the Cronkite evening-news set. The other half was for radio, and beyond that the radio studios. There were big clocks high up on the wall showing the time in Paris and Joburg and Bonn, and below them big bins containing telex traffic—GOING DOWN DIXIE STOP ONPASS TO HIGLEY BIRD BOOKED FOR FIVE PEYEM GMT MY ETA TWELVE NOONER THIS DAY THAT IS 12:00 9/7/78 GMT BIBIFONOW JOHNSON—and desks full of radio editors holding two and three phones at a time yelling, "Get studio five to pick up on one-five, Roth's filing from Moscow." A constant buzz and clamor.

I was lucky. When I got down to the network, the older people from whom you'd learn weren't just anybody, they were the Murrow Boys, the last of the gentleman broadcasters. Doug Edwards once read a script I'd written about Omar Bradley, and stayed around afterward to reminisce. "One day years ago I was sitting in a studio not too unlike this one, and Ed Murrow came in, and Peggy, he had the stench of death on him, literally an odor. I said, 'Ed, you look awful. What's the matter?' And he said, 'I have just come from a place called Auschwitz.' "

When you wrote a good script, you wanted Doug Edwards with his beautiful voice to read it, or Dallas Townsend, the star of the *World News Roundup,* who knew everything about broadcasting, and if you were curious and sincere he would tell you. Charles Collingwood, who at my age had reported for Murrow from the Battle of the Bulge and had ad-libbed with such precocious authority—"They say this one is by the book, but nobody ever wrote this book, this is a new book, and Omar Bradley its brilliant author"—would tip his hat to me in the elevator. If he was the Duke, Osgood was the Prince, the most gifted and sweet man. All the strange and difficult people in radio, and there were a number of them, could count on him for a friend.

It was a few years after Watergate. CBS was at its height and the news division was at its height and TV was at its height, but network radio was reaching bottom. Local radio stations with entertainment formats—rock and roll and talk—were doing fine. But network radio had lost steam. Television was where you put today's stars, radio was where you put yesterday's. Radio management was where they put the men who'd been unlucky. There was a whole floor of them upstairs, tall white men sitting at desks making decisions that didn't really have to be made.

When people asked what you did, you didn't say, "I work in radio," you said, "I work in the news division." The wife of a television executive sat next to a radio star at a fancy dinner. "What do you do?" she asked. He told her. "Really?" she said. "I had a radio once." A guy at local bragged, "I'm on the radio!," and the person he said it to said, "That must be uncomfortable." When we went out to cover caucuses and primaries, TV stayed in a big hotel in town, radio stayed in a mom-and-pop motel on the outskirts. We called it Radio Shack.

We felt like clerks in an abandoned railroad station, hearing the echoes of a locomotive that doesn't stop here anymore. But the best writers came from radio. They knew a word is worth a thousand pictures and believed, as Osgood did, that radio was the more creative medium: TV gives everyone an image, but radio gives birth to a million images in a million brains. Radio people were also, alas, a type: perhaps a little pedantic, perhaps finding a little too much joy in the grammatical errors of others. They read books. There was even a physical type: A lot of the men who were on the air had unusually large heads. I used to wonder if their heads got big because their unusually big voices caromed around in them. There weren't too many women on the air because we were just breaking in, and because of a certain bias: Management felt women didn't communicate the proper authority. (Once I auditioned for an on-air job in local radio, and the news director took me aside. "Your voice," he said, "it has no balls." I still haven't come up with the right answer to that.)

I auditioned for an opening on the *Morning News* and spent a week sitting across from Charles Kuralt. At four o'clock in the morning he'd squeeze into the anchor position and read wire copy with a grunting intensity. He was one of the only writers I ever saw who seemed to write the copy first in his head; all we saw was the typing. He'd sit there heaving, tie askew and white shirt wilting, chain-smoking unfiltered cigarettes, nodding to himself. He looked like a factory foreman running behind in stock. Hours later, combed, powdered, and wearing a fresh blue shirt, he'd lean into the camera cool and unflappable, perfectly urbane. TV is such a liar.

CBS, like all the networks, all media, was shaped in part by a certain political spirit.

They call the *Times* "the good gray *Times*," they call the BBC "Auntie," and when I was there, I thought of CBS as "the Schoolmarm," for flourishing within it was the sometimes tender impulse to provide moral instruction to a nation badly in need of it. It was a CBS tradition—Murrow on McCarthy, Cronkite on Vietnam, the correspondents of the thirties and forties warning what was happening in Germany. CBS drew people with a mission.

It was not a place where one wore labels such as conservative or the even mustier liberal, and no one claimed to be a Democrat or Republican. Lack of affiliation was presumed; to label was to confine, to admit one is unalive to the complexities.

My peers at the network, the writers and producers in their late twenties and thirties, thought of themselves as modern people trying to be fair. There are conservatives over here and wild lefties over there—and us, the sane people, in the middle. If you made up a list of political questions—should we raise taxes to narrow the deficit; should abortion be banned; should a morning prayer be allowed in the schools; should arms control be our first foreign-policy priority?—most of them would vote yes, no, no, yes.

And they would see these not as liberal positions but as decent, intelligent positions. They also thought their views were utterly in line with those of the majority of Americans. In a way that's what's at the heart of our modern political disputes, a disagreement over where the mainstream is and what "normal" is, politically and culturally. I think a lot of the young people at the networks didn't really know what normal was in America, and I hold this view because after working six years in broadcasting and three in New York, I no longer knew what normal was.

A small example. Once I wrote a radio script in which I led into a story by saying, "This Sunday morning you'll probably be home reading the papers or out at brunch with friends, but Joe Smith will be . . ." A middle-aged editor listened as he walked by the studio and approached me afterward. "Peggy, a small point but maybe not so insignificant: This Sunday morning most Americans will be at church."

He was, of course, correct. But I forgot. I wasn't at church on Sunday mornings, I was in a restaurant on Columbus Avenue eating mushroom omelets and reading the Arts and Leisure section of *The New York Times*.

There were interesting divisions of age and class at CBS that complicated things nicely. There were technicians and engineers and custodial staff and couriers and the guys who ran the mail room and secretaries—and they were often from the lower-middle class and were considered blue collar. Then there were the writers and producers upstairs, the executives and on-air talent—the white collars. They were often well educated and sometimes thought of themselves as intellectuals.

The blue collars lived on Long Island or in Queens or Staten Island and made a lot of their money in overtime, which was heavily taxed. They lived on their own kind of common sense and had a nice natural hatred for bullies, most especially management. They voted for Reagan.

Some of the older white collars at CBS had prep-school names like Bud and Shad and Chub and Chad. They were intelligent Protestants who lived in Connecticut and had been educated out of the narrowness of their backgrounds into a more acceptable liberalism. I believe their prime educator, when they were just starting out in the fifties, was Mr. Joe McCarthy.

They were the first in their families to vote Democratic; they wept when FDR died. They had earned their liberalism, swimming upstream in the frosty waters of Greenwich and Larchmont, and it was hard not to respect a politics that was so hard-won. But . . . it is perhaps true that they had been born into a class that understood explaining to the disadvantaged to be part of its burden. Now their influence has ebbed, but when I got to CBS they reigned, and their influence can still be seen in broadcasts such as *Sunday Morning*, a wonderful old village explainer of a show that likes to tell us that racism is a bad cruel thing and so is war bad and cruel.

The young white collars, the boomers, my friends, were perhaps less compelling. There was something poignant about how hard they worked and all the things they wanted, but . . . had anything been hard-earned for them? They too had known privilege, but a privilege so prevalent—for everyone had had braces and a Schwinn and piano lessons—that they did not know that they were lucky. In fact, they had a sense of deprivation, and what they were deprived of, I believe, was the generational pride born of adversity: the boomers hadn't had their trauma yet.

They didn't have much in common with people who have wedding receptions at the VFW and die in the veterans' hospital. I used to think they picked out their politics as they picked out their clothes, with thought and care, but it did not occur to them that they might be shopping in a store with a limited inventory: the university of the sixties and seventies, the press, what the smart people say on TV. They had everything going for them, including fifty thousand dollars a year at the age of thirty-two, and yet they felt obscurely besieged.

I remember a young bureau chief who would sit back, his bearded chin jutting into the air, as he challenged his colleagues on just how soon they'd turned against Vietnam and what they'd done about it. And a young producer who railed against tax and social-spending cuts in the kitchen of her Vineyard home. (Asked why she, in her work, used the phrase "right wing" and never "left wing," she replied, "Well, 'left wing'—if you say that, it sounds like McCarthy!") The right looks into the heart of a place like CBS and sees these young people ruling; the young looked out dark-eyed, frustrated at their inability to change the country.

I remember the night of the 1980 elections. All of CBS was gathered in a huge studio up above the newsroom. Big, crisply cut graphics saying CBS NEWS dominated one wall, the set for television another. Tucked away in a corner was radio, where I produced the coverage of a regional desk. For the first time the network would be fully computerized. Everybody in the room had a screen on which he could punch up information on races throughout the country.

There was a sense of expectation and excitement. America would soon know who its next president was, and there was only one way the people would find out: through us. We had a mission, and we wanted to do our best, to be great. It was Cronkite's last election night. I watched him across the room calmly patting his tie and laughing with Bob Schieffer and Roger Mudd.

Late in the afternoon, a few hours before we were to go on the air, the first exit-poll information was to be available on the computers. Everyone started to punch it in. The room was bustling with laughter and oaths, but little by little it quieted. It was as if an invisible cloud of gas had descended. Soon there was only the dry tap-tap of computer keys as people punched up and repunched a nightmare. Something extraordinary is happening, Reagan is winning, he's not only winning, it's going to be a landslide. It's not just Reagan, it's McGovern out, Frank Church out—it's carnage! Those my age (I had just turned thirty) sat staring,

slack-jawed, at little green words on little green screens. They commiser-
ate. "Can you believe it?" "God, I can't believe it."

I say nothing until I see a fellow Reagan supporter across the room.
I lift my fist. "Yo!"

"Yo," he answers. Ashamed of my joy, I go back to work.

Later, at 2:00 A.M., we went to a local bar. A young producer named
Al, a smart and civilized fellow, said with slump-shouldered sadness,
"What is happening to us? What is happening to this country?"

"I think we awoke from our slumber," I said.

"You're not upset?"

"No. I think the country probably had enough of everything that
wasn't working, and now they want a change."

"Well, they're going to get it!"

I became the backup writer for Walter Cronkite's commentary
show, a solid, well-written show that offered five minutes of intelligent
thought each day.

I was finally going to meet Cronkite, the great Cronkite. My first day
I got in early, read the wires, and wrote a show that was real Walter,
avuncular and yet no-nonsense, deeply current and yet with a certain
historical view. I must have written ten drafts. It was 3:00 P.M.. The
show had to be piped out of the network to the affiliates at 3:56.

I called Cronkite's office and said I had radio all done, and if he could
come by in the next twenty minutes—

"Walter's out today," said the secretary.

My heart sank. "Out? Who's gonna do radio?"

"Dan Rather's doing the show tonight. Why don't you ask him?"

He came into the studio walking fast, shook my hand, read the script,
looked up, and said, "This is good. Let's go."

Rather. How to explain Rather. I knew him at a hard time, the early
days when he first got the Cronkite job—for a year after he was anchor
they still called it the Cronkite Show in house—and ratings were down.
Then ratings were up and he expanded—a sweetness came out, and a
sensitivity, though there was still about him, I thought, a frustration,
a bristling. I would think, This is the sadness of the man who got what
he wanted. Now he's stuck with it. And is it enough, and was he right
to want it all his life, and doesn't he really want to get back on the road
and chase a lead and hustle a secretary for the sheriff's home number

and get the story and get wrecked that night with the boys in the bar? Now he is a statesman, when what he really wants is to be what most reporters are, adult delinquents. That bristling quality—it was restraint.

We worked together the rest of the week, and the last day we went downstairs for coffee. He wanted to know what I wanted to be. I said short term I wanted to fill in when Cronkite's writer was away—

"Done."

—and long term I wasn't so sure.

"Do you want to be a producer?"

"No, I don't want to live in the Holiday Inn. I don't even like to fly."

"Want to be on-air?"

"No, I don't really speak well on the air."

He looked at his coffee.

"I don't really know what I want to do. I know I'm a writer. CBS used to be a great writer's shop, but that's—"

"Less so now."

"Yes."

"While you decide, write radio for me when Walter's out, and when I come in you'll get the radio job if you want it. Okay?"

When he took over from Cronkite I took the commentary job, and our first show was on March 31, 1981. I was so nervous that I couldn't have any distractions, so I didn't answer the phone or listen to the radio. I finished early, took an elevator down to the newsroom, and bumped into Doug Edwards, who shook his head and said, "Isn't it awful?"

"What?"

"Reagan, didn't you hear? He's been shot. They don't know how bad. Terrible, terrible."

I had to sit down it was such a blow.

The show was canceled. I spent the afternoon trying to track down John Hinckley's parents for an interview, and watching over and over on a monitor as Reagan was shot and James Brady lay in shock in a pool of blood.

A few months later I walked into Rather's office and found him pacing the floor. It was the morning after John Hinckley had been found not guilty by reason of insanity. Rather was astonished and angry. We did a piece on it that became somewhat controversial. A radio editor wanted to pull it because it was more like an editorial than a commentary, which was true. But sometimes you have to do an editorial and not a commentary.

"There was a dreamlike quality to what happened in the courtroom yesterday. It was a dark dream full of movement: The jury walks in and hands up the verdict, the judge mouths the words on the paper, the assassin nods his head forward and backward and closes his eyes. The parents cry in happiness, and the government lawyers are struck dumb. The spectators look at each other in astonishment and turn to each other with words, and the judge snaps, 'There will be order here!'

"The dream jumps. In a suburban home sits a witty and competent man whose life was quite ruined by the young man who nods and closes his eyes and hears that he is not guilty of committing ruin. The dream ends with a question: Who tells James Brady?"

Break for a commercial, then:

"The jury has spoken, their judgment is final, and that is as it should be. But something is wrong here. Years ago Clarence Darrow made a speech to the inmates of a Chicago prison, and he told them, 'You are in here because you do not have money.' Oh they wanted to hang him for telling the truth. But money talks, and in the Hinckley case money yelled and banged on the table and won the day. The cleverest lawyers were hired, the most expensive psychiatrists. The Hinckleys committed a considerable part of their considerable wealth to the case, and when it was over, the victorious defense attorney smiled and said, 'Another day, another dollar.' There's a legal maxim for you.

"Something is wrong here. America's prisons are full of poor blacks and whites and Hispanics, and their crimes are the usual assortment of human transgressions. What does the Hinckley verdict say to them? It says, 'Your big problem, boy, is that you are not a millionaire's son, and you went after a grocery clerk. Next time go after a president. This will help you with your insanity plea, because this is what the plea can mean: If you commit a big crime then you are crazy, and the more heinous the crime the crazier you must be. Therefore you are not responsible, and nothing is your fault.'

"The insane are among us, it is true. But so are the calculating. And what they learn from this verdict is that you can do anything; you can wait like a jackal and shoot a man in the head and leave him for dead and buy your way out with clever lawyers and expensive psychiatrists.

"Something is wrong here. If John Hinckley has the will (and he has shown he is willful) and the way (and his family is rich), he will probably down the road ask to be released from St. Elizabeth's on the grounds that he is no longer dangerous. And sooner or later a panel of experts may nod and say yes, yes, because of the logic of his request. An expert will testify, 'Hinckley only shot people to become famous and now he is famous so he no longer has a reason to shoot people so he's no longer dangerous so we can let him go.'

"Something is wrong here. Wrong about this age of millionaire assassins and high-powered lawyers and cool talk about the secrets of the mind—and no talk about old abstractions like responsibility and punishment and sin."

Well, all right. It was the day after the verdict and we were hot under the collar. But we were engulfed by telephone calls from people saying thank you for caring about this and voicing how we feel. They were appreciative for unalloyed, unexpected passion on a subject that was not, for once, a matter of left and right.

We had fun on the show. It had a following. It was even followed in Washington. One day when I'd been doing the show for a year, Dan got a call from a fellow who worked for the president. He told Rather, "You got to the old man." We'd done a piece that afternoon on how the veterans of Vietnam were gathering in Washington for the unveiling of the Vietnam Veterans' Memorial. And Ronald Reagan wasn't going. We said maybe the boys deserved better, and if the president thought about it he'd probably realize he didn't have anything more important to do that day than show his respect for the veterans of that war. If he thought about it.

Dan was told the president heard it on WTOP, the Washington affiliate, and his aides thought, This is bad publicity. The president put on his coat and went to a service for the veterans.

People always ask me how Rather and I worked so well together when we disagreed on everything. But we didn't disagree on everything. He's as corny and emotional about America as a dunken YAFfer. The astute television essayist Tom Shales has noted something I thought only I knew: Rather and Reagan have a lot in common. Here's Rather as Reagan: Once I walked into Dan's office for our morning meeting and it was a slow day and neither of us could think of a topic for the show. We started to shoot the breeze, and somehow got on the subject of the San Jacinto monument. Dan talked about the Alamo and how little kids in Texas were taught state history as if it were as important as national and world history. He spoke of the first time he saw the monument gleaming in the sun and started to recite the words on it, then stopped—and I looked up, astonished to see him wiping away tears. "I'm sorry," he said, as surprised as I, "But that is some kind of thing to see, and I guess I got reminded of some old days. . . ."

It's hard to imagine Reagan being quite so emotional, but he would have shared the sentiment.

We did disagree on a number of issues, but we worked it out. I went to him after I'd been working with him a few weeks and told him we had political differences, more than I knew going in because I hadn't paid a lot of attention to his career.

"All right."

"I find you to be somewhat liberal in your views, and I am somewhat conservative."

"What kind of conservative are you? You want to dance at the Annenbergs', or what?"

"No, I'm the lower-the-taxes-on-poor-people type. What kind of liberal are you, the dance-at-the-Harrimans' type?"

He laughed. "We'll make a deal: We'll work out what the topic is every day, and I'll tell you my view and the way I want it to go. If you disagree, you've got five minutes to change my mind. If you succeed, we do it your way. If you don't, you'll still get to give a fair presentation of your side, but we do it my way. Ultimately it's going to reflect my views. Because it's my show."

It worked fine for three years. I always found him to be open-minded and fair, and he became my friend and is to this day. He is, of course, the nemesis of the right, which is understandable given the history, but frustrating for his friends nonetheless. It sounds weak, or only senti- mental, but I always want to say to them: He wouldn't be if you knew him. That he is a symbol of the Northeast liberal establishment is somewhat ironic. He was never of them—I once asked one of the Bud Shads what Rather was like in Vietnam, and he sniffed, "He wore bright yellow socks."

Anyway, I think the real key is that Murrow is still the Everest of CBS, and Dan's a mountain climber. And Murrow didn't become Murrow by standing for nothing. It was Murrow who said, "Some stories don't have two sides." At Auschwitz he was right. But the news isn't always Auschwitz. (Actually, if you get down deep maybe a lot of stories *are* Auschwitz, but TV doesn't get down deep.)

In time I knew what I wanted to do, what I yearned to do. I wasn't a journalist, I was a partisan. I yearned to help the president whose views I shared. I ached to write his words. For four years I'd been listening to his speeches in a studio and I knew he was tired. I felt not only yearning but an increasing sense of terror: Soon it would be over, for a presidency is a train that leaves a station at a certain time and arrives at its destination at a certain time, and it had been four years since the "All aboard" was sounded.

I felt like Mr. Roberts—I was missing the war! In Washington they were fighting for ideas, and here I was sailing from tedium to apathy with a side trip to torpor.

I had no connections in Washington, knew no one in the Republican party, no one who'd worked for Reagan. But I was right for the job, I knew it. So I did a number of things, from telling everyone I knew what I wanted to do ("Get those thoughts into the air," said Terri Belli, Rather's secretary) to praying that God would open a door. (I know now I was asking for a small miracle, but I believe in miracles. The way I see it, life isn't flat and thin and "realistic," it's rich and full of mystery and surprise. I think miracles exist in part as gifts and in part as clues that there is something beyond the flat world we see. I also think they happen every day, from the baby's perfect shoulder in the sonogram, to saints performing wonders. I think saints are with us, watching and taking part, every day. The Blessed Virgin also. I think she's very much on the scene, functioning as a friend to mankind. When there are reports that the Blessed Virgin appeared before Mexican farm workers in Oklahoma, I think maybe she was there. Which is a reason I read the tabloid press—it keeps track of sightings. I think this accounts for some of the popularity of the *National Enquirer* and *The Star*—it's not just Oprah's diet and who is Roseanne Barr mad at this week. They tell you stories about miracles without the requisite skepticism; maybe because they think their readers are dumb. The mainstream press ignores these stories; if you asked a young producer why, he'd say, "Because we don't do science fiction." This sounds like I have a lot of faith; I do; I was taught to have it, and it took. But it shouldn't sound like I'm holy because I'm not—I'm just your basic bad Catholic, utterly believing and yet full of the flaws that make for real interesting confessions.)

By 1984 it had been years since I'd gone to church or thought about what I believed and why. But by the mid-eighties I was changing.

I had no great Paul-falling-off-the-horse moment (unlike a woman I was to meet in Washington who one day was driving along the roads of suburban Virginia when suddenly the reality of Christ came crashing down upon her like a roof. As she drove shakily through the junction she'd entered, she looked up to see the street sign: Damascus Road). I just started to go to church again.

I also told everyone, "I want to work for Reagan—do you know anybody?" I told Joe Sobran, a *National Review* editor who was also a weekly contributor to CBS Radio's *Spectrum* series. People always used to bring visiting conservatives around to meet me, as if to say, "See? We have one too." Joe was encouraging of my hopes, but at a loss as to how to help me. He went to a fellow *National Review* editor, Kevin Lynch, who picked up the phone and called his friend Ben Elliott, the head of the Reagan speechwriting department. Ben, as Kevin knew, was in a quandary: He needed a new writer soon, like yesterday, and it had to be someone who could handle a lot of work because this was an election year, and it also had to be someone who was a little different. Had to be someone whose work Dick Darman would respect.

And one day Ben called. CBS News isn't exactly a garden where they grow Reagan speechwriters but that didn't put him off because he'd worked at CBS himself years before as a producer in syndication, and he liked journalists, and was the coffee in the cafeteria still bad?

He asked me to send him everything I'd written in the past five years. Then he asked me to come and talk.

We met in his big corner office in the Old Executive Office Building, within the White House complex and across the street from the West Wing. It was evening. It was such a tall office and looked so impressive, so well appointed. Only later would I notice the couch was frayed and the carpet faded. But that night as I walked in and saw the Washington monument just outside the window, and the shadows of the flags flapping against the smooth stone . . . it glittered.

"Why do you want to work here?"

"Because I want to help the president."

He nodded.

"And I believe in him. I guess everyone gets a president, one president in their adult life who's the one who moved them. For me, it's Reagan."

He smiled. "Me too."

His skin was thick and pale, and there were rings under his eyes. He was tired, but it was clear he was also happy. He had a family in Virginia, a wife and three children. He had called himself in an interview a "bleeding-heart conservative," which was just about right. The moment I remember of him best now was one day months after our first interview. Michael Jackson had come to the White House to promote some antidrug campaign, and all the top staff brought their children and took the seats up front on the White House lawn. A quarter-mile beyond were the children of Washington, mostly black, watching from the gate. Ben stared at them and shook his head. "They're the ones who should be here," he said. "They're the ones who deserve it." A small thing, but Republicans, then, rarely thought like that, or spoke like that.

A few weeks later he called and asked me down to meet Dick Darman, to whom speechwriting reported. The second time I'd heard that name. I pulled the clippings on him and found out he was James Baker's chief aide, meaning he was the chief assistant to the chief assistant to the president.

I never see him now without thinking of that night. Ben walked me over from the EOB to Darman's West Wing office. Dick introduced himself, leaned back and giggled. Later I thought of the words for his first impact on me: merriment stripped of illusion. He was young, perhaps forty, with thick brown hair and sharp brown eyes and trousers three sizes too big buckled up with a belt that was too long. A man who'd lost weight but who hadn't changed his wardrobe after the loss; a realistic man, perhaps, or a pessimist.

"I'm sure you've heard all about this White House," he said. "That there's a great deal of infighting, and we're split into separate warring groups which leak unpleasant things about each other to the amusement and delight of the media, which are not slow in passing it on." His eyes sparkled with amusement at his glibness. I nodded yes, it's a shame you have to read that sort of nonsense.

"It's all true of course."

"Oh."

Ben interrupted. "Dick, don't scare her."

"She's not scared."

"That's right," I lied.

He asked if I knew the CBS White House correspondents, Lesley Stahl and Bill Plante. Not well, I said.

"Do you know the real power around here, Susan Zirinsky, the producer?"

"Only slightly."

"You must be very important. Why do you want to leave a powerful man like Dan Rather to write speeches?"

"Well gee, the president's almost as powerful as Dan."

"Almost. If you are offered and accept this position, what do you want to do next?"

"Commentary on a network," I improvised.

"Well, I'm not sure this will advance you on that goal. There has been a good deal of back and forth between the White House and the networks as you know. Moyers, Diane Sawyer. Though you'd be doing it backwards. But I don't suppose that will hurt you."

Back in Ben's office we talked some more. I asked him how the office worked. He leaned forward with his elbows on his knees and rubbed his head where the hair had been.

"Do we meet with the president?"

He massaged his eyes.

"I mean, who exactly do we answer to?"

"Well, there are lines of authority. . . ."

"Do a lot of people see the speeches?"

"Well, some people do before the president does, but of course it's his speech."

"Does he get much involved?"

A sigh. "The president is old, and he's been shot, and he's tired. He has a lot on his shoulders. . . ."

"This is a hard job, isn't it?"

"Yes. But in spite of all our problems it is deeply satisfying." He told me he wanted to hire me, and would try to do it.

A few weeks later, in Manchester, New Hampshire, where CBS had set up a news bureau to cover the primary—in fact, it was Primary Day—Ben called. I was there to write, with Paul Fisher and John Mosedale and the *Evening News* editor, Lee Townsend, the television special Dan would anchor that evening.

"I got you okayed by the big man. I'm sorry it took so long, there were problems."

"I was okayed? I'm in?"

"I wrote the president a memo telling him we should hire you but letting him know you work for his favorite anchorman. He said fine, no problem."

"Who was the problem?"

"Someone took a run at you. I think the feeling was what if you're someone who comes in here from the media and works the campaign and then does a big exposé?"

"Hey, that's a good idea."

I asked Bill Moyers if I could speak to him. He'd had a wonderful primary. Mondale was supposed to win but that morning, as everyone else in the hotel was looking at room service and reading the *Times* and the *Post*, Moyers was out at the Laundromat, the diner, the bank, the cafe and the candy store. He kept hearing, "I thought I'd vote for Mondale but when I woke up this morning I thought no, I'm gonna vote for Hart."

Bill came on the set and made an announcement. "I have news for you. Gary Hart's going to win tonight, and I'm taking bets." He was, of course, correct.

I like Bill because he's a malcontent, nothing's ever good enough, he's got high standards and expectations and he's always frustrated. He's a terrific writer for broadcast, with that nice old courtly edge—he doesn't go somewhere, he's summoned by an intuition.

We went to a bar in the hotel where cameramen passing themselves off as producers were trying to pick up secretaries passing themselves off as campaign advisers. I told him the story and said, "I'm right to go, right?" Not that I doubted it, I just wanted to talk.

"Peggy, in the history of our country, how many people have worked in the White House? In these two hundred years, how many people have worked for a president? Five thousand? Tops? You have been given an opportunity you cannot turn down. It's part of the American experience. And when you're done with it you'll know more than you do now."

And some advice: "If they ask you to write an antimedia speech, don't."

I went to see Dan. A few weeks earlier I'd told him I was talking to the White House, and he'd said, "You're gone, I can feel it."

This night I went to his makeshift office off the set and sat on a crate and told him I was leaving. He offered as I'd hoped he would a raise, and said as I'd hoped he would that I was irreplaceable.

"You're the best boss I ever had."

"You'll soon be saying that to the new one."

I called my mother. She said it was wonderful and then paused, and I knew she was fighting something. She lost. "My father always said, Stick with the Democrats. They're the party of the working man."

"When Grandpa said that, it was true. It's not anymore, Mom."

"Maybe you're right."

The CBS I left was different from the CBS I'd joined in Boston ten years before. The media consultants had had their way, and so had the accountants, and suddenly men and women who had been with the company thirty years were being informed their services were no longer needed.

A year and a half after I left CBS, Andy Rooney wrote me a note. "CBS has not been a good place to be. Everyone feels tired. They got rid of some dead wood but a company, like a forest, needs some of it. And they got rid of a lot of wood that wasn't dead, too. I think a great many of us are feeling we are loyal to something that no longer exists, and it makes us feel foolish."

When I joined CBS in New York, there was a great and aged correspondent in a foreign bureau who had suffered from a lingering illness for many years. He filed stories perhaps twice a year, and if an accountant looked into it, he would conclude that the correspondent was not pulling his weight. But he had once been great and done great work for the greatest of the networks. And so he was kept on, at full salary, year after year.

Now CBS has done away with that kind of thing, and a young business-management major might say good thing—you not only cut down costs, you cut down everybody's bloated sense of entitlement. But it wasn't a sense of entitlement the old way produced so much as a sense of investment, an assumption that outstanding work from the worker would engender outstanding fidelity from the company.

CBS not only has a right to make big profits, it has a responsibility to its shareholders. And yes, technology has changed things, and yes, a lot of money was wasted along the way, a lot of charge cards flashed in a lot of frog ponds.

But what the accountants and their bosses did not understand is that when you "waste" money by keeping a great man who has passed his prime on the payroll years after his daily contribution has ended, the widest impact is not on the great man but on the people who work around him.

They realize the company cares about them in a careless world, and they decide to care about the company. And so they come up with their share of the bargain and—I could pick from many examples—decide, as the correspondent Bruce Dunning did, to fight his way onto the last plane out of Da Nang, where he huddled on the floor and kept his tape recorder rolling and reported live as the plane barely made it up, as desperate people fell from the wheels. He didn't stop talking, and you could hear the terror of what was happening through the terror of his shaking voice. There has never been a better moment in broadcast journalism. Dunning was later demoted.

CBS saved money, but it spent loyalty as if it was going out of style, which perhaps it is. Rather captured it. An executive was wondering aloud about the effect of the cuts on office morale and the sense of tradition. "Listen," Dan said, "this place has all the tradition of a discount shoe store."

A week before I left, I went to the Washington bureau with the *Evening News* crew for a few days. I called Ben and we had lunch at the White House. It was a sunny afternoon in March. As we talked I looked across the room and there, sitting at a big round table, was James Brady. His wife was at his side, and friends who laughed at his jokes.

James Brady who was shot the day the president was shot, James Brady who lay in shock as the camera lingered on the head in the pool of blood. My colleague, James Brady. I work here now.

As we left, Ben bent toward the wheelchair and said, "Jim, this is our new speechwriter." Brady's eyes were merry. He squeezed my hand.

I left CBS on Friday, March 31, 1984, three years to the day after our first show, which was the day Reagan was shot and Brady wounded. A perfect three-year arc for a thirty-three-year-old woman beginning her third job since leaving college. Not that I pay attention to such things.

Rather's good-bye rang in my ears. "Don't let 'em scare you."

* * * * * * * * * * *

THREE

The President's House
Is Many Mansions

Y ou there, citizen, standing on E Street looking in: What do you
see? A white and stately mansion on a softly rising hill, a great house
at rest on a wide expanse of lawn, the sort the fabulously rich enjoyed
many years ago. The grounds are perfect, soft green and smoothly hilly.
Encircling it all is a tall iron fence of deep dull black with golden eagles
and golden stars halfway up the bars.

Citizens stand and peer in. Some put their faces between the bars
as if they were watching a baseball game or a building going up. But
others will not touch this gate, even it has a mystique, for it guards the
stately mansion on the softly rising hill.

How do you feel, outside this gate peering in? As if it's another world
in there. (It is.) How do you feel, inside those gates looking out? As
if you're in the middle of something special, the way you felt in the
cafeteria in high school when you sat at the most popular table, or at
a tutorial in Cambridge, England, the day you thought, No one in the
world is getting a better education than I am on this day in this place.

Come see the whiteness on the elevation. Come, come in, I have
cleared you in, I have given your name to the guards. They have put

it through the computer and checked you out and now they smile; they have a pass for you to wear around your neck. "Visitor," it says. Wearing it will make you feel foolish and proud.

It is different here, come see. Everything is so well tended, the flowers, the trees, (the president's soft hands).

This is the first thing you'll notice: The white walls go right into the ground, past the grass and into the dirt, just like any other wall and any other grass, and you'll see this and think It's really here, the White House, and I can touch it. And when you touch it, what do you touch? Jefferson could have put his hand on just this spot. (Everyone who works here thinks these thoughts, at first.)

There is the whiteness of the paint and the play of the sun; the shadows look so clean and well defined. The flowers are so beautiful against this house, so crisp and rich.

And: It sits so heavy. What a thick-walled house. If you stand outside a few feet from an entrance, what you hear are birds. Sound from within does not escape; you must enter this place to hear it.

A Mute and Stately Mansion

When people find out you work in the White House they tell you about the time they were there, and if you ask them what the weather was like they say it was pretty, a sunny day, bright and warm. They all remember it this way.

Come in to the lower-level West Wing entrance. This is the entrance the staff members use, the one the Cabinet secretaries walk into as their limousines idle on West Exec. This is the entrance you never see on the news.

Come in through the double doors and pass the white walls covered with photographs of the president and the first lady doing the work of the people. Here the president leans over a child's hospital bed, here he is signing a bill in the Rose Garden, meeting with Soviet dissidents, chatting with the pope, laughing in a balloon drop—action pictures for an energetic age (or an age that hopes to find itself in movement).

An old clock down the hall softly tolls the hour, people pad by, a man walks in with a frisky brown dog who pulls at his leash. "First mutt" says the guard, who mock-bows as they pass.

Tell me, because I know: It is smaller than you expected—so much power crammed into such small space—and homier too, all those Girl Scout cookies on the desk with yellow stickums that say, "Mr. Jackson, $4.50."

Here is a thing: The people are so nice here. (At least when they don't know you.) There is a culture of politeness. (Or so it seems.)

Secretaries speak: Their voices lilt, are lambent, have a most moderate music in them. "Hello," they say, "hello, how nice, oh do." Their voices warm and purr.

They smile, the special assistants smile and the press aides, the guards smile, and when you go by the kitchen the cook looks up from the mist, lifts his eyebrows, and laughs, and the president just walked by and winked at you, and the other day the vice president said, "What a pretty baby" to the picture on your desk.

Everyone is well dressed, so that when the people of America visit they will see handsome adults doing the business of the nation. All of the men wear blue suits, not gray or black but blue, from Brooks. If a new aide walked in in a gray double-breasted jacket with shoulder pads no one would say a thing, but later he would hear what they said when he left the room: What is he, a gigolo? The women make you think of these words: handsomely put-together. They are not quite chic; there is something of a fifties feel to the perfectly applied lipstick and the conservative shape of the gold. The White House look is ten years behind the fashion times (if you remove the seventies).

Come, look in the mess, on your right, through the open doors and up to the lectern where Diane the steward memorizes her list of reservations. She knows you by name and gives you a personal smile, cocks her head and escorts you past the kitchen where the trays are stacked and where Majorette the steward is rinsing down the coffeepot and singing, again, too loud. She will be mildly reprimanded again, she will sing too loud again, to your delight. "Blue moon," she is crooning, "you found me standing alone, without a dream in my heart—hi, how you today, honey, without a love of my own. . . ." Peek inside the senior staff mess, a small wood panelled room with dark thick carpets. Men murmur at tables; something in the coolness muffles the clatter.

Come, up the stairs, toward the press office, past the Norman Rockwell portraits of members of the press corps in the thirties and forties. There is such implicit affection in these old pictures. The reporters sprawl, doze and drop their ashes on the Persian rug; they were regular people once.

Walk on: Here the blond press secretary stands caressing a coffee cup and talking to the dean of correspondents, who looks like the kind of fortune-teller who would enjoy telling you the part about the accident at sea. Walk on.

Through the door at the end of the short hall. To your left is the Cabinet room with its long shiny table. When this room is empty it is roped off like something at the Smithsonian, but soon it will be full of Cabinet secretaries, who sit at the table, and their aides and aides to the president, who sit in a row of chairs along the wall. Now and then unscripted things occur. Here is a contributor to spontaneity, barreling Bill Bennett, who walks in thinking Holy smokes, I'm in the White House. I am a member of the Cabinet of the United States, holy smokes!" The honest never get over it.

Walk on a few paces to the Oval Office, which sits cool, still and soundless but for the mellow ticking of an ancient clock. It is the brightest spot in this bright house; even the basest most mundane metal would shine in this room. You stand in the doorway looking in. You would like to touch the red velvet rope but you don't, you stand straight and stare. You have never been here but there's so much you remember, Kennedy finding the holes in the floor from Ike's golf shoes, Roosevelt shaking the martini shaker and booming out, "Babs, who's home?," peppery Harry writing letters. You have to make eye contact with someone and shake your head.

Turn away down the hall past Deaver's office, toward Baker's, and stop for a moment. Look at the walls: The pugnacious part of history is happening here. The oils, the copper and brass—

The art of this house is a masculine art, the heavy art of a masculine age, the rough ragged bronze of America's West: a sun-beaten cowboy breaking a colt, an Indian, mounted, surveying the land, another, his brother, galloping past. So many Indians mute and stopped; they look so real and radiate such life.

The guards should tell children, "They say late at night when these halls are bare that just at that moment when midnight is coming—they say there's a sound that comes on like an echo, a soft singsong chant and the beat of a drum. They say it's the spirits of Cherokees chanting, they say it's the sound of the night before battle, when warriors asked the gods to protect an ancient honored spot. I personally do not know, miss, but that is what they say."

The art of this house is a masculine art, great ships clash on the bounding main, and the air is thick with cries of men. If paintings made sounds we would duck from the din.

Come into this aide's office and look out the window. Do you notice? It's always springtime here. The Parks Service is constantly digging and replanting. Whatever is in bloom is always in bloom here. Little men in olive green come in and do their silent digging, taking out the old plants and putting in the new ones, so nothing ever droops here and the color is always the brightest. (Nothing is allowed to fade here, everything is perfect and impermanent. It makes one slightly anxious.)

At Baker's office turn right. Here is a friendly office. It is empty now, and awaits its occupant. Look before he comes.

It is a little larger than most, a little finer. A couch, a small Persian rug, a coffee table with hinges, three easy chairs, a fireplace with a big mirror above, two portraits, a U.S. Grant and a Jefferson by Matthew Jouett—when you look at an oil of a president in the White House, you think to yourself, There must be no better example of this kind of picture in the world—the de rigueur models of boats, an eighteenth-century schooner and a nineteenth-century sailboat.

A simple office, not imperial, no boast. The candle-holders on the fireplace and the lamps on the little tables could have been picked up on sale at a department store, but the desk is beautiful, heavy old blond wood shined to such a gloss that it looks as if it is encased in glass. The top drawer looks like the top drawer of your desk at home—a snapshot of a grandchild, scissors, pens and paper clips, a newspaper clipping and a ruler, not neat but all thrown in. Behind the desk, a breakfront with family pictures and the day's *Wall Street Journal* and a little stand with the one thing every office in the White House has: a television set. Which always goes on at six-thirty, for the first feed of the network news.

On a little bookcase there is a small picture of a tennis star framed in silver and inscribed with affection to the office's inhabitant. *To Vice President George Bush,* it says.

Outside again and downstairs, and people nod hello. Everyone uses correct grammar, not only the correct grammar of using the right words in the right order but a grammar that assumes grace (The cleaning lady says, "Excuse me, but may I take this? Thank you."), and most of the people you meet are relatively happy because they're at the top of

America and at the top of their game and they are well known in circles that count to them and the president called today and you know what he said, it was so funny.

They are living the happiest time of their lives, and some are like soldiers in a war, so busy living it years will pass before they look back and say, "You know, that was the vivid time, that's when I was living my life." And some control the size of their joy by remembering it can't last, it's all just a chapter, a train I got on that will soon get to Bayonne. And some don't notice their happiness, they're too busy.

Here is one who knows his joy. Stand back against the wall near the door and see him enter:

> *The bright young aide walks briskly,*
> *pushes back the door with a great oiled whoosh,*
> *stands poised for a moment, inhaling,*
> *legs firmly planted,*
> *a moist smile starting on his moist pink lips.*
>
> *The brisk young aide walks brightly,*
> *breezes through the door, stands poised,*
> *head tilted forward as he listens for a moment*
> *to the West Wing hum,*
> *thick-thighed legs firmly planted in the moment,*
> *for this is his moment.*
>
> *He stands in his thick-thighed stillness*
> *but there is about him a sense of moving forward,*
> *a suggestion of propulsion, a stiffening*
> *as he stands all vest-bursting energy*
> *and panting radiance. He sniffs, knows,*
> *stiffens, tightening to the slap of the moment,*
> *to the yes,*
> *to the yes of the sharp, dry smell of power waiting to be*
> *touched and kneaded, soothed.*

Nods briskly at the guard, rounds the corner where the elevator is, nods brightly to the aging arms-control negotiator who stands conferring with the senator. They wait for the doors to open.

But the brisk bright aide bounds by,
rounds the elevator, takes the stairs three at a time
propelled by joy and heat,
by that smell, that hum,
hurls himself toward the second floor,
takes the bend, legs like pistons,
and then bursts, bursts into the hallway—
where the Secret Service men subtly move their hands to
where they carry metal.

He stops, smiles, slows, walks by,
panting slightly, heartbeat up,
a panting pant that passes.

Regains his posture, pats his tie, feels for a cigarette, remembers not to,
walks into the Cabinet Room with a grave slow gait, nods gravely to no
one in particular and takes his seat along the wall.

He loves this place loves it loves the power and the cleanness, loves
the brightness, loves it loves it . . . and why not? Action, fun, power,
history and a future full of money! Because when you get out of here,
if you bothered to make your contacts and keep them happy and make
no enemies or rather no important ones, if you paid attention and
planned ahead and achieved a certain amount of standing you could
get out (when the getting was good, when the administration was just
beginning to peak, when it was a seller's market) and parlay it into a
nice job with Shearson Lehman or Salomon and start pulling down two
hundred K, and that's before bonuses, and buy a good English suit and
a pair of hand-tooled shoes. At least if you were a Republican, which
our aide certainly is! If you were a conservative it was: back to the think
tanks! back to the ivy! back to the column or the talk show (or the
book!).

Now is good, but what's coming is so good that he smiles in yearning
pleasure. Nostalgia for the future is what he has, a yen for what will
be. He sits back, smooths his mustache, purrs.

What the high-level aide said before he left. He said, "This is what
I most remember." He said, "I don't have a lot of feeling about the

usual places one might mention, the Cabinet Room or the Roosevelt Room or the Oval Office. I have the biggest reaction to odd places like that." He points to the entranceway of the West Wing.

"That's where I used to stand and grab people and get things done. These peripheral places—a spot outside the Cabinet Room where I grabbed Jim Baker and got him to agree to something, an area against the wall just outside the Cabinet Room. That's where the real work of the White House gets done, in small places, in a hurried conversation in the hall."

The hurried conversation in the hall—where policy got okayed or knocked down and careers got a boost or a shove, in the hurried conversation in the hall, with the men with their heads bent, nodding.

And this is what they'll remember and be surprised about years later: that when the decision was being made you weren't looking into somebody's eyes, you were staring down at the carpet. And in your dreams for the rest of your life, when you feel anxiety it will usually be a against a backdrop of a dense low-pile almond-beige carpet with a light-checked weave.

Everyone is happy here but not everyone is good.

There is a split, a distance, between how people act and the dreadful things they're doing, for the white and stately mansion is a place of intrigue and betrayal. People are leaking stories on the phone or subtly undermining colleagues, and you never really know what's happening here, what's taking place, you never know what the exact facts are— and because it is history and history has a thousand tellers, you never will.

You cannot tell how people get along by observing them. You cannot tell how two people feel about each other by how they act. You have to talk to them separately, behind the office door, or you have to talk to the press, because reporters always know.

You know this, don't you. It's like this where you work. The White House is only more so.

You leave, and as you do, mind relaxed, for the first time you notice what you had not seen on your way in, when you were so dazzled by the mansion. You notice what is on the grounds:

A smart young marine, a full-bird colonel in olive green, and movie stars dressed like queens, and queens.

And Indians on their way to meet a friend, dwarfs on their way to see the president for a photo op arranged by a right-to-lifer, basketball players in from the Rose Garden, where they were honored for winning the big game, chauffeurs leaning against gleaming limousines, a young servicewoman carrying "the football," painters in white splattered overalls, and the girl from the Parks Service waiting to put in the tulips, and fix-it men, furniture movers carrying a couch into the office of the deputy assistant who just got promoted to full assistant, Filipino stewards in gray slacks and blue blazers pushing a cart of club sandwiches for the vice president's meeting with the influential columnist from the *Post* . . .

Famous faces, *Nightline* jockeys, mystics and leaders of movements, Phyllis Schlafly with her two long waves of hair parted down the middle looking like there's an eagle on her head.

All of them being stopped somewhere along the line by a guard because they weren't wearing their passes, which they hate to wear because it mars the perfection of the uniform.

It is like a movie set, the White House and its grounds. It is like the MGM commissary in the 1940s, where no one thinks it's odd to see a Cowardly Lion eating tuna fish next to Robert Taylor dressed as a Yank in the RAF. Surprise is expected here.

You can forget, because you work here, what this house is. You can forget when you walk in to look up and peer closely at the white paint on the north portico and see the patches of roughness and know this is one of the spots that was licked by the flames of the British when they tried to burn us down in 1812. You can forget to go into the East Room and stare at the portrait of Washington that Dolley Madison saved when the British were coming. You can forget to stand there and wonder what it was like when Teddy Roosevelt sat in this garden, leaned on this mantel, laughed on this spot. You can forget you are surrounded by your country.

And then you see it, the child in the mess. Staffers bring their friends and family into the mess and the friends and family, they are from America. They walk in proudly, shyly, moving like people who have unexpectedly been called onstage.

Three children, teenagers, sit at a table with a speechwriter. They hear a sound that comes from the ceiling, and one of them asks, "What's upstairs?"

"The Oval Office."

Another sound. They are looking up.

"That would be the president." The speechwriter looks at her watch. "Yup, they're serving him lunch about now. He's probably just moving his chair so they can put the tray." They look up, awed, their faces like the faces of the children at Lourdes.

And suddenly you remember. They remind you. Which is why everyone who works in this house says to family and friends, Come, come in, I have cleared you in, I have given your name to the guards— come see the whiteness on the elevation.

FOUR

* * * * * * * * * * * *

I First Saw Him as a Foot

I first saw him as a foot, a highly polished brown cordovan wagging merrily on a hassock. I spied it through the door. It was a beautiful foot, sleek. Such casual elegance and clean lines. But not a big foot, not formidable, maybe even a little . . . frail. I imagined cradling it in my arms, protecting it from unsmooth roads . . .

—Yanked from my reverie by the movement of an aide, who bends past the foot and murmurs, "You're in luck, Mr. President, the meeting with the speechwriters is canceled." The foot stops, then wags more merrily still. Talk and light laughter. Someone closed the door.

I was finally to meet the boss; we had waited outside the Oval Office and everything was fine until an NSC official walked in and saw a speechwriter with whom he didn't get along. "I'm not going to a meeting where I'm on an equal footing with him," I heard him say as he huffed down the hall. The meeting was canceled.

Ben was embarrassed. For some reason I thought I should say something. "But I'm wearing my red silk, does he think I wear it every day?" No one laughed.

Anyway, I'd seen his foot. At least I'd have a story for my friends.

· · ·

Joining the Reagan White House as a speechwriter was like joining CBS in radio. Right church wrong pew, right company wrong division. There was an odd and general feeling, a slight snicker, perhaps the snicker the guys in the plant reserve for the PR types who float through now and then: You're part of the wind machine while we do the real work on the assembly line! But there was more and it was mysterious. At first I thought it was personal because people were so eager to tell me about my colleagues, that this one had caused great consternation when he had leaked his grievances to a columnist back in the early years, and that one had played his guitar on Air Force One. "What does he think this is, the Carter White House?" an aide to the first lady had sniffed.

In time I thought part of the problem was the speechwriters' comportment. They tended to be sad sacks and complain, and resentment isn't a magnetic personal style. But I also thought it might be that they were speechwriters in a White House so dependent on rhetoric that the people around the president came to see it as an act of loyalty to dismiss the people who wrote the script.

Things I didn't understand were always happening. A few weeks before I started I went to the White House Correspondents' Association's annual dinner, at which I met one of Larry Speakes's assistants.

"Pete, this is Peggy Noonan," said my colleague Deborah Potter. "She's going to work with you guys and write for the president."

"Why?" he said, unsmiling.

"What?"

"Why leave a network to write speeches for us?"

"Oh, because I'm stupid and have no future at CBS."

"She likes Reagan," Potter interjected. "She wants to help you guys."

"Oh. That's nice I guess. Good luck."

The same evening I had seen Jim Baker across the room, introduced myself and to my delight found that he knew who I was. As I walked away he called out, "Remember, when they shoot at you, just duck and let them hit me."

I sublet an apartment up in the Northwest section of town in a fine old building populated almost exclusively by old women. I would tell cabdrivers, "The Westchester, please," and they'd get to the driveway and turn to me and say, "I thought this was an old people's home!" There were New Deal widows who had come to Washington from all over the country in the thirties and forties to work on the Hill and at the agencies; they met a guy and had kids and now he was gone and now the women of the Westchester met in the evening in the lobby, powdered, sweet-smelling, silver-haired, buzzing softly in their patterned dresses. They always said hello.

My first days at work what I remember was walking the high marble hallways and tall, cool stairs of the Old Executive Office Building. (An aide told me, "When they're new they walk right down the middle, when they've been here a while they hug the walls." He was right.)

The EOB is part of the White House complex, within the gate but separated from the West Wing by a short street called West Executive Avenue. Most of the White House offices were in the EOB, and people who worked there called it: the White House.

I was introduced to the staff. "Peggy is from CBS, where she worked with Dan Rather, and their show was nominated for many awards—"

"The Lenin prize!" said a bearded speechwriter.

"Now Dana," said Ben.

"Ben, when are we going to see the president again?" he asked. "It would really help us to meet with him and hear what he's thinking about."

"I know, Dana," Ben said.

"How long is it since you met with him?" I asked.

"More than a year."

"It's more than a year since you saw the president?"

"Well, since we met. We see him all the time. We wave to him."

They gave me a little office that faced a courtyard that never got the sun. I could look out and see the exhaust system of the EOB. An old radiator hissed forlornly, carrying into my office the metallic rumblings of the deepest insides of the old Victorian building. It was dank and clanked.

Sig, the lady who assigned furniture, came in and looked around. She had a sweet, comic way about her as she shyly asked me what I do and what my title is. I had been warned that you didn't get nice furniture unless Sig thought you were important, so I puffed myself up nicely and said important things with an air of authority. She smiled and wished me well. That afternoon she sent down a broken chair and a bookcase with water stains.

I loved that funny office. I used to sit there in the late afternoon in a red velveteen chair and read the papers of the presidency in the glow of an old lamp. In the White House they keep big, thick volumes of the speeches, utterances and meetings with the press of the presidents, all the presidents. I'd take a few volumes from the library upstairs and read them at random. In time I knew I was looking for the grammar of the presidency, the sound and tone and tense of it. And I knew where to go: to the modern president who had sounded most like a president, the one who set the standard for how the rest should sound. I went to FDR.

I'd hold those heavy volumes and turn back the pages, breathing in, smelling the musty smell. I'd pick a year at random, thumb through and stop. FDR on the campaign trail, on a campaign train. And nei-thuh does my little dog Fala . . . All those head-wagging sentences, rounded, declarative, naturally written and naturally voiced. You could see it on the page even if you hadn't read it all your life that the thing about Roosevelt was that he was shrewd and sunny, not hurt by man's sin but relishing its many varieties. A man who felt that life is good, life is being up there in Dutchess County sitting at a great table with all the chicks, eating a big spring lunch of beefy red tomatoes and potato salad and mayonnaise and deviled eggs on the old china with the flowers almost rubbed off. Talking, entertaining. And did you hear what Joe Kennedy did? He stood there hard-mouthed and determined in the middle of my office and pushed off his suspenders and let them drop so I could see his legs! I guess he wants St. James's pretty bad! Nice place to wash the Irish off!

I knew he liked the poem "Invictus"—"I am the master of my fate / I am the captain of my soul"—and saw now that he had absorbed its rhythm so that it had become his own triumphant cadence, a sound that echoed not only in his speeches but in his recorded conversation. He had small press conferences in his office, informal affairs, a half-dozen of the boys ringed around the big desk and FDR discoursing on the world, spinning the globe in his mind, putting his finger on a spot and looking down. "Now in England, on the other hand . . ."

I'd think, This is how Reagan should sound.

· · ·

It was hard for me to make friends. Not that people weren't nice, they were, but we did not have similar lives. The men and women my age were not like New York people. They were married and had two little children; they had such settled lives. And I was shy, and when I am shy I look impassive and when I look impassive I look formidable, and some people were shy with me.

It was a daily challenge for me to walk into the mess by myself. Young men would look up, look down, and continue to chew. Women would look up, nod pertly, look down, and chew. But mostly there were men, men in suits, and when they gestured the light caught their presidential cuff links. In time I forced myself to go, unaccompanied, to the big round staff table where those without lunch partners sat.

I would listen: This is like a tutorial, I thought. These people are like the bright, intense people in college who couldn't stop talking about Hawthorne and Tennyson and the Lake poets. Only the topic was public policy. And there was a freshness to it.

Now I know it was the authentic sound of the Reagan revolution, buzzing around me.

"Peg, hi, Mike Horowitz, OMB! Heard all about ya, welcome!" He turns back to the men, throws his arm over a chair. "Now the thing we have to keep in mind in welfare reform is the fourteen-year-old kid in the inner city who has been unwittingly encouraged by this great lumbering government of ours to take steps in her life that are ultimately harmful to her. She's had a baby she's not equipped to care for, she's just made her mother a grandmother at the age of thirty, she's stuck now without an education, without options, with no particular promise. She has been used and abused by the very system created to help her! And who will speak for her? No one, because precious few in this debate care about anything but the biases and demands of their own constituencies. Thus: stasis. Pass the catsup!"

"Yes," says Doug Holladay of OPL, "you're right, but that gets us back at least in part to values, and the role they play. And that brings up the sometimes delicate question of how to effectively bring back and encourage those values by which all of us of all colors have lived in this country for generations, for centuries."

"But without being labeled irrelevant to the debate or sentimental about a past that never was," says Judi Buckalew of OPL.

"Let me fill you in on what is happening in our sincere if admittedly at this point inadequate attempts to overhaul and improve our farm program and see if you can't draw some surprising parallels," offers Fred Khedouri of OMB.

"Wait, here's Lenćzowski," says Horowitz of an NSC staffer. "John, that statement of yours that a lot of the people who are pushing for an arms agreement must just love signing ceremonies, because without a serious commitment to verification, it's all a charade was just—super! Fred, go ahead."

It was music to my ears. All these intelligent, well-motivated people talking about important things and trying to understand America. It was music.

Little by little I settled in. There were times when I thought, and I wasn't sure if I was right but I felt that I was viewed as . . . a little different. Not quite an oddball, not quite a strange one, not quite a walking occasion of sin, though those phrases came into my mind. A secretary told me, "You dress different." I was at that time partial to long black skirts and soft black boots. "That's not so bad," she said, "but everybody here at your particular level wears suits with a sort of man-tailored blouse and a scarf or a tie. But what's really different is your hair. You have this long, free-flowing hair. Most of us have shorter, neater hair."

A young woman took me aside and said, "I heard you had wine in the mess."

"Yeah."

"And smoked cigarettes."

"Oh yeah. It was my friend's birthday and we were celebrating, and I guess we stayed too long. Was it . . . sort of noticed?"

"I heard about it."

"Was it disapproved?"

"Well . . . it wasn't considered average."

What was considered average?

I went to lunch with a man I met at a brunch, a lobbyist for a big insurance consortium. "The Carter folks used to hang out at a bar on Pennsylvania Avenue called Sarsfield's," he told me. "It was wild, it was a zoo. Sunday was the big night. All the bartenders and waitresses from around town would go there to drink and the Carter people would show and there'd be fights in this corner and heavy drinking over there. It was wild those days."

"Is there a Reagan hangout?"

"Nope."

"I didn't think so. You know, no one has ever said to me, 'After work let's go for a cup of coffee.' At CBS people were always going out. Here there's nothing. I think they go home and they fall asleep at eleven-oh-three and get up at five-forty-five and go jogging and then they eat cereal with the kids and correct their homework at the table and come in at seven-fifteen with their briefcases and say, 'Good morning! What can we do to advance traditional values today?' "

The social ecology of the White House and the EOB was interesting. There was the difference between the East Wing and the West Wing. The East Wing was the first lady and her staff, and they were considered not so serious. They also seemed more acutely aware of status and money and style. They read *W* and the fashion magazines. "Those folks don't seem so chatty and friendly," I told a friend who'd been observing the White House since 1980. "Good," she said. "You don't want them to like you, you don't want to fit in."

The West Wing was the presidential side of the White House, where the important men and the important meetings are. There were more groups and subgroups.

There was a group of young women who were the daughters of millionaires. Here was Miss Catsupfortune, there Miss Daddysalobbyist. They were in their early and midtwenties, and they were assistants to special assistants and secretaries. They wore pretty scarves and they were pretty and some of them were funny and the White House was their social whirl. "I love them," said an older woman. "They're our Sloane Rangers. If Charles had married an American . . ." and she pointed at a porcelain blonde in old lace.

At war with them were southern girls of modest means, middle-class girls from Winston-Salem who were famous back home because they worked at the White House. They had southern drawls and a kind of down-home shrewdness. The girls from the South called the rich girls the Whitestockings, because they wore white patterned hose. (Others called them the Debs or the Dumb and the Restless.) The southern girls resented the rich girls because they thought they didn't have to do good work, which was maybe true, and were protected in ways others weren't, which was probably true. The Debs sensed the class resentment, and understandably resented it. (The best answer to such things is George Bush's: When he was accused of being born to rich parents in Connecticut, he said, "I couldn't help where I was born, I just wanted to be near my mother at the time.") The Debs fell back on their strong suit: being glamorous and looking down.

There were movement conservatives with serious demeanors and New Right intellectuals from Harvard and Stanford and lost people from New Jersey and supply-siders from the Philadelphia Main Line. There were born-again Christians in their inexpensive suits and their not-quite-right glasses. They had gone to state schools and loved to talk about the kids. They didn't quite fit in either.

And there was the college thing.

I am in the mess, at the staff table, trying to maintain eye contact. Hello, how are you, what college did you go to?

"Fairleigh Dickinson in New Jersey."

"I never heard of that," he says.

"That's okay," I say.

"You don't seem embarrassed," he says.

"Am I supposed to be?"

"Of course not," he says stoutly.

It was odd people were always asking me what college I went to, because I came to town at thirty-three, and that's not the first question you ask when a grown woman walks in. ("Didn't they care about that at CBS?" said a writer who is a friend. "Not in the newsroom," I said. "Dick Salant cared," she said.)

I asked about it. I was told: a) they're just trying to make conversation and discover if there's any connection between you, b) they're snobs and want to know if you're on their level, so they find out your college and extrapolate from there, and c) what do you expect, it's a totally masculine culture.

Which it was. It wasn't like New Jersey, where the housewives control life, or New York, where bright men and women rub shoulders and bump against each other a little too hard as they try to get ahead. I had entered a place where men were completely in charge. And one of the things men use to start sizing each other up is: college/Ivy League/sports. Also: The thing at the heart of the White House experience is impermanence, you only have a certain amount of time. In the mess you want to be the first to have a fact and an opinion that both catches the new person's identity and underscores your own: "Yes, she does seem bright; she went to Radcliffe, but before my wife."

. . .

There was a man in Ben's office, squatting on the floor, telling the secretaries dirty jokes. I thought, That's what an advance man is. He said, "Hi! I'm Art Laffer! Hear about the Polish lesbian who likes men?" There was a man standing in an office. I'd gone in to get a pencil sharpener and saw him waiting for someone. He was big, and he slumped like Columbo in his trench coat. His eyes were so sad. "I'm Lyn Nofziger," he said. "Have fun here. Have a good time."

I walked the halls with a cleaning woman named Miss Hall. This is where Nixon made them tapes. Who else is in these offices? I don't really know, honey. I just know who's neat and who's a mess.

I walked into a speechwriter's office, and he introduced me to his friends: "This is Peggy Noonan, who took the woman speechwriter's job."

My first speech was what former speechwriters have called "Rose Garden Rubbish," though I never heard that phrase when I was there. It was a Rose Garden appearance in which the president would announce the Teacher of the Year. You would think this would be easy: Praise teaching, announce the winner, praise her, and that's it, neat, nice, five minutes. But it was my first speech so I included a defense of the West and an analysis of Bloomsbury's contribution to Keynesian notions of expediency as illustrated by the famous "In the long run we're all dead." It ran a little long.

I got my information on the teacher from a researcher who got it from the advance office. I got advice on the tone from Ben—don't go too long because it's hot in the Rose Garden and he's standing in the sun and reading from cards and that's not his best read. It's an annual speech, ask Research for copies of what he's said in the past. "And remember, it always has to be positive with him. Never 'I'll never forget,' always 'I'll always remember.'"

I listened, I tried, I froze. The president would be saying these words! (They would go in the books!)

I stared at a whiteness waiting for words. The blood pounded softly in my ears. "Teaching is a very important profession." Scratch that. "Teaching is arguably the most important of professions for—" Strike "arguably." Scratch the whole sentence, it's so blah blah. "Teaching is a profession I would have considered, but . . ." But. But they paid better at Warner's.

"We are here today to honor . . ." Strike today. Remember the waterfront shack with the sign FRESH FISH SOLD HERE. Of course it's fresh, we're on the ocean. Of course it's for sale, we're not giving it away. Of course it's here, otherwise the sign would be someplace else. The final sign: FISH.

Ben had said, If you get in a bind call Bill Bennett at the National Endowment for the Humanities, he's brilliant and he cares about teaching.

I called his office. He called me back from an airport.

"I'm a new speechwriter for the president and I need some help. The subject is teachers. He's announcing the Teacher of the Year. I hate to bother you but—"

"When do you need it?"

"Now."

"Oh, nice to have time. Okay: *A Man for All Seasons,* Sir Thomas More's speech to Richard Rich. Rich is a bright young man not sure of his future. More tells him, 'Be a teacher.' Rich says, 'And if I'm a great teacher, who will know it?' More says, 'You, your students, God. Not a bad audience, that.' Or words to that effect. Beautiful speech, and true. Look it up, gotta go, bye."

I used it. The President to my pride and disappointment did not change a word.

The day of the ceremony I went to the Rose Garden. It was a warm humid day in April and the sun was strong. The press was gathered in front, looking around, scoping the joint. Their eyes never stop: Who's that talking to Deaver, Who's with Baker? I stood in the back behind a row of chairs.

The president bounded out of the Oval Office into the sunlight and stood at a lectern on the grass. He cleared his throat. "Thank you, ladies and gentlemen."

It was him. I began to pace back and forth. I began to swallow, and wet my lips. It was so exciting to finally see him with him saying my words which I wrote on my typewriter with my hands. I looked up at the roof and saw the little window where Caroline looked out when her father honored the astronauts. I looked at the Colonnade. I looked at the grass, my shoes; I looked at . . . the Secret Service men, who were looking back. They stared at me, blank-faced and ready. One of them was walking toward me.

"Would you like to sit, miss?"

"Oh no, not really. I'm not a guest, I mean I'm not supposed to be in the audience, I'm not supposed to be here, I'm—"

"Who are you please?"

"Oh I'm the new speechwriter. I wrote this and I'm nervous that's why I'm pacing, I'm sorry would you like me to leave?"

"No." he said, nodding, his tongue pressing against his cheek. "It's all right. As you were. Proceed."

First big stupid thing I did:

I got a call I didn't want. The first lady's chief of staff wanted me to come over to the East Wing to work on a speech for Mrs. Reagan.

I went to Ben. "I mean no offense but we settled this before I came. If I were a man I could write for her but as a woman they'll say I'm the first lady's speechwriter who now and then does a speech for the president."

Ben sighed. "I knew this would happen. I told them you're not here for that."

"Can we do anything?"

"She's upset because she doesn't like her speeches. She doesn't think Peter's stuff is muscular enough."

"Well I'm a girl and I'm not muscular either. Girls are sissies and don't use verbs."

"Nice try. Look, do it this once and if he asks again I'll take care of it."

I wrote a nice bad speech, so sugary she'd have to lick her fingers afterward. "My life didn't begin until I met Ronnie." "I can tell you as a mother that nothing, nothing, is as important as the welfare of a child." The kid didn't miss a cliché. Peter, the speechwriter she'd rejected, offered hopefully, "When she talks about drugs she likes to say things like, 'The things I've seen would make the strongest heart break.'"

I figured if Peter wrote that and she didn't like his work, I should write it too.

I sent it in. Jim Rosebush called. "Congratulations," he said, "she loved it!"

A week later he asked that I "polish up" another speech. I went to Ben. "There's nothing wrong with helping out a little," he said. A week later Rosebush called.

"I want you to write another speech."

I said I'd have to check that out. He said, "I'm sure there's no problem. The president's speechwriters write for the first lady. She *is* the first lady of the country, you know."

I said, "I know but I came down here to write for the president and—"

"Well, if you think you're too good—"

"No, no, but I just want to write for the president."

"Well, we'll see."

A moment later Ben called. "Go."

I called Rosebush's office and offered to come over. He asked exactly when I'd be there. "Ten minutes," I said. "No, make it twenty," he said. "Okay, twenty."

"Twenty on the dot," he said.

He offered a seat and proceeded to talk about the weather and politics and how did I like it here. Odd, I thought, this busy man killing time.

Mike Deaver walked in.

"What's all this about?" he said with a scowl as he threw his briefcase onto a chair.

"This is Peggy Noonan," said Rosebush, "who is refusing to write speeches for the first lady."

"Ughuh," I choked.

"We need her help, but she doesn't want to help us."

Deaver looked at me.

"Mr. Deaver," I said, "I don't want to be unhelpful but I joined up here a few weeks ago to write for the president. I'm sure the first lady is going to be very important to the campaign and I'm sure she'll have a lot of speaking engagements, and—and I think she'll need a lot of help. But I can't do it because that's not why I came here."

Deaver looked at me. "Well I don't think we're going to settle this here," he said. "We'll work this out later. Jim, since I'm here, let's finish our talk about . . ."

I gathered my papers and ran. "I have to get a speech to the president," I said over my shoulder at Rosebush, who was making little pyramids with his hands and tapping them together.

I made a decision. I was not going to become the first lady's speechwriter and I was not going to keep worrying about it. I called Darman. This is important, I said. He chuckled and told me to come by.

I told him what had happened. "I'm going to have to leave here and go back to New York and my nice job writing for CBS News unless we settle this, and I must tell you I can't settle it by agreeing to write the first lady's speeches. Ben promised I wouldn't have to do it, I was worried about it from the beginning because I'm a woman and—"

"You're not going to write the first lady's speeches. It will be taken care of. Any other problems?"

I was taken aback, and a little disappointed. Here I was all wound up; I wanted to have to insist.

"No."

"Are we enjoying our job?"

"We are coming to terms with the facts of our employment."

"I'm pleased. Do come again."

"Thank you, it's been a pleasure."

"Me too."

A few days later I passed Rosebush and a few of his assistants as I walked along looking at the portraits of the first ladies in the part of the White House known as the residence. "Will you be coming by soon?" he asked brightly.

"No!" I said brightly. "I will not! Talk to Dick Darman! Thank you! Thank you! Goodbye!" I kept walking.

What I should have done, of course, was act very friendly and explain with some pain that I'm just unable to do it, Jim, but if there's ever anything else I can do for you . . . Or I should have said I was eager to help, but Dick and Ben wouldn't free me up, the election, I'm working so hard. . . . Instead, I did a very un-Washington thing. I showed an unseemly joy in my victory.

The fact is, and this has been a problem all my life, when I don't like somebody I just can't make believe I do. I don't mean I'm too genuine to fake a regard I do not feel, I mean I'm too proud not to show it when I think someone has overstepped the bounds. (To make it all worse, when I am really mad I can be blunt as a blunt instrument. A friend once told me, "It's okay to call a spade a spade, but you don't have to call it a shit shovel." Anyway, I'm getting better as I get older at maintaining a reliable if unspectacular civility. But this may only be because I'm getting tired.)

Anyway, Rosebush scowled. His assistants scowled. I had made enemies. I didn't care.

I have asked myself since: If I knew then that the first lady was the major and decisive force she was in that White House would I still have rejected the call to write for her? And the answer, I think, is yes.

A few weeks later I was walking through the East Wing when I saw the first lady and her entourage coming my way. I'd never met her and didn't know if I was supposed to look at her and make eye contact and say hello or leave her to her privacy, of which she had not had much these many years. I decided to look to see if I could see anything interesting in her eyes. She looked at me in a way that seemed to have no meaning. Then she looked down at what I was wearing which was, unfortunately, a wrinkled khaki skirt and a blue workshirt and heavy walking shoes with white woolen socks. Not exactly White House issue, but I was going walking. She looked me up and down and I swear her mouth curled. She looked away and said something to an aide. The next time I saw her I hid behind a pillar.

Second big stupid thing I did:

I was invited to the mess to have lunch with Maureen Reagan. I think Nancy Risque in the Congressional Affairs Office arranged it. I got there late. Maureen was already there. Her face was like the face of Bette Davis in *The Private Lives of Elizabeth and Essex* when Errol Flynn did something impertinent. I couldn't think of any good conversation. She did not appear to be attempting to think of any. At one point someone mentioned the board game Trivial Pursuit, and I piped up that I'd heard the Canadian version was better. There was silence as I remembered what I'd read about the Canadian version in yesterday's *Washington Post:* that unlike the American version it contained the question "How many months after their marriage was Ronald and Nancy Reagan's daughter Patti born?"

The phone rang. Saved by the bell. A steward brought a phone to the table and murmured to Miss Reagan. "Mr. Baker's office," he said. She picked it up, listened, glowered, slammed down the phone. "Goddammit," she spat. "Let's go." She left in a huff. I lingered over coffee and thought, You just made a bad impression on a powerful person with a volatile temperament. Congratulations, you're doing really well.

Third big stupid thing I did:

I was writing the president's remarks for a luncheon for a Republican women's group. Maureen Reagan was involved with the group. I knew how to recoup my mistake: I called the East Wing and said that I would soon be finished with the speech and would like Maureen to look at it. They called back: Miss Reagan wants the speech immediately upon its completion.

I wrote a good speech, a fine speech. It connected things that had never been connected, it asserted itself, it was intellectually substantial and yet marked by a kind of sunny, big-chested bonhomie. I sent it over and waited for the raves. The next morning Maureen called me personally.

"Page two," she said.

"Yes?" I smiled.

"Kill it."

"What?"

"Kill it. And three. Page four, second graph, kill."

"Gee, Maureen, I don't know. Don't you think this is pretty good? Where I mention the rise of the conservative columnists and Safire and all the percolation of ideas on our side—"

"Are you refusing?"

"Well, I don't know. I'm saying though that—"

Click.

I had the distinct impression my rehabilitation program had not achieved the desired effect. I sat in silence. I had done it again but it wasn't my fault, I was really trying, I meant well. But . . . is the president's daughter really supposed to control what he says? That's really dumb, that's really—

The phone rang.

"Peggy? This is Dick Darman. I see you're already making an impression. I've just spent the past twenty minutes saving your job. Miss Maureen Reagan was over here telling some very important people that you should be fired."

"Oh no."

"Did you say no to her?"

"No, I just, I didn't say no but she wanted me to do some things that I thought were wrong."

"All right, listen to me. Are you listening?"

"Yes."

"This is what you say when Maureen Reagan tells you to do something. You say, 'Yes Maureen, you bet Maureen, right away Maureen.' Do you have that?"

"Yes."

"Good. What are you going to say when Maureen Reagan calls?"

"Yes Maureen you bet Maureen how high Maureen."

"Even better. And when you're done you call me and tell me what stupid thing you agreed to, and I'll take care of it."

Yes Dick, you bet Dick.

I had a Maureen Plan after that. I was going to apologize and whatever she told me I was going to do and I was going to be very eager about it. But she never called again. A few years later I sat two people away from her at a table at a big dinner. She made believe she didn't see me. (Maureen says she never told anyone I should be fired.)

I hoped to meet the president. I continued writing speeches. They were not the most important speeches, but each had a weight of its own, and I strove to make each special. I thought about the audience. I would think how happy they were to be near the president and how each deserved something special, something personal. I experimented with jokes and witticisms in parentheses at the top of the page; I did not endear myself to the researchers when I asked them to go back again and again to find out who the leader of such-and-such an organization is and what his nickname is and has he ever met the president? And in the town where he's speaking what are the people talking about, is there a local problem like a garbage scow nobody wants, does the local school have a winning team, what's the big local department store and are they hiring? Anything to make it seem as if someone thought about this speech and these people.

I would write them and send them in; the president would voice them and never complain.

I will always remember—actually I will never forget—the first time I got a response. I received a speech back from the president, and in the upper right-hand corner where he put his initials to show he'd read it there was the usual RR, but beneath that I saw his faint script. "Very Good," it said.

I stared at it. Then I took a pair of scissors and cut it off and taped it to my blouse, like a second-grader with a star. All day people would notice it and look at me; I would beam back in quietly idiotic manner. In the mess one of the president's lawyers, Peter Rusthoven, nodded hello, saw the paper, read it, put his head in his hands and screamed softly. That was my favorite reaction.

I met him face-to-face my fourth month there. I had been lobbying, of course. "I can't write well without hearing the person I'm writing for talk in conversation," I told Ben. "If you think he sounds stale maybe it's because the speechwriters haven't met with him in more than a year," I'd tell Darman.

Finally, after the president returned from Europe, where he had attended the fortieth anniversary of D-Day and given the address at Pointe du Hoc, I was to meet him. With Ben and Dick and the entire top staff. That was one of the odd things about the Reagan White House: Wherever the president was his top staff was. They'd sit there in a row in his office like frogs on a log. I used to wonder, Don't they have work to do?

(A digression: What I learned from seeing them operate is that you don't just elect a president when you vote, you elect a staff. A modern chief of staff is, in a way, an assistant president; in the Reagan White House he sometimes seemed to be co-president.

(It's the chief and his chiefs who persuaded the president as to the agenda and how to pursue it; it's the chief and his chiefs who persuaded him as to personnel decisions and how to make progress with Congress. It's the chief and his chiefs who revealed, through daily conversations and lunches and dinners with journalists, the nature and character of the presidency; and it's journalists who shape our perceptions and history's assumptions.

(I decided that history really is biography, and you could map the probable trajectory of an administration by making a deep study of the chief and his chiefs. If the head of NSC is not relaxed about his personal powers, beware: He will attempt to show his mastery through some scheme that will more likely illustrate his inadequacies. If the new chief has an ego to beat the band, beware: He'll trip over his vanity, and take the president tumbling with him. If the chief's chief aide is a fellow of modest talents then realize: When the chief and the president get in trouble they will not have a first-rate person to help them.

(By the time I left the White House I thought all this was an immutable fact, an unstoppable trend. But now, it seems, Bush is turning it on its head.)

. . .

We waited outside the president's office. An aide inside opened the door—the doors in the West Wing don't make a sound, you feel the air and that's how you know they're swinging—and motioned us in.

There he was, behind his desk, turning toward me: big tall, radiant man, impeccably tailored. He twinkled at me. I was the new one, and the only woman. He walked to me and took my hand. It is the oddest thing and true even if everyone says it: It is not possible to be nervous in his presence. He acts as if he's lucky to be with you. Well, he says, it's so wonderful to meet you, please, sit down, well, so!

We sat, I in the spot on the couch immediately to his right. I don't really remember what we talked about. There was no reason for the meeting other than the new speechwriter's unhappy and let's have him meet her or she may leave. The president sat up straight in his chair, a piece of beige plastic in his ear. I was surprised how big his hearing aid is, or rather how aware of it you are when you're with him. There was a quizzical look on his face as he listened to what was going on around him, and I thought, He doesn't really hear very much, and his appearance of constant good humor is connected to his deafness. He misses much of what is not said directly to him, but he assumes it is good.

The meeting lasted half an hour. Conversation ambled. The president looked around sometimes as if to say, What are we doing here, folks? I felt guilty at taking his time.

The night before, Mario Cuomo had given his speech to the Democratic Convention. Everyone agreed it had not been a great speech, but I thought it had been a speech of great power. Good or not, it sure had got under the president's skin.

He looked at me. "Larry Speakes says all the reporters have been asking questions. I asked him to draw up a list of what they're saying at the briefing. I just got it and sat down and wrote my answers for the news conference. Would you mind if I read them to you?"

Would I mind. Hey buddy, I don't have time to sit around listening to the leader of the free world speculate on how to answer his most eloquent critic. "Oh please, yes."

He retrieves the list from his desk and reads off the answers, some of which are snappy. I smile. It's all facts and figures about the economy. "Seven million new jobs created, six hundred thousand new businesses incorporated—if that's depression, let's have more of it!"

As we leave, he takes my hand. "You know, a while ago I wanted to call you about something, but . . ." He can't remember.

"Peggy wrote the Pointe du Hoc speech, Mr. President." Eager Ben.

Reagan lights up. "That's it. That was wonderful, it was like 'Flanders Fields.' I read it upstairs, and when I read something, I like to look up at the corner to see the name, and I saw Noonan. I meant to call you and never . . ."

"Oh that's okay."

"But it was wonderful. Were you there? Well, after the speech the original Pointe du Hoc fellows came up and told me how much they liked it, and there were tears in their eyes. And you know, I talked with this fellow—the day before, when the Rangers recreated the climb up those cliffs, this fellow went up with them just as he had forty years ago, and he made it to the top with those kids. Boy, that was something."

"Boy, that was something." That's how he talks, like a happy working-class American boy of the thirties.

I had been in the White House less than five months at that point. I had seen how the White House works and how speechwriting works. What I was learning was what Dick Darman said at Ben's good-bye party two years later: that speechwriting in the Reagan White House was where the philosophical, ideological, and political tensions of the administration got worked out.

Speechwriting was where the administration got invented every day. And so speechwriting was, for some, the center of gravity in that administration, the point where ideas and principles still counted. For others—at the State Department, for instance—speechwriting was a natural and unhappy force of nature, a black hole from which no sophisticated thought could escape.

What an apprenticeship I had. I had better tell you, before I tell you about that, what a speech is to me.

FIVE

"Speech! Speech!"

A (The use of man, here, is generic; I mean man and woman; he also means she.)

speech is a soliloquy—one man on a bare stage with a big spotlight. He will tell us who he is and what he wants and how he will get it and what it means that he wants it and what it will mean when he does or does not get it, and . . .

And he looks up at us in the balconies and clears his throat. "Ladies and gentlemen . . ." We lean forward, hungry to hear. Now it will be said, now we will hear the thing we long for.

A speech is part theater and part political declaration; it is a personal communication between a leader and his people; it is art, and all art is a paradox, being at once a thing of great power and great delicacy.

A speech is poetry: cadence, rhythm, imagery, sweep! A speech reminds us that words, like children, have the power to make dance the dullest beanbag of a heart.

Speeches are not significant because we have the technological ability to make them heard by every member of our huge nation simultaneously. Speeches are important because they are one of the great constants of our political history. For two hundred years, from "Give me liberty or give me death" to "Ask not what your country can do for you," they have been not only the way we measure public men, they have been how we tell each other who we are. For two hundred years they have been changing—making, forcing—history: Lincoln, Bryan and the cross of gold, FDR's first inaugural, Kennedy's, Martin Luther King in '63, Reagan and the Speech in '64. They count. They more than count, they shape what happens. (An irony: You know who doesn't really know this? Political professionals. The men who do politics as a business in America are bored by speeches. They call them "the rah rah." They prefer commercials.)

Another reason speeches are important: because the biggest problem in America, the biggest problem in any modern industrialized society, is loneliness. A great speech from a leader to the people eases our isolation, breaks down the walls, includes people: It takes them inside a spinning thing and makes them part of the gravity.

All speechwriters have things they think of when they write. I think of being a child in my family at the dinner table, with seven kids and hubbub and parents distracted by worries and responsibilities. Before I would say anything at the table, before I would approach my parents, I would plan what I would say. I would map out the narrative, sharpen the details, add color, plan momentum. This way I could hold their attention. This way I became a writer.

The American people too are distracted by worries and responsibilities and the demands of daily life, and you have to know that and respect it—and plan the narrative, sharpen the details, add color and momentum.

I work with an image: the child in the mall. When candidates for president are on the campaign trail they always go by a mall and walk through followed by a pack of minicams and reporters. They go by Colonel Sanders and have their picture taken eating a piece of chicken, they josh around with the lady in the mall information booth, they shake hands with the shoppers. But watch: Always there is a child, a ten-year-old girl, perhaps, in an inexpensive, tired-looking jacket. Perhaps she is by herself, perhaps with a friend. But she stands back, afraid of the lights, and as the candidate comes she runs away. She is afraid of his fame, afraid of the way the lights make his wire-rim glasses shine, afraid of dramatic moments, dense moments. When you are a speechwriter you should think of her when you write, and of her parents. They are Americans. They are good people for whom life has not been easy.

Show them respect and be honest and logical in your approach and they will understand every word you say and hear—and know—that you thought of them.

The irony of modern speeches is that as our ability to disseminate them has exploded (an American president can speak live not only to America but to Europe, to most of the world), their quality has declined.

Why? Lots of reasons, including that we as a nation no longer learn the rhythms of public utterance from Shakespeare and the Bible. When young Lincoln was sprawled in front of the fireplace reading *Julius Caesar*—"Th' abuse of greatness is, when it disjoins remorse from power"—he was, unconsciously, learning to be a poet. You say, "That was Lincoln, not the common man." But the common man was flocking to the docks to get the latest installment of Dickens off the ship from England.

The modern egalitarian impulse has made politicians leery of flaunting high rhetoric; attempts to reach, to find the right if sometimes esoteric quote or allusion seem pretentious. They don't really know what "the common man" knows anymore; they forget that we've all had at least some education and a number of us read on our own and read certain classics in junior high and high school. The guy at the gas station read *Call of the Wild* when he was fourteen, and sometimes thinks about it. Moreover, he has imagination. Politicians forget. They go in lowest common denominator—like a newscaster.

People say the problem is soundbites. But no it isn't.

A word on the history: "Soundbite" is what television producers have long called the short tape of a politician talking, which is inserted into a longer piece voiced by a reporter. Imagine a speech as a long string of licorice; the mouth-sized bite the reporter takes as it goes by is the soundbite.

The cliché is to say, "It all has to be reduced to a tidy little thirty-second soundbite." But soundbites don't go thirty seconds, they go seven seconds. Or four seconds. When I got to the White House I never met anyone who had heard of soundbites or thought of them, and the press never wrote of them. I used to tell Ben, "What we're going to see of this speech on TV is five seconds that a producer in New York thinks is the best or most interesting moment." Then I'd tell him what they were going to pick. I knew because I used to pick them. Now people who don't understand soundbites talk about them all the time.

Soundbites in themselves are not bad. "We have nothing to fear . . ." is a soundbite. "Ask not . . ." is a soundbite. So are "You shall not crucify mankind upon a cross of gold," and "With malice toward none; With charity for all . . ."

Great speeches have always had great soundbites. The problem now is that the young technicians who put together speeches are paying attention only to the soundbite, not to the text as a whole, not realizing that all great soundbites happen by accident, which is to say, all great soundbites are yielded up inevitably, as part of the natural expression of the text. They are part of the tapestry, they aren't a little flower somebody sewed on.

They sum up a point, or make a point in language that is pithy or profound. They are what the politician is saying! They are not separate and discrete little one-liners that a bright young speechwriter just promoted out of the press office and two years out of business school slaps on.

But that is what they've become. Young speechwriters forget the speech and write the soundbite, plop down a hunk of porridge and stick on what they think is a raisin. (In the Dukakis campaign they underlined them in the text.)

The problem is not the soundbitization of rhetoric, it's the Where's-the-beef-ization. The good news: Everyone in America is catching on to the game, and it's beginning not to work anymore. A modest hope: Politicians will stop hiring communications majors to write their speeches and go to history majors, literature majors, writers—people who can translate the candidate's impulses into literature that is alive, and true.

A speech is also a statement of policy. Sometimes it is This Is What We Must Do About the Budget and sometimes it is Why We Must Go to War, but always it is about plans and their effect on people: policy. It is impossible to separate speechwriting from policy because a policy is made of words, and the speechwriter makes the words. A speechwriter is obviously not free to invent out of whole cloth, but—by articulating a policy he invents it.

An example: If an American president goes to Berlin and stands next to the Berlin Wall, it is one thing (and one kind of policy) if he says,

"The American people support the German people." It's quite another if he says, "I am a Berliner." The first means, "We support you," the second means, "We really mean it, we're really here, and if we ever abandon you it will forever be a stain on our honor." Sorensen knew it, Kennedy knew it, and the crowd knew it.

In the Reagan administration there was an unending attempt to separate the words from the policy. A bureaucrat from State who was assigned to work with the NSC on the annual economic summits used to come into speechwriting and refer to himself and his colleagues as "we substantive types" and to the speechwriters as "you wordsmiths." He was saying, We do policy and you dance around with the words. We would smile back. Our smiles said, The dancer is the dance.

It was a constant struggle over speeches, a constant struggle over who was in charge and what view would prevail and which group would triumph. Each speech was a battle in a never-ending war; when the smoke cleared there was Reagan, holding the speech and saying the words as the mist curled about his feet. I would watch and think, That's not a speech it's a truce. A temporary truce.

How were speeches made in the Reagan administration? Here's an image: Think of a bunch of wonderful, clean, shining, perfectly shaped and delicious vegetables. Then think of one of those old-fashioned metal meat grinders. Imagine the beautiful vegetables being forced through the grinder and being rendered into a smooth, dull, textureless purée.

Here's another image: The speech is a fondue pot, and everyone has a fork. And I mean everyone.

This is how a speech came about:

First, the president's top advisers would agree for him to accept an invitation to speak at a certain time or a certain place. If NYU invites the president to deliver a commencement address, someone on the president's staff might note that this would be a perfect spot to unveil the administration's new urban enterprise-zone policy. The invitation is accepted.

The speech is then included on the weekly and monthly schedule of presidential appearances. The writers would get the schedule, read it, complain about the work load and lobby for various speeches. When more than one writer wanted a speech, the decision was made by the head of the speechwriting staff—Ben Elliott, who also functioned as chief speechwriter. Ben made his decisions based on merit. I say that because he gave me a lot of good speeches.

Each speech was also assigned a researcher. There were five young researchers when I got there, and they were usually assigned more speeches than they could do well. I learned to rely on the research people not for creative input—ideas, inspiration, connections one wouldn't have thought of—but for fact-checking, at which they were uniformly reliable and sometimes spectacularly diligent.

A writer usually had a week or two to work on a big speech, or a few days to write a small one. I'd ask research to gather pertinent books from the White House library and to go through Nexis and pull out whatever there was on the subject at hand. They'd also get me the president's previous speeches on that subject or in that place. Research would get precise and up-to-date information from the advance office on the who-what-when-where-why of the event. And then I'd begin, haltingly, to write.

You may be thinking, How did she know what to say? At first I didn't, but after a while I figured it out. As for point of view, the president's stand on any given issue was usually a matter of record. He'd been in politics twenty years, and his basic philosophy wasn't exactly a secret. As for new initiatives, various agencies would phone in directives. Ben would get a call from the Department of Energy, for instance, asking that we mention some new energy initiative in the speech in Boston on Sunday. Ben would pass the word to the writer and a paragraph would be inserted.

In the research phase I'd read a lot and take notes and think of phrases and snatches of thought and type them out, and then take them home and stare at them. When I was in the writing part on an important speech I never read pertinent reference books. I would read poetry and biographies, the former because the rush of words would help loosen the rocks that clogged the words in my head, the latter because biographies are about the great, and the great lead lives of struggle, and reading about their epic pain put the small discomforts of a speech in nice perspective.

I always kept Walter Jackson Bate's biography of Samuel Johnson nearby, and Stephen Vincent Benét's *John Brown's Body,* and the Bible (especially the Psalms), and Ezra Pound's *Cantos,* though I don't think I ever understood a one. It didn't matter, the anarchy of the language and the sweeping away of syntax had force.

Also, Pound helped me with the State Department. I used to be visited by people from State who wanted to help me write. I always thought of this as the descent of the Harvardheads. They all had thick, neat, straight-back hair and little bitty wire-rim glasses and wives named Sydney, and there was only one way to handle them in my view and that was to out-Sydney them. So a man from State would come in and see the books on the coffee table and the first thing he'd do is signify:

"Oh, Pound," he'd say.

"Yes," I'd breathe, with the gravity of a Radcliffe beatnik who'd just met Lenny Bruce in a basement in the Village.

"Took a gut on Pound at Yale. Of course that was before the Deconstructionists."

"Don't laugh. They might have helped." Snap snap.

"So." He seats himself on the couch, readjusts the pillows. "Beijing. How go our efforts."

With State guys you had to remember that if you dropped the right cultural references they'd realize it might not work if they patronized you, and if they couldn't patronize you they didn't have a style to fall back on to shape the meeting so they were a little less sure, which is precisely the way you wanted them.

I'd write and rewrite. I'm about a fifth-draft speechwriter. When I was new in the White House it helped me, I think, that I was changing from writing on an electric typewriter to writing on a word processor. On a word processor you have to exert so little pressure on the keys that it didn't really seem like official writing, it felt like playing on a children's typewriter. That helped free things up.

I'd also walk around and talk to people. I'd turn to someone in the mess and say, "I'm writing a speech on Nicaragua. If there was one sentence on that subject you could communicate to the American people, what would it be?" I got some interesting and helpful answers, but I can't remember any of them.

I chain-smoked when I wrote in those days. I'd be dizzy from the chemicals. I'd do anything to avoid writing, and then I'd force myself to sit down at the computer—Edna Ferber wrote in her diary, "I could not lie down to my work today," an assertion whose implications I do not choose to ponder except to say I know what she means—and I would write very badly at first, very clunkily and awkwardly. It wasn't even grammatical. When people would come by and say, "Let me see," I'd shield the screen with my hands.

The whole speechwriting department was computerized, so I'd write my first draft on a floppy disk, and my secretary would print it out. Then I'd rewrite it from there, and ask her to run it out again. Then she'd give it to me, and I'd rewrite again. Each draft would get a little better as I relaxed and got tired. I was relaxing because I wasn't desperate because: at least I had something on paper. Then, on about the fourth draft, I'd see that I'd written three or four sentences that I liked, and that would relax me further: At least there's something of worth here! That would get my shoulders down. Then I'd really barrel.

I'd read over the final product and realize that once again I'd failed, what I thought was witty was only cute, what I thought was elegant would seem so only to the ill-read, and that imagery didn't come close. I'd hand it in, having reached the deadline. I would tell Ben, "It isn't up to snuff and I'm sorry." He would say calmly that he was sure it would be fine. I would go for a long walk and rationalize my failure: I was tired, they were working me too hard, you can't get blood from a turnip or juice from a stone or whatever the hell.

I would get it back from Ben. He would not have changed it much, but he would have written little exclamation points along the margins, and sometimes on some sections he would write, "Excellent!" And I would be shocked that Ben's critical faculties had failed him. Then I would read over the speech and realize for the first time that it was actually pretty brilliant, so delicate and yet so vital, so vital and yet so tender.

My secretary would incorporate Ben's changes. Then the speech would go out into the world for review. This is where my heart was plucked from my breast and dragged along West Exec, hauled along every pebble and pothole. This was my Heartbreak Hill, my Hanoi Hilton, this was . . . the staffing process.

In staffing, a speech was sent out to all of the pertinent federal agencies and all the important members of the White House staff and the pertinent White House offices. If the speech was relatively unimportant perhaps twenty people in all would see it and comment on it. An important speech would be gone over by fifty or so. The way the system was supposed to work was that the reviewers were to suggest changes, additions, and deletions. The key word here is suggest. They were also supposed to scrutinize all factual assertions and make corrections where necessary.

In the first administration Dick Darman received, along with the speechwriter, a copy of each suggestion, and it was Dick who had the final say on which suggestions must be included and which could be ignored. I didn't always agree with Dick's decisions, but he was open to appeal. More important, I could see his logic. He also didn't mind offending people if it meant preserving a script. I doubt anyone ever pressured him into accepting a change that was frivolous or unhelpful. He didn't care who got mad.

In the second administration a young Regan aide was given control, for a time, of the staffing process. He incorporated many more suggestions than Darman, which was in the short run bureaucratically wise because it made the twenty people who wanted changes think he was smart and easy to work with, and alienated only the speechwriter. But in the long run it proved unwise because it contributed to the diminution in the grace and effectiveness of the president's rhetoric that marked the second administration. It was the first administration that was the fondue pot, it was the second that was the meat grinder.

(The aide's problem was not that he wished to be perverse. It was that he simply could not tell the difference between good writing and bad. It was said of Donald Regan that he did not know what he did not know. His aides were oblivious to what they were oblivious.)

Speeches in the staffing process were always in danger of becoming lowest-common-denominator art. There were so many people with so many questions, so many changes. I sometimes thought it was like sending a beautiful newborn fawn out into the jagged wilderness where the grosser animals would pierce its tender flesh and render mortal wounds; but perhaps I understate.

There were at any rate two battlefields, art and policy, and sometimes they intersected.

The art problem was . . . delicate. Most of the people in the staffing process thought of themselves as writers, which is understandable because everyone is. Everyone writes letters home to Mom or keeps a diary in weight-loss class on What Food Means to Me. Not everyone plays the piano so most people don't claim to be pianists, but everyone is a writer, and if you're a writer why can't you write the president's speeches?

Complicating this is the fact that there's an odd thing about writing as an art: The critical faculty often fails. When people who can't paint try to paint they can usually step back when they're done, smile a rueful smile, and admit that painting's not their talent. But when people who can't write try to write they often can't tell they're not good. In fact, they often think they're pretty close to wonderful, and they're genuinely hurt—and often suspicious—when told otherwise.

I always wanted to handle these people with a lovely finesse, a marvelous grace. I wanted to do it the way Gerald Murphy did when he told the off-key singer, "Ah yes, and now you must rest your lovely vocal chords." But because I always felt threatened—the people most insistent about changes were always more powerful than I—I would sputter. "I'm sorry," I'd say, "but that doesn't work. It's not quite right. Well, it just doesn't. It's just not—oh look, it's just dumb, I'm sorry it's dumb but it is, it's shit." It's a wonderful look an undersecretary gets when you tell him this. His eyebrows jump up right over his hairline, and that's only the beginning.

The policy problem was . . . well, the policy problem was the reason we were all there every day. The policy problem was government. Government is words on paper—the communiqué after the summit, the top-secret cable to the embassy, the memo to the secretary outlining a strategy, the president's speech—it's all words on paper. Government draws aggressive people who feel that if government is words on paper then they will damn well affect the words. After all, this is why they came to Washington: to change things, to make a difference.

Speechwriting naturally started rows because debates and arguments would go on for years but finally at some point policy had to be announced and articulated in speeches. By the very process of writing and declaring we were throwing down the gauntlet. The battles were not only hard-fought, they were sometimes bizarre. Once, when I was new, I was assigned a speech in which I was to write about our conservation policy. I didn't have the faintest idea what our conservation policy was. There were few previous pertinent speeches to go by. I spent a lot of time phoning around asking people, "What the heck am I supposed to say?" I'd get little suggestions here and there.

Then one night a bland young man came into my office and said, "The office of"—here he lowered his voice—"uhpolicydecisionoptions, here." And he placed on my desk a nice typed list of our most recent conservation plans and priorities. I was delighted, and built the speech around it.

Then I sent the speech out. Then I ducked, because the incoming mail was fierce. My phone lit up with people screaming, "Where did you get that? Who told you that? It's all wrong." In the mess a man I didn't know pressed me aggressively, and finally I told him look, a guy walked in from some office and told me this is what's supposed to be in the speech, and I believed him.

The man sat back and shook his head. "Somebody must've found out you were new." There had been internal disagreement over various conservation ideas, he said, and I had been tricked into advancing the agenda of one group. When the speech went out people thought I was taking sides, and got mad. But at least the speech forced everyone to focus, and the policy disagreement was resolved. (I never saw the man who'd come into my office with the list again, by the way. I still wonder where he was from.)

Serious policy issues were not the only thing being worked out in the speech fights. There was plenty of vanity on display, and willfulness, and even now and then the existential willies. "Here's this speech," says Mr. Harvardhead, "and the president will say it and my friends will hear it and tomorrow excerpts will be in *The New York Times* and— and I'd better jump in there and make my presence felt! Because if I don't then I haven't affected the process! And if I haven't affected the process then I haven't used my power, and if I haven't used it then maybe it's gone, because Washington's a use-it-or-lose-it town—if you don't flick the switch then nobody knows if the current's still there, and if it's not then I'm not powerful. And if I'm not powerful then who am I? I decide therefore I am! Command is my essence! If I'm not powerful I will dry up and blow away like the dead leaves of November! If I am not powerful . . . I will die!"

All the suggested changes would come in by a certain deadline. I'd take the ones I thought helped the speech and the ones Darman told me to take. Then we'd send the speech to the president for his suggestions. He'd make changes here and there and send it back to speechwriting. At that point it was supposed to be frozen. But that's not what happened. What happened was the final battle would be fought on the plane, in the limousine, on the couch in the Oval Office. The speech was never really frozen until the president had said it; it was never really frozen until they were typing, from the audiotape, for inclusion in the big books.

My first big speech was for the China trip in the early spring of 1984. The president was going to the People's Republic to meet with its leaders, take part in some serious talks, make a series of speeches and remind the American electorate of his foreign-policy expertise. Ben was going to do the major speech to the Chinese parliament and I would do the speech to the students of Fudan University. Ben told me that no matter what the State drafts said, we would talk about democracy. Get across to the Chinese through the very vigor of our language what a lifting thing freedom is, take those thirsty minds and pour in cooling drafts of truth.

The State Department draft for Fudan was just fine and a little boring. It's not interesting to say, "America loves freedom," it's interesting to say, "Freedom to us is newspapers that everyone can buy on the street corner, newspapers that get to say just about anything about anybody—including me, and I'm supposedly the top man, and sometimes I don't like it a lot but I always know, all of us know, that bruised feelings and some anger are an inevitable part of the process as we look for, find, and publish the truth. Freedom to us . . ." and so on. Be specific, personalize. Make it real.

I wrote a draft and Ben liked it and we sent it out. Within days a young man from the State Department called and introduced himself—he had a name like a child's toy—and proceeded to correct the speech line by line. I sat there and steamed.

"Ah, yah. Perhaps we'd better start with the more egregious problems. The paragraph in which you say, 'To many Americans, China is still an exotic place—beautiful and far away. In a way you are, for many Americans, like the dark side of the moon—unknown, unseen, and entirely fascinating.' The dark side of the moon will have to go. The Chinese are likely to find it grating."

"All right, if you say so."

"Ah, yah. The reference to hardworking Americans."

I had written this little section that pleased me about how we Yanks are not dread hegemonists but honest dealers not out for territorial gain. I liked it because I was using proletarian imagery against Communists, which is one of my favorite things to do. "We are a fair-minded people. We are taught not to take what belongs to others. Most of us, as I said, are the children and grandchildren and great-grandchildren of immigrants—and from them we learned something of hard labor.

As a nation we toiled up from poverty. And no men living are more worthy to be trusted than those who have worked hard for what they have. None are less inclined to take what is not theirs."

"What's wrong with that?" I said.

"It sounds anti-rich."

"No it doesn't, it just sounds pro-poor."

"It sounds as if you're suggesting the wealthy are not to be trusted."

"They're not."

Silence.

"That was a joke. Look, we're not offending anybody. I'm doing a number of things in that section including obliquely knocking down the perception some of these kids have been given that Uncle Sam's just a rich, cold, greedy power."

"You are clearly ascribing certain virtues to the poor that you by implication deny to the rich."

"Oh come on."

"You don't think there's a contradiction between our promotion of economic growth and our lauding of the special virtues of the poor?"

"Oh this is nonsense. I'm not even sure what we're talking about but it's nonsense. Next."

"You refuse to change it?"

"Next." I was learning.

He paused.

"An even bigger mistake," he continued, "is the ending. The river metaphor."

"The river metaphor is lovely."

At the end of the speech the president was to speak directly to the students:

"You know, as I do, that there is much that naturally divides us. Time and space, different languages and values, and political systems that are not, in truth, the most compatible on earth. It would be foolish not to acknowledge these differences. There is no point in lying for the sake of friendship, for a friendship based on fiction will not long withstand the rigors of this world.

"But let us, for a moment, put aside the words that name our differences. Think of what we have in common—think of the things that unite us.

"We are two great and huge nations on opposite sides of the globe.

We are both countries of great vitality and strength. You are the most populous country on earth. We are the most technologically advanced. Each of us holds a special weight in our respective sides of the world.

"There exists between us a kind of equipoise. Those of you who are engineering students will perhaps appreciate that term. It speaks of a special and delicate balance . . ."

The president then speaks of the political issues State said must be mentioned: the US and China together condemn the invasion of Afghanistan, share a stake in preserving peace in Korea, etc. Somewhat dry and semi-true, but State insisted. Then:

"I have been happy to speak to you here, to meet you in this city that is so rich in significance for both our countries. Shanghai is a city of scholarship, a city of learning. Shanghai is your window on the West; it is the city in which my country and yours signed the communiqué that began our modern friendship; it is the city where the Yangtze meets the East China Sea, which itself becomes the Pacific, which touches our shores. The Yangtze is a swift and turbulent river, one of the great rivers of the world.

"My young friends, history is a river that takes us as it will. But we have the power to navigate, to choose direction, and make our passage together. The wind is up, the tide is high, and the opportunity for a long and fruitful journey awaits us. Generations hence will honor us for having begun the voyage . . ."

Well, I thought this was just real nice. But the young man from State with a name like a child's toy did not.

"The river metaphor is politically unhelpful," he said.

"How?"

He brought in his breath in a way that made me think of how missionaries must have sounded years ago when pressed on fine points of Scripture by the savages.

"Ah, yah. To begin with, the 'history is a river' claim is more in line with standard Marxian theory regarding historical determinism than it is with the idea that man can affect his fate."

It took me a while to absorb this.

"You mean you think Ronald Reagan in saying history is a river will be spreading Communist propaganda."

A sigh, softly.

"That's not the way I'd put it, but if you must."

"Look, history is a river is not Communist propaganda, it's poetry. It's not a dialectic, it's not literal, and you can't apply those logical standards—"

"So you concede it's not logical."

"I concede nothing, I concede it's literature."

A few days later we got a long memo from State, cc'd all over the place, that said, "We have a few problems with the 'History is a river' metaphor as presented. The notion that history 'takes us where it will' is closer to fatalism and the Marxian belief that the future is determined by preset forces than it is to our own Western notions. It also tends toward sacrilege, which we mention given the emphasis on religion earlier in the speech. While there is power to navigate on a river, it is only the power to avoid obstacles as you proceed on the river's course. Rivers almost always flow only one way, and at best there are only two ways to go. With the exception of where rivers meet the sea, there is rarely if ever an appreciable tide that affects navigation, and unless the wind is blowing in the proper direction, it is more a nuisance than an inducement to sail."

We went back and forth, I lining up my ducks and the man from State his. The speech went to China with "history is a river." There was an argument over it there, State lost the struggle to have it removed but won the struggle to get a word inserted: "may." As in, "history is a river that may take us as it will." I guess they figured that way Marx may or may not be right.

The day after it was given, *The New York Times* front-paged the speech, and under "Quotation of the Day" they printed, "My young friends, history is a river . . ." I clipped it and sent it to State.

There were two other things that happened with that speech. In a short section on the things that helped shape the American character I had written that most Americans had derived their spiritual knowledge from the Bible of Moses and the Bible of Jesus Christ. The State Department repeatedly deleted the references to Moses and Christ, for no obvious or stated reason. They'd just always X it out in any draft they saw. I puzzled over this and asked about it. In time I came to think of it as an illustration of an odd small fact: The people who run our foreign-policy bureaucracy are so used to bending over backward to show their openness to and approval of other cultures that after a while any positive and explicit reference to their own culture seems a faux pas. I think State reflexively saw a noncritical reference to Moses and

Jesus as something that could be perceived as a put-down of Buddha.

The other thing was that in the debate over the poetry, we all missed a factual mistake. I have a poor grasp of certain aspects of physical reality and never caught the error in "the tide is high" in "history is a river," the error being rivers don't have tides, oceans do. At the last minute somebody caught it in China. It was changed to "the current is swift," which has, perhaps, less buoyancy and more of an undercurrent of slight threat—but it was a good catch and did the trick.

But what I learned was that I would have to watch out at the White House, as I did at CBS, for the kind of editors who want to sit around and give you their opinions on things instead of concentrating on the text and catching your factual mistakes. Catching mistakes is hard, you have to know things like facts and numbers and names; you have to be awake. Anybody can have an opinion. This is not to say that good editors don't notice things like the quality of the writing, they do, and when it's low they hope you'll be fired, which you probably will be. But the first thing a good editor does is catch your dumb mistakes; all else, as they say, is commentary.

What I also learned from Fudan was that: a) people see funny things in speeches, and b) everybody was going to debate everything. I also learned how the Chinese report a speech whose content they disagree with. In Chinese press accounts the next day they omitted references to the Bible, the Declaration of Independence, and the contributions of two Chinese immigrants to the United States: the architect I. M. Pei and computer entrepreneur An Wang.

What I learned from the Pointe du Hoc speech was that to the men of the Reagan White House, a good speech is really a sausage skin, the stronger it is the more you shove in.

The Pointe du Hoc speech was scheduled for a month after the Fudan speech—June 6, 1984, the fortieth anniversary of D-Day. It was to be the central speech of the spring European trip. The setting was the windswept cliffs of Pointe du Hoc, where forty years before a group of American Rangers had climbed into France in one of the bravest hours of the longest days.

When I was assigned the speech I was overjoyed. Ben was surprised. "I hired you to write this speech."

The subject matter was one of those moments that really captures the romance of history. I thought that if I could get at what impelled the Rangers to do what they did, I could use it to suggest what impels us each day as we live as a nation in the world. This would remind both us and our allies of what it is that holds us together.

I worked hard, walked the circle around the Washington Monument, paced the halls, ran into an advance man. "You the girl doing the D-Day speech?" *Come here so I can kill you.* "Yeah."

"Can I give you advice? We'd like it to be like the Gettysburg Address."

Oh.

I walked into Ben's office. "They'd like it to be like the Gettysburg Address," he said.

Oh.

"Also it's going to be on live TV in the States on all the networks, so it's considered a big political event. Apparently Deaver wants it as part of the Reagan film at the convention."

I went by a speechwriter's office. "Do you think it's fair that you write this speech?" he said. "I mean you haven't been here very long, and you haven't been in the service like————"—he mentioned another speechwriter—"and you don't know what it's like to fight."

The head of advance came to my office. "Look, I want this to be like the Gettysburg Address. . . ."

I threw my hands up. "What do you guys mean when you say that? What did the Gettysburg Address do?"

He threw a hand in front of his face and moved his fingers up and down. He was saying, The Gettysburg Address made people cry.

I shook my head. "The Gettysburg Address wasn't a tearjerker. What happened at Gettysburg was in itself so moving and dramatic that Lincoln knew he had no choice but to use cool words to convey the meaning. 'Fourscore and seven years ago our fathers brought forth upon this continent a new nation, conceived in liberty, and dedicated to the proposition that all men are created equal. Now we are engaged in a great civil war, testing whether that nation or any other nation so conceived and so dedicated, can long endure. We are met on a great battlefield of that war.' "

I hoped to impress with my mastery of my discipline. He stared at the pleat on his knee.

"People didn't cry to it they thought to it, it was a new kind of poem."

He fingered the pleat. "Well, I'm not going to argue," he said.

I drifted around waiting for the speech to come; sometimes they do. I don't mean they come complete, I mean the basic shape and bits of the literature of the speech start to present themselves. But the only thing that came was a phrase: *Here the West stood.* I tried writing on weekends, writing at odd hours. I tried writing a letter to my aunt. "Dear Aunt Peg, They died for a cause and the cause was just," it says in my notes. I ran out of time; the work got done.

I had decided on a plan. The first paragraph would be full of big, emotional words and images so advance and Mike Deaver would be happy. And so it began:

"We are here to mark that day in history when the Allied Armies joined in battle to reclaim this continent to liberty. For four long years much of Europe had been under a terrible shadow. Free nations had fallen, Jews cried out in the camps, millions cried out for liberation from the conquerers. Europe was enslaved, and the world waited for its rescue. Here in Normandy the rescue began. Here on a lonely windswept point on the western shore of France."

Then:

"As we stand here today the air is soft and full of sunlight, and if we pause and listen we will hear the snap of flags and the click of cameras and the gentle murmur of people come to visit a place of great sanctity and meaning.

"But forty years ago at this moment the air was dense with smoke and the cries of men, the air was filled with the crack of rifle fire and the boom of cannons . . ."

What I was doing here was placing it all in time and space for myself and, by extension, for the audience. If we really listen to and hear the snap of the flags, the reality of that sound—snap . . . suhnapp—will help us imagine what it sounded like on D-Day. And that would help us imagine what D-Day itself was like. Then your head snaps back with remembered information: History is real.

Then move on to what happened. This part was a little for the average viewer but mostly for kids watching TV at home in the kitchen at breakfast:

"Before dawn on the morning of the sixth of June, 1944, two hundred American Rangers jumped off a British landing craft and ran to the bottom of these cliffs. Their mission was one of the most difficult and daring of the invasion: to climb these sheer and desolate cliffs and take out the enemy guns. The Allies had been told that here were concentrated the mightiest of those guns, which would be trained on the beaches to stop the Allied advance. Removing the guns was pivotal to the Normandy invasion, which itself was pivotal to the reclaiming of Europe and the end of the war."

I wanted American teenagers to stop chewing their Rice Krispies for a minute and hear about the greatness of those tough kids who are now their grandfathers:

"The Rangers looked up and saw the big casements. . . . And the American Rangers began to climb. They shot their rope ladders into the face of these cliffs and they pulled themselves up. And when one Ranger would fall another would take his place, and when one rope was cut and a Ranger would hurtle to the bottom he would find another rope and begin his climb again. They climbed and shot back and held their footing—"

I wanted this to have the rhythm of a rough advance:

"—and in time the enemy guns were quieted, in time the Rangers held the cliffs, in time the enemy pulled back and one by one the Rangers pulled themselves over the top—and in seizing the firm land at the top of these cliffs they seized back the continent of Europe."

Pause, sink in, bring it back to now, history is real.

"Forty years ago as I speak they were fighting to hold these cliffs. They had radioed back and asked for reinforcements and they were told: There aren't any. But they did not give up. It was not in them to give up. They would not be turned back; they held the cliffs.

"Two hundred twenty-five came here. After a day of fighting only ninety could still bear arms.

"Behind me is a memorial that symbolizes the Ranger daggers that were thrust into the top of these cliffs. And before me are the men who put them there.

"These are the boys of Pointe du Hoc. These are the men who took the cliffs. These are the champions who helped free a continent. These are the heroes who helped end a war."

The day he gave the speech it was at this point that the cameras cut to the Rangers, all of them sitting there on their folding chairs, middle-aged, heavy, and gray. One of them began to weep. But maybe that's just the way I remember it because that's the way Deaver used it in the convention film.

"These are the boys of Pointe du Hoc" came out of another conversation with the head of advance. He was still disappointed in the speech because it wasn't moving enough. He told me that the other speech of the day, by the speechwriter Tony Dolan, which consisted of a sweet and emotional letter from a young woman named Lisa Zanata to her father, who had fought at Normandy but hadn't lived to see this anniversary, had made him cry. I said wonderful, that speech will make 'em cry and this one will make 'em think and the day will be a hit. He kept saying, "But they'll be there, they'll be there," and suddenly I realized, He means the Rangers.

But they would be scattered throughout the crowd. No, he said, the Rangers were going to be sitting all together in the front rows, sitting right there five feet from the president.

Oh, I didn't know. Oh. Well then he should refer directly to them. He should talk to them. He should describe what they did and then say—

The phrase came with ease because I had just finished Roger Kahn's lovely memoir of his beloved Brooklyn Dodgers, *The Boys of Summer.* O happy steal: "These are the boys of Pointe du Hoc . . ."

The speech went on to talk about the rebuilding and reconciliation at the end of the war. The State/NSC draft that I'd been given weeks before wanted the president to go off on this little tangent about arms control, and as I read it I thought, in the language of the day, Oh gag me with a spoon. This isn't a speech about arms negotiations you jackasses, this is a speech about splendor. But of course I did have to mention the Soviets, because a subtext of the speech was, The things that held the Allies together then hold us together now, even if we forget to know. Our alliance was always a successful effort to stop totalitarians.

"Why did you do it? What impelled you to put all thought of self-preservation behind you and risk your lives to take these cliffs? What inspired all of the men of the armies that met here?

". . . It was faith and belief; it was loyalty and love.

"The men of Normandy had faith that what they were doing was right, faith that they fought for all humanity, faith that a just God would grant them mercy on this beachhead—or the next. It was the deep knowledge . . . that there is a profound moral difference between the use of force for liberation and the use of force for conquest. They were here to liberate, not to conquer, and so they did not doubt their cause . . .

"They knew that some things are worth dying for, that one's country is worth dying for and that democracy is worth dying for because it is the most deeply honorable form of government ever devised by man. They loved liberty and they were happy to fight tyranny . . .

"In spite of our great efforts and our great successes, not all of what followed the end of the war was happy or planned. Some of the countries that had been liberated were lost. The great sadness of that fact echoes down to our own time in the streets of Warsaw, Prague and East Berlin. The Soviet troops that came to the center of this continent did not leave when peace came. They are there to this day, uninvited, unwanted, and unyielding almost forty years after the war.

"Because of this, Allied forces still stand on this continent . . ."

All of this for the purposes of history but also for that young man with the soggy Rice Krispies in his mouth.

"Today, as forty years ago, our armies are here for only one purpose—to protect and defend democracy. The only territories we hold are the graveyards where our heroes rest.

"We in America have learned the bitter lessons of two world wars: that it is better to be here and ready to preserve and protect the peace, than to take blind shelter in our homes across the sea, rushing to respond only after freedom has been threatened. We have learned that isolationism never was and never will be an acceptable response to tyrannical governments with expansionist intent."

Then a plea for peace with the Soviets, a reiteration of fealty to the alliance, a vow to the dead: "Let our actions say to them the words for which Matthew Ridgway listened: 'I will not fail thee nor forsake thee.' Strengthened by their courage, heartened by their valor and borne by their memory, let us continue to stand for the ideals for which they lived and died."

The speech got stripped down by advance and by Deaver's office. For some reason they thought the networks were going to pull the plug after eight minutes. I don't know why they thought this since the networks had allotted more time than that, and after they aired the cut-down version of Pointe du Hoc they had to fill for a long time. About half the cuts made me bleed.

At the beginning, the part about hearing the snap of the flags and the click of the cameras was cut here and there to save time, and what remained was of diminished power. There were some good catches: NSC changed the "boom" of the cannon to the more elegant "roar," and "rushing to respond only after freedom is threatened" to "rushing to respond only after freedom has been lost."

But after they cut the speech down they kept shoving stuff in. Deaver's office kept telling us to put in the phrase "pride and purpose." Deaver liked it. He also wanted us to use "prepared for peace." Deaver apparently liked *P*-words.

Advance kept telling us to put in "selfless effort" and "impossible odds" and "indomitable will" and "courage" and "bravery." NSC wanted, "It is fitting here to remember also the great sacrifices made by the Russian people during World War II. Their terrible loss of twenty million lives testifies to all the world the necessity of avoiding another war."

That started a nice little war. I was upset because the speech was losing part of its literature to save time and they kept shoving in last-minute policy and I had to keep cutting lines to make room. But it was more. The insert on the Soviets had that egregious special-pleading ring that certain bureaucrats get when they deal with totalitarians, and it was going to rob the speech of some of its authenticity. And the Soviets didn't take part in Normandy; they weren't at that party, why stop the speech dead to throw a fish to the bear? For what? So the Soviets could say thanks, we're so moved we'll change our behavior? There was a secondary reason for fighting it: If I held them off till they left and they fought for it on the plane or on the helicopter on the way to Pointe du Hoc, they'd have to scribble it in and they wouldn't have time to take something out. So at least I wouldn't lose more of the text.

That's what happened. The insertion did no harm except for slowing the speech with buzz sounds that everyone knows are buzz sounds. It was the first time a dispute over a speech I'd been involved in got leaked to the press. *Newsweek,* the following week, reported, "In Normandy, his elegant speech on the cliff had gone through several drafts to pencil out anti-Soviet rhetoric. Pentagon hard-liners at first opposed any reference to Soviet losses in the war. Secretary of State Shultz insisted on a compromise: In the end, Reagan noted that Soviet troops are still there (in Central Europe), 'uninvited, unwanted, unyielding almost forty years after the war'—but then he did recall the 'terrible' loss of twenty million Soviet lives and called for East-West reconciliation."

You could hardly be wronger than that report was. The reporter was a professional (Eleanor Clift, who did a candid and unusual thing recently when, as a guest yeller on *The McLaughlin Group,* she frankly and happily identified herself as a liberal) whose primary source, I believe, was a gentleman of similar ideological views who had worked, as a Carter appointee, at the NSC and who, brought in to help on European trips, was an active participant in the battle for the Soviet reference and who tended to reduce these things to a fight between the forces of light and rampant Reaganism. He was also the guy who said, "We substantive types, you wordsmiths."

Other odd things happened. Bud McFarlane kept rewriting the end. Where I had "borne by their memory," he'd put "sustained by their sacrifice." I'd say to Ben and Darman, "I'm the writer, right, and he's the policy maven, I mean that's what he's always saying, right? So you'll tell him to stop writing 'sustained by their sacrifice,' right?" Right, they'd say. Then we'd get another draft from NSC: "Bud wants 'sustained by their sacrifice." He'd X my phrase out, I'd X his phrase out.

I told Ben: Look, this guy who talks like a computer, who in fact probably *is* a computer—I'm going to interface with him and tell him to leave my work alone.

Ben told me: He's a computer with more power than you and he's the computer who'll be on the plane, and we'll all try very hard to preserve the integrity of your work.

My version prevailed. I don't know why, since McFarlane was on the trip and at the speech site and I wasn't. He must have forgotten. Or maybe Darman thought it was my turn to win one.

I wondered, Did the president know of the controversies and disagreements that raged about him? Did he write, at night, alone, in his diary, like Claudius: "They all think I am unaware, but I know of their m-m-m-machinations, I am not as d-dull as they imagine, or as removed."

I don't know. I think the fellas just . . . handled it. "Aw, something in speechwriting's holding it up, but we took care of it and the draft'll be here in what, Dick, by lunch? You can read it over lunch, Mr. President."

A year later, when speechwriting was beginning to fall apart, I had a fantasy. Someday the president would look up from an inadequate or less than striking piece of work and a look the fellas had never seen would cross his face. "There's something curiously lifeless about this thing. Let me see the earlier draft."

He'd get it and see all the changes.

"Listen," he'd say, snapping the draft impatiently on his knee, "this started as something good and now it's common, boneless and banal. Who had the temerity to change this speech? Who made these changes in my name without my authority? This early version is clearly superior—can't you knuckleheads see that? From now on I want to run the staffing process, or there'll be hell to pay."

Sometimes he'd fire people. Sometimes he'd say, "Get me Noonan. Hello, Peg? Your long national nightmare is over. If anyone tries to tamper with your work again you just tell them to dial G for Gippuh, got it?"

I learned how it had been for other speechwriters at a dinner at William Safire's. It was the first annual dinner of the Judson Welliver Society. Welliver, the first presidential speechwriter (his title was "literary executive secretary") coined the phrase "the founding fathers" and wrote "most of the public utterances of President Harding and was largely responsible for Calvin Coolidge's reputation for eloquence."

The quote is from *our* founding father, William Safire, who'd been noodling on the idea of a society for former and current presidential speechwriters for years, and who opened his spacious and capacious house in Chevy Chase to us on a frosty autumn evening. I walked in, and there arrayed before me were my heroes. Ted Sorensen, Richard Goodwin, Arthur Schlesinger, Jr., Safire, Buchanan. Doris Kearns, Goodwin's wife and author of *Lyndon Johnson and the American Dream*. Clark Clifford. I turned right and heard Chris Matthews of the Carter administration telling Schlesinger, "When I was in college, at night before I went to bed, after I'd done my work, I'd read *A Thousand Days*. That was my candy." I turned left, and Jack Valenti was saying, "Speechwriters have a unique distinction in Washington— none of us has ever been indicted."

The Safires had prepared a sit-down dinner for forty or so of us, and it was warm and full of tribute. One of my generation, Dana Rohrabacher, rose and made a graceful tribute to the greats of the previous generations, to the wonderful words of the Kennedy, Johnson, and Nixon writers.

One of Eisenhower's speechwriters told of how he and Ike were talking one day about speechwriting in general and about the great warrior-orators. Eisenhower, suddenly resentful, said, "You probably think Doug MacArthur was the great silver-tongued orator of the army. Well, who do you think his speechwriter was? It was *me*!" As he told the story you could hear the old speechwriter's bitterness.

(Years later Ronald Reagan turned to me and said, with wistfulness, "I used to write my own speeches, you know.")

A speechwriter named Milton Friedman ("There's Milton Friedman the economist, and he has the economic answers, and there's Milton Friedman the speechwriter, and he has the economic problems!") told of how he wrote a speech for Nixon that acknowledged for the first time that the United States would indeed be pulling out of Vietnam eventually. It was something that needed to be said, Nixon told him. Somehow Friedman managed to keep a copy of the script away from Henry Kissinger. When Kissinger finally saw it he yelled to Friedman, "How dare you end a war without staffing it out!"

One of LBJ's speechwriters said, "I was on the phone with Johnson one day at home, and my daughter skipped into the kitchen and told my wife, 'Mommy, Daddy's talking to Mr. Yessir!' "

Valenti again: "Ours was a life of fleeting anonymity. Every morning Johnson poured spoonfuls of humility through our clenched teeth."

I realized as I listened that all that I'd been feeling had been felt before, that the speechwriter's lot is frustration, and it was ever thus. While most of them maintained a good deal of affection for the presidents they'd served, they'd also experienced disappointment and occasionally resentment. "Of course, Truman in those days had little time to give direction—who has time for a speechwriter, anyway?"; and "Look, the longest talk I ever had with Carter was the day I left."

Most of them had had moments when they felt they were doing literary facading, putting attractive exteriors on empty buildings to please the passersby. But the bitterness was fleeting; given a chance to stand by their man again, it was clear they'd stand and deliver.

★ ★ ★ ★ ★ ★ ★ ★ ★ ★ ★

SIX

I Am a Camera

The city was never finished. I would walk out of the EOB that first year in my tan walking shoes and purple cotton sweater and I would go in search. I would go down an avenue, turn a corner, go to one of the places where the people of Washington really live, downtown to the stores where they shop or up near the river where they cool themselves on a summer day, and no matter which way I turned I would come up against the symbol of modern Washington: a long tall crane bent and cracked against the sky, surrounded by a plywood construction fence and the deep ggggrrrrrr-kahpoohmmm-ggggrrrrrr of a city being torn down, rebuilt, and torn down again.

I was searching for Washington, for the sense one gets when one finally knows a place, the confident sense that being truly oriented gives. I would look and wonder: is this it? This space between the monuments, this corner where the storefront meets the broad bleached sidewalks—is this absence it? Where is the culture, where is the town?

I looked for a permanent apartment. When I first moved to Boston I had wanted to live on Beacon Hill in a town house on cobblestone streets, but I couldn't find one and wound up in Cambridge. When I got to New York I wanted to live in a walk-up in Little Italy near a neighborhood club where the old men sit outside in the sun, but I couldn't find one and settled for the Upper West Side. When I moved to Washington I decided to hold out until I found an apartment in the place I wanted to be: quiet, genteel Georgetown.

People at work told me to go there looking for For Rent signs because there was so much demand and it was so constant that renters didn't have to advertise in the papers. One Saturday morning I saw a sign and knocked on the door. The elderly gentleman who answered looked at me for a moment. "It's only the basement and not good enough for you, I won't even show it. You should find something nicer! Enjoy life!" I laughed and said all right.

"Come back if you're in terrible trouble!"

I asked his name.

"Kierkegaard!" he said merrily. "Mr. Kierkegaard!"

I found a little apartment on Thirty-third between N and O. It was the basement of a town house and it smelled faintly of mildew and fresh paint. It was in the heart of Georgetown, and it had shiny deep blue tiles on the kitchen floor, and when you stood near the front door and looked down the hall through the open back door you could see a patch of pale grass and a few feet beyond that an old white fence; it gave a sense of foreground and background, of depth. I liked it. It was too expensive. I moved in the next week.

Georgetown was beautiful and genteel and newly full of crime. Young men had started coming in and holding people up on the street, and some of them were so inexperienced that they used Magnums, and everyone warned each other, "Don't walk around after dusk!" The wife of Commerce Secretary Malcolm Baldrige had made more news than she wished when she publicly called Georgetown dirty, noisy and unsafe. I would think of this at night as the students of the universities ran up and down the small alley next to my house throwing beer bottles at each other's heads. I'd been living there six months when I found out the Baldriges lived across the street. One day we were introduced. They were tall and old and beautiful.

"You live there?" said Mrs. Baldrige, pointing.

"Yes."

"I witnessed an incident of sexual intercourse in front of your home recently."

I could not think of a proper response.

"A couple in a car," she said.

"Coupling?"

"Yes, and quite obviously."

"Wow. I never saw that myself. What time was it?" Poor woman must be up all night.

"Four o'clock in the afternoon."

I met a neighbor, a tall old man in a black cape who walked his two tiny high-strung dogs each morning in front of my house. "It certainly is nice to have a new neighbor. I hope you have better luck than the other girl who lived there!"

"What happened?"

"Oh, I don't want to upset you, and it doesn't matter. She just was a girl with bad luck. Always lock your door."

"I'll probably imagine it's worse than it is."

"Well, but only because you insist. She went out one night after dark, not late, and got some milk at the little store there on M. And she came back and saw that her door was unlocked, but it was closed and she assumed it was all right. She went in and there was, unfortunately, someone waiting for her. She was raped. At knifepoint. Big carving knife against her throat. Very sad. But I have to go. Come Felix, come Heather!"

He turned and called back, "They never found him. The man. Still at large."

"What happened to her?"

"Moved, of course."

I was walking to work when I thought, This isn't the way it's supposed to be for me anymore. I am tired of being alone. I am ready to marry.

It was a change for me, not only to declare the desire, but to have it in the first place. I was for my generation a not unusual 33-going-on-34. I had had a lot of boyfriends the past twenty years and one engagement, two relationships of significant duration only one of which was a disaster, and no particular desire to wed. I had wanted it in the abstract, in some semidistant future, but not now, not here. I believed in marriage as an institution; I also believed if I married I'd wind up in one. I would think of William Carlos Williams's lament: "I am lonely, lonely./ I was born to be lonely,/I am best so!"

It wasn't only my temperament, it was the times. When I was a child

I didn't want to be a wife, I wanted to be a widow. I wanted to be like Jackie Kennedy in the lace mantilla, I wanted to be beautiful and tragic and go on boats, to be frail and exquisite in white linen with big sunglasses. I wanted to do whatever I wanted and not feel any pressure to get married, but I wanted the respect society gives to a woman who has merged and mothered and then, through no fault of her own, wound up alone with a lot of interesting men around to help with the kids. Gloria Steinem was part of it—a widow in a lace mantilla with aviator glasses—and Katharine Hepburn, K-K-K-Katy telling Merv or Dick, "I really don't think men and women can live togethuh! I think the best we can do is live near eachothuh and visit now and then!" Marriage had no cheerleaders when I was young.

But now I was changing, now I realized I wanted a live husband who would stay with me and be my beloved friend and talk with me at night as we watched TV and read *The American Spectator* and wore wool socks and moved our feet back and forth in a happy way. I was losing my yen for solitude.

I told my friends, "If you meet a nice man who's single, and ideally of the Catholic persuasion, this is my number, which you are to vouchsafe to him," and enjoyed their reaction, which was applause. I waited for the future to reveal itself.

In the meantime there was work and its demands, and friends, and my walks.

On weekends friends would visit from New York, and we'd walk along the cobblestone streets and I'd show them what I knew. This is Ben and Sally's house—that's what they call them here, the Bradlees; this is where Kennedy lived when he was elected president, and look at this across the street, this plaque: IN THE COLD WINTER OF 1960–61, THIS HOUSE HAD AN IMPORTANT ROLE IN HISTORY. FROM IT WAS FLASHED TO THE WORLD NEWS OF PRE-INAUGURAL ANNOUNCEMENTS BY PRESIDENT JOHN F. KENNEDY. Imagine a world in which reporters would put up such a plaque. What another era!

This is the old church where everyone who's Catholic goes because it's the big Catholic church in Georgetown. This is Martin's Tavern, where Harry Hopkins used to go and have a few pops. Also Whittaker Chambers met with Alger Hiss here. This is where Eric Sevareid lives. A congressman this guy I know knows lives here. See that window?

From that window one bright summer morning, a morning thick with the smell of roses, a pretty young woman threw a flower, meaning to surprise her father as he left the house. But she missed; the father walked on; the flower landed on the sidewalk in front of a young soldier who was on his way to the train that would take him to the ship that would take him to the trenches of France. The soldier looked up in surprise; the girl looked down. A breeze came into the open window; her hair moved. She smiled. He took the flower and put it between his teeth, rakishly, like a sheikh in the movies, and walked on. But after a few paces he stopped dead still, turned, walked back and took off his cap and placed it on a picket of the white fence that enclosed her house. He laughed, threw the duffel bag over his shoulder and bounded off. Three years later there was a knock on the door. The young woman answered. It was the soldier. "I've come for my hat," he said. The girl was Alice Roosevelt and the father was old Teddy and the soldier was John Hadley Dos Passos Fitzgerald Smith, who became the great love of her life. I made that up.

You could make a great deal up as you walked the streets of Georgetown because parts of it looked exactly as they had a century before, the old houses bunched together brightly, their wooden shutters thick and buckled from the paint of a hundred years. One morning at dawn I walked along the streets during a snowstorm, and all the stop signs and mailboxes were covered with a blanket of snow, and all of Georgetown looked as it must have looked a century before. You could imagine old Walt Whitman sweeping off his hat and trying to look into the eyes of the tall man with the homely weathered face. You could imagine the metallic click of the horse's hooves as Booth galloped west from Fourteenth Street. You could imagine the senator in sunglasses cruising in a white convertible and smiling at the girls in their summer suits. You could imagine . . .

And that was the secret, that was how I found Washington. I realized that yes, Washington is the thick suburban carpets of Northwest and the crick of the sprinkler turning, it's Georgetown and the towpaths and the Kinney downtown, it's the Hill and the senate office buildings . . .

But if you really want to find it you have to realize that the Washington that lives in your imagination is realer than the Washington that is. And this is the second thing: There are really only two kinds of buildings in Washington, the sandstone and marble ones, which are permanent, and everything else, which is torn down and rebuilt and torn down again (the crane, bent and cracked against the sky).

In the sandstone and marble is democracy and those who work in them are democracy and with each presidency the nature of the democracy changes.

Therefore and thus: To find Washington in the eighties, you had to find the era itself, the Reagan era.

Just see it. Don't expect, just see.

I am a camera.

The young man in a tux made his way across the crowded room. It was a Christmas party in a narrow old Victorian newly purchased by a congressman from the Midwest and his pregnant wife. The lights in the ceiling caught the moisture on the young man's smooth, bald head; it glimmered like an ornament. "Merry Christmas, Peter," I said as he reached our side. He nodded curtly and turned urgently to the man I was with. "I've just come from the Property Rights Task Force. We have to talk."

The new head of the National Endowment for the Humanities, William Bennett of Harvard, Williams and Brooklyn, New York, was attending his first White House dinner. He was seated near the important presidential aide Michael Deaver, who was going on about the wine.

"Do you like this wine?" he said to Bennett.

"Yes, it's a fine wine," Bennett said.

"Good year, don't you think?"

"Good enough for me."

"Delicate bouquet."

"Yeah."

"You've probably guessed what vineyard."

"Not really."

"But you know the region."

"No."

"Oh come."

"Look, I don't know anything about wine."

Deaver sat back, pale with disappointment. "And I thought you were an intellectual," he said.

The Roman Catholic bishop stretched, and rearranged his bulk in the chair as he took questions from the pleasant young journalist. The bishop had been a proud originator and contributor to the U.S. Catholic bishops' letter on the economy. He had with passion and authority scolded the administration for its adherence to antediluvian policy and sharply espoused greater spending for the poor. He had no doubt looked forward to this interview as an opportunity to expand upon his views, but the young journalist's references were so distressingly arcane. He must be trying to impress me, the bishop mused. Well, I'd be nervous too if I were twenty, twenty-five years old and going yackety-yack with a prince of the Holy Roman Catholic and Apostolic Church. But who is this economist he keeps referring to?

"Keynes," said the young journalist.

A blank look from the bishop.

"John Maynard Keynes. An economist who has been, uh, actually rather dramatically influential in this century in terms of public policy. British. Keynes."

Silence.

"I'm afraid I've never heard of him," the bishop said pleasantly, careful not to dampen the enthusiasm of one so young. "But I'm sure you're right! I must take some time and look into it!"

Everyone wore Adam Smith ties that were slightly stained from the mayonnaise that fell from the sandwich that was wolfed down at the working lunch on judicial reform. The ties of the Reagan era bore symbols—eagles, flags, busts of Jefferson—and the symbols had meaning. I had a dream: The ties talked; they turned to me as I walked into the symposium. "Hi, I'm a free-market purist!" said the tie with the little gold curve. "Hello there, I believe in judicial restraint!" said the tie with the liberty bell. "Forget politics, come fly with me!" said the tie with the American eagle.

You'd be in someone's home and on the way to the bathroom you'd pass the bedroom and see a big thick copy of Paul Johnson's *Modern Times* lying half-open on the table by the bed. Three months later you'd go back and it was still there. Everyone had read Jean-François Revel's *How Democracies Perish* and could discuss with ease Jeane Kirkpatrick's analysis of authoritarian versus totalitarian regimes. In the

Reagan years you hated to go out on Saturday night before the McLaughlin show, and when you got to the restaurant, you could get a laugh by saying, "Issue One: the appetizuh!"

You knew you had arrived when you'd been a prediction. I had a dinner party and we talked about the paradox of fame in Washington, so intense and yet so fleeting. I said, "Raise your hand if you've been a prediction on McLaughlin." Four people did, including a woman who drawled, "I have been both a topic and a prediction—twice. I just wanted to share that with you." Someone threw a roll.

There were words. You had a notion instead of a thought and a dustup instead of a fight, you had a can-do attitude and you were in touch with the zeitgeist. No one had intentions they had an agenda and no one was wrong they were fundamentally wrong and you didn't work on something you broke your pick on it and it wasn't an agreement it was a done deal. All politics is local but more to the point all economics is micro. There were phrases: Personnel is policy and ideas have consequences and ideas drive politics and it's a war of ideas—ideas were certainly busy!—and to do nothing is to endorse the status quo and roll back the Brezhnev Doctrine and there's no such thing as a free lunch, especially if you're dining with the press.

I was asked to write some short remarks for the president's appearance before CFA.

What's that? I said.

Conservatives for America.

Oh, what's that?

Grass-roots conservative organization pushing the president's program. Lehrman heads it.

Lou Lehrman? I thought he was in New York, gonna run for governor again.

He was, but they got nervous he'd come down here and talk to the president, so they gave him CFA to keep him out of town. He thought it was an honor. He got rolled.

(He got rolled—he took a lickin' and kept on tickin'—it was a done deal.)

•   •   •

It was an age of vivid talk, not poetic but serviceable, communicating as much as possible as quickly as possible, a quick bite of the cigar and a spit of sound.

A moderate was a squish and a squish was a weenie and a weenie was a wuss. Bureaucrats with soft hands adopted the clipped, laconic style of John Ford characters. A small man from NSC was asked at a meeting if he knew of someone who could work up a statement. Yes, he knew someone at State, a paid pen who's pushed some good paper. I thought he was going for a laugh and looked around for someone to start it with. They were nodding and taking notes.

They called it "the movement," and they said it with an unconscious reverence, the way antiwar kids in the sixties said "the student mobe." It was a cause, a belief, and it mattered if you were a longtime movement activist or a new arrival, a movement person or just another Honda-driving-Hermes-wearing-wuss. He goes way back in the movement, they'd say, He's movement from way back. Yeah, she's good, she's hard-core.

"They don't know what to make of you," said a new friend. "You don't quite fit the categories."

"I know," I said. "They hid me from this lady who apparently checks you out when you're new here and asks you whether your parents are Republicans and did you vote for Reagan in '76 in the primaries and does your family give money to the party? I'm not from a Republican family and they don't give money to parties and in '76 I voted either for Ford or the Libertarian, I forget. But what could that lady do to me?"

"It's her job to make sure people who've worked long and hard in the movement and/or the party get the jobs before the ones who didn't earn it. She could cause you a lot of trouble."

"Well loyalty's good but they shouldn't be keeping people out, they should be happy I'm here."

"Well, do good. And keep hiding."

There were all kinds of people at the revolution (and much uneasiness at the barricades!). There were libertarians whose girlfriends had just given birth to their sons, hoisting a Coors with social conservatives who walked into the party with a wife who bothered to be warm and a son who carried a mason jar full of something Daddy grew in the backyard. There were Protestant fundamentalists hoping they wouldn't be dismissed by neocon intellectuals from New York, and neocons talking to fundamentalists, thinking, I wonder if when they look at me they see what Annie Hall's grandmother saw when she looked down the table at Woody Allen.

There was a shift occurring, a shift of style and class. You could see it most easily in the generations. In Washington the older Republicans, the ones over forty-five, looked the way a Hollywood screenwriter would have a Republican look: Wadsworth Worthington III, a man of pinstripes, parentage and pedigree. An older Democrat is a guy named Vito who talks with his hands and wears a lumpy gray suit—he looks like a walking, talking toaster—and represents the wards of Newark.

But with the young it was all changing—and the clichés hadn't caught up! Up on the Hill or at the White House the young rough-looking guy from a state school is probably either a Republican or a conservative, and the snooty sniffy guy with a THANK YOU FOR NOT SMOKING sign on his tidy little desk is a Democrat. (The nation as a whole would not see this until the summer of '87, during the Iran-*contra* hearings, when the majority counsel [that is to say, the Democrat lawyer] was a straight-laced Ivy League nanny rapping Ollie's knuckles with a fan; and the minority counsel [the Republican lawyer] was a burly, easygoing guy with a big head of hair and a five o'clock shadow and a name that ends in a vowel except that it doesn't. He is Richard Leon, Republican, and the Democrat—that twitchin' hippie guy, as they said at night in the bars of America—was John W. Nields, Jr., of Yale and points east.)

It was all changing (and the clichés hadn't begun to catch up!).

The young people who came to Washington for the Reagan revolution came to make things better. They had such spirit, such idealism. They looked at the flow of money in America and they said, "See those taxes you put on families? Cut that money, lower that amount, leave them more money for shoes and the mortgage and vacations." They looked at where freedom was and what it did to people and where freedom wasn't and what that did, and they wanted to help the guerrilla fighters who were trying to overthrow the Communist regimes that had been imposed on them ten years ago while we were all watching

60 Minutes. The thing the young conservatives were always talking about, the constant subtext, was freedom, freedom:

> *we'll free up more of your money,*
> *we'll free up more of the world,*
> *freedom freedom freedom—*

It was the drumbeat that held a disparate group together, the rhythm that kept a fractious, not-made-in-heaven alliance in one piece.

I was in the White House mess with a Mujahedeen warrior as my guest. He was gruff and taciturn in his rough robes and his—turban?—that thing they wear on their head like a canvas towel. Conversation was rough going. What is the condition of your troops in the field? I ask. The Mujahedeen warrior's P R representative looks to see if he understands. "We need help," he says. Are you making progress against the Soviets? "The Russians fight, we fight, we win." He has been all over town in his heavy robes in the heat, up on the Hill and all around, talking about the cause to the extent that he talks, and hoping to raise funds. We look at our menus. The polite, attentive Filipino steward approaches and holds out his pad, his pencil poised in the air. The Mujahedeen warrior turns his turbaned head. "I will have meat," he says.

There were young men who were always just in from the bush or back from the border. They hated communism because communism was the state sitting on the individual, so they went to where the individuals were fighting back and joined in however they could. Jack Wheeler came back from Afghanistan with a Russian officer's belt slung over his shoulder, Grover Norquist came back from Africa rubbing his eyes from taking notes in a tent with Savimbi.

They reminded me of Ernest, Dash and Lillie getting drunk at "21" and hitting the New York intellectuals for money to fight the Fascists of Spain; there was the same sense of idealism, and adult delinquency. How can we turn our backs on the democrats of Central America? they'd ask late at night in a bar somewhere. How can we not help them fight the fascism of communism in Nicaragua (which is how the conservatives said it, Nicker-AH-gwuh, as opposed to Nee-kuh-DAH-goo-ah, as in Dan-YELL, as in I am a leftist former nun / this is my bible, this is my gun. You could tell who was on what side by how they pronounced the country.)

This was the movement:

A group of Young Republicans, angry and hurt at Washington's acquiescence in the recapture and apparent beating of a Soviet sailor who'd tried to jump ship in American waters, rented a tugboat, pushed out into the Mississippi, and crowded the decks, yelling encouragement to any other Soviet sailor who might try to jump. They had a motto: "College Republicans—It's not a job, it's an adventure." They picketed public-relations firms that fronted for Communist governments and called the rich Republicans inside whores.

And: one day a man walked into my office in the EOB in 1986, his face red with excitement. He said, "Did you see this?," and he read from something he'd torn out of a newspaper. His fingers trembled.

"Soviet dissident Anatoly Sharansky said Tuesday that he told President Reagan during a half-hour White House meeting that the President's hard-line anti-communist speeches were so popular with the inmates of Soviet forced labor camps that snippets of news about them were secretly communicated from cell to cell. Sharansky, 38, who was released February eleventh after nine years in Soviet prisons and labor camps, said that prisoners usually learned of Reagan's tough rhetoric through accounts in the Soviet press intended to inflame the public against the president. But he said the news had the opposite effect among the prisoners in the camp system known as the gulag. . . . Sharansky said that news of Reagan speeches was passed from prisoner to prisoner, despite camp rules against such activity. 'There are ways of communicating in the cells, even the punishment cells,' he said."

They were great days.

In the Reagan era people sent each other letters that said things like, "Many thanks for Macedo's new monograph; his brand of judicial activism is more principled than Tribe's," and "Thank you for yours of October 15 in which you outlined the appropriate criteria by which a reform of the current system can and should be judged." Sometimes they ended with "Soldier on!" This is how you know you're in a certain time: People write letters as if history will read them. (A secret of the people of Washington: They keep their letters and memos for the museum that will someday be built for them.) They sent each other articles and clippings with little yellow stickums that said, "If this gets into the hands of the Russians, it's curtains for the free world!"

People were thinking. That doesn't quite express it. People were driving intellectual bulldozers and knocking down rotting old ideas. Richard John Neuhaus identified the collapse of the dogmas of the secular enlightenment, the collapse of such dogmas as "Religion is only a crude superstition," Paul Johnson identified the error at the heart of this most killing century as man's tragic falling in love with the state, Jean-François Revel identified the inherent inability of democracies to consistently and convincingly recognize and respond to real challenges, George Gilder wrote not of the practical but of the humane nature of the free market, Michael Novak noted the collapse of the sophisticated assumption that the education we give our children can or should be value-free.

There was a collapse, on the honest left, of what remained of the assumption that we can judge communism by its professed aims rather than its realities, a collapse of the dominance of liberalism, a collapse of the left's ability to mold the debate.

Fall, fall, fall (or so it seemed). And in that collapse we saw: opportunity. And the chance to build.

Up on the hill the highly partisan atmosphere was occasionally soured by evidence of real personal contempt—for Congress in the eighties was so divided and contained camps reflecting such utterly different points of view on the essential questions that in some ways it was like the Congress of the 1850s, the Congress before the cataclysm, the Congress in which Preston Brooks caned Senator Charles Sumner on the floor of the Senate. There were enemies of Sumner who were happy he would be disabled for years.

Randolph and Sumner were one thing, and it was different now (though one day in 1987 a member of the Conservative Opportunity Society told me at lunch, "I had a terrible nightmare last night that Jim Wright killed Newt Gingrich"), but still: How could two men be more different than Jesse Helms and Barney Frank, Henry Hyde and Stephen Solarz?

Such division! The Democrats of the House looked down the street and saw the White House, the imperial presidency and the shallow president. In the White House they looked down the avenue as they sent down their defense appropriations, and what they saw was Heart-break Hill and all the unhelpful efforts of the Downeys, Dicks and Dodds.

But for all that, some things transcend. Maleness transcends, the rough, anarchic humor of men in powerful places transcends. The members were held together at least to a degree by a leveling crudity, by the common coin of sexual sameness. At the subcommittee hearings the thick-haired congressman was unrelenting in his questions, but he only half listened to the answers, because as soon as he'd spoken, he'd turn to his esteemed colleague and whisper, hand cupped over his mike, and without any apparent hint of irony, "Third row back, the blonde." New lobbyist from Detroit, an esteemed colleague would say. "Way on the left, the legs." New secretary in Fred's office but I understand they're close.

When you went to the Monocle or Anton's the members would greet each other heartily as they passed each other's tables, and if they got into a discussion of some vote they had taken that day they'd say, for the consumption of the people at the table, "But I told him it was economically unfeasible and practically unworkable," and then one would bend down and say to the other member, "I told him to go screw himself twice, once fuh me and once fuh you. I don't believe the pair on this guy." He straightens, smiles. "Very nice meeting you, have a nice evening."

They had jokes. What kind of body language tips you that a pol is lying? Well, it's not when he tugs at his tie or straightens his cuffs, and it's not when he moves his hands like this. What gives it away that a pol is lying is he moves his lips.

After every tragedy there was one thing to look forward to: the jokes, the instant jokes, the ones that start in New York and L.A. Something awful would happen and every press secretary on the hill would take at least three seconds to shake his head in sadness before racing to the phone to call a producer at one of the networks and say, casually, careful not to betray his hunger to be the first in the member's dining room with The Joke, "So what're they saying, yeah oh God oh-ho that's cruel gotta go," and then they'd get on the phone with the boss, the majority counsel, the girl third row back, and say:

"What did Rock Hudson say when his doctors asked him how he got sick? I don't know, ya think I got eyes in the back of my head? What did Rock Hudson and Donald Manes have in common? They both screwed Queens before they died. What's Claus von Bülow's favorite song? 'When Sonny Gets Blue.' What was Jessica Savitch looking for when she went into the canal? Roger Mud. Hey, she always wanted to be an anchorwoman."

Q: Was it sexist? A: Was it male?

Whenever one large congresswoman stood to make a speech, one member would always turn to another and say, "There she is, living proof that the Indians slept with the buffaloes." It was such a well-known joke, such a regular routine that once when she stood to speak her esteemed colleagues took a shortcut, and wafting from the well came an impromptu chorus of "Buffalo gal, won't you come out tonight."

In Washington in the eighties you would meet people from the Hill and the agencies and as you got to know them you would realize there was this funny thing that was accepted by everyone in Washington: The staff is more important than the senator or the agency head. The staff is almost always considered superior to the principal—more intelligent, more informed, more thoughtful.

I would talk to the members of a big man's staff, and after a while it would come out: the attitude.

"I'll tell him why we ought to do it this way," would become:

"Don't worry. I'm not sure he has that much interest in the specifics" would become:

"Don't worry, he won't mind" would become:

"Don't worry, he won't notice" would become:

"Don't worry, he won't care."

More and more the candidate was the front man; more and more he was just the talker. Our Senate and House candidates, even some of our presidential candidates: they are becoming like anchormen. They are becoming handsome speakers. 'And now *Eyewitness News* at eleven, with Dick Gephardt and Al Gore, the weather with Mike Dukakis, Paul Simon with a movie review, and Jesse Jackson with the Bruins."

At the end of the Reagan era all the presidential candidates looked like local TV news guys.

At the end of the Reagan era they had all gone to the same TV coaches, and they all talked the same way. They talked with their voices low and cool, not going to the mike but letting the mike go to them, moving their hands within the frame for emphasis, moving their hands the same way, with the same studied, predictible natural mannerisms. The thumb and forefinger together pinch-of-salt point-maker, the flat-palm-pushing-out emphasis-maker, the thoughtful pyramid as he ponders, the here's-the-church-here's-the-steeple as he coolly offers the cool riposte . . .

Stepford candidates with prefab epiphanies, inauthentic men for an inauthentic age.

I went to a brunch where a quick and angry young editor from *The New Republic* sat and talked with some young conservatives. Naturally it turned into a debate. He went back and wrote, If they're so interested in the family how come none of them are married? How come none of them have kids? I ponder this.

Yeah, said someone at lunch, you guys don't believe in God, you just believe in religion. I ponder this.

I went to a party where a former Carter speechwriter tapped my arm. If your conservative-opportunity-type congressmen like patriotism so much, how come they all dodged Vietnam? Talk about your war wimps! I ponder this.

Yeah, said someone across a dinner table, if conservatives are so interested in traditional values how come half of them are faggots—I mean total flaming lulus? (This is how it was: Conservatives would never talk like that because everyone knows conservatives are bigots; liberals could talk like that because everyone knows liberals live in terror of pressure groups.)

There was idealism to the movement and a sternness, an unforgiving quality. A woman who toiled long and hard at the White House, who tried to serve the president and balance the right against the middle she was surrounded by, said, "You never build up any equity with those people, you're always starting over again, back to point one. You always have to prove yourself, and you can never deviate from the line."

It was a hard place. Some of the movement conservatives just weren't very . . . well, the hard-core movement people were so . . . well, you know how it is with intense people in an intense environment, and so many of these guys are fish who swam upstream, and add to that the difficult natures that politics often draws and movements draw, and

. . . and add all that up and you get . . . well . . . what you get is a bunch of creepy little men with creepy little beards who need something to seethe on (State Department cookie-pushers! George Bush! the Trilateral Commission!) some hate to live for. These are not people who mourn when someone disappoints them, they like it. More proof of human perfidy! More proof of the ugliness at the core of the human heart!

He was a big man in the first administration and now, near the end of the second, he sat back on a thick couch and talked. "Everyone had to get labeled," he said. "People talk in shorthand in this town and they tag you so they can talk about you. So you get labeled like a can of pineapples. Neocon! Pragmatist! Idealogue! Hard-liner! And you don't even know it's happening until it's happened, and once you're tagged that's it."

Once you were tagged you would find yourself fair game for the side that was opposed to what you'd been tagged as. And when they'd start gunning for you, you'd run for shelter to the people who'd been tagged the same way you had. And they'd take you in. So you'd owe them something. And you'd try to take their side, and their enemies were your enemies.

"It was the labeling, wasn't it," I said, "that hardened positions?"

"In large part, yes."

"But there was so much shooting in the halls that you had to know if it was a buddy or a belligerent."

"The reasons don't matter. We all got labeled. And most of us lived up to them."

Here is Craig Fuller, assistant to the president, big-bearish and friendly, walking down the hall not too quickly, not too slowly, giving nothing away. He has on his face half a smile—a friendly, open look that invites greetings (and gives nothing away). He had learned by the end of his first year at the White House that younger staffers were watching his face and the way he moved for signs of a clash or a victory. They would see him angry and think, It must have been the staff meeting this morning; they must have had a fight about . . . that personnel thing. I bet Meese really went ballistic! An hour later Fuller would get a call from *Newsweek*. "Craig," they'd say, "is it true what

I'm hearing about blood on the floor?" He got used to this, to the fact that no one would ever believe he was in a bad mood because the cleaners lost his shirts.

The place swirled with rumors. "Mike Deaver asked me where the stories were from," Fuller later said, "and I said it's that we live in a fishbowl. You walk along the halls and there's three to four hundred people watching. And if you're visibly upset with me at a meeting it's only a few hours before my staff gets called. But they never see you and me alone, working it out and laughing it off. They never see Meese and Baker calmly and amicably working it out. They just saw the letting off steam at the meeting. They watch me, they read the schedule, they see your face. They're Kremlinologists of your face."

It doesn't matter who he is. He is a member of the Cabinet, but he doesn't look the part. He looks like a working man, with big shoulders and alert eyes. He was often called controversial.

He believed in things, and one of his problems was that every time he said something the sentences had meaning and the meaning was unmistakable. This forced the men around him to respond with sentences that also had meaning. In this way disagreement was crystallized and division defined. This wasn't helpful. It was assumed he didn't understand that you have to be vague in order to give both yourself and the other guy maximum feasible maneuverability, which is what people in Washington want because it's how you survive. You don't get pinned down, you don't go out on a limb, you don't act as if an idea is more important than a colleague.

He didn't murmur softly at the Cabinet table, he leaned forward— he had a reputation for leaning forward—and said those sentences. "What I think about before I open my mouth," he said, "what goes through my mind, are the words to an old Chuck Berry song, 'I got a chance, I oughtta take it.' "

Well-meaning people who'd been in town a long time tried to take him under their wing and help him understand how to get along. "You don't have to be controversial," they'd say. "You don't have to provoke people." Years later he would say, "They thought, understandably, that I was a rather callow fellow, that I didn't understand. But the thing is I was here and I wanted to be candid and talk about big problems and see if we couldn't move some things forward. Why not? That's what we're here for."

What he was saying was unusual. He was saying, I know that in Washington most people in power give first attention to protecting their careers, and putting yourself out front on various national problems increases the chance that your career will be hurt. But if I lived like that I'd think: For what? It would make my time here pointless, so I tried to do what I thought was right while also trying to protect my career, because I like this job and this is a great office and it's nice to be a Cabinet secretary.

Once he was invited to a dinner party with people of high repute in a splendid house with fine food. These people were the permanent Washington, Potomac royalty, the unchanging inside; they lived in a world of tacit assumptions and assumed understandings, a world in which it is de rigueur to talk about left-wing fanatics and right-wing fanatics, a world in which when you call to RSVP, the person who answers always somehow makes you feel like . . . a total yahoo. He wanted to be liked. The talk was of the day's events. Someone mentioned the big demonstration that had held up traffic for what seemed like hours, and a woman with pale hair exclaimed, Oh those anti-abortion people, they're so awful!

And the man who was controversial said, Yeah, well, abortion's pretty awful too, don't you think, the ending of a life?

And as he finished that sentence he looked at her, and her eyes went mmmmmmm-nice-to-see-you, and she looked away. He wasn't invited back.

He was at a museum opening or a cultural do—"One more corporation spending one more million on bad art"—where he was seated with three patronesses. He made conversation. "Too bad we couldn't give some of this money to hardworking English teachers instead of this goofy stuff," he said. Mmmmmmmmm-nice-to-see-you.

I admired him. It's hard, when you're trying to get along and stay inside, not to betray the convictions that brought you here. No, it's more human than that: Most people don't want friction and discord all around them all the time, they want things to be calm and nice, and it can be hard to strike the right balance between the correct social impulse and the correct moral one. He was trying. A lot of people don't, or don't for long.

I mentioned my admiration to a friend who worked at the networks. Yes, she said, I understand, we oughtta get him on *Face the Nation*.

Oh he'd be great, what story?

I don't know, anything. He's so controversial.

At a reception or a party there were rules. One is that people are allowed to quickly turn away from you once they've determined you do not have any clear utility to them. If you cannot help them in their rise, if you are not famous or influential or important, or if you're important but not in their field, they will simply turn away. The calculation and execution are done with an economy that no one decries.

How to disengage: Begin by signaling your disinterest. Do not maintain steady eye contact. Peer over the person's shoulder to see if someone important is within reach, and when you see your escape, say, "Oh gosh, there's Joe, the report, I hate to but I've got to—" And run.

Or: Pleasantly hold up your part of the conversation as if it interests you but repeatedly peer about turning your head from side to side with a big goony smile that says, "This is great, my first party, and I just have to get in the middle of it and experience it!"

Or—this one is popular in conservative circles: Peer morosely into your drink as the person drones on and then, just when he desperately tries to say something funny, look up with a pained expression and shake your head as if to say, "I'm in too much political pain to laugh— I'd better go home."

Departure lines did not have to be convincing. Standard good-byes of the Reagan era were:

"Well, time to do the room and advance the agenda!," and "I have to find my wife." (If someone says, "You don't have a wife," the answer is, "All the more reason to begin the search!")

In Washington the aging wives of important men have champagne-colored hair and quiet demeanors. They've been through this so many times, so many receiving lines and so many parties, so much small talk and tall talk, and when they finally meet you it's hard for them to muster up any real enthusiasm unless you're the boss or the boss's wife or someone who's famously rich. For everyone else it's this: a quiet and disinterested hello. Not hello, nice to meet you, not hello, howdyado, just hello . . . and a nod. And on to the next as they move along the line, frail in their beaded dresses.

· · ·

Dinner is served. Candlelight, soup, a crisp white wine. Stuffed sole, salad, raspberries and cream. Coffee, cognac, laughter. Things start out in a murmur; everyone sits up straight. By the time the evening is ending they're draping their arms over the pretty girl's chair. Cuff links catch the candle's glow, laughter turns languid, "Ya know, I think I will" follows "Have some more brandy" and anecdotes are less perfectly articulated, and funnier.

Down the table they speak of economics, and as my partner on the left turns away from them to me, he glides into conversation: "Do you like to discuss economic issues?"

"I surely do not."

"And what is it you like to discuss?" His eyes sparkle. He is the secretary of state.

"I like to discuss. . . . mmmmmmm, perestroika, and whether it is as real as this candle or flickering as this flame."

He laughs. He thinks, She wants to discuss no such thing, but he indulges her. They speak of the difficulty of change.

I am at a dinner at the home of Donny Graham, publisher of *The Washington Post,* son of Katharine, brother of the writer Lally Weymouth. An achieving man from an achieving family, but with a résumé rather different from most: He served in Vietnam and returned home to become a cop on the beat in the District. He and his wife are bright and warm and live in a section of Washington where normal people live, in a nice-not-grand frame house.

There are twenty or so of us, some people from the administration, some writers and editors from the *Post.* I see Lee Atwater, whose face and name I know, though I'm not sure what he does. Something about politics upstairs. I say to him, "Hi, this is nice, I don't know why I'm here, do you?"

"Ah don't know, but I think this is Meeting the Yuppih Republicans."

Graham approaches with his hand on the arm of Meg Greenfield, the gifted columnist and *Post* editorial writer. She offers her hand.

"Meg runs our op-ed page," says Graham.

I think to say the truth—I know who you are, and I've admired your work enormously since I was a kid—but don't because one mustn't gush, and one certainly mustn't make references to one's relative youth when talking to great ladies who are not only a bit older but a bit shorter. I opt for a laconic, "Oh, *Post* op-ed page, that counts."

"Gee, thanks," she says dryly; and steps over my body to join the others. (Three years later I saw her again at a party. I wanted to say that every time she writes about her early days in town, during the Kennedy years, I think, I wish she'd write more of this and say things you can't say in columns, because I'd learn so much. I blurt, "I think you should write your memoirs." She gives me the gee look. "Perhaps I will. Someday." (Excuse me, I have to go put my head on the tray with the melon balls.)

After dinner we sit on couches. Graham is bright-eyed, tapping his fingers together. He wants to talk about Vietnam; he wants a spirited conversation. I can see disagreement and debate coming, and wish to deflect. A low-key conversation gets going and I'm listening and disagreeing with this and that and soon I am bloviating quite nicely: "But we were trying to protect the people of Asia from communism, and if we'd achieved our objective we wouldn't have had the carnage that followed, we wouldn't have had the current Vietnam and the Khmer Rouge and the boat people—"

And a pretty woman with brown hair, the wife of an editor I think, interjects with passion, "Yeah, well we know that *now*. It's easy to say that *now!*"

I am too surprised to answer. Some of us knew that then. Some of us said so.

We look at each other a second. Our heartbeats are so elevated you can see the silk jump. There is going to be a collision. I swerve. "Oh well," I say, and move my hands.

Overheard on a reception line:
"So, how's tricks at Justice?"
"You know him, you saw him on C-SPAN."
"I loved your testimony!"
"Norman one, Gore zero."
"Will I see you at the Wicks'?"

Everyone had read *Advise and Consent* and at least one other of Allen Drury's wonderful old novels about Washington. We had read them in the sixties, when we were young, and they were part of the reason we were here. They had given us a sense of what Washington is or was or could be, and most of us, living in Washington in the eighties, had at least one moment where we thought, This is like Dolly's salon, or He's like Leffingwell, or I bet he's patterned himself on Harley. We never said these things to each other, ever. But we thought them.

We'd read all the Washington books, Drury and Teddy White and *Death of a President,* read them at an impressionable age, and we saw the town through the eyes we had when we were fourteen. Which contributed, I think, to the sense of cognitive dissonance some of us had, the gap between expectation and reality.

A perceptual problem: the textured nature of reality in the books versus the flatness of the reality in the room.

Another way of saying this is: Life is a big thing, it's got size, and you shouldn't be applying your passion to puny things. Life is a struggle for the human heart and the human spirit, a struggle between good and bad for good and bad. But so much of the human drama in Washington is comprised of . . . lesser stuff. A member of the Cabinet told me of his surprise: "In this town it's not for sex or power or even money that people will do things, grovel and do all sorts of things. It's for the president's box at the Kennedy Center! In New York they kind of go by what you know and what you do, but Washington's more a town of status, of the right parties and the right circles. Such—small stuff! Such thin gruel!"

In Washington in the eighties a man would attempt suicide when he thought his career was over, and later he would say, I did it because I had failed my country, and failure and defeat are difficult for someone with my admittedly achieving nature to countenance. He did it because he's a patriot with high standards. Not, I did it because my anguish is so huge, so ineradicable, that to remove it I had to try to remove myself.

It never occurred to him that he didn't have to make a statement.

I got the news that Bud McFarlane had tried to kill himself as I drove one morning along the Georgetown Pike, a hilly winding road in northern Virginia. I heard it on the radio as the car in front of me disappeared over a ridge.

So he wasn't a computer. I thought of the words that came to my mind the day I heard Bud quit the White House: the fluttering heart within.

A reporter called a week or so later. Did I know that Bud's scheduler had called to say that a reporter and photographer were invited to interview him as he recovered at home?

"He's doing photo ops of the convalescence?"

"Yes."

"That can't be true."

"It is," she said. "He apparently wants to talk about why he did it."

She asked if I had any thoughts. I said I did, but not for attribution, so no one will know that I talked to a reporter, no one will know I was a source. This is the Washington way.

I said, we live in an inauthentic age and everyone knows this but you have to wonder, has it got so bad that we do spin control on our suicide attempts, robbing even those moments of their true size, their true anguish? Do we render now even these cries of the soul tinny and insubstantial? And isn't this really very NSC, to turn your own suicide attempt into just another crisis that has to be handled, just another crisis of many. . . .

The reporter says she has spoken to another former administration official who had said of Bud, not for attribution, "At the White House I would see him, and afterward I would think of Hemingway in 'The Snows of Kilimanjaro'—'How did this leopard climb so high?' "

"Ooooooooh," I said.

"Yes," said the reporter.

She tells me she has just spoken to someone at the White House who had told her, not for attribution, that they didn't talk about the suicide attempt at the senior staff meeting that morning. Nobody mentioned it. The man said, "The reason is, we don't know how to deal with those things."

"That sounds true. A howl of pain is one message they wouldn't get on their beepers."

"That's good—can I use it?"

Yes. Not for attribution.

The story came out a few days later. It quoted Bud explaining that he had refound his will to live after watching a Frank Capra movie.

A few days later a publisher called the reporter. "That story was wonderful, and that 'howl of pain'—do you think there might be a book in that?"

A few days later: another call from another reporter. She said, "I'm calling about Regan's reaction to Bud. Did you hear it? Incredible. I have a source who swears to me that when Regan heard that Bud had attempted suicide and survived, Regan said, quote, That poor son of a bitch can't do anything right, unquote.

"Oh my God."

"Have you heard anything or know anything?"

"Not at all. What do White House people say?"

"They say, 'It sounds like him.' But I can't find anyone who knows it's true."

"God."

"Yeah. If you hear anything."

"Yeah."

In the park across from the White House were gathered each day the mad. People who had the secret to world peace, people who communicated with other species, people who heard voices. There was a man who handed out leaflets. "Are you being mind controlled by the subliminal radio? The government has developed a vast secret department involved in the study and advancement of mind control of individuals and groups by the silent radio. As a dog hears a silent whistle these persons hear a silent radio, which sounds the same as thoughts in their minds." The pamphlet continued, "Please write your questions or thoughts to me. If you don't receive an answer it is because of mail censorship. American Civil Liberties Union states they know nothing about mind control by silent radio. All the other organizations state the same. Many liars live in this world."

There was a man who lived in a cardboard box in front of the EOB. On cold days he surrounded himself with cellophane and wore a hat. There was a hand-lettered sign propped up against his box. It explained the injustices that had been visited upon him throughout his life. Day in and day out he sat there, cold and sullen. Now and then I would say hello. He made believe he didn't hear. Or perhaps he didn't, though the sign did not say he was deaf. In Washington in the eighties, as in every American city, the street people no longer tried to arouse an empathy or create a connection that might prompt a hand into a pocket. They often sought to menace.

There was a street person who waited until nightfall to roam the streets outside the EOB. He mumbled and was obscene. He frightened the women leaving the building. He frightened me. In another era various factors would have inhibited him, but this was the eighties, and the work of homeless activists had convinced the unstable that they had a wholesome and immediate job to do: challenge society's complacency and agitate for the dispossessed. In Washington in the eighties the insane were coolly used to advance ideological aims—cruelty in the name of a higher compassion, engineered by men and women who were lauded in the press for their decency and concern.

Was that it?

Well, for me. In part. To a degree. But just as Washington was the context in which the Reagan revolution ruled, the city itself lived within a context, the context of America in the eighties. Which was, in all, a strange place.

Prosperity and economic growth—abundance, such abundance, the profusion of material goods pumped out by a modern free market—the culture was vibrant (shallow, but vibrant), and the country's style had become so egalitarian that everybody wore pretty much the same jeans and the same sweats and ate the same Häagen Dazs (they wore different watches—the rich showed their riches on their wrists). . . . And: peace, an uneasy peace, an it-can't-last peace, an as-long-as-you're-not-in-Beirut peace, a we-could-all-blow-up peace, but peace.

And still an unease. Were we living through an era or a moment, was this an epoch, a real time like the twenties and the flappers or the sixties and the hippies (did it make it realer if we had a two-*p* word like yuppie?), was it an age or an aberration, was it the real thing, or merely the Ritz?

It wasn't like the seventies, where you could name the strangeness and cite examples of it. In some ways we'd improved greatly. America had been through therapy and *est,* had gone to the Betty Ford clinic and agreed to make its bed; we no longer said "recreational drugs," "victimless crime," or "quality time" without a guilty smirk, and as for the sexual circus of the seventies, we had long since quit the high wire.

By the eighties we were able to stand up, regain our balance, peer around, and see a quiet and pervasive dysfunction; all about us things weren't working anymore.

There was hardly a major corporation that wasn't adrift in some way, confused about its mission.

The airlines were no longer capable of prompt and efficient service, the networks were being run by midlevel executives from General Electric and the news divisions were falling apart (told to cut, the producers had no idea where; told last night's show was great, they stared back at you, eyes dilated: What had made it good, how could they do it again?). Congress was no longer capable of performing even its most essential duties (it hadn't passed a budget in five years!). All these power centers—they had forgotten the mission! They had forgotten the point! The Catholic Church could not decide if its job was public policy or the redemption of souls so it failed at both, offering pilgrims hungry for sustenance tepid homilies on defense spending. The nation's churches had nothing to say about sin. In Hollywood it had been more than a decade since art had escaped the system and thrilled the adults of America ("Why, the future, Mr. Gittes, the future!") The ayatollah had done it to us twice and the shuttle had gone kaboom, leaving the neighborhood optimist embarrassed at the cookout.

We seemed sometimes like a large dysfunctional family, bumping into each other in the kitchen every morning and saying excuse me, pardon me, (get out of my face!).

We were experiencing the dislocations prosperity allows: Everyone gets to free-lance, to dabble, to be the prince of somebody else's province. By the end of the eighties there was barely a power center in the country that could not echo Ray Donovan's sad plea: "Which office do I go to to get my reputation back?" (One of the three memorable lines of the eighties, the other two being Madonna's reaction to the discovery of pornographic pictures she'd posed for when young—"So what?"—and Howard Simons's, when asked how bad his cancer was—"Let's put it this way, I'm not flossing anymore.")

Across the ocean the Berlin Wall began to come down. Sad places we'd written off four decades ago were recalled to life and America, the great spokesman and practitioner of freedom in this century, was stunned and moved by an idealism we'd promoted just by being, and lost, so many of us, along the way. We looked at the tapes of Tienanmen Square, and the exodus from East Germany, and our eyes filled with tears, and I think it was part wistfulness. Oh to be young and romantic about freedom. Oh to know in your heart that democracy is a gift, like faith.

SEVEN

Knee Deep
in the Hoopla

Dick Darman walks into my office, crisp shirt, crisp tie, brisk stride. He sits on the couch and motions to me. It is the summer of '84, I have been in the White House six months, I've just written one of the first of the president's campaign speeches.

"Let me point out a few of the things you're doing wrong." He placed a speech on the coffee table and tapped it lightly with a pencil.

"On page three, in the second full paragraph, the sentence beginning, 'I will be frank.' To begin with, the use of 'I will be frank' carries within it the suggestion that our president is not always frank, which is untrue as we know. But that's not what bothers me. What bothers me is what follows: 'I am worried about' such and such."

He tapped the pencil.

"Understand: This president is never worried. This president is concerned."

Ah.

"Now. The section in which you thoughtfully provide instructions for the president, telling him to take off his jacket as he says, 'So I'm rolling up my sleeves and I'm ready to' blah blah. Now—"

"I like that because it's surprising, he never does anything like that and the TV producers will use it, it's a good picture and—"

"I know I know don't tell me what I know. Peggy: The president doesn't like to do things like take off his jacket and speak in his shirtsleeves."

"He'd look great."

"Do you know what the president's wearing when he's relaxed, by himself, at his desk in the Oval Office?"

"No."

"He wears his suit jacket and a tie knotted neatly at the neck. He never loosens his collar. He never rolls up his sleeves. He is fastidious. Your directions are not pertinent to his style."

"Okay."

"All right, here. This line is almost good but you have it wrong. You have him say of the Democrats, 'They've gone so far left, they left America behind.'"

"You don't like that?"

"I like part of it. The way it's put it sounds as if they've gone so far left they've left America in their wake—as if they've progressed and America hasn't."

"It does?"

"Yes. Try it this way: 'They're so far left, they've left America.' Period."

"Oh."

"Otherwise you're doing well. You're getting his sound. Actually you may be recreating his sound, and it sounds very natural to him." He laughed and walked out.

The famously difficult Darman, a man with scores of admirers and even more detractors, who described his virtues as if they were vices. And so he was not subtle but Machiavellian, not clever but devious, not proud but egotistical, not forceful but a bully. I suppose he was all of these, and more.

I think of the words Bill Moyers spoke in a eulogy for a friend: "He was the most difficult man I've ever known, and the one most worth the effort." In those days I did not know Darman well enough to say that; all I knew was the dervish of the White House and the blur he made as he levitated through the halls, his white shirt billowing behind him. He yelled and made the secretaries cry, but only if they were good at their jobs. He never made incompetents cry; he never even saw them.

He was different, not government issue. He looked at things with a keen eye and isolated quicker than most what was special about the painting, distinguished about the writing, unique to the individual. He could look at the landscape and see before anyone else the unexpected problems that would emerge. His risibility was partly the result, I think, of a kind of sensitivity. Once at a small meeting someone said something stupid for the second or third time and I quickly looked at Darman for his reaction and saw him actually involuntarily shudder, like a cat who'd been hit by scalding water from the counter above.

And yet, in a difficult administration he was one of the few who maintained strong bonds of friendship. Craig Fuller, David Stockman and Jim Baker were all his friends, and are. Few in that place in that time could claim so many close ties.

The White House during the presidential campaign of 1984 always seemed quiet and serene. No hustle and bustle, no things yelled in the hall. It was a polite place in a meaningful endeavor. When I think of it now I see an empty office with streams of sunlight and a fly buzzing softly in the corner.

Years later Mike Horowitz, the counsel for OMB, would tell me, "The '84 campaign was a kind of dream. We all wafted through it, a dream period where nothing happened. . . ." Some of us, he reminded me, figured it was our job to make sure something happened by getting the president to wage a campaign of ideas, a campaign that would produce a mandate he could use to govern. Instead it was, in Lance Morrow's phrase, a campaign of "blithe triumphalism." They took him out like a torch and carried him through the streets and schools . . .

There was the inevitable split between the White House and the reelection campaign, the latter pushing for a more aggressive stance against the Democrats and the White House mandating a more above-the-fray, these-are-our-triumphs approach. I hoped for a speech in which Reagan would paint a picture of where America is and where we want to go, specifically and with spirit. Then he could take his landslide and declare, This is what the American people have chosen to support; this is the vision we share and this is what we're going to do, bing bang boom.

The president would leave with a speech in the morning for a day of campaigning, and we'd wave good-bye on the South Lawn as the helicopter lifted. The people who went with him would come back with glowing reports of crowd reaction and response. But soon we started hearing the folks at the campaign thought it was all too "ivory tower." They wanted a rougher Ron, a more pugilistic approach in which the president lambasted the Democrats.

Dick Wirthlin, the president's pollster, weighed in at a meeting with the speechwriters that summer. He told us, "We had a sixteen-, seventeen-point lead in May and June. The Democrats were wrangling, and we had our planets perfectly aligned. But then the convention, and they got some bounce out of it."

He broke it down. "When we ask, 'Are you better off now after four years of Reagan', the answer is yes. But when we ask 'Are you safer,' people say no. Although a big part of it is crime in the neighborhood. People think that Ronald Reagan is capable, inspires confidence, a leader, gives moral leadership, delivers on his promises, and may start an unnecessary war."

We laughed.

"At the same time they trust him to negotiate a meaningful arms-control agreement. Firm hand on the tiller." He cleared his throat.

" 'Fear' will be a big part of the Democratic attack. 'Fairness' will be another—the rich versus the rest. 'The Future' will be the third part—four more years of Reagan means cuts in Social Security, tax breaks for the rich and a war in Central America."

What to do? "Stress the record. Talk of Mondale's unfairness. 'Tax and tax, spend and spend'—we can't say that enough. Mondale gets a lot of negatives, two negatives for each positive. People think he would increase employment, but they're afraid inflation will come back under him."

And the other *F*-word?

"The Democrats will try to take the family issue away from us, values, etc. And we won't let them. And we've got to reach out to the young, who are very patriotic."

I had put together a stump speech that was used in the early fall, but after the failed first debate the campaign rose in influence, and I was instructed to redraft it, making it sharper toward the opposition. For each appearance we'd write a new top—a new first few graphs saying it's nice to be in Ohio/Texas/New Jersey and come on up here,

Dick/Bill/Tom. I wrote with Reagan's admonition to Ben Elliott in mind: Specificity is the soul of credibility.

What follows is most of the stump speech, annotated. It was given two and three times a day, every day, the last two weeks of the campaign. (The thing about a stump speech is that it has to appeal to many different audiences. Our typical audience in '84 was composed of college students in university auditoriums. Twenty-year-old juniors were twelve when Jimmy Carter was elected; he was the first president a lot of them really remember. They were sixteen when Reagan came in, so he was the first president who was vivid to them. Anyway: thus the slightly professorial tone.)

"Abe Lincoln said, 'We must disenthrall ourselves with the past, and then we will save our country.' Four years ago that is what we did. We made a great turn; we got out from under the thrall of a government which we had hoped would make our lives better, but which wound up living our lives for us."

(Hyperbole is the soul of oratory, at least in the last days of a campaign.)

"The power of the federal government had, over the decades, created great chaos—economic chaos, social chaos . . . Our leaders were adrift, rudderless, without a compass.

"Four years ago we began to navigate by certain fixed principles. Our north star was freedom, common sense our constellation. We knew that economic freedom meant paying less of the American family's earnings to the government. And so we cut personal income-tax rates by 25 percent. We knew that inflation, the quiet thief, was stealing our savings—and the highest interest rates since the Civil War were making it impossible for people to own a home or start an enterprise. We knew that our national system of military defense had been weakened—so we decided to rebuild and be strong again. This, we knew, would enhance the prospects for peace in the world. . . .

"What, already, has come of our efforts? A great renewal. America is back. . . ."

(Ben Elliott's phrase from the '84 State of the Union)

"—a giant reemergent on the scene—"

(An echo of a Teddy Roosevelt line)

"—powerful in its economy, powerful in the world economy, powerful in its ability to defend itself and secure the peace.

"But now, four years after our efforts began, small voices in the night are scurrying about, sounding the call to go back, go backward to the days of confusion and drift, the days of torpor, timidity, and taxes."

(I think it was "torpor" that made them call it "ivory tower.")

"My opponent this year is known to you. But perhaps we can gain greater insight—"

(A teacherly locution from an aged wise man)

"—into his leadership abilities and his philosophy if we take a look at his record."

(A steal from Al Smith's famous "Let's look at the record.")

"To begin with, his grasp of economics is well demonstrated by his economic predictions. Just before we took office, my opponent said our economic program is 'obviously murderously inflationary.' That was just before we lowered inflation from 12 percent to 4.

"Just after our tax cuts, he said the most he could see was 'an anemic recovery.' That was right before our economy created more than 6 million new jobs in twenty-one months . . .

"My opponent said decontrol of oil prices would cost the American consumer more than $36 billion a year. Well, we decontrolled oil prices—and the price of gas went down eight cents a gallon.

"I was thinking about all this the other day, and it occurred to me that maybe all we have to do to get the economy in absolutely *perfect* shape is to get my opponent to predict absolute *disaster*!"

(FDR looks up and wags his head; the crowd roars.)

"He says he cares about the middle class, but he boasts, 'I have consistently supported legislation, time after time, which increases taxes on my own constituents.' Doesn't that make you eager to be one of his constituents again?"

(Pause as the answer rolls in: Noooooooooo!)

". . . He voted sixteen times in the U.S. Senate to raise your taxes. But this year he has outdone himself . . . If he is to keep all the promises he's made to this group and that, he will have to raise taxes by the equivalent of $1,890 per household. That's more than $150 a month. It's like having a second mortgage. And after the Mondale Mortgage we're sure to see more than a few foreclosures!"

(With a fed-up face, as the boo roles in.)

"I happen to believe my opponent's policies are as bad as they can be. I think his tax plans will be a hardship to the American people, and I believe it will bring our recovery to a roaring stop. But I'll give it this:

At least it gave me an idea for Halloween. If I could find a way to dress up as his tax program, I could go out and scare the devil out of the neighbors!"

(Take the sting out of the boo with down-to-earth humor. The witticisms in the speech came from fellow speechwriters, researchers, a professional joke writer, and Reagan.)

". . . But I'm not finished here, there's so much more to say about my opponent. His grasp of foreign affairs is demonstrated by his understanding of world events.

"Some time back he said the old days of a Soviet strategy of suppression by force are over. That was just before the Soviets invaded Czechoslovakia. And after they invaded Afghanistan, he said, 'It just baffles me why the Soviets these last few years have behaved as they have."

"But then, so much baffles him.

". . . After the Sandinista revolution in Nicaragua . . . he said the 'winds of democratic progress are stirring where they have long been stifled.' That was right before the Sandinistas slaughtered the Miskito Indians, abused and deported church leaders, slandered the Holy Father, and moved to kill freedom of speech. . . .

"More recently, my opponent failed to repudiate the Reverend Jesse Jackson when he went to Havana, stood with Fidel Castro, and cried, 'Long live Cuba . . . long live Castro . . . long live Che Guevara. . . .' My opponent never has disassociated himself from that kind of talk.

"I could say of his economic program that he will either 'have to break his promises or break the bank'—but I won't say it because Senator John Glenn, a Democrat, already has.

"I could call his economic program, 'A collection of old and tired ideas held together by paralyzing commitments to special-interest groups'—but I won't, because Senator Gary Hart, a Democrat, has already said that.

"I could predict that he will create deficits more than twice what they are now. But I won't, because Senator Fritz Hollings, a Democrat, has already said that . . ."

(The quotes are from a comprehensive research book put together by Ken Khachigian and his assistants at the campaign.)

"The truth is, if my opponent's campaign were a television show it would be *Let's Make a Deal*—you get to trade your prosperity for the surprise behind the curtain. If his campaign were a Broadway show it would be *Promises, Promises.* And if his administration were a novel, it would only have a happy ending if you read it backwards."

(Take that!)

"Now, I have probably been going on too long here."

(Reagan is one of the few politicians in America who could say that and count on a Noooooooo, turn to the press and smile a Cheshire smile: See how they love Daddy?)

"But the point is we were right when we made our great turn in 1980—we were right to disenthrall ourselves with the past—we were right to take command of the ship, stop its aimless drift, and get *moving* again. And we're right when we stopped sending out SOS and started saying USA again!"

(Well, all right, but in 1984 every time the president spoke before college kids, they'd interrupt him constantly with chants of USA! USA!—an echo of the chant at the 1980 Olympics when the American hockey team pulled off its spectacular win over the Soviets. So we figured: Don't fight it, use it.)

"And let me say here that the 1984 election isn't just some kind of partisan contest. I was a Democrat once, for a long time, and I always respected that party."

(This and what follows was aimed at dealing with the embarrassment nice people feel about turning Republican.)

"But in those days, its leaders weren't the Blame America First crowd."

(A steal from Jeane Kirkpatrick's wonderful speech to the convention two months before.)

"Its leaders were men like Harry Truman and John Kennedy, men who understood the challenges of the times. They didn't apologize for the totalitarians of the left, like Castro. They didn't reserve all their indignation for America and all their apologies for the Soviets and the Sandinistas of the world. They knew the difference between freedom and tyranny, and they stood up for the one and damned the other."

(Yayyyyyyyyyyy!!!!!!)

"To all the good Democrats"

(Good Democrats)

"who respect their tradition I say: You are not alone and you are not without a home."

(Come in, come too)

"We're putting out our hands and we're asking you to come walk with us . . ."

"All of us, together, are part of a great revolution. and it's only just begun, and we will never stop, never give up, never."

(Calling Dr. Churchill)

In the end, it worked. But it wasn't a good enough speech in terms of content, not enough fiber, too much sugar. What it included was fine, but it needed more—it needed to be specific about the future and the president's plans. The critics were right, I think, to criticize the Come-on-baby-let-the-good-times-roll aspect—but that aspect was unavoidable after the first failed debate, when no one wanted to put forth a more high-risk strategy.

The last day of the campaign Marlin Fitzwater, who was then an assistant to Larry Speakes, told Francis X. Clines of *The New York Times* that I'd written the speech. (Most reporters thought the campaign guys on the plane wrote it, because that's what the campaign guys told them. I was shocked when I got to the Reagan White House to learn that this was normal behavior, less a vice than a tradition. At CBS I never heard of a writer claiming to have written a show he didn't write, though the reason was probably the union-fee rules: You had to list what you'd written each week when you put in your hours to be paid. But in the White House there was no such system, and people lied with gay abandon, and I was constantly taken aback.)

Clines is one of the best prose writers in the working press. When I was just out of college I used to clip essays he'd written about New York in the *Times*, essays of great beauty, fluidity and knowingness, and tape them to the walls of my room. The day of the election he wrote a small story in the *Times* saying that the last day of the campaign reporters had asked the president if he would miss the stump speech. "Do you miss boils?" Reagan replied. Which for a while gave me a nickname I didn't need.

I wrote Clines a note asking if it was true the press, at the end of the campaign, used to recite whole sections of the speech with the president. He said yes, and the use of "torpor" was an accomplishment—but Eisenhower's military-industrial complex speech ended with the word "love."

A great trick, he said, in a political speech.

· · ·

I said earlier that after the president's failure in the first presidential debate the campaign rose in influence, but that doesn't quite convey what the mood was like in the White House after that debate. The Invincible Man had failed, and in public. It was the first time Ronald Reagan's countrymen ever saw him cast about and seem not up to the battle, and I don't think he ever completely recovered his pre-debate aura.

There was some panic and finger pointing. A gifted member of the White House staff was about to be sacked when he heard about the plan for him to take the fall. He went to a high campaign official and said: throw me over the side and I'll take some of you with me. The high campaign official smiled his sly-fox smile and said, "Now never mind son, you know we'd never let you go."

After the first debate I went to one of the daily press briefings. I liked to go to them now and then and sit in the back with the cameras and watch. One day I got a transcript of a briefing that gave a good sense of what the mood was like in October 1984, shortly after the first debate. It showed the class cut-up dynamic that not infrequently prevails in the pressroom, and the frustration of the press.

"Q" means a reporter is talking; they're always unidentified on White House transcripts. Speakes, of course, is the spokesman Larry Speakes.

SPEAKES: [In the next debate] the President's not going to do anything different . . .

Q: Well, he's going to present a coherent summation this time, is he not? . . . (Laughter)

Q: [Paul Laxalt] said that you're going to get out of the ivory—the president's going to get out of the ivory tower and go into the streets. Do you accept that characterization of where the campaign has been?

Q: Or where it's going? (Laughter)

SPEAKES: No change in campaign planning at all—steady as she goes . . .

Q: Larry, there was a man on *CBS Morning News* this morning who said he was Ronald Reagan's makeup man—

SPEAKES: How long did it take you to find that fellow? You ought to be ashamed. (Laughter) I mean, *Good Morning America* might do that—but *CBS Morning News*? I don't know . . .

Q: What about the President wearing makeup after all . . .

SPEAKES: He does not wear it as President, I can guarantee that—I wasn't there—

Q: Has he forgotten that he used it?

SPEAKES: I wasn't there in *Death Valley Days.* (Laughter)

Q: Does the President still say he doesn't . . .

Q: And he never did?

Q: Except for powder, right Larry?

Q: Who does his hair, Larry?

Q: . . . Larry, Pete Teeley [the Vice President's press secretary] is quoted as saying Ferraro is bitchy. Is that now the consensus? (Laughter.)

SPEAKES: I thought the word was "witch."

Q: No—

Q: No, seriously—

Q: It's a debate within the campaign.

Q: Shhhhhhh . . .

SPEAKES: We're the presidential campaign. We'll leave the Vice Presidential viewpoints to the Vice Presidential Press Office and the Vice President's wife.

Q: Well, have you inquired of Teeley . . .

Q: Have you or anyone else inquired of Teeley whether he in fact said that? He's quoted in *The Wall Street Journal* as saying this.

SPEAKES: Yes, I spoke to Teeley, but the subject didn't come up.

Q: How come these unpleasant subjects never come up? . . .

Q: Why is it that when you're asked about a Mondale slipup you'll refer people to the Mondale campaign, when you're asked about something Teeley says you refer to the Bush campaign; when you're asked something about a Reagan slipup, since you are his press spokesman why don't you comment on that? I mean—

SPEAKES: Well, Lou . . . how long have you been covering politics?

Q: Longer than you've been a press spokesman.

SPEAKES: Well now—you know how the game's played, though.

Q: It's not usually played like this.

Q: Is that a confession on your part?

SPEAKES: No, I'm not confessing to anything—I'm just stating the facts.

Q: Game's suddenly gotten serious, hasn't it? . . .

Q: Was the Laxalt news conference [in which the president's friend Senator Paul Laxalt of Nevada accused the White House staff of "brutalizing" the president in rehearsals before the first debate] a surprise, and what he had to say a surprise?

SPEAKES: The Laxalt news conference was not a surprise.

Q: —what he had to say?

Q: —about brutalizing—

SPEAKES: We didn't write a script for him, if that's what you're asking.

Q: You didn't? That's a stunner . . .

Q: Mondale is saying that the President's practice of embracing dead Democrats amounts to political grave robbery—(Laughter)

Q: Necrophila—

SPEAKES: Well, my viewpoint is, these Democrats are a lot closer to President Reagan's philosophy of government than—

Q: They're dead. (Laughter)

I sometimes felt sorry for the White House press corps in those days, a perhaps eccentric emotion, but a lot of them had worked twenty years to get to the top, to the White House, and here they were stuck in little booths doing little real reporting—their work is, in many ways, a protracted jolly deathwatch—doing trips and flagging soundbites, and dealing with Speakes, who at the end of the briefing was asked about the president's preparation for the second debate. "That's for me to know and you to try to figure out."

Those were hardworking days. I'd get to work about 9:30 A.M., late for the White House, and stay till 10:00 P.M. or so. I'd lean back in my chair and see the helicopter take the president off to Air Force One in the morning and then write whatever I was assigned (a new top for the stump for an appearance in Ohio, a new speech for old people for a just-scheduled appearance at a nursing home) and walk around, go into people's offices and say hello, go back to the word processor and write some more, lie down on the floor, read for a while, walk some more and bump into people who'd been out with the president and hear how it went. . . .

I was always asking to go on one of the trips but speechwriters weren't allowed. I'd tell Darman, How can I write not knowing how what I'm doing is being received? How can I write not knowing what works and what falls flat, and where the president has to pause for breath, and what clumsy construction is tripping him up?

One day in October they let me go. I was going to go on Air Force One with the president of the United States to the University of Alabama, where he would give the stump speech to thousands of adoring students. (It was the great story of the campaign, how America's young people loved Pappy.) I was so excited I dressed nicely, with an expensive sweater and a truly adult Norma Kamali black linen skirt, and I resolved to keep a friendly, open adult face on.

It was a sunny day, brilliantly sunny.

We rode in limousines from the White House to the airfield. We rode right up to the plane. I said my name to a military aide who was standing with a clipboard at the bottom of the ramp and who checked off names as we jogged with just the right amount of casual energy up the stairs. At the top I turned to see what the president sees when he stands and waves—a terminal with little people waving back—and turned into the coolness of Air Force One. There it was: the West Wing hum. And the West Wing aroma, flowers on the airplane.

There was a name on each seat. There was no boisterousness, no loud talk. People had brought newspapers, and read them as we rose. I was too excited to read but I didn't want to look that way so I read the *Times.* People walked by. A steward. Would you like anything, ma'am?

Yah (with a yawn), think I'll take some coffee. (This isn't my first time here.)

I rustled my paper and looked around in a bored fashion.

Next to me was Ken Khachigian, who had written one of the campaign kickoff speeches on Labor Day and who had given the president the old Jolson line that became the tag line of the campaign: "You ain't seen nothin' yet." Ken introduced me around. I don't really remember who they were. Intense men in suits.

The famous smooth takeoff was smooth. Air Force One macho: No one wore seat belts. I unbuckled mine. Soon we were above the clouds and the president walked back to say hello. In those days he liked to change into sweatpants as soon as the plane took off, and with his white shirt and tie and cuff links, the sweatpants gave him an unexpectedly youthful, insouciant look. I'd seen it in magazines. But this morning he wore his suit and walked from chair to chair. Ken reminded him who I was, and the president said of course of course and talked about the day ahead.

"Did you see that thing on CNN last night about Social Security?" he said.

We shook our heads.

"There were all these Democratic politicians, and they were talking about how I threaten the system."

He shook his head.

"I don't blame some of these old folks for how they feel about me. If I were old and I listened to that stuff I'd think I was terrible too."

Pause.

"Wait a minute, I am old!"

Hearty laughter.

When the plane landed we got in a motorcade and sped off, driving fast over empty highways. We took a ramp off a highway and proceeded toward the main shopping area, past the First Alabama Bank, past the Piggly Wiggly and Kentucky Fried Chicken. There were little clusters of people on the sidewalks. Finally there were enough people so that they formed one long, unbroken line. It's funny how they reacted to us.

There's no official way to act when a president goes by anymore. Once joy was the appropriate reaction, or excitement or enthusiasm. But now people are embarrassed to act that way unless they're in a big crowd. When it's a line one or two deep they don't know how to act. They don't want to jump up and down because, after all this guy is probably just a future unindicted co-conspirator and only a chump would jump—so they just stand there.

But then the big black cars with the flags pass, and in spite of themselves they get excited and want to do something, so they give these restrained little hurrahs. They don't jump but they do a little hop, and they don't wildly wave their placards but they hold them up and bob them back and forth a moment.

They didn't know (you never know, not since Kennedy) exactly which long limousine was the president's, so they jumped and waved at the first three cars. Then they stood quietly, arms folded, staring ahead. Until the media car came—an open truck with cameramen and technicians and photographers spilling over the side and taking pictures into the wind. Then they jumped real jumps and applauded and yelled things and waved their signs. They were acting out joy for the cameras.

There was a sign that said, THEY SAID OUR COLOR WAS A YELLOW

RIBBON—WE HOISTED THE RED WHITE AND BLUE. There were a lot of signs like that. It was curiously flat. Poor Mondale, how must it be for him.

Then the school and the boom boom of four thousand Adidas on the planks of huge bleachers and the speech, followed by the Crimson Tide wave—an Oooooooohhhhhh that went from one side of the huge gym to the other like the wind through grass. . . .

Then into the cars, out onto the highway in the sun, no traffic, smooth, just us and the mournful wail of the sirens of our police escort—and then the evening's photo op, an impromptu stop at a local McDonald's (impromptu in modern politics having the same meaning as spontaneous in Gore Vidal's *The Best Man:* How long will the demonstration last, Governor? This spontaneous demonstration will last approximately seven minutes and thirty seconds.).

They stopped the motorcade in the parking lot and the president got out and his aides got out and they all walked in, surprising the patrons. When I got inside the president was making awkward chitchat with someone who stood near him. He was supposed to order a Big Mac or something like that but when it was his turn on line he didn't seem to know what to say. He stared up at the menu and then at the young black girl at the counter, who stood with a slouched, muscleless awe. He looked at her, she looked at him, he looked at the menu. He didn't seem to have the faintest idea what a Big Mac was. Someone whispered to him. He brightened and nodded. He seemed relieved to hear he could get a hamburger here.

He took his tray, his aides took their trays, they went to a table and sat.

The president bit into his burger. The cameras taped him eating. People stood around him clicking cameras. The president chewed in a sort of ostentatious, chewy way. The aides chewed.

Then something nice. There was a young white girl, nineteen or twenty years old, standing a few feet from me with a baby in her arms. She was thin and, except for the baby, alone. She held the baby tensely and stared. When the president and his aides stood to leave she involuntarily took a step back, but then she stopped as if she were thinking, No, I'm an American, I belong. The president and his aides were walking her way.

"Mr. Reagan," she said softly.

Her eyes were luminous. She stood there in her pink shorts and her beige halter top and her pale skin. They were walking past her to the door.

"Mr. Reagan," she said.

And he looked at her and saw her, and a rush of warmth came from him, and he put his hand on her arm and smiled at the baby, who looked up at him. They talked. The president patted the baby.

Something in it redeemed the day.

Outside we scrambled for cars. I had been assigned the back of a crowded sedan—when you travel with a president, you get a little booklet that tells you not only what car you're assigned to but who is in it with you, and as soon as people get it they read it to see if they're being treated with respect, and if their enemies are.

I made it to the sedan. To my left, the president's secretary, puffy and aggrieved, heaved soft complaints into the air. She always seemed as if she were afraid someone was going to ask her to take a letter. To my right another secretary, a bouncy blonde named Barbara who burbled with delight.

I was between them in a backseat built for two. There was a pile of gear in the middle of the floor and no room for my feet, which I placed on top of the pile. My knees were almost at my throat, an interesting look. We hit a bump and I jumped; I was sitting on the phone. We lurched to go, we lurched to stop. In the front seat were two big, chubby boys, volunteers from the local Republican club, who were having a hell of a time talking on the radio. Now and then one of them would turn around and honk, "You girls all raht back thayuh?" The president's secretary stared at them, hot needles coming from her eyes.

Back to the plane and off to another speech. This time I saw that everyone was sitting in his own separate seat doing his own separate work, all of them together but really apart. They did not speak with comfort and familiarity to each other. I didn't feel I belonged. Now I wonder, Did anyone?

I remember Margaret Tutweiler, an aide to James Baker, knitting in the seat in front of me and saying to Senator Strom Thurmond as he boarded as a guest, "Senduh, you just sit right down here next to me and we'll catch up." She belonged, or must have felt she did.

The president came back and asked if we'd seen the girl with the sign.

"She was standing by herself on a little hill just up above the people there, and she held up a little sign that said, 'Mr. President I'm your favorite poet!' And I knew it was the girl who wrote me a while back and sent me her little poems, you know, and they were very good, and I wrote her back and said from now on you're my favorite poet. And there she was." He shook his head.

"I wish I could have stopped the car and gotten out and given her a hug."

We arrived in another southern city for an outdoor rally. There was an old courthouse from the Civil War era, which was lovely to see. It's always such a relief in modern America when you find a building that's old, that's weathered some times and is still there. The president spoke, it went fine, we scrambled for our cars and sped away. I watched again as we drove slowly through the town, the people jumping a little for the president and higher for the media car.

I was reading those days a poem by Vachel Lindsay:

> *I brag and chant of Bryan, Bryan, Bryan,*
> *Candidate for president who sketched a silver Zion,*
> *The one American Poet who could sing outdoors,*
> *He brought in tides of wonder, of unprecedented splendor,*
> *Wild roses from the plains, that made hearts tender,*
> *All the funny circus silks*
> *Of politics unfurled,*
> *Bartlett pears of romance that were honey at the cores,*
> *And torchlights down the street, to the end of the world.*

Once it was like that, wasn't it? Torchlight parades and red-faced boys with big bass drums, hurrahs, huzzahs and rallies. Now this—this joyless endeavor, this arranged marriage, this enactment of the process.

Whatever happened?

You know what happened.

I was on the campaign trail in '80 and '84, interviewing housewives who hosted caucuses in Iowa and businessmen who'd just voted in New Hampshire; I produced election coverage; I wrote a president's election speeches. And this is what I know:

It's true what Andy Warhol, the only artist ever quoted in the Reagan era, said, but when you get your fifteen minutes you're going to be reduced to a photo op and a soundbite, and they're going to be the truth about you long after you're gone.

In the eighties television reached critical mass, reached the saturation point. It was no longer only the thing that takes the place of the fireplace, the thing we gather round to hear of myth and story; TV had by the eighties become not the final arbiter of reality, but reality itself.

We are no longer obsessed with television we are addicted to it (half the people in the stadium watch the game on the monitors, half the people at the convention watch the demonstration on the monitors), and we are not only addicted, we are saturated (the monitors are all over). It isn't enough that they're experiencing it; it isn't real unless it's ratified, and television is the ratifier.

HOW DID IT GAIN SUCH SWAY?

By the Reagan era the traveling salesman, the man who drove his wagon into the neighborhood to sharpen the knives, the Fuller Brush man, the Avon lady, the vacuum-cleaner salesman, the tinker with his horse, all the people who used to come into the neighborhood and break the tedium, break the loneliness—all of these were gone. The once-a-week mobile libraries that came to the middle-class neighborhoods in the sixties and gave something to look forward to to the woman on the stoop with the housedress on and three kids fighting for her lap—they were gone.

But in the Reagan era Bill Cosby came to visit, and Hugh Downs and Pizza Man and Counselor and Michael J. Fox and the theme to *St. Elsewhere*—they were there, come to say hello, to give you someone to commune with. . . .

You sit there content, the smoke curling out of the tray. The world is still out there it is still there it is pumping through the cathode ray, and I am here I am whole and I know this sound, it is the theme music of The Love Boat *and it lifts my spirits: It is familiar it is part of life I hear the sound of me in it I hear the room I live in I am here, and this is life.*

For our politicians and our poor, two groups with a special interest in the illusory, TV is the mother in the Skinner box; for the children in our increasingly dysfunctional homes TV is a soft, warm blanket; their favorite shows are about healthy families.

TV has not only changed our habits and social customs and our way of looking at the world—it has, I believe, changed our way of experiencing life.

We have stopped wanting to star in a television movie and have begun more and more to experience our lives as made-for-TV-movies. (The brisk young aide a few chapters back—one of the young men he was based on breezed past me in the West Wing one day, and as we paused near the doorway of the Roosevelt Room, I said, "Memorize it so you can tell the set designer when they make the made-for-TV-movie of your life." He smiled, but his unwavering eyes said *yes*.)

WE'RE ALL SOPHISTICATED NOW. WE'RE ALL NATIONAL. WE'RE NOT LOCAL ANYMORE.

The culture of our country used to be made up of the sum total of local pockets of local culture. There was the South and the Deep South and the Breadbasket, there was Out West and Brooklyn, and all these places were different. The people in these places had accents, regional accents, and they read the local paper and listened to the local DJ and got the news on one of the local affiliates and it was read to them by a guy who'd been there for years. There was local entertainment, the fairs or the grange or the local Y; you read local columnists.

But now—and this was the big thing you could see, if you were looking, on the campaign trail in America in the eighties—the sheer weight of national is flattening regional, the sheer weight of network is flattening local.

We all watch the same TV shows, receive and repeat the same cultural references, hear the same jokes, read from the same syndicates, see the same commercials, and we're starting to talk alike, with air-conditioned voices, like people from nowhere, like the anchor on TV. (There is a hurricane down south and a local man is telling the TV reporter what happened to his house. You hear his voice and think Oh nice, an accent. But his accent is not nearly as deep as his father's, and is deeper than his son's.)

Increasingly when reporters go out there to cover an election—when they go out there to test and write of the mood of the people—they find they cannot find it.

(I turned to Dick Darman after the trip back to the airport and said,

Dick, does the sameness get to you? He seemed surprised, and laughed. No, he said, it makes it all easier.)

What does this have to do with politics?

THE DISAPPOINTMENT ON THE
CAMPAIGN TRAIL

The reporter goes to the luncheonette on a side street in Des Moines. It is the 1984 caucuses, and he is looking for the local angle. How do people feel about the candidates? What's going to happen? How do they feel about being subjected to such overwhelming media scrutiny? . . .

He goes to the counter, throws a leg over the round red leatherette seat—I look, he thinks, like a cowboy mounting his horse outside the saloon—and orders coffee from a woman in a waitress uniform. She looks like Flo on *Alice.* He asks what kind of pie today, makes a joke, introduces himself.

"I'm Joe Smith from *The New York Times* / *The Washington Post* / NBC. Editor back home wants me to get the local angle"—he rolls his eyes to show irony, a tribute to the waitress's sophistication—"so we can tell New York what the natives are thinking."

"Any way you can help me out," he says. "Like how do you feel, for instance?"

If this were a 1930s movie, she'd be flustered. "Hey, Helen," she'd yell into the kitchen, "This fella's from *The New Yahrk Tahms,* and he wants to know what we're thinkin'!"

But this is not the thirties, or the sixties, or even the seventies, and she is not fazed.

She says, "Sure, hon, you local or network?"

"Uh, network," he says.

She says, "Brokaw's doing pretty well against Rather. You folks must be happy."

He says, "Let me ask you a few questions."

She says, "You gonna tape me or go live?"

He says, "Uh, tape actually, but before—"

"You got a crew?"

"I can get one, but let's talk first—"

"Ya'll gonna hard-mike me or what?"

Is she a good interview? She talks in perfect eight-second soundbites and it is totally unconscious, it's the wordbursts we use now to communicate, wordbursts full of verbs and huffs and puffs. If she were a neighbor at the local fire and a crew from Channel 7 came in and asked her what happened (as it has), she would say (as she did), "I just looked out my *window* and I saw *billows of smoke* and I ran across the street and there he was with *a child in his arms* and he *threw him* and *ran in again!*" In cue: "I just looked . . ." Out cue: ". . . ran in again." Runs: 06.

Why does she talk like this?

Does it have anything to do with the three and a half hours a day of television she watches and the radio news that she has on in the car? But it's also the way people talk to Sonny on *Miami Vice*, it's the way we've been taught to communicate: in quick, vivid wordbursts. Like: "You keep talking about your new ideas, but I keep thinking of that woman in the commercial—'Where's the beef'?" And: "I don't think age is an issue—I don't hold my opponent's relative youth and inexperience against him."

SHE'S GOT THE STYLE DOWN, BUT CONTENT IS A PROBLEM.

"Let me ask you," says the reporter, "what you think of Mondale."

She says, "Well, the people around here would probably not like his position on the farm problem but I don't think they dislike him personally."

"Do you like him?"

"I think he may do well because of all his money and all. He has the best organization."

"Yes, but do you like him?"

She stares. What is the soundbite supposed to say? She doesn't know her opinion! She only knows her opinion of local opinion. (We are all commentators now.)

All right, he thinks, switching gears. "What do you think of Hart?" She thinks in a hurry. Last night John Chancellor said voters find Hart cold.

She says, "I think he's kind of cold, myself." The reporter goes back to the newsroom and writes a story: "Gary Hart has a 'people problem,'

and that's not political professionals talking, that's down-home Io-
wans." Cut to Flo, who articulates her opinion with modest authority.
She is . . . authentic, the voice of the true America! She watched it that
night eating Häagen Dazs out of the container, which is what Caroline
Kennedy was doing as she watched the same show on Park Avenue.

She is important, Flo. She is the disappointment on the campaign
trail: Reporters go out there to find out what out there is thinking, and
find there is no out there out there.

WE ARE ALL ACTORS NOW.

We are all actors now. We get our mannerisms from TV and our
opinions from opinion leaders, and all this without knowing. We became a nation of actors not by design but because we could not resist
(no one can resist) the irresistible tug of all those things we see on the
tube. The politicians are actors playing out their anger at injustice and
their desire to get this country moving again; our anchormen are actors
as they look away from the TelePrompTer for a minisecond in the
middle of the "tell" story, disengaging themselves from the machine
to show that they are moved. The reporters are actors as they act out
the somber tone needed to convey pathos in the minute-thirty report
on the death of the little girl, the TV preacher as he begs for forgive-
ness, the boxer as he explains how he did it, the man at the dinner table
moving his hands the way intellectuals do on TV.

Everyone in America now explains a moment in their lives by saying,
"It was like a scene out of————." Whatever—*Marcus Welby, Gone
With the Wind, I, Claudius,* and everyone in America is seeing an
invisible camera.

(Ollie standing ramrod straight in his uniform in the hearing room
with his hand held high: That was Ollie's Gary-Cooper-as-Billy-Mitch-
ell moment. And that image will live longer on tape in the network
archives than Ollie will, and that moment will be "the truth" forever.
And so his gaze was steady and his eyes sincere, and when he wanted
us to know he was moved there was a catch in his voice, and when he
wanted us to know something was important he lowered his voice and
slowed his delivery, and when he wanted to show he was hurt he'd nod
and purse his lips and his eyes would grow moist.

(He was not so much a liar as he was an actor acting out the truth;

it never occurred to him not to act; it was his way of communicating; he is modern.

(After his testimony one of the networks, in an attempt to assess how well he'd done, turned to the movie critic of the *Los Angeles Times.* The next day another newspaper reported the American people found Ollie to be "performing well." They were not being cynical.)

The senators at the hearing base their characters on kinescopes of the Army-McCarthy hearings and the mob hearings of the fifties, on Joseph Welch and Estes Kefauver (and the network cameramen, playing to the same script, zero in on the witness's hands, hoping they'll clutch and unclutch nervously like Frank Costello's).

Politicians are no worse than most people on this, they're just more so. They feel such an affinity for artifice!

Gary Hart borrowed his mannerisms and physical style from John F. Kennedy, who was as fascinated by Hollywood as Hart is. Hart's best friend was Warren Beatty, whose movie *Shampoo,* its characters and their small-time corruptions, grew out of his experience in the McGovern campaign, which Hart managed. Hal Haddon, a close friend of Hart's, once said that Beatty was fascinated by Hart's life and Hart by Beatty's. "Politicians and actors—each one thinks that the other has a better scam, and they're just curious."

I drive along the hills of northern Virginia and the man at the Amoco does a Johnny Carson and the woman at the little store is doing a flinty old woman routine and I think about this as I drive into town to see the president and the first lady at the White House Correspondents' Association dinner. The president stands at the podium and calls Nancy to the stage. They look out at the black-tie audience.

He says, "Nancy, would you like to say a few words?" She looks out, deadpan. "Any words of welcome?" Again, deadpan. "Can't you even think of one nice thing to say to the press?" he pleads. Beat beat, and then: "I'm thinking, I'm thinking!" It is a perfect Jack Benny, even using the face he put on when they said, "Your money or your life."

They are at their best when they are performing.

Increasingly this is true of their countrymen.

WE'RE RUNNING OUT OF TIME. COULD YOU SUM THIS UP?

Well, Bryant, what I'm saying is—

You've already established you feel TV reached its zenith in the Reagan era but—

Yes, and the political result was this: When I was in the White House, TV was no longer the prime means of receiving the presidency, TV in a way *was* the presidency—

Uh-huh—

—and decisions were made with TV so much in mind, from the photo op to the impromptu remark on the way to the helicopter, that the president's top aides who planned the day, were no longer just part of the story—it was as if they were the producers of the story. They were the line producers of a show called *White House,* with Ronald Reagan as the President. And this wasn't particular to that White House, *it was simply a trend that achieved its fullness in the Reagan era.*

All right, thank you. And now we're going to go to Willard and—

I learned to move my eyes in a sincere way from you.

—check the weather. Thank you.

HERE'S THE SCARY PART.

We are more sophisticated about television than ever before, we've seen *Network* and *Broadcast News,* and the opening shots of *West 57th* and its string of quick, nervous cuts of a control room with directors yelling, "Give me video!" But our sophistication means nothing; for all our knowledge of TV, it still fools us. We are like people who go to a magic show knowing it's all strings and mirrors and still being thrilled when the lady gets sawed in half.

SOMEDAY

Some president is going to put TV in its place. Someday a smart man or woman will come in and say, I don't exist to feed that thing. Get it back in its cage—I have a country to govern. It will be an interesting presidency. (It may be Bush's.)

We had another meeting with the president.

Dick Darman told me Mike Deaver was talking to the president and thought he heard him say he'd like to meet with the speechwriters about the election but apparently that's not what he said but anyway the meeting was set up so we're going.

It was nice the way Dick always made sure I didn't get too excited.

The president was his genial self. It was eleven-thirty in the morning, and his office was flooded with sunlight. Ben, Dick, Ed Meese, and Mike Deaver all took seats.

I sit on his right and talk begins of the campaign. He is in a thoughtful mood, talkative, even softly garrulous.

"Now there's gonna be shrinkage," he says. "We've done fine, but sooner or later we'll start to lose some points. And I wonder if the time hasn't come to pick a forum and make a statesmanlike address about the economy and the deficit in particular. So that we can analyze, factually, some of their proposals and what they would really mean. I mean, we'll give them credit for their motives and the best of intentions, but then we should say, 'Here is why these things won't work, here is their unintended result.'

He looks at us expectantly, but everyone is scribbling furiously and no one looks up. When he has meetings like this he can never make eye contact with anybody because we're always busy writing down every word he says. He winds up talking into the air.

But it is a good idea: a calm, statesmanlike approach, forget the one-liners and the applause lines—calmly lay out your case. What a relief.

"Let's give them our own specifics, really give them chapter and verse. Our program is a success, while we didn't get what we wanted completely from Congress it is working and it's taking hold. And we can demonstrate that with figures."

He looked around; had anyone caught his enthusiasm? Nothing but the tops of heads as half a dozen pens scratched half a dozen legal pads. The old grandfather clock by the door issued its muted tick tick, like the dashboard clock of a BMW. I looked at Mike Deaver, who had a dreamy look on his face.

"We will go over what the revenues will be, for example, if we continue with a four-percent growth rate—that would mean how many billion, and if a five-and-a-half-percent growth rate that will be however many. And get across that growth is going to take away a lot of the deficit with time."

He paused, looked around. I looked up and nodded a very definite sort of nod.

"And I want to talk about economists and economic predictions. You know, I know those fellows. I majored in economics in college. And believe me, those fellows have a Phi Beta Kappa key on the end of their watch chains, and no watch!"

Meese said, "Mr. President, we have a number of quotes from economists, on when they've been wrong."

The president nods. "The profession isn't up to the problem it has to analyze."

The president continues, we all take notes, and—

Beep beep!

I looked up. No one moved or indicated that they had heard anything funny. The president continued talking.

Beep beep!—louder now. I look around, realizing it's one of those modern moments, someone's beeper or computer watch telling him to take his pill—but no one makes the movements a beeper owner would make.

Beep!

No patting of the pockets or readjusting the watch. They look at the president as if beep beep isn't happening.

I look at him too. He continues talking.

Beep beep!

Is it coming from . . . the couch? But they're all sitting there looking at the president in their pleasant low-affect way—

Beep!

—or could it be the chair? It's coming from the president's chair.

Beep!

No, it's coming from his head! His head is going beep and no one will tell him! He opens his mouth and—

BEEP!

—looks at me in a quizzical way. He shakes his head, brings his hand to his ear, sticks his index finger in, pulls out . . . his hearing aid. It was not a nuclear alert.

Beep.

He looks at it and turns it over.

"This darn thing! New batteries and the darn thing goes off all the time anyway!" Shakes his head, puts it back in and continues. I look at everyone. Low affect. I look at Ben. Ronald Reagan wouldn't lie there with a look like a dead carp if someone's hearing aid went off, he'd help the guy and tell a story. I smile at Ben and Darman. They look away.

The president returns to his theme.

"You know, back in the twenties I think they did a report for Herbert Hoover about what the future economy would be like. And they included all their projections on industries and restaurants and steel, everything. But you know what they left out? They left out radio! They left out the fantastic rise of the media, which transformed the commercial marketplace. And those were economists talking about the future!

"And now they make their projections, and they leave out high tech. A couple of days ago Dick Lugar told me that now in Indiana— Indiana!—one out of eight workers is working in the high-tech field. And no one is really catching on to its importance to the future and the economy.

"Anyway," he finishes, "what I want is the kind of speech that there ain't no rebuttal to!"

Meese in again: He wants us to hit hard on family themes in some speech down the road.

"Yes. And we can mention Social Security. Say that there are some who suggest some of our deficit problems are due to the size of Social Security, but that's not so. Social Security is not a part of the deficit; it's funded entirely by its own fund, and if you reduced benefits—and we never would—but if you reduced benefits, that saved money would simply revert to the Social Security trust fund. So no, we won't lower Social Security to reduce the deficit."

I looked at Darman. He looked like a man on a reception line trying not to show pain after his toes have been stepped on by some fat fool.

The president leans slightly forward. "You know, we couldn't say this, they'd hang me, but one of the things wrong about Social Security is we broke up the three-generation family. Now, I never had that kind of family—my grandparents were dead before I was born—but we went too far, and we allowed older people to live on their own, and originally it was just supposed to be a few dollars to help them out. And now they can live apart. And it broke up the three-generational family. That's why that show, *The Waltons,* was so popular, because the whole family was together."

Darman can't stand it anymore, and leans forward. "Well I think Mr. President that technology played a part—mobility, the enabling of the American family as a unit to leave one part of the country for another, the—"

The president nods. "It was the rise of the city, too," he says. "You know, those sleepy old towns where generation after generation lived. And then the kids in the Midwest left; there was nothing in those towns—Lord, that's why I left! And they wanted to see the world, so they went to the cities. . . ."

I was in heaven. People were talking about the world.

The president returns to the economy, and as he speaks some more he does something—an oldism. He stretches his legs out, soles of both shoes planted firmly on the floor . . . and he moves his toes up and down. And watches them. Sort of feeling his muscles, feeling the movement. He wiggled them and stared at them, as if he were thinking in a child's singsong, "My feet still move and my legs still move, and I still have muscles, and they all move. . . ." I laughed. He looked at me and laughed.

As we leave he says to Ben, "That Italian-American dinner went great. The speech. You know, it was almost embarrassing. There's Ferraro, and she's Italian, and she goes in and there's applause but also some boos. And when we went in they started actually to cheer 'Four more years' over and over. Did you hear about the dress? No? Well, we get there and we're ready to go in and they come to us and say Ferraro forgot her dress, she's waiting for it upstairs, and can we please stay in the waiting room because there's this protocol—after a president is introduced no one else can be introduced, and that would be rude to her, so can we just wait?

"Well, we wait for about twenty minutes in this little room. And finally I called over this fellow and I said, Boys, those folks out there are waiting to eat, and we're being rude. And if there's any protocol I hereby declare it waived. And we went in."

He laughs. Then the quizzical look. "I don't know about that wait. I think we got rolled." He shrugs, good-naturedly. Everyone gets rolled.

I bounded outside, past the president's secretary who sat, puffy and aggrieved, hurling soft complaints into the air, through the door, out through the West Wing, back across to my office.

I would be able to say, "Well, I was meeting with the president the other day, and he says—" for weeks. And he had opinions, he had something he wanted to do.

Days later Ben told me to forget about the economics address, it wasn't going to happen. I was surprised. Why not? The fellas don't want it. Why? They think your friend Lesley Stahl will say, "In a defense of his much-criticized economics program, the president insisted that things are better." They think it'll play defensive, like Mondale's scoring off us.

What does the president say?

Ben shrugged.

I spent election night with some researchers and speechwriters at a little party at Ben's house in Arlington. It was anticlimatic. Ben's pretty wife made a buffet, and his children sat in our laps. Darman called Ben to say, Well done, the president made his victory statement out in California, we went home early.

Weeks later Darman's office called. Dick wanted to come by, would I be in? Minutes later I turned from the word processor to see him standing with a big white piece of paper framed with a big black wood border.

"This is your commission," he said. "You are now a special assistant to the president of the United States. Here is his name, Ronald Reagan. And here is yours."

I laughed and clapped my hands.

"A battlefield commission," he said. "Well deserved."

I was happy, but I also think it was during the campaign that I started to feel a kind of disorientation. I would wonder, Who's in charge here? I could never understand where power was in that White House; it kept moving. I'd see men in suits huddled in a hall twenty paces from the Oval Office and I'd think, There it is, that's where they're making the decisions. But the next day they were gone, and the hall was empty.

At the center of it all, at the center of the absence, was Reagan, whom I adored and who confused me. For years I would ask his friends, Who is he? Tell me stories, make me understand. Who was that masked man?

EIGHT

Who Was That Masked Man?

He was to popular politics what Henry James was to American literature: He was the master. No one could do what he did, move people that way, talk to them so that they understood. A demagogue would have begged for that power; he didn't even care. That's part of why he had it. He didn't have to be the man pulling the switch, he wasn't in it for ego; he was actually in it to do good.

He was probably the sweetest, most innocent man ever to serve in the Oval Office. He was a modest man with an intellect slightly superior to the average. His whole career, in fact, was proof of the superior power of goodness to gifts. "No great men are good men," said Lord Acton, who was right, until Reagan.

Toward mankind in general he had the American attitude, direct and unillusioned: He figured everybody is doing as much bad as he has to, as much good as he can. He wasn't artless, or an angel; he didn't seem to expect a great deal.

He was a happy man. He trusted life. But then so much that had happened to him had been lucky and good. His mother loved him. The fellas knew what they had. Once Deaver took Darman aside and said, "Listen, Dick, I don't care what else you do but make sure you do this:

Get that face on television. This is a face that when a baby sees it, the baby smiles." Back in '80 in the debate with Carter, it was the little man who winced versus the Emperor of Ice Cream. Carter didn't have a chance.

How to capture him, how to say what you saw and imagined without it being twisted by one side or another. Tell the truth and the left will seize it as a flag, tell the truth and the right will wave it as a banner. No matter what you say about this man it winds up being somebody's propaganda.

Here he is, at his desk in the Oval Office, a bright, rounded room of gravity and weight.

He is answering his mail. He looks up as you enter and blinks his moist eyes. His suit is brown, of a dense, substantial weave, his white shirt as bright and uncreased as a shirt in a department store; a tie striped in earth colors is knotted at his neck. You imagine him patting down the collar and trying out a smile.

"Well," he says, as he stands and rounds the desk. He walks toward you softly (I never remember hearing his footsteps).

"Hello!" you say smiling, as he puts out his hand. As your hands touch and then clasp you think: I am standing here shaking hands with the president of the United States, right now, this second. The thought so takes you that you forget to let go. He lets you keep shaking. He is used to this. He rarely lets go first.

He stands there in his tall brown suit looking down with soft, kind eyes, and you are surprised by the pinkness, the babylike softness of his skin. The soft neck, and something you hadn't expected: the air of frailty.

He gleams; he is a mystery. He is for everyone there, for everyone who worked with him. None of them understand him. In private they admit it. You say to them, Who was that masked man?, and they shrug, and hypothesize.

James Baker said, He is the kindest and most impersonal man I ever knew.

An aide said, Beneath the lava flow of warmth there is something impervious as a glacier.

Mother Teresa said, In him, greatness and simplicity are one.

A friend said, Behind those warm eyes is a lack of curiosity that is, somehow, disorienting.

A power source cool at the core. A woman who knew him said, He lived life on the surface where the small waves are, not deep down where the heavy currents tug. And yet he has great powers of empathy. There is a picture of the president and his aides watching TV moments after the shuttle *Challenger* blew up. It is shot from the angle of the television set. On the faces of the men around the president we see varying degrees of interest, curiosity, consternation. Only on the face of Reagan do we see horror, and pain.

Through the force of his beliefs and with a deep natural dignity he restored a great and fallen office.

He was so humble and unassuming that his aides were embarrassed a few days after he was shot to find him in a little bathroom off his hospital room, down on his hands and knees on the cold tile mopping up some water he'd spilled from the sink. He hated to make a mess for the nurse, he said. He wanted to clean it up before she came back, and could they get him some more towels?

Imagine a president with no personal enemies. This has never happened before.

Imagine a man nobody hates, or no one who knows him. He was never dark, never mean, never waited for the sound of the door closing to say, "What a fool," didn't seethe, had no malice. People could tell he trusted their motives. It brought out the best in the best of them, who acted better for the compliment, and the worst in the worst of them: They nodded with mild surprise when they saw his trust, looked into his eyes, and saw . . . nothing. They thought he was an empty house, and they were second-story men.

I'll tell you something surprising: This sunny man touched so many Americans in part because they perceived his pain. They saw beyond the television image, they saw the flesh and blood, they felt those wounds, they caught that poignance.

The reporters and correspondents and smart guys, they missed it. But the people saw. They thought, Look at the courage it took at his age to be shot in the chest by a kid with a gun and go through healing and therapy and go out there again and continue being president, continue waving at the crowds as he walks to the car. Think of the courage that old man had!

Stop shaking his hand for a moment. Stop loving him. This is what you should say: "So where did you come from, Mr. President, and who are you, really? What are the forces that shaped you, and why are you so odd?"

"I'm not odd," he would say. "I'm only odd for a president."

Imagine the sound of a river, the burly Mississippi, snaking its way through soft defeated acres; it fights for every inch it gets, pushes and claims, pushes and claims. Its tributaries, sluggish and slow, push through Illinois, past Dixon, past Tampico, where, in the year 1911, he is born. Mark Twain has been dead a year, Keynes is just out of college, Lindbergh in grade school. It is all so long ago.

He is the second son of a disappointed father and a handsome mother; he bright and dour, a skeptic chasing his dreams with no great joy, she Bible-quoting and resolute.

Listen: a fly buzzing against an old screen door looking for a way out—the gentle slap of the cord of the shade on a sill—and upstairs, second floor, the boy on the bed reads a book about plumed knights. The kids call him "Specs"; his face is earnest, too boyish to be pretty. In the pictures of his childhood he is not always smiling, as he is as an adult. In the town there are still men who fought in the Civil War; each year they march in the Memorial Day parade. He spends hours with a set of old tin soldiers.

The town itself—houses made of wood, a flatness to the landscape, no great wealth.

("There was nothing in those towns," he said to me. "Lord, that's why I left.")

"What you have to remember is that this boy was a loner. He was often alone, reading and dreaming. He looks back on his boyhood with nostalgia, but it's very clear in his writings, his autobiography and interviews, that he always had a place to be alone.

"Look at that childhood, the mom a do-gooder who took part in the local plays, who was strongly Christian and devout. Always taking in strays, and scolding people who weren't helping the poor or taking people in. And minorities. She was always down in the local hospital or the jail, volunteering.

"He's so nonjudgmental. He doesn't judge people's motives or morals, he doesn't cast aspersions on how they live and what they do. He got this from his mother."

—Nancy Reynolds, a longtime Reagan friend

His career both in Hollywood and Washington was devoted in part to celebrating the traditional family, but he didn't come from one. The Reagan children called their parents Nell and Jack, who in turn called their sons Moon and Dutch. They were always moving. Jack had jobs but no profession. The mother was dominant; she ran the home. It was, all in all, more like a Reagan era family than a family typical of its time.

"I think he must have suffered a terrible hurt in his youth, because he closed himself off. He didn't become involved with people. The people he worked with, they were all interchangeable. He didn't become immersed in their lives, and they didn't touch his. He was closed off."

—an aide to Ronald Reagan

The father was an alcoholic but the son rarely speaks of it. He offers, when pressed, a memory: He was coming home from somewhere one day when he was a teenager, and saw his father passed out on the porch. In front of everybody, the whole neighborhood. He dragged him inside and closed the door. It is part of the lore.

"Kids of alcoholics," said Nancy Reynolds, "are hurt. Their mothers are always so embarrassed, and they're hurt for them. There's shame and embarrassment and pity. The shame that you're so ashamed. And it's a little frightening, because alcoholics are scary."

There is a book called *Adult Children of Alcoholics* by Janet Woititz, Ph.D. It was one of the silent best-sellers of the Reagan era, a self-help book that I read when I was trying to understand Reagan.

"Children who live in alcoholic homes take on roles. 'Look at Emily, isn't she remarkable? She's the most responsible child I've ever seen . . .' If you were Emily you smiled, felt good, and enjoyed the praise . . .

"You might have been more like Barbara and become the class

clown. 'Gee, she should really be a comedian when she grows up. How clever, how funny, how witty!' And if you were Barbara you might smile, but underneath you wondered, 'Do they know how I really feel? . . .'

"You began to live in a fairy-tale world, with fantasies and in dreams . . . You lived a lot on hope . . . Because you believed you had to keep these feelings [of tension and disappointment] to yourself, you learned to keep most of your other feelings to yourself . . ."

Adult children of alcoholics do not know what normal is.

"Throughout life, to keep others from finding out that they don't know what they're doing, they guess at what is appropriate . . . You have no frame of reference for what it is like to be in a normal household. You also have no frame of reference for what it is OK to say and feel. In a more typical situation, one does not have to walk on eggs all the time. One doesn't have to question or repress one's feelings all the time . . ."

Adult children of alcoholics have difficulty with intimate relationships. Because they lacked reliable and consistent love from one or both parents, building a relationship with another person is very painful and complicated. Because they have been disappointed and manipulated, however subtly, many of them wind up with "the colossal terror of being close."

"As a result of your fear of abandonment [children of alcoholics never know what their parents will do and can't rely on them] you don't feel confident about yourself . . . So you look to others . . . to feel OK. You feel OK if someone else tells you that you are OK. Needless to say, you give away a great deal of power . . . you give the other person the power to lift you up or knock you down . . . You feel wonderful if they tell you that you are wonderful, but when they don't these feelings no longer belong to you."

I always had the feeling he came from a sad house and he thought it was his job to cheer everyone up.

He was a compulsive entertainer: He couldn't not do it. Before he entered a room, he would pause at the entrance and prepare. He sucked in his breath, straightened his shoulders, sucked in his stomach—he would sort of blow himself up. His upper body would get higher, and when he turned he was sort of swiveling. Then he would walk that smooth walk. (A screenwriter told me, "Actors always try to get the walk first. John Travolta told me he knew he had Tony Manero when he got the walk.")

He would bound into a room, acknowledge the applause with a nod, and begin his remarks. He needed a joke at the top to relax him; he still had some stage fright. He would make a small speech, put the cards back into his pocket, wave and nod again, and as he left he would walk backward, edging out of the room like a vaudeville hoofer shuffling off stage right. All he needed was a cane, a straw hat, and a glove—*Is everybody happy?*

Right up until the end, right up until they were closing the door, he maintained eye contact with the people in the room—the audience—and if he saw an unsmiling eye he stopped and tarried. (It was a generous impulse, wasn't it, to want to give people a lift? Or was it only or partly that he needed that laugh, needed the approval?)

It was the lonely empty middle of America and he wanted out, so he joined the migration of ambitious kids out of the small towns and into the media of the big cities. (They were already including this cultural phenomenon in the movies, with Jack Carson sprawled across the counter telling the soda jerk he was going to get out of this one-horse town, this two-bit hamlet.)

It was lonely where he came from and he turned to the world, to a place where the world was synthesized, distilled, where a Swiss mountain village was just down the block from a western town, where life was denser. He turned to Hollywood, the Hollywood of the Depression—the place that cheered up a nation.

He came of age in the middle of the most eager-to-please city in the most eager-to-please era in the most eager-to-please country in the history of the world. Scott Fitzgerald summed up the ethos when he said of one of his heroes, Dick Diver, "He had the American disease—he wanted to be loved."

In Hollywood in those days movie stars knew the names of the heads of the state chapters of their fan clubs, and they were happy to cooperate with the fanzines and the popular press—no one punched photographers in those days—and they were happy to give autographs, and movie posters were colorful with the stars smiling out, and there would be a zany blonde with her eyes crossed in comic confusion and a dancer hurtling himself against a wall to make 'em laugh, and it was zany, hilarious, tons of fun. . . .

And there was little sense of "I can't offend my own dignity," no sense that you were stooping to entertain. There seemed nothing embarrassing about making yourself a little silly for a laugh, to cheer people up. His adult sensibility was shaped in this place.

Maybe there was a sense of imported dignity, of class, in the British colony, but the mood of Hollywood in the thirties was also set by the refugees from vaudeville and burlesque, the Bert Lahrs and Jack Bennys. In the show business of Lahr's youth an out-of-work actor would smudge the collar of his shirt with greasepaint before he walked down Forty-second Street, so everyone would think he had a job. (The young Reagan, eclipsed by the mischievous Errol Flynn in a publicity photo, quietly built up a mound of dirt around his feet as the photographer changed the film and the setups, so that by the time the last picture was taken he was taller than most—and even with Flynn.)

Federico Fellini once spoke of sitting as a child many years ago in a room with a curtain in a small Italian town. It was a makeshift movie theater that sat a hundred. He would sit in the darkness with his friends and watch the movies from America.

Years later he talked about what it did to his spirit to know that somewhere there was a country where people were laughing and dancing on the tops of skyscrapers, who were rich and spirited. Even if it wasn't quite true that any place was this happy, it gave him an intimation of joy, of civic comity, that he ever after associated with film, and childhood, and America.

I believe that we all have had this feeling, and that it has helped explain America to all of us.

Yankee Doodle Dandy with its buoyant patriotism, *Young Mr. Lincoln* with Henry Fonda saying good-bye to Springfield, *Bataan* and *Sands of Iwo Jima,* where the platoon is a cross section of America, and at the end, when it's one of the rough poor kids who takes a bullet, it's all right because we know that somehow he more than the others understands the magic of our country. *Born Yesterday,* when the blonde gives the businessman what for . . .

All these movies have taught Americans about America. All of us who are adults now, that's how we got our sense of our country, from the movies. All of us, including him.

For years I had an intuition that his idea of the presidency and how to be president was influenced by a scene in *Yankee Doodle Dandy,* the big hit of 1942. An actor playing FDR gives a presidential medal to George M. Cohan in a private little ceremony in a room in the president's house.

Jimmy Cagney, as Cohan, is properly awed. The FDR character is down-to-earth and expansive—he has all the time in the world as he makes the visitor feel at home. They reminisce. Cagney/Cohan speaks of his birth—born red-faced and squalling on the Fourth of July as the cannon went off in the public square in celebration.

The FDR character listens, adding in his rich radio announcer's voice that there's something special about the Irish, they wear their love of country right out there where everyone can see it. He gives Cagney/Cohan the medal, saying it is for his contribution to American patriotism through the writing of such classics as "Over There" and "Grand Old Flag."

Cohan is so moved he can barely speak. He stands, takes the president's hand. "My mother thanks you," he says, in the family's old vaudeville sign-off, "my father thanks you, my sister thanks you and, I assure you, I thank you."

He takes his leave, is handed his hat and coat by an old Negro butler, and begins his descent down the broad white stairs. But he cannot contain his emotion, the jaunty habit of a lifetime asserts itself: He begins to dance down the stairs. Soon he is doing a wonderful, joyous step-by-step tap, as the music builds. He walks on to Pennsylvania Avenue, where a parade of soldiers is passing by. He joins the parade and joins in the song they are singing, "Over There."

The scene in the president's office is one of the most beautifully played in all the history of the movies, the dancing down the stairs one of the most moving.

And I always thought—I knew—that that was the movie and those were the scenes that Reagan kept in his mind as he greeted his visitors and sang their praises. It gave him a beautiful sense of how to be president, how to make people comfortable, how to make them aware of their own bigness, as if America noticed their work and appreciated it.

A lot of people, after meeting him, wanted to dance down the stairs.

He didn't work from the inside out, he worked from the outside in. He saw the role and put it on, like a costume. He had respect for the set and respect for the character he played, or rather the title and circumstances of the character. He really always played himself; the vivid have no choice. That's why he seemed both phony and authentic. Because he was. He was really acting but the part he played was Ronald Reagan.

The White House always seemed like a set. "I used to feel sometimes it was a stage," said a man who worked there. I wasn't surprised when I heard what Reagan said twenty years earlier, when he was asked, "What kind of governor will you be?" He answered, "I don't know, I've never played a governor."

When Al Haig left—he'd repeatedly threatened to resign, and finally they accepted—the president had to go into the pressroom and take questions. He'd just been given the letter of resignation, had read it, and now he was telling jokes and making everyone laugh as he ambled toward the pressroom. "Whoa there" said James Baker as they approached the door, "we better get serious here."

"Oh don't worry, I'll play it somber," said the president—who stepped, in the next second, in front of the reporters with a face so serious you could call it . . . well, somber. An aide who stood behind him noticed how he held his feet—one curled nonchalantly around the other, as if he didn't have a care in the world. But from out front you couldn't see.

Was part of it that he lived in California, breezy, take-it-easy California? Fred Allen would have laughed seeing a guy from Hollywood become president, would have loved President Ronald Reagan for his perfect reflection of what's dangerous about California—that life is so soft there, it's like moving through a lovely haze of warm gelatin. Reality offers no resistance, all movement eased by baby oil, everything warm as a womb and moist, all the people on the beaches slicked up with balms, oils, and protectors, like those babies born with a thin covering of white wax. . . .

Existence asks so little of them, why stir? Why disturb the slumber of their universe? (His hands were soft and small and pale.)

He wasn't only a man who had to be loved. He had courage.

All through the fifties and early sixties, when he had his last chance to become a star, all through that time the convictions he held were unfashionable. The important people, the sophisticated people who'd been successful, who produced and directed the serious movies and who owned the great newspapers and produced the hit sitcoms, all looked down on his politics.

But he held to the unfashionable. This man who wanted to be loved stood fast to his views and voiced them even though he knew the cultural leaders (by whom he wanted to be accepted, in whose movies he wanted to star) had contempt for what he thought.

He could have adopted the corporate liberalism of Hollywood, the happy conviction as they raked in the money that they really cared about the working man.

But he wouldn't play. At the dinner table at the dinner party it was, "Isn't the asparagus wonderful, isn't this lovely wine?," but then when someone made a reference to Communists and someone else said, "At least they're trying to help the little man," he'd answer, "Well, I got to know them in my union days and you can be sentimental about them but they sure won't be sentimental about you, or the proletariat, or the workers, or whatever they're calling them. They aren't sentimental people; they're hard as nails. And killers, also. Look at Poland, look at Stalin and the kulaks, and they count on us not to notice. But . . ."

And the crystal would hit the linen ever so softly, and his cultural betters would think, He's obviously sincere, but he's so . . . simplistic. Or: unsophisticated. Or: such a radical, and dangerous.

Look at him on abortion. It took courage to oppose an option that at least 20 million Americans had exercised since *Roe* v. *Wade,* when the issue isn't a coalition-builder but an opposition creator, when the polls are against you and the boomers want it and when you've already been accused of being unsympathetic to women and your own pollster is telling you your stand contributes to a gender gap. . . .

But he puzzled it out on his own, not like a visionary or an intellectual but like a regular person. He read and thought and listened to people who cared, and he made up his mind. And suddenly when they said, "The argument is over when life begins," he said, "Well look, if that's the argument: If there's a bag in the gutter and you don't know if what's in it is alive, you don't kick it, do you?"

Well no, you don't.

He held to his stand against his own political interests (where were the anti-abortion people going to go?) and against the wishes of his family and friends. Nancy wasn't anti-abortion, the kids weren't anti-abortion, and people like the Bloomingdales and his friends in Beverly Hills—they did not get where they are through an overfastidious concern for the helpless. He was the only one of his group who cared.

You forget what it takes to think the unpopular thing, for a politician. But they all want love, that's their game, they want to agree and build bridges and reach out. They all suffer from the American disease.

There's a funny thing in life, but one way to keep people close to you is by not giving them enough. I used to wonder if he ever noticed that with people who give a lot of themselves, you sometimes lean back—but with people who give little you often lean forward, as if they're a spigot in the desert and you're the empty cup. It is the tropism of deprivation: We lean toward those who do not give. Did he ever think in these terms? (What did they teach him on the soundstage at Warner Bros.? Always leave 'em wanting more.)

Was this a part of his relationship with his children?

There was a reporter one day back in the seventies, a respected reporter who had an interview with Reagan. He mentioned to the former governor that he had read that Reagan's father had never gone to one of his son's football games. And Reagan nodded that it was true. And the reporter said, Do you ever see your father in you?

Reagan blinked. This least introspective of men, this living proof that the unexamined life *is* worth living, looked away, his eyes fluttering. Was a realization forming there?

Once in the early winter of '88 a group of White House people were at a brunch, and one asked, "How is Maureen?," and everyone told funny stories with a certain edge, and someone said that it was impressive how she always got the old man to back her up on stuff, and someone said, "Yes, how does she do it?"

A smart woman said, "Because he's afraid of her." Perhaps, and why wouldn't he be, and not only of her but of all of them. He must have felt such guilt! He couldn't match their demands or meet the constant unspoken needs, the rebuke of this daughter's doleful gaze, the challenge of that daughter's aggression, the soul-killing sunniness of the son—how to be a father to him? Who would have taught Ronald Reagan to be a father? (Donald Crisp? But what did Donald Crisp say behind the set?) He wanted them to be happy and succeed, but he didn't know how to do the father role. The world was a more manageable place than the home front; he didn't know what to do, had no ideology to guide him, no politics of the family to inform him, and for once his instincts failed.

He must have felt guilty—and angry. Why do I feel bad? my father never did anything for me and I turned out okay, I never asked for anything, I made my own way, why do they demand so?

"This," said a friend of thirty years, "is a man who can't afford to think bad things. . . . When people were rude to him he'd get a pained look. He'd never be rude back. It wouldn't occur to him.

"He's totally satisfied in his own little world," she continued. "He doesn't like to go out with the boys; he's happy to stay home with her. Left totally to his own devices, he'd read and ride and walk and work.

"He's not a gregarious man. He's not driven to talk to people. He's—there's a shy streak in him that's part of his charm. I've never seen him stride into a room and say, 'Hi, I'm Ronald Reagan!' the way they do. He'd never do that. He'd never interrupt somebody's meal. He'd never impose. You'd never see him glad-handing. He's actually quite self-contained."

It was probably the closest White House marriage since the Grants. You'd think of them like this: as a unit, total and complete, self-sufficient and self-supporting. Just the two of them, quietly eating dinner off the trays in the residence, up at Camp David, holding hands on the couch as they watched a movie, all alone, eating from the same bowl of popcorn.

It couldn't have been easy for her as first lady. She wasn't really temperamentally suited to the role, not that anyone could be. Jackie Kennedy used to talk about the big heavy curtains on the upstairs windows, that trying to open them was like pulling down canvas sails. Even the name, she said, was awful. "First lady," sounds like a show horse.

Stand at a window in the residence and one of the first things you see is the cast-iron gates. They make you president and give you a big house and a lawn, but the house is in the middle of downtown and you can't lose yourself on the grounds unless you don't mind being stared at by a few hundred people yelling, "Hey, First Lady! Hey, Nancy, over here!" They almost throw walnuts at you, as if you were a squirrel.

There's no escape, no chance to get out of the house, take a brisk walk, go for a run, shop, drop by the neighbors', go by a church and sit quietly, go to a diner and have a cup of coffee, read the *Post* or the *Daily News*. A first lady is caught: She sits and seethes.

And they take so seriously, both a president and his wife, what they read in the papers. The criticism from the columnists, the bad headlines, the knowledge that dawns on you little by little, day by day, that it's your own aides who are feeding the *Post*, your good friends who, prominently quoted in a story saying something supportive, are also the unattributed longtime observer, as in, "But even Mrs. Reagan's closest friends concede a coolness between her and her children. 'They hate each other,' said one longtime observer."

A jail that leaks, a satin-pillowed jail. She took comfort in the phone, into which she issued the long complaint of a fretful nature caged. She relied on her friends, who were, many of them, *Women's Wear Daily* Republicans who kept the conversation on the surface things. They showed a lot of sympathy. And admiration.

"Listen to me: Without Nancy Reagan, Ronald Reagan would have been nothing but a grease spot on the road."
                                        —a longtime friend of both

They called her Evita, they called her Mommy, they called her the Missus and the Hairdo with Anxiety. They resented her because usually in a big place there's only one person or group to be afraid of, but in the Reagan White House there were two, the chief of staff and his people and the first lady and hers—a pincer formation that made everyone feel vulnerable.

When I was new I asked a woman about her.

"She's okay, at least until she gets into one of her No More Wire Hangers moods." I laughed.

"And of course there's when she glides down the great stairway like Gloria Swanson in *Sunset Boulevard* and says, 'They had faces then.'

What you say, in case this happens when you're around, is, 'Mr. DeMille is ready, Miss Davis!' "

I laughed again.

"She's okay. Just don't cross her. Or let her think you crossed her."

It is well known and still true: Her power was everywhere, in personnel, in who rose and who fell; she was on the phone with McFarlane about foreign affairs, on the phone nixing and okaying trips and events, arranging to closet the president with this policy analyst or that, calling to get the speeches earlier. She was everywhere.

What did she believe? She wasn't a liberal or a leftist or a moderate or a détentist; she was a *Galanosist,* a wealthy, well-dressed woman who followed the common wisdom of her class. She didn't worry about the effects of burdensome taxes on the individual, she worried about the effects of the deficit on her husband's popularity; she disliked the *contras* because they were unattractive and dirty and probably raped people; she disliked SDI and the defense buildup because they were not popular in the polls. And when she got on an issue, she was, in Deaver's words, "like a dog with a bone."

A story I was told by a woman who got it from the friend in the story:

Mrs. Reagan was upset, in the 1984 campaign, about her husband's references to the so-called social issues, and called a friend. "I want you to tell him he has to stop talking about abortion," she said. "It's turning everybody off. He already has those people, it does him no good." The friend agreed.

Nancy arranged a small dinner party upstairs and it was festive, with stories and fun. The president was having a good time. Nancy signaled to her friend by raising an eyebrow: now. But the friend thought, The timing's not right, he's having fun, and ignored the signal. Again the raised eyebrow: now! The friend turned away.

At the end of a presidential anecdote the first lady leaned forward. "Ronnie," she said, her eyes flashing, "Jane here has something to tell you."

Jane cleared her throat and sang for her supper.

"What do you think, John?" Nancy asked another guest when Jane finished.

John began to say what Jane said. Two sentences in, the president interrupted. "Nancy," he said, "I know what you're up to and it's not going to work. I'm not changing my mind on this now, and it's not going to work."

And he placed his napkin on his plate and took a sip of water, and that was that.

None of this is news, and yet it is still surprising, and conservatives still haven't got over it. The columnist George Will not infrequently lunched with the first lady, and made no secret of their friendship. Pat Buchanan, observing their closeness, was reminded of William F. Buckley, Jr.'s ill-fated support of a celebrated New Jersey murderer: "She's your Edgar Smith!" he'd tell Will, laughing.

She took no prisoners. Once, near the end of the administration and after the death of her mother, when she was angry with her daughter Patti, she gave *The Washington Post* an interview that made the skin crawl. Patti is nothing like my mother, she said. My mother was kind and considerate and loyal. My mother was nothing like Patti, there was nothing selfish or self-centered about my mother. She was asked about Patti's absence. Ron more than makes up for that, she said.

Mike Deaver was her best friend but I thought he didn't like her because he did two things that struck me as revenge. One was his book, which paints her between the lines, and sometimes not so between, as a bully through such compliments as "Many times, Nancy will react to a problem by wanting to do away with the person who created it; or by simply trying to change whatever course or direction has caused her husband to be criticized." (Lucky she wasn't married to Lincoln.) The other was that he arranged for a writer who was not a partisan but a serious historian to come and observe and be Ronald Reagan's official biographer. When I heard about Edmund Morris, I read the book for which he'd won a Pulitzer Prize, *The Rise of Theodore Roosevelt*. It was majestic, elegantly written and unfooled by charm. I thought, Deaver did this to get back at them.

For what? For the million phone calls and the disengagement, for the 1980 campaign when John Sears fired Deaver and the Reagans let it happen, and then, after Sears himself was fired and they made clear they expected Deaver to come back, he did. I don't think he ever forgave them their cool expediency; I suspect he never forgave them that he came back.

•   •   •

Always someone would say, But how can anyone criticize? She wanted to protect her husband like any good wife! It's not for herself but for him, and even if she's wrong in some of her decisions, at least she's making them with good intentions!

I would listen and wonder. This was another view, from a man who had spent almost five years with the president in his White House.

He said, "Mrs. Reagan is the lady in the star. She basks in the glow of the sun. Without the sun—her husband—she is unseen. All of her effort is aimed at those actions which she feels enhance her husband's power, his brightness. It doesn't matter to her what actions are taken. She has no loyalty to ideas or to a political party, and she doesn't care about the political process or any known philosophy. All she cares about is, is it good for Ronnie?

"The point is her decisions were aimed at one thing, and her decisions were not necessarily wise. In fact, usually they weren't. She surrounded herself—and the president—with people who were, essentially, rich and trivial. They added nothing to him and could do nothing for him. But they're her friends, and they did her bidding.

"It wasn't altruism," he said, "that motivated her; it was ambition. She wanted to be a star too, remember. She wanted to be star too."

What about the disengagement? I never understood how broad it was or exactly what it was, but I know his boredom with governance was something those who worked for Ronald Reagan got used to. Twenty years ago they were saying things like this, which appeared in a profile on Reagan in the June 1968 *Ripon Forum:* "He is most certainly not, as some have charged, a puppet on a string . . . but his unfamiliarity with his own legislative program is striking . . . Governor Reagan sees himself as the man responsible for setting the basic thrust and direction of government, but he would rather forget the details . . ."

I went to a smart and sophisticated man. If Reagan was so disengaged, I said, then how did the White House run? How could someone so uninvolved run it?

He said, "The presidency is a self-defining office. It's pretty much what you make it. If you want to read every bill and schedule the tennis courts, you can do that. If you want to treat it like a photo op and sit in on the big meetings and then turn to your advisers, get the consensus and go with it, you can do that. It's what you make it. There isn't much you actually have to do."

But how did his will get imposed? If he didn't take a leadership position in forming policy and initiate actions and talk to people, how did he rule?

"He didn't. The idea of Reagan ruled. Everybody around him had a good idea of who he was and what he would do. He'd been in public life for twenty years, they knew what he stood for. Though not everyone had a fully formed idea. There were those who'd read the book, and those who'd seen the picture. Stockman, Darman, Marty Anderson—they'd read the book; they had an elaborate and detached sense of who the president was and what was going on.

"But the old California crowd, the kitchen Cabinet, the Meeses, and Bill Clark. They had an impressionistic sense of what was happening. They'd only seen the movie."

An aide named Fred Khedouri, a brilliant and subtle man who helped run OMB for David Stockman, told David Hoffman of *The Washington Post*, "I don't think [the president] was all that passive. . . . He didn't just do what he was told. . . . But another element of this is that through some mechanism I don't pretend to understand, he wouldn't get asked things that he wouldn't agree with. You could say he didn't have to do anything . . . because there was a kind of self-control or self-censorship by the staff. People wouldn't bring him something if they knew he would be averse to it."

Lesley Stahl took me aside at a lunch one day in 1986 and said, "I'd give a lot to reconcile these two things: that Reagan is, so the rumors have it, disengaged and uninvolved and lazy—and yet on certain issues he is totally unmovable, wouldn't give in no matter what the pressure. How could he be so uninvolved and yet cling, with determination, on taxes and SDI?"

A lot of people used to wonder that. In time I thought this:

Taxes and SDI and abortion were issues that captured his imagination. He could *see* how taxes hurt and frustrated the hardworking middle-income guy with a growing family; he could *see* how SDI could, with a perfectly directed laser beam, shoot down a missile or put it off course; he could *see* the fetus kicking away from the needle. And once he could imagine these things, these people, he could not abandon them. The job he liked most when he was young was lifeguard.

And he was convinced; he hadn't spent years thinking about these things for nothing, he'd come to his conclusions the hard way, by thinking and questioning and trying to understand, and he knew, just knew, that he was right. He trusted the American people's common sense, and he trusted his own. (In the fifties and early sixties, while the other people in power in the eighties were joining government and learning its language, he was going from plant to plant for GE, shooting the breeze with the workers in the cafeteria, the guys on the line telling him what they thought. More than any president since Jackson, he spent the years before power with the people, the normal people of his country.)

No amount of criticism would change his mind. The left could hurt him and make him defensive but the right couldn't make a dent. Once, after Reykjavik and the Daniloff-Zakharov swap, the president held a White House meeting with members of the conservative community and, as he walked to the meeting from the Oval Office, he turned to Mari Maseng, the young head of the Office of Public Liaison.

"They think I'm a wimp, don't they?" he said.

"Oh no," she said.

"Yes they do." He shook his head, resigned. But it didn't seem to bother him terribly. He didn't believe that anyone could seriously doubt his conservative credentials; he had faith in his ability to be intelligent and tough, and if the others didn't they were wrong was all. And there was a bit of *Le droit, c'est moi*—if I do a thing it is by definition conservative, bub, because I damn well define conservatism in our time.

The fellas would come and give him the options and lean forward with their hands clasped lightly together. They'd say, "Mr. President, it's lookin' like this is really our only choice, and it's not so bad. . . ."

"Not bad at all," another would chime in. "In fact, I think we may have been handed this one. Looking back, we may realize—".

"That it was more of a victory than we knew," says another.

"Well, okay," says the president, "if you think that's the best we can do, okay."

Thus were compromises agreed to; thus was history made. He was almost always willing to go along, one of the fellas told me. An aide told me:

"The president never picked Jim Baker as his chief of staff; Mike Deaver and Stu Spencer did. And they did it with the purest of motives: to keep Ed Meese from getting the job. They thought he was too disorganized, an embarrassment waiting to happen. They picked Baker because he was smart, because he had a sense of organization, and because he knew something about Washington. It was August of '80, before election day, but they knew they were going to win, they knew the numbers; Wirthlin had already told them. And Deaver and Spencer talked to Governor Reagan. They said, 'Governor, we need to talk about this. You didn't express a firm view, so we thought we'd work it out.' That was Deaver's mantra, Work it out, we gotta work it out. And Mike usually had an intuition of what Reagan would like, what he'd prefer. 'We think you really ought to consider Jim Baker. . . .' And the president would nod. 'Well, fellas, if you think so . . .' "

"I loved it there," said an aide who had just left the White House, "but it can be a terrible place. The backstabbing, the leaks to the press, can all make it so godawful unpleasant. It was marvelous and awful in the West Wing. In the Nixon White House everyone was shooting at us from the outside, so inside there was camaraderie. There was more loyalty to each other—at least among the nonconspirators!

"But in the Reagan White House it was backstabbing and knifing each other and anonymous sources killing each other with the gossip.

"And you have to lay it on ol' Dutch. He wouldn't crack down. He should have stopped it. And he could have. But he didn't. It just wasn't his style to get involved."

A woman who was a personal friend of the president and who knew most of the players said, "He hates confrontations, and the staff was tearing itself apart and there were leaks in the newspapers and he knew it—and he ducked it. He just ducked. He should have called them in and said, 'Boys, I don't like what I'm reading and I want this chaos to stop right now. I'm walking out that door and when I come back I want it settled, I want it to be history.' That's what he should have done. But he hates that scene."

He hates that scene. And when those who were loyal to him and his beliefs were done in, he managed not to notice.

At first the fighting between the so-called ideologues and the so-called pragmatists was gentlemanly, and if it had been left solely to the principals, it might have stayed so. But a dynamic kicked in: Because the president interacted with relatively few people, the members of his top staff became more important to their own staffs. Jim Jenkins was White House counsel, but he reported to and interacted with Ed Meese. Margaret Tutweiler reported to and interacted with Jim Baker; advance and scheduling worked for the president, but they reported to Deaver. And so each staff in a way saw its principal as president, and each fiefdom fought the others, protecting their "president," which embittered the process.

"This administration was so punishing on the staff," said a veteran. "It ground up so many people. The Nixon people, there were friendships formed there that are the tightest friendships to this day. It was a tough White House, but maybe that bonded them. Here it tore them apart. The Californians who came here as friends—Meese, Clark, Helene von Damm, Nofziger, Deaver—they were all close. But little by little it imploded. Somehow in this White House they moved away from each other. They drifted apart."

This is something else those who worked closely with Reagan all said, though they all refused to elaborate.

"All of us used him," a former high aide told me. "We wore him out."

Months after he had left, I sat across from Donald Regan at a dinner and asked, "What will history find out about the president that it doesn't know now?"

His face literally darkened as he leaned forward and pointed. "That he was used. The people around the president used him like you wouldn't believe. History will tell the story. He was used mercilessly—and the historians will tell it."

Conversation in a restaurant, 1987:

"You know what the deal was? He was surrounded by people who used him, and the way they made it up to him was they kept other users away from him. But they couldn't tell who was a user and who wasn't because they—how to put it?—had a tendency to project. So they were constantly seeing bad motives. It was not unusual to hear them saying

that so-and-so—an ambassador, a secretary, it didn't matter—is just
trying to use the president, and they won't have it!"

"You mean they didn't want anyone horning in, making a stake on
their claim."

"That's right. The users called themselves his protectors, and the
only tragedy—and I'm not sure it was a big one, though on reflection
perhaps it was—is that they did keep away people who actually might
have helped him. They surrounded him like a fence. And he didn't
know."

There was something else at work with the people around the president, something I noticed when I'd been in the White House a year.
It was that people were afraid not to like him. They were afraid to get
mad at him because his goodness was so famous, such an accepted part
of the air of the place, that to dislike him was tantamount to admitting
a serious inner flaw. Those who grew impatient with him or frustrated
or resentful tried to cover it up. But sooner or later—and you really saw
this in the Regan years—what they were thinking could be seen in a
sentence shot out, in a look or a shake of the head. They were thinking
something like what Sergeant Warden said of the captain in *From Here
to Eternity*: "He'd choke on his own spit if I weren't here to clear his
throat for him." They'd say, with a certain edge, "The president isn't
a detail man" (The fool doesn't know Antarctica's the one on the
bottom!); they'd say, "The president is a big-picture man" (He
wouldn't know a fact if it ran up his nose!). You could see it in Deaver's
book, all the unexpressed hostility seeping out in those 'The president
of course has an amiable temperament, but he's usually content to
allow someone else to make the decisions' sentences.

Most presidents find a place to hide.

Nixon, overwhelmed by the Oval Office, took refuge in the Old
Executive Office Building. Carter took refuge in minutiae. Eric Sevareid once walked in and saw Ham Jordan, who talked about the shape
of things and the forces at play in the world. Then he met with Carter,
who talked about the arcana of an insignificant bill. Afterward Sevareid
told colleagues, "I get it—Jordan's president and Carter's the chief of
staff."

Reagan took refuge two ways. The first is that he never really took the size and measure of the physical plant.

Remember those stories in the early years that he didn't know where his own top aides' offices were? When I first got to the White House I thought it was untrue. Then a top aide told me, "Look, he would have had a general sense of where Baker's office was and where Meese's was because he saw them walking away. He knew they were down the hall because they never said, 'When I was upstairs in my office.' But why should he know where their offices were? Everyone comes to him."

But it's not normal, I said. It's normal to walk around the physical plant and see who's where and what it's like. LBJ went on walks, Kennedy did, Nixon. Johnson would have been checking to see whether the chief of staff has better furniture, Kennedy would have been finding out who's got a pretty secretary.

But Reagan withdrew from the White House, staying sealed in the Oval Office and the residence and pretty much ignoring the fact that he worked where Lincoln trod and Jefferson dined. He never took the dimensions of the place, and so he avoided taking possession of it.

He also took refuge in the mail, in writing letters to children who loved him and old ladies who needed him. Ann Higgins, the woman who ran the president's mail operation, used to send him fifty or so letters from the two hundred thousand a week he received in that time, and sometimes—and it wasn't all that rare—he'd call and ask for more.

I think he saw that people pour out their hearts to presidents, and in a democracy, particularly a modern democracy, it's important that they know they have at least a chance to make it through to the top guy. He knew this naturally. He answered letters from citizens with the same kind of care and respect that he gave to a letter from Thatcher or Kohl.

People thought he was their friend. They'd send him pictures of themselves and their families. The original letters would come back to Ann, but she noticed he always removed the pictures. They started showing up in the pockets of his jackets and coats and in the drawers of the lamp tables in the residence.

He got more mail than most presidents, at one point receiving 8 million letters a year, almost twice the presidential average.

He wrote about ten letters a day, not counting those he wrote to personal friends who contacted him at his special post office box. He had a name-card file of people he'd been writing to for half a century, and when he was president he was still writing to them.

When he had surgery, people wrote in and told him of their ailments. "There's something in Americans that makes them describe their sicknesses in loving detail. We know the country's temperature—literally!" Higgins said.

He wrote regularly to two old ladies who live by the side of the road in Sacramento. Twenty years earlier, when he was governor, he met Miss Jane and Miss Sally, who lived with their brother and made beautiful leather goods, saddles and belts and things you keep a knife in. Every Christmas they would send him a present. It was a tradition. When he was president they would write him in the autumn and say, Don't forget to tell us what you want, and he would tell them, sometimes drawing it out on a pad.

And what they got in return, aside from hundreds of letters from Ronald Reagan over the years, was that every time their horse got sick and had to be treated, they'd ask the president to drop the vet a line to thank him. That's how they paid their bills, with the letters. Everyone knew this, including Reagan, who laughed and kept on writing, "Dear Doctor Smith, How nice to hear you were able to help Dassy-doo when he stopped eating. . . ."

Once he got a letter from a little girl who was upset because her father wouldn't let her keep her horse at their home in the suburbs. She poured out her heart to him because, she said, she could tell from all the pictures she'd seen that he really loved horses too. And he wrote back by hand a long letter telling her of his sympathy. And then he said, But a horse needs space and sun—they need to run free. He told her, It will help you, maybe, if you could try these things: work part time at the nearest stable and rent a horse on Saturdays, and read books about horses and write to trainers and riders and ask them about how they do their jobs. . . .

His aides were always getting calls from weekly newspapers out in the hills asking, Did you know the president has promised to look into Mrs. Elma Fogelby's Social Security problem and also invited her to the White House for a cup of coffee, and are you guys always this nice?

The press aide would sigh, and get the Social Security straightened out, and make sure she got in when she came.

· · ·

Citizens sent him gifts and he used them. When school children in Allingtown, Connecticut, sent him a bunch of yellow notepads with FROM THE DESK OF PRESIDENT REAGAN stamped on top—it was cheap yellow stock, it looked like something they'd done in shop—he used it for years.

A citizen sent him stationery with a nerd with a long nose peeking over a wall and the saying "No More Mr. Nice Guy!" He sent notes to George Shultz on them.

He sent money to strangers and friends. Once he wrote someone a check for a hundred dollars, and the recipient couldn't cash it because it was signed Ronald Reagan and the cashier at the bank said that was worth more than the amount. Ronald Reagan had to call the bank and arrange for it to give the money. This happened a number of times.

And he met with the people he wrote to. Once Ann Higgins asked him to call the Rossow family of Connecticut to congratulate them on their fine family. At the time Mr. and Mrs. Rossow had fourteen children, most adopted and many handicapped. The president not only called but, typically, asked to speak to everyone in the family including five-year-old Benjamin, who was born with only a brain stem. He not only spoke to them, he invited them to visit. A few weeks later two vans drove up and deposited the sixteen Rossows at 1600 Pennsylvania Avenue. They stayed with the Little Sisters of the Poor, who made waffles in their happy kitchen.

This happened all the time in Reagan's White House. You'd walk by the Oval Office and there was a family full of people with no legs nodding hello to a dwarf who was bringing a message from the doorman at the Mayflower, who'd get a reply. No one else ran a White House like this, none of the modern presidents.

A political analyst sipping a six-dollar glass of orange juice across Lafayette Park at the Hay Adams would say, "Reagan understood that kindness you retail." It's true he had the instinctive knowledge that everyone is moved by the letter Lincoln wrote to the mother who'd lost two sons in the war while no one remembers his decision to push for better wool in the Union Army blankets, but it was more.

Ronald Reagan was utterly egalitarian. He never thought he was stooping to these people, he didn't think he was better, and he was possessed of an intuitive sense of the purpose of royalty. He would have instinctively understood Oliver Goldsmith's exclamation of the common man's love for the king: "I flee from petty tyrants to the throne."

There was too much deference in him. He was too deferential to the more sophisticated, to assertive people with impressive degrees. He even deferred to his secretary, writing his letters in longhand, neatly printing out the entire name and address on the top of the page so she wouldn't have to look it up. Sometimes he didn't have the zip code, and he'd be apologetic and ask if she could please look it up if she has a minute.

The first Cabinet meeting I ever went to, I was mildly shocked at how the president strained to show interest. As an earnest young man in horn rims stood with a pointer and spoke at some length about the commercial possibilities of space the president, his lips pressed thin, leaned forward in a physical attitude of concentration. But one eye was slightly out of focus, and his gaze was trained unmoving above the speaker's head. His head was cocked as if he were listening, but he wasn't.

I turned back to the young man and watched his pointer and thought of space, and capsules, and free floating, and stars, and a landing, and feet, and, in my reverie, turned toward the president, who looked at me and winked. I smiled. He recocked his head and watched the spot over the young man's head.

I thought, He knows I'm bored. He just told me he's bored too, it's okay, that's government.

Pat Buchanan eagerly awaited his first Cabinet council meeting on economic issues. He sat behind George Shultz, who was in a heavy phase. Pat had to stretch his neck to see past him.

It was a fractious meeting. The subject was grain exports, and Shultz started exploding at Block about trade wars and Block started yelling back and Stockman jumped in and exploded at someone who exploded with a defense.

While everyone shouted, the president reached toward the middle of the table and pulled over the bowl of jelly beans. Then he dreamily, delicately began to pick out his favorite colors. Buchanan watched in astonishment: My God, what in heaven's name is with this guy?

The president caught Pat's astonished face, and winked.

Pat sat back and thought, This guy knows what's going on. He thinks, They're having an argument here, and I'm not getting into it; let 'em work it out. It's not just passivity; he knows what he's doing.

The president smiled, and Buchanan thought, All right.

Gary Bauer was at an issues lunch in the Cabinet Room. It was just after Black Monday and people were talking about the causes of the crash. The president launched into an analysis of the recent comparisons to 1929.

Why, at that time, he said, just like today, the president was urged to raise taxes—and he did. They urged him to sign a protectionist trade bill—and he did. And the result was the longest depression in our history. And—

Bauer shot up. Those were his words. The president *did* read his memos. He looked at the president, who paused and looked at Bauer . . . and winked.

That wink, thought Bauer, said, I read what you send, and I agree.

Becky Norton Dunlop sat along the wall in a Cabinet meeting and listened as someone said something she knew to be untrue. She winced and shook her head no. She wondered if the president believed what he was hearing. She turned to look, and saw him looking at her. He winked. And the wink said, I know, I don't believe a thing this guy's saying either.

Everyone who worked for him, when they were leaving I'd ask, "Did the president really know who you were, do you think?" And they'd straighten and say, "Yes, I think he did. I was in the Cabinet Room"— or the Roosevelt Room or the hall—"and for a moment our eyes connected, and he winked. And I realized, He knows who I am."

We made so much of those winks.

He could make a decision and live with it. No micromanaging the desert rescue, no debating how many helicopters and tell Charlie Beckwith to call me when he gets there. Reagan might not have known how many helicopters were used, but a Reagan raid would have succeeded. He knew how to say yes, and he knew how to trust.

When Bud and Ollie said they could get the *Achille Lauro* terrorists the president said do it, and they did. He could listen to the options on Grenada and go, could make a decision on the Falklands and stay with it.

During a Persian Gulf crisis, at an NSC meeting called after Iran hit an oil tanker flying the U.S. flag, the president came in and listened to the options. Someone suggested the United States hit three or four Iranian military points, including perhaps an Iranian naval vessel. Iran would get the message, and it would put a dent in the ayatollah's air of invulnerability.

The president said no. I don't think we should hit an Iranian ship, he said, because they didn't hit one of ours, and it would be wrong. They hit a commercial tanker, so we should hit a commercial entity. I want the retaliation to be proportional, he said.

He made it clear that he did not want a large loss of life, and added, But if any attempt is made to interfere with our forces I want our men to know they have the maximum discretion. They should go with their judgment.

In the end the United States hit an oil platform that carried military antennae and other gear. It made an impression.

Reagan also had a romantic's sense of what will capture the public's imagination. Once they were debating the future of space. It was back before the *Challenger,* and they were talking about which direction the program should go in. Some said we ought to go in the direction of unmanned space probes, like *Voyager.* The president listened. David Stockman had almost zeroed out funding for NASA; a low-key approach seemed right.

But later, at a lunch with space enthusiasts, the president said, We've got to have a space program, and we're going to have a space station—a manned space station.

"He had a vision," said an aide who was there. "It was his insight that we have to have people in space not only to experience it and tell us about it, but to capture the imagination of the public. People don't respond to machines, he thought, people respond to people."

"Space captured his enthusiasm," said Craig Fuller, who was involved in the space decision. "But some would argue that there was no follow-through on this issue, and that was true to an extent. That was the downside."

That was Reagan too: He lived in the headlines, he didn't do updates.

• • •

I guess the most special thing of all was the humor. It was like Lincoln: Those who knew him and were asked what he was like would start to smile, and the smile was because of the funny thing he'd told them that they couldn't forget.

I say hello to a Secret Service man and ask how the president is. He laughs and says, "Did I tell you about Lucky? This morning he wouldn't sit down, and he wouldn't be still. He was real balky and barking. The president leans down and pets him, all sweet. Dog growls. President pats him and smiles and says in this nice voice, 'Man's best friend.' Then he puts his hands around Lucky's neck and starts to strangle him."

Once when Deaver saw the president trying to train the dog in the Oval Office, he said, "Watch out, he's going to pee all over your desk." Reagan said, "Why not? Everyone else does."

He loved stories and one-liners, loved to do accents; his humor was sometimes racy, but never around ladies. And there was a knowing quality, an edge. After the homosexual scandals of his first administration as governor, an aide worried that more homosexuals might still be on the staff and cause another scandal. Reagan leaned back with a merry face. "Well, Truman Capote's coming to visit. We could always tie a rope around him and let him troll the halls. . . ."

Years later, the day before he went into the hospital for an operation, he met with the vice president for their weekly lunch. The doctors would, the next day, insert tubes into various parts of his body to make sure everything looked as it should. This caused an unusual problem for the networks. The president's organs of reproduction were involved in the procedure—should they be portrayed in the graphics? Drawn or not? And if yes, well . . . well, as a network producer said at one of the evening-news planning sessions at one of the networks, proportion becomes an issue. Presidential size, full view? If it's not big, is that an editorial statement? An unintended slight, yet more proof of liberal bias?

Each news show handled the problem in its own way. Most used a variation on a drawing of an adult male's intestines, and a tube being sneaked into the lower intestine from—well, from somewhere into something.

But one news show used a drawing that was somewhat more realistic, showing the tube running through what it would really run through.

To avoid the question of proportion, not to mention taste, they drew only a small portion of the organ.

It happened that the president saw the graphic on TV. Later, at their weekly lunch, he mentioned it to the vice president and deadpanned, "Gee, George, they didn't tell me they were going to cut it off, maybe I better think twice."

Bush started laughing and couldn't stop. The rest of the day he'd chuckle at odd moments and when pressed he'd say, "Reagan," and laugh more. He loved Reagan.

Not long after the president was shot, the doctors told him to get into his pajamas every afternoon and take a long nap. He happily followed orders. One day he couldn't sleep and started padding around in his pajamas and robe. There were some workmen having their sandwiches at lunchtime on the floor outside the Lincoln Bedroom, where they'd been painting. They looked up and saw this apparition— Reagan in his robe blithely proceeding toward them. They lowered their sandwiches and stared. Reagan padded by and without missing a beat said, "Gee, fellas, I didn't know there were any good restaurants this far out."

Like Lincoln, Reagan was occasionally reviled for his penchant for jokes and stories, but only by the intelligentsia. Normal people liked it fine. Newspapers and magazines ran his joke of the week; *The Washington Post* had a Reagan joke file. It was like the profusion of paper booklets produced when Lincoln was president, with titles like *Abe's Jokes—Fresh from Abraham's Bosom* and *Old Abe's Jokes, or, Wit and Wisdom at the White House.*

Because Ronald Reagan was so open and sweet-tempered, people tend to expect his humor to be broad and sweet, and since that's what they expected, that's what they saw. But there was a genial blackness to his humor. He always liked those stories about the guy who said to his friend, "I'm sorry to hear your wife ran off with the gardner," and the friend says, "That's all right. I was going to fire him anyway."

"The teacher was trying to impress on her students that winter had come, and they should try to avoid colds. And so she told a heartrending tale about her onetime little brother.

"As the story went, her little brother was a fun-loving boy, and he went out with his sled and stayed out too long, caught cold and then pneumonia, and three days later he died.

"When she finished with the tale, there was dead silence in the room. She thought she had really got through to them when a voice in the back said, 'Where's the sled?' "

He used humor to illustrate a point, defuse a moment, clinch a deal. Once a Republican senator who was trying to convince the president of his loyalty in spite of his refusal to back the White House on a difficult vote, said, "Sir, I'd jump out of a plane without a parachute if you said jump, but—" And Reagan leaned forward and said, "Jump!" The senator changed his vote.

A man I know asked a psychologist, What's the most important thing my son can get from me? The psychologist replied, A sense of humor. The man asked, Why? The psychologist said, Because humor is the shock absorber of life; it helps us take the blows.

Humor allows us to step out of the moment, look at it, and sum it up with no great reverence. It is a gift nature gives the mature intellect. (If a presidential candidate is lacking in humor then forget him, don't vote for him. He lacks the presidential sensibility; he'll never succeed with Congress or rally the will of the people.

(Jimmy Carter, though diligent and earnest, was not capable of wit; he could not, for instance, poke fun at himself, which must have made him feel left out. LBJ had a kind of rough and bawdy humor that was not without a streak of cruelty—all in all a wit not suited to public consumption. Richard Nixon had little humor; Gerald Ford wasn't exactly rapier-quick. There was no modern president to equal Reagan but JFK, whose answer to the question, How did you become a war hero?—"It was easy; they sank my boat"—is utterly reminiscent of the man who deadpanned of his role in *Bedtime for Bonzo*, "I'm the one with the watch.")

Wit penetrates; humor envelops. Wit is a function of verbal intelligence; humor is imagination operating on good nature. John Kennedy had wit, and so did Lincoln, who also had abundant humor; Reagan was mostly humor.

A few years ago at the official opening of the White House press briefing room, which was built over what had been the president's swimming pool, Reagan blithely told the reporters there was no truth to the rumor the floor was hinged. He added the place was now wired for sound—why, just by pressing a button, we can get helicopter noise to drown out your questions. Then he cut the ribbon, adding that he'd been practicing all morning on Ed Meese's tie.

He told jokes about age because other parts of his repertoire were now foreclosed. As he told a dinner for Russell Long in 1985, "In my position any more I have to be very careful of whether there is any ethnic note to any joke that I tell. But I find that I can still tell jokes about people getting old."

He told a classic Reagan:

"It's a story about an elderly couple who were getting ready for bed one night, and she said, 'Oh, I just am so hungry for ice cream, and there isn't any in the house.'

"And he said, 'I'll get some.'

" 'Oh,' she said, 'you're a dear.' And she said, 'Vanilla with chocolate sauce.' She said, 'Write it down, you'll forget.'

"He said, 'I won't forget.'

"She said, 'With some whipped cream on top.'

"And he said, 'Vanilla with chocolate sauce, whipped cream on top.'

"And she said, 'And a cherry.'

"And he said, 'And a cherry on top.'

" 'Well,' she said, 'please write it down. I know you'll forget.'

"He said, 'I won't forget. Vanilla with chocolate sauce, whipped cream, and a cherry on top.'

"And away he went. By the time he got back, she was already in bed, and he handed her the paper bag. She opened it, and there was a ham sandwich. And she said, 'I told you to write it down—you forgot the mustard!' "

It got him in trouble sometimes. After "We begin bombing in five minutes," the aides of the first administration were frustrated because they knew his humor wasn't being directed. They used to say to him in the morning, "Mr. President, you're going to get asked such-and-such along the way today, and you have to think about what you're going to say." And he'd come up with a line, a smart-aleck line, and he'd get the laugh. Then someone, sometimes Baker, sometimes Darman, would say, "Mr. President, I think we're going to need a less dramatic answer. How about if you say such-and-such?" The president would nod, and smile. And later that day when Sam shouted the question, he'd give the low-key, reasonable answer the fellas asked for.

After the humor was the good nature, the invincible good nature. Ego ties us all in knots, but not him. Amazing, since all presidents are monsters. We make them that way. They're all king babies after a while—too many bells rung and answered, too many aides laughing too heartily at the mild joke. In the years he's in the White House, a president never even feels the cold. I mean this literally: He never feels the cold. He is barely allowed to walk into the frigid air (the photo op waiting for Gorbachev, yes, otherwise no), never mind waiting there for a minute; presidents aren't allowed to wait; presidents aren't allowed to stand in a distracted manner in the driveway and look at their hands. There is always someone with a coat, always someone saying, This way, sir, to the car, always saying, Sir we should wait inside.

Control the environment! Can't chill the franchise! But all this protection, all this attention, all this being served and bowed to—it would twist the healthiest nature and bring out whatever little devils lurk within.

For Reagan, it was quite literally disorienting. "It's the funniest thing," he told a reporter, "but when you're in this job, you forget where things are. When I used to be able to drive my own car I'd have a sense of where things are geographically located. And when I've driven in this town, before I was president, I knew where the hotels and monuments and such are. But now, being driven everywhere in the back of the car and not navigating—it's the oddest thing, but you lose track of where things are."

He never got to see the fronts of hotels anymore, never walked in where other people do. The limousine would take him and his party and the agents and his staff through a big back entrance. He went in where they stack the green plastic bags. "What was that line from *Kitty Foyle?*" he said. "She used it to describe coming into Chicago on the train. 'It's like seeing civilization with its pants down.'"

He had a tact and delicacy so great that I suspect no one has ever been embarrassed in his presence.

Once he went down to Jacksonville, Florida, to meet with a big group of high school students. And a boy stood up and asked a question, a young kid with a thick southern accent and a speech impediment. No one could make out what he was saying. When the student finished the president leaned forward and said, "You know, I'm awfully sorry, but I've got this hearing aid here, and I can't understand. I'm so sorry," he said, as he put his hand to his ear. And the boy nodded. "That's all right," he said, with sympathy and grace.

Once there was a big rally in Washington during the bicentennial of the Constitution, and everyone made speeches. The Chief Justice was there and the majority leader of the Senate, and Bob Dole. And a student got up and spoke for three minutes in front of all these great personages, and he finished his remarks too early and ad-libbed, "And now, the president of the United States."

No one moved. The boy looked over at the president and made a gesture with his arms that said, Hey, buddy, get the lead out! And the president laughed, quickly took to the podium, and apologized for his slowness.

Bill Bennett, the secretary of education, was there. "That boy's gesture is more eloquent than any statement about what democracy is. You don't do that to George the Third." You didn't do it to LBJ, either.

Bennett had another story.

"I called him the day he was to go on TV and talk about Iran-*contra.* Every time I called him I was either put straight through or he'd call back within the hour. He returned my calls quicker than anyone else in the administration.

"Anyway, I called him before the speech and said, 'Mr. President, far be it from me but—I'm sure you're getting a lot of advice but—but can I give you one more piece?'

" 'Sure, Bill,' he said.

" 'Word is you're going to take responsibility and acknowledge mistakes, and that's fine. But, sir, don't underestimate what your enemies want from you. They want you to humiliate yourself; they want the hair shirt. But you can't do that, sir. You're the leader of the free world. You're the leader of a great and proud country, and you can't abase yourself.'

" 'I agree,' he says.

" 'But if you don't give them what they want they'll say you didn't go far enough. That'll be the line.'

" 'Bill,' said the president, 'I'll take responsibility, but you don't have to worry about the other.'

" 'This is big tonight. . . .'

" 'Yeah,' he said.

" 'This is big as they get.'

" 'Yes.' "

Bennett felt like a coach before the big game. He found himself moved and excited.

"This is Rock Falls," he said. He'd been saving that a long time. Rock Falls, he'd once read, was the team the president's school played in the big annual football game back in Dixon.

"You mean Sterling," said the president.

"Huh?"

"Sterling. Sterling was the big game."

"Oh. Yeah. You're right. I stand corrected."

Reagan was an unfazed man.

All presidents wind up lonely, even the ones who didn't start out that way. That old house, the hollow echoes in empty halls.

I don't know if Reagan was any lonelier than most. I think he was solitary. Mari Maseng, when she left the White House, went to say good-bye to him. As she left, her eyes filled with tears. "I think of him alone," she told me. "He seems so alone." George Bush thought so too.

But if you asked him, if you looked in his eyes and asked if he was lonely, he would be surprised. Why no, I—I certainly have a lot to keep me busy. No, I can't say I'm deprived at all, no.

I think he was lonely but had grown so used to it he didn't notice. Lonely but not unhappy, like a productive poet.

They say he was like Willy Loman, going through life on a smile and a shoeshine and telling his sons you've got to be liked. Well, he was Willy without the angst, and he was Ben too. Remember Ben, Willy's brother, who visited the Lomans and dazzled Biff and Happy before he disappeared into the darkness? "Why, boys, when I was seventeen I walked into the jungle, and when I was twenty-one I walked out. . . . And by God, I was rich."

He was Willy, and Ben—"The jungle is dark but full of diamonds, Willy"—and the homespun father in *Splendor in the Grass* who says, "Always drink plenty of milk."

(When Nancy Reynolds had been working for Reagan for a few years back in Sacramento, she realized that as long as she had known him, whenever he had something to do after work, he'd bring along an extra pair of shoes and change them in the car. Finally she asked why. He said, "Nancy, my father was a shoe salesman, and he always told me that when you change shoes you get a new lease on the day—it makes you feel all fresh and rejuvenated to let your feet be in another shape. I always bring a second pair of shoes, no matter where I go.")

But most of all he was the Gentleman Caller, Tennessee Williams's gentleman caller who comforted a shy girl and touched a demoralized family—the enthusiastic strop-snapping American male, striving, planning and calculating but a good fellow, one with compassion there to be tapped.

His warmth overcomes; he is gently humorous. He talks of the Wrigley Building and the Century of Progress—"What impressed me most was the Hall of Science. Gives you an idea of what the future will be in America, even more wonderful than the present time is!"

The great comforter:

"Why, man alive, Laura! Just look about you a little. What do you see? A world full of common people! All of 'em born and all of 'em going to die! Which of them has one-tenth of your good points! Or mine! Or anybody else's, as far as that goes—Gosh!"

The King of Can-Do:

"Take me, for instance. My interest happens to lie in electro-dynamics. I'm taking a course in radio engineering at night school, Laura, on top of a fairly responsible job at the warehouse. I'm taking that course and studying public speaking. . . . Because I believe in the future of television! I wish to be ready to go up right along with it. Therefore I'm planning to get in on the ground floor. In fact I've already made the right connections and all that remains is for the industry itself to get under way! Full steam—[His eyes are starry.] *Knowledge*—Zzzzzp! *Money*—Zzzzzzp!—*Power!*

"That's the cycle democracy is built on! . . ."

They said he lived by symbols and mythic figures and that's why he was so drawn to those *Reader's Digest* stories about the airman who went down with the wounded gunner, and why he was so moved by movies.

But in turning to myth wasn't he being American? Johnny Appleseed, Paul Bunyan, Casey Jones—a hundred years ago when we were settling the West and families full of children close in age were living by themselves, with no one else for miles, no one else within sight—a huge lonely country telling itself stories in isolated cabins, a huge lonely country going to the movies and believing what it saw, that Ty Power was brave and Spence strong, a huge lonely country turning on TV and shooting the existential breeze with Ralph Kramden and Rowdy Yates and then . . . Reagan.

Who understood the loneliness, knew it in his bones, and wanted to assuage it. For eight years he did.

★　★　★　★　★　★　★　★　★　★　★

New Terms

Just before the New Year's of 1985 Ben called me to his office. "Baker's leaving, and Darman. They gave Baker Treasury, and Darman's his number two."

"Who's in?"

"Don Regan. They did a switch, they switched jobs."

"Wow, what did the president say? Well I guess he said yes."

"I guess he did."

Sometimes in the days before he left Darman would call from the mess where, unlike him, he had taken to reading the papers and not worrying about time. He would ask me to join him. He seemed as if he'd lost some of his investment in the place; some level of engagement had been blocked, some plug pulled from the wall. Now here he was, softly turning the big pages of the *Times* and talking to me in a way that at first seemed aimless and unconnected.

The president is a very kindly man but it's hard to know him. Inevitably and in spite of themselves people have a tendency to expect to forge some kind of bond with those with whom they've been involved in a big endeavor, but those bonds, when forged, can be illusory; and sometimes they are never forged at all. It's only human to want to connect, but sometimes in life . . . And listen, Peggy, you're the kind of person who needs intellectual engagement, you crave connection, but you're not on his radar screen and you never will be.

As he talked I thought, This is a man who has been surprised by life, who didn't know until the end that his emotions had been engaged. He's warning me. He's saying, Don't get hurt here. I thought, that last time we talked, I am going to get hurt, and I'm always going to remember his warnings.

In January Baker and Darman were not yet out, Regan and his staff were not yet in, and the inaugural and the State of the Union loomed. A few weeks before, Darman had instructed me, Ben, and a speechwriter named Tony Dolan to write individual drafts of an inaugural address and forward them to the president by December 26, when he would leave for the ranch to celebrate New Year's.

I was excited, of course. An inaugural address is part of the collected works of our democracy, a lasting part of the literature of each presidency. I read every inaugural address that had ever been given. There were surprises. Calvin Coolidge's was clear as crystal and written with a kind of dry fluidity; it didn't ask you to like it. Jefferson's second inaugural was surprising in its sourness. Not quite "You won't have Jefferson to kick around anymore," but close, and it ended with a subdued little tirade about the irresponsibility of the press.

But the most striking thing was how every inaugural since John Kennedy's was an imitation of that great Kennedy/Sorensen address: the 'Ask not' syntax, the "Never negotiate out of fear, but never fear to negotiate" balance (you've heard it—"Let us always bop bop bee dop but let us never boop boop be doop")—the modern-stately tone ("tempered by war, disciplined by a cold and bitter peace"). A speech that was perfect for one brief, shining moment in '61, but less perfect in '64 and '68 and '72, and '76, when Johnson, Nixon, Nixon and Carter did their variations.

I knew that for some of the people who would review Reagan's speech, the more Kennedyesque the better. But Ken Khachigian, who had written the first inaugural with the president, had broken away with an address that was conversational, sentimental and, to me, marked by a plain western unpretentiousness. Which was fitting, since Ronald Reagan was the first president since Kennedy to be undaunted by his memory.

I gathered up my notes and took them north for Christmas with my family. I worked on the draft in my apartment on West Seventy-fifth Street in Manhattan, which I was still holding on to; I hoped to keep it, and by extension my New York life, for a long time. Which is funny, since the neighborhood had changed a lot since I'd moved in seven years before, and I didn't like it as much anymore. In 1977 Seventy-fifth Street was still called the Upper West Side, a mixed neighborhood with apartments that went for $370 for a one-bedroom, and little bodegas and candy stores and neighborhood bars for the meat-loaf crowd.

There was crime, but there was a rough neighborliness too. Once when I was new I saw a lovely tableau of neighborhood people joining in to chase a young mugger until he dropped a pocketbook—a whole line of them wearing jogging outfits, business suits, waitress uniforms and, at the end, the fellow from the shoe-repair shop, his apron flapping in the wind. Often I pulled the 5:00 A.M. shift at work and I'd wait for a cab in the dark on Columbus and Seventy-fifth, where there was a candy store owned by an old man named Joe. When he saw me out there by myself he'd come out and throw around bundles of newspapers so I wouldn't feel alone. He never said a word save "Good morning." He had white hair and a thick European accent. Once when he was giving me change I saw a string of blue numbers tattooed on his arm. Our eyes met, and he looked away.

There was a kind of menacing romance to the neighborhood, a cross between *My Sister Eileen* and *Panic in Needle Park*. In the brownstone across the street there was always a window that was open in nice weather, and when you walked by you could hear a young woman doing her singing lessons. Down the street it was piano lessons, and up here through the window someone was singing along to the Demon Barber of Fleet beat beat Street.

But in the boomtown atmosphere of the eighties the West Side became chic. All the rich young arbitrageurs and producers needed somewhere to live, and they bought and renovated the brownstones and grabbed up the apartments, and suddenly *New York* magazine was calling it the new Left Bank, and then, more pointedly, the Yupper West Side. They doubled old Joe's rent and doubled it again until it was over two thousand dollars a month, and he closed up and left. It's a chic jewelry store now. The bodegas and shoe-repair shops closed down and reopened as expensive clothing stores and trendy shoe shops.

Tap-a-Keg, the bummy bar where people went to dance and play pool and snort coke in the bathroom opened a fern bar down the street. Even the Donegal Inn, a true meat-loaf bar on West Seventy-second that drew to its long brown bar a cast of characters with names like Betty Boop and Lana Turner's Mother and thin men hoisting boilermakers—even it was getting chic. I knew it had gone too far when I went to a neighborhood restaurant with my family and an intellectual in a corduroy jacket violated my airspace to hiss, "Do you have to smoke?" When the health nazis move in a certain degree of neighborliness moves out; and yet I not only chose to stay, I was loathe to leave.

I stood near the window looking out. The doorman across the street was the same old guy in gray pants and a gray shirt. For years I thought he was an old Irish guy from Queens, and then I found out he was a millionaire and he owned the building. The man who sat on the sidewalk with his big dog was still there, still striking up conversations with strangers walking by.

I worked in an uninspired state, mostly because I knew that what I was writing would have to be seriously altered because it didn't include the president's thinking. The only part that I managed to write with any excitement was the ending, in which I attempted to evoke something of the national spirit, to lasso it for a moment, present it, bucking and kicking, and let it go again.

I celebrated Christmas in New Jersey with my family and took the 8:00 A.M. shuttle back to Washington the day after, rewrote the final draft, and got it in by 3:00 P.M. The president took it and the others to the ranch.

For a week we hear nothing. Another week: nothing. The size of my disappointment is a revelation: I realized I had always wanted to work on this big speech with this great man, it had been a picture in the back of my head that would come forward for a moment and give me the shiver that signals the possibility of future happiness.

I would go to Ben and say, "You know, I don't mean to be impolite, and far be it from me to be critical of a genuinely great man who has turned this country around, but I was just wondering if it's not unusual that the president of the United States appears to be taking no interest in his inaugural address."

"Uh-oh, here it comes," he said, as he waved his hands in the air.

"I'm serious. Has he been in touch with you at all? He knows his inauguration is coming up, right, on account of he won the election and they always inaugurate the elected president in America. He knows, right?"

Ben did the Ben sigh. "Look, he has his own way of doing things, and complaining won't help. I think we're going to meet with him and talk with him, but if not we'll just have to do our best. That's the way it is, and it shouldn't come as a surprise to you by now."

Then news: Word came from the Oval Office that the president had been working on his own draft, taking lines and sections he liked from the three speeches he'd received and weaving them into his own. He wasn't ignoring it, he just hadn't loved what he'd been given. On January 14 we received the president's draft. We'd been warned it would take some work by James Baker, who told Ben that when the president had handed it to him, he'd said, "Maybe I'm losing my touch."

It wasn't anything like what I expected. It wasn't broad and thematic; it was chock-full of facts and statistics and percentages. I thought, How unlike him. Ben said no, this is the essential Reagan; everyone thinks he doesn't give a fig for facts but he loves his factoids, loves his numbers.

I wrote a memo saying the way I see it, an inaugural address is a tone poem and should not defend but declare, then sent it to Ben, who sent it to Darman, who staffed the speech to Dick Wirthlin, Baker, Stockman, Fred Fielding, and a few others. Their comments were timid—I gathered they knew whose work they were criticizing—but there seemed to be a consensus that the speech would benefit from a more clearly defined theme.

Ben and I incorporated the suggestions as best we could and disagreed, near the end, on what tack to take. Ben felt it was necessary to keep as much of the president's own work as possible while improving the speech in general. We'll keep this section, written by RR, and add on this section, which helps it.

My approach was bolder and dumber. Either let the president's version go as is (the president would like giving an address he'd written in its entirety) or tear the whole thing up and rewrite it, and maybe the president will love it and maybe he'll hate it but do it right and send it in. The worst that could happen was that we'd wind up with the speech we'd already got.

Ben's voice rose with a cutting edge.

"You still don't get it, do you? If we let it go as it is and it's a flop

I'll be fired and you'll be fingered. Someone will have to take the fall, and Speakes'll be out there leaking that the president received some very bad drafts, and maybe we'll have to make some changes in that department. And if we send a whole new original speech in it's like an insult. He worked on it, this is what he wants, and we've got to work with it."

He was right about everything except, I think, the president. I still think that if we'd written him a note saying, "We did the whole thing over and we think this is much better"—and Darman let the note go through—he would have been receptive. He would have been especially receptive if Ben wrote a note that joked with him a little about what we were up to, but Ben couldn't joke with the president. I think he felt that in all badinage there is an implicit assertion of equality, and Ben was too modest to make such a claim.

The reworked draft was sent to the president. A day later we got it back. The president had written two words on the upper left-hand corner: "Just fine."

The press saved the speech. The reviews were uniformly good. It wasn't a great speech, but the press, full of people anticipating the Great Communicator communicating greatly, heard it and couldn't believe it wasn't great. So they said, It was very good but somewhat . . . restrained in tone, somewhat low key, yeah, that's the ticket. It was . . . the Gipper communicating softly and in a subdued manner. (The press often did this for us. A lot of reporters thought Reagan's rhetoric was effective because of the way he said things, not because of what he said. They saw him as a great communicator as opposed to a communicator of great things. So they didn't understand why it worked when it worked, and when it didn't a lot of them couldn't tell.)

The day of the inaugural they canceled the parade because of the cold; they even moved the address from the steps outside the Capitol to the rotunda. I watched in my office. As the president raised his hand and took the oath, a nameless niggling anxiety came over me. Something was wrong, we'd overlooked something and the president was about to make a mistake. It was . . . it was . . . oh jeez, it was the end of the speech; we forgot to change it when the ceremony was moved inside! I ran into Ben's office. "Is there any way we can get someone in the rotunda?"

"What."

I told him. He shook his head. And anyway they'd never be able to change the TelePrompTer or the cards.

When the president got to it, we watched and winced:

"And as we continue our journey, we think of those who traveled before us. We stand again at the steps of this symbol of our democracy—"

AAAaaaaggggghhhhh.

Shush! Ben said.

"—well, we would have been standing at the steps if it hadn't gotten so cold!"

A ripple of laughter spread through the rotunda.

"Now we're standing inside this symbol of our democracy. And we see and hear again the echoes of our past . . ."

"Thanks, Pappy."

"An easy save by the Gippah," said Ben.

After the speech I went to the Hay Adams to meet Andy Rooney for lunch. Andy is, I think, an original, acerbic and funny and cynical and sweet; I hadn't seen him since I left CBS. Now on this crisp brilliant day we were in the upstairs yellow dining room eating fish on white china and talking about presidents and history. People at the other tables looked and turned to each other, excited. As we left a small stream of them approached and said hello. I thought of Will Rogers's shoe. The tip of the shoe of the statue of Will Rogers in Statuary Hall is always brighter than the rest of the statue, the dullness having been rubbed off by the hands of tourists who pat Rogers's foot as they go by, as if to say hello. That's what it was like being with Andy, people patted him.

I walked back to the EOB. Gusts of wind lifted swirls of snow and carried them high through the air. Pennsylvania Avenue was empty; the ice made a dry crunch. Four years earlier on this day it was cold but not as cold as this. I was producing the parade coverage for radio, working up there in the big network booths that had been erected across from the White House. My correspondent was George Herman, who stood at the mike, described what he saw, and removed his hat every time the flag came by. During a commercial I asked him about it. "I always take my hat off for the flag," he said. "It's the flag of our country. It's the least I can do."

A week later I saw a copy of a letter that had gone in to the president.

January 21, 1985
(Inauguration Day)

Dear Mr. President and Mrs. Reagan,

Do you remember, on Saturday, January 19th, 1985, just two days ago, you and Mrs. Reagan left the Convention Center after the Gala at about 10:15 P.M., and your limousine came down New York Avenue to the White House?

Do you remember a woman waving to you both madly at the corner of 13th and New York Avenue? You both looked over and waved and smiled so warmly. Well, that was me!!

The reason I am writing to remind you is that, do you realize that I was your "Parade"? Since the official one was cancelled today, I was your parade! I just wish I had had a flag at the time. You both looked fabulous, and I was thrilled to see you . . .

It was signed by a woman who lived in Washington. Ever after the phrase stayed in my mind, becoming somehow an anthem for those days. I was your parade.

The next night I had an interesting date. Some weeks before I had gone to the White House staff Christmas party, which was always fun because you got to pose with the president and the first lady, who, poor them, stood together in, I think, the Red Room, as members of the staff (actually, commissioned officers and up—I'd just made it) waited on line to say hello and smile as a photographer quickly snapped a picture.

I was with a fellow who worked on the Hill, a friend of a friend. He was fortyish, handsome, and silly. I knew what he was as soon as I met him: the kind of man who liked to fall for a woman—that's how he'd put it—argue with her, and then, alone and abandoned, lick his wounds in a semi-Byronic swoon. He was funny and made me laugh. We walked in and immediately saw a friend of his, a long, tall ambassador and her escort, an attractive man with gray hair and a black eye patch. Introductions all around, the talk turns to politics; I withdrew to the East Room and the famous Christmas tree. It was beautiful. I turned. There was someone behind me. The man with the eye patch. "Hello," I said.

"Hello."

"Lovely, isn't it?"

"Yes. You write speeches for the president."

"Yes."

"I'm surprised. Rarely do great beauty and writing talent go to-gether."

Reader, once Ethel Merman went to a very bad Broadway musical that starred the not sufficiently talented lady friend of one of the authors. A friend of mine sat near Miss Merman and found it much more fun to watch her than the stage. At one point the not sufficiently talented lady reached for a high note, missed by a mile, and Ethel Merman turned to her escort and said, "Oh buhRUHthuh!"—which, because of her fabulous vocal power, was heard more widely than she'd intended, inspiring laughter and applause.

That is what I thought of when the gentleman with the eye patch said what he said. Oh bahRUHthah. And: nice to leave your date and follow another woman into a room and flirt with her.

I said something, he said something, I began to walk on, he said, "Could we go to dinner some time?" I said, "Oh guhguhbluhbluhbluh-buh." We were intercepted by our dates and parted.

The next morning I walked into Ben's office to talk about the party when the man with the eye patch stood up and said hello. "You know Richard," said Ben.

"Yes, we met last night. Hello."

"I asked her out, and I think she said no."

Ben smiled.

"I wanted to see you, so I made an excuse to see Ben."

"You're very direct."

"Yes, I am. Are you free for lunch sometime?"

"Yes, I could do lunch."

"Good, when?"

"Uh, well, I could today I guess."

He pulled an appointment book from his jacket pocket and said, "I'm busy today. And tomorrow. And next week. I'm okay the Wednes-day of the last week in January."

"I'm busy Wednesday the last week in January. I'm booked all winter except today."

"Looks like one of us will have to readjust our schedule."

"Ooh!" Ben laughed.

We decided on dinner and here we were at an Italian restaurant known for its impossible-to-read hand-scrawled menu, and he was tell-

ing me of his life. He is an economist for a business organization,
lobbies the hill for tax cuts. No, the ambassador isn't his girlfriend.
She's a friend, she thinks she needs an escort to functions, and I like
to go, but no, it's not a romance, and what about you and that guy from
the Hill? A friend of a friend.

What do you want out of the next five years?

I want to achieve things with my writing, I want to do meaningful
work, and I want to get married and have children. In fact, I decided
just recently to get married this year but then figured that's a dumb
thing to decide so I won't get married this year but the key thing is
that I articulated to myself the desire to—

He was thumbing through his calendar. "I'm free Thursday."

"What?"

"To get married."

"Oh, ha ha." (Oh bahRUHthah!)

Working on the State of the Union was fun, and for some reason
it was easy. Baker's group was on its way out and Regan's on its way
in and no one owned the speech. So I wrote part, Ben wrote part, we
sewed it together and sent it to staffing. It was a good document,
dynamic both in terms of policy and style, tightly written and always
moving forward. Some speeches just lie there. This speech never
stopped except for now and then when it idled for a change of pace.
(Note to young speechwriters: People are used to commercials, they're
used to a break in the action. They need daydream time every few
minutes. Also, when a speech is densely argued it can be exhausting to
follow. So what you want to do is offer two or three minutes of the good
stuff and then pause, switch gears, and include the boring, obvious stuff
that you don't want to put in but somebody makes you. That's where
people will daydream. Then wake 'em up with good writing and continue the flow.)

Ben felt that this was a good time for the president to reassert his
opposition to abortion and some of his reasoning. I thought it a good
time to bring some of the reasoning up-to-date. A number of people
I knew, friends who were approaching their middle thirties, were trying
to have children and, for a variety of reasons, having trouble. One,
who'd been a newswriter with me in Boston and become a close friend,
was trying to adopt and finding it very difficult. One of the unan-

ticipated results of *Roe* vs. *Wade* was that people like Judy couldn't find babies they wanted to adopt anymore.

This is what I wrote:

"I believe that when we allow ourselves to take the lives of our smallest, most vulnerable members, we coarsen ourselves as a society. And it is surely a terrible irony that while some abort their children, so many others who cannot become parents cry out for children to adopt. Abortion has emptied the orphanages—and emptied the cradles of those who want a child to love.

"Our nation has made great strides in helping unwed mothers bring their children to term. Churches, private agencies and individuals are housing, feeding, clothing and treating young mothers, helping them to keep their children or put them up for adoption. This great movement has spread across the country like wildfire."

Dick Darman did not like anti-abortion language (in the speechwriting business the word "language" is used in place of "argument" and "words"), partly because the president's stance did not reflect, he said, the will of the majority of the people, and partly, I think, because he himself did not support a ban. We talked about it once. He brought up the polls and said it's an 80–20, I said if you polled the German people in 1939 killing Jews would be an 80–20, he said you can't squander political capital, I said the courage to take unpopular stands *is* this president's capital, he referred to Prohibition and back alleys. I don't know what I said but I probably conceded yes, people will still do it and they'll get hurt, you're right, and more than a change of law is needed—but a change of law is needed.

(I know I lose some people here. I don't have a single woman friend who agrees with me on abortion, and the woman who edits this or sets the type is steaming. But it's what I think. When people say abortion is a visceral issue I think they mean it's purely instinctive: One's instinct is either to rush to the aid of the frail thing that will be killed or rush to the aid of a freedom that could be lost—and there is no room for compromise. But I'll tell you something that some members of the antiabortion movement are privately wrestling with. I had a talk the other night [it is late autumn '89] with an antiabortion activist who is a distinguished writer and thinker. I told him of my growing fear that moving for something like a constitutional amendment when so many women want to keep the abortion option open was—maybe right now not the answer. If we just pass a law and everybody breaks it, what have we gained? There would be so much resistance, so much added pain inflicted on young girls, so much profit made by bad people, by the worst of our society. And since the decision to abort is made in a single woman's mind . . . maybe what we really have to do is keep changing minds. He surprised me. "I know what you're saying," he said, "and I think about it too." Maybe the real battlefield is in literature and the arts, in the media, in the fields of political debate. Republican politicians hate to talk about abortion, and then once a year they line up behind a bill to ban it. They have it backwards. They should talk and talk and not move until they have the people. Maybe in this case action must follow concensus, or the action will be meaningless.)

I sent a shorter version of the speech to Darman, who sent a shorter version to the president, who added, "Tonight I ask the Congress to move this year to ban abortion unless it can be proven that an unborn child is not a living human being, and I submit the burden of proving that should fall on those who want a license to destroy the unborn."

After we sent the president a copy for final review, Ben received a call from one of the new people Donald Regan had brought in. He told Ben, "The president says it's much too long."

Ben was stricken. For once he came into my office to wail. "He'll cut it, he'll put in his numbers. He'll decide to cut five lines per page and he'll cut all the music out." His head was in his hands.

I was delighted to get to be the wise one who comforts and cautions. "It can't be that bad."

He said nothing.

"Let's call Darman and scream!"

"I've already made calls. Darman has no real responsibility for this anymore. Regan's people have no emotional investment in this speech."

"Regan does. It's his first big speech, if it's a hit he's a hit."

He shrugged.

A few hours later he called.

"I've got good news and bad news."

"Good first."

"Fred Ryan called. Deaver okayed the heroes."

"Great."

"And the president has a cold. He's cleared the decks this afternoon, and I can see him up there with his pen."

"Oh listen, he'll make some changes, we'll incorporate them, we'll be forced to cut some national sewer-commission stuff that's boring anyway, and we'll send it back to him and it will be a tighter more elegant speech and he'll write 'Just fine' in the corner."

"No, we'll have Mrs. Reagan down our backs if it's not shorter, she'll blow her top."

"We'll make it shorter, it'll be fine. We'll cut the boring stuff. Come on. Speak softly but carry a big Bic. This is fun, this is what we're paid for."

Ben again, that evening.

"I just spoke to Baker. He says the president likes the speech but he wants to cut it from thirty-five minutes to twenty-five. That's approximately one third."

"What did you tell him?"

"I told him we should make the cuts."

"What did he say?"

"He understands. He said, You two cut it and I'll go in tomorrow for my last meeting and break my pick on it."

"We're gonna miss him, aren't we."

"Probably."

The "heroes in the balcony" was a Reagan White House tradition that I'd long thought was hokey and corny. But, I was told, the first lady and Mike Deaver liked it and so did the president, who'd been doing it ever since Lenny Skutnik threw himself into the freezing Potomac to rescue people after the Air Florida jetliner crashed into the Fourteenth Street Bridge.

The night of the State of the Union I sat in the gallery of the House of Representatives. Ben had lent me his ticket and I watched with excitement. As the president neared the end of his address I looked over at the balcony across the room and saw a pretty, proud young Indochinese woman in a gray wool tunic clutching the hand of a frail old black woman.

The sight of them made me realize I was wrong. The heroes in the balcony was a metaphor for all the everyday heroism that never gets acknowledged. It was for kids, to show them what courage is.

"Tonight I have spoken of great plans and great dreams. They are dreams we can make come true. Two hundred years of American history should have taught us that nothing is impossible.

"Ten years ago a young girl left Vietnam with her family, part of the exodus that followed the fall of Saigon. They came to the United States with no possessions, and not knowing a word of English. The young girl studied hard, learned English and finished high school in the top of her class. This May is a big date on her calendar. Just ten years from the time she left Vietnam, she'll graduate from the United States Military Academy at West Point. I thought you might want to meet an American hero named Jean Nguyen."

The young woman in the gray tunic stood and bowed to the applause.

"There's someone else here tonight. Born seventy-nine years ago, she lives in the inner city where she cares for infants born to mothers who are heroin addicts. The children, born in withdrawal, are sometimes even dropped at her doorstep. She heals them with love. Go to her house some night and maybe you'll see her silhouette against the window, as she walks the floor talking softly, soothing a child in her arms. Mother Hale of Harlem—she, too, is an American hero."

The frail old woman stood.

"Your lives tell us that the oldest American saying is new again: Anything is possible in America if we have the faith, the will, and the heart. History is asking us, once again, to be a force for good in the world. Let us begin—in unity, with justice, and love."

And *love*. The president had cut a number of words in that section, but not the last.

Take that, Francis X. Clines.

When the winter of the heavy speeches was over we summed up. I had become used to being unusually frank in my conversations with Ben; I didn't have many other friends there, and he got all the candor I'd normally parcel out. The White House wasn't the kind of place where you made close friendships; you made alliances. I had allies, and we talked to each other with a well meaning semi-openness. But with Ben I was myself, and I think he was unselfconscious and trusting with me.

I told him that the past few months I'd been getting a bad case of that ol' debil cognitive dissonance. The president is clearly an intelligent man, but I get the impression sometimes his top aides don't think so. And a lot of them don't think he's right. I had the feeling the president himself had picked it up. Maybe that's why he's so deferential.

"There are people here who say that's why the first lady is so protective of him."

"Because he's surrounded by people who think he's not smart?"

"Because she thinks he's not smart. That's why she's so protective and fierce, because she really thinks he'd do anything he's so innocent and dumb."

"That's why she reads his speeches and works things out with Deaver before they tell him the schedule."

"That's why she's such a tiger."

"That's how a mother is when the child is endangered."

"Yup. First she growls, then she gets her paws up."

"Then she shows her fangs."

★ ★ ★ ★ ★ ★ ★ ★ ★ ★ ★

TEN

George Raft

Here is Don Regan gliding down the hall, his unsmiling aides in a phalanx behind him. He breezes past me, pulls out a sentence and shoots: "Ya did good on the State a' the Union." He passes in a breeze, pauses down the hall and turns so that I see him, hands in the pockets of a light gray suit.

He is like . . . George Raft! Those hooded eyes, and the silky way he moves—all he needs is the fedora and a quarter to flip in the air and a zoot suit with a reet pleat and a drape shape to please his baby.

He is a character, he is cool, you can see it all the minute you meet him, he loves his power and his fame. But he has the Irish disease: He cannot resist a good line (I would think of Leo Rosten: "Who is a hero? He who suppresses a wisecrack."), and he cannot resist appearing to be tough and mean when in fact, inside, you could tell, he wasn't so tough and he wasn't so mean. Some men have to act worse than they are.

He was certainly convincing. I kept a small collection of Regan characterizations. He was "a Wall Street sharpie" (Hugh Sidey), "abrasive" *(Time)*, "high-handed" *(Time)*, "fatally flawed" (David Broder), a "dangerous" man who "does not know what he does not know" (George Will), "a blundering and dissembling Chief of Staff" (Broder again), and "a great guy whom I admire for his humility and kindness" (I made that one up).

Don Regan was, we all know, enamored of the salty observation, the colorful metaphor, and he'd rather go for the good line than keep a prudent silence. And so he said he cleaned up after the circus parade, and he didn't even notice that if he followed the logic of the metaphor he was suggesting his boss is a large, turd-dropping elephant, an image that would have made the president laugh but would have rattled Nancy's teacup pretty good. And he couldn't resist the truthful observation that most women don't know throw weights from a shoeshine, without having the wit or humility to add, "And neither do I, and neither do men!"

John Dean called the Nixon White House Macho Mountain, and Regan would have fit in. He would have been able to let Bud twist slowly, slowly in the wind, would have appreciated the sardonic edge of "modified limited hangout," would have laughed on Marine One as Colson said, When you've got 'em by the balls their hearts and minds will follow. He was in fact very much the kind of man who would express the difficulties of other men in terms of their genitalia.

Reporters liked him at first, not only because he was good copy but because every now and then you could look up from your pad and catch the wry twinkle in those eyes, a look that said, Of course I'm full of it, so are you, we all are, it's all a glorious con, welcome to life.

There was something of the charming rogue in him, and there was a decency too. I did not enjoy his tenure at the White House—he was, for Ronald Reagan, the beginning of real trouble—but you had to see the poignant quality. I wrote a speech for him once. Jim Baker never asked the president's speechwriters to do one up for him, but Regan had no reluctance to issue such a request, and I was delighted to comply. He'd get to know me and like me and we would be friends. I went to his office and sat at his table, and he tried to tell me what he wanted and he was awkward. He expressed himself badly and knew it, which made him drum his fingers and finally blurt, "How did you get to be a writer? Where did you learn it?"

I thought, I make him nervous as a writer, as a woman. I was surprised; all my life I always think nervous is my job. I told him I went to Fairleigh Dickinson, but it didn't make him feel any better.

A year after he left the White House, I met him at a small party. We discussed Tip O'Neill's recently published memoirs and his surprisingly harsh portrait of the president. I asked him if Ronald Reagan had liked Tip O'Neill. Regan came alive.

"He tried to! He wanted to like him, he thought it was good for the government if they got along and could work together. Sometimes they'd have a meeting and Tip would be there and they're laughing and getting along and it's very warm. And then"—Regan made a fist and punched it into his palm—"Tip would leave, go up to the Hill and turn on him just like a snake! It was treachery. And the president would say, 'What's wrong with that guy?,' and finally I said, 'Mr. President, you don't know it because you're from the Midwest, but there's two kinds of Irish, lace curtain and shanty, and that man is shanty Irish and they'll turn on you like that.' " He snapped his fingers. "It's just the way they are. They'll turn on you, ya can't trust 'em for anything."

That was Regan, not only the Jimmy Cagney language—shanty, the guy's a rat, and the horse you rode in on (when Supreme Court nominee Douglas Ginsburg was forced to withdraw his nomination, I asked Regan what a chief of staff should do to recover from such a fiasco, and he said, "Ya mean after saying every four-letter cuss word you know, and then maybe some you don't, and after knocking back a stiff one or maybe two, ya mean after that?")—but in the visceral, almost too responsive edge. Someone was always knifing, sandbagging, bashing or snookering some jackass, Joe Shmo, or betrayer.

I can tell you both as a woman who grew up listening to old Irish ladies take their tea and cigarettes on an oilcloth table, and as someone whose friends have suggested she could always join the circus as the only living human exclamation point, that the Irish often see aggression and affection in exaggerated form. They take it all so much to heart, and they sometimes speak with a certain violence of expression. No one ever ignores you they turn their back on you, and no one ever assists you they really come through.

Perhaps it is because they have a religion that deals with big things—betrayal and redemption and love—but a lot of Irish Catholics don't do understatement, they're afraid they'll be misunderstood by their friends—or their enemies. (Perhaps at the heart of the Irish-Orangemen tensions of the past century is the fact that half the Irish were taking, "Uh, yes, well, it's over here" for "Get out of my store, you bum.") (Perhaps I overstate.)

Regan's aides were . . . How to sum them up. They were not as vivid as their boss, and I think that's part of the reason they were there.

There were four of them but when people thought of them they thought, There are three of them. It was one of those funny things, but even when they were thought of en masse there was something diminished about them. There was David, who was in charge of the paper flow; we sometimes called him "Yah Yah Understood," because that's what he said to us on the phone before he ignored what we were saying. There was Al, who dealt with policy and who had the forlorn look of Stan Laurel after Ollie bopped him on the head. There was Tom, who became famous, perhaps unfairly, as the aide charged with finding the joke du jour for Mr. Regan's morning meeting with the president, and Dennis, who would be spoofed in a witty piece in *The New Republic* as "America's Guest," so much did he enjoy being entertained at expensive dinners paid for by the networks and the mainline press.

For a while I kept clippings on them too. The one before me now is from *Time* magazine. It says, "The NSC staff is sharply critical of Regan and the handful of aides, known as the 'mice,' he brought with him from the Treasury Department. 'They have a track record of being willing to tar anybody and everybody if it helps distract attention from their own foibles,' says an NSC staff member." Years later a senior aide to the president was just as direct: "They were guys who just wanted to be there. They wanted to be in the picture laughing with the king. They were pilot fish for the shark, they were derivative, they were Regan's little boys."

They had a lot of nicknames. They were the Chief Fella's Fellas, they were Delusions of Adequacy. But the name that became famous, the one that ever after clung to them, came from an OMB official who approached me one day after I'd had a disagreement with Yah Yah Understood. He said, "Don't feel bad, they're the three blind mice." Ever after when tensions were bad, it made us feel better to refer to them as the mice. *Newsweek* picked it up and once it spread it stayed because it was: perfect. People gave each other mousetraps as a joke, and I was told, though I never saw one, that traps were even placed in the corners of the West Wing lobby.

After I worked with them for a while, after I saw them floating in the halls in a great whisper, with Mr. Regan in the middle, I would think of Prufrock:

Am an attendant lord, one that will do
To swell a progress, start a scene or two,
Advise the prince; no doubt, an easy tool,
Deferential, glad to be of use,
Politic, cautious, and meticulous;
Full of high sentence, but a bit obtuse;
At times, indeed, almost ridiculous—
Almost, at times, the Fool.

They were in a bad position, charged with creating a successful second administration when no one had done that since Eisenhower in 1956. They had inherited a staff the most talented of whom were the most exhausted. They had to be better managers than the first-termers and better thinkers, and they were not more talented.

The problem for me as a writer was that the mice had control of my work. Some of them liked to look at speeches. Some of them liked to write them. I knew I was in trouble when I got a note from Dennis one day, early on. I had written for the president the phrase "The Constitution, as you know . . ." He had circled the last three words. If they already know, he challenged, why do we have to tell them? I began a memo explaining that "as you know" is a polite thing to say when you're reminding people of something they may have forgotten, or repeating what is known for effect, or telling people something they really might not know, but you don't want to appear to be assuming they are uninformed or . . . And then I thought, When someone wants to argue about "as you know," there's more going on than "as you know." I didn't send the memo.

"There are people who barely feel poetry," said Jorge Luis Borges, "and they are generally dedicated to teaching it." I took it as my mission to resist the pedants, ignore the pedagogues, spoof them, fight them, pick them up in their little mouse chairs and throw them out the window. But I also knew that I would lose, that in the history of the world the crude power of mice tends to prevail over the more subtle power of words—in the short run. But in the White House the short run is the only run there is.

Anyway, that's what I know now. What I knew then I got from my tours through the halls, where I asked everyone I knew.

. . .

Here is Marlin Fitzwater, assistant to Larry Speakes. He leans back in the chair in my office and takes a cigar from his pocket. He is portly and pink, so people think he is jolly, but his eyes are shrewd and miss nothing, and he does not expect the right thing to happen.

"If you ask a big question, I get to smoke."

"You know you can smoke." In the eighties the White House was smoke-averse; people had come to think it fair to wave their hands and wrinkle their noses when you lit up. More of the fastidious disdain that blights the era. Sam Donaldson had harassed the last few smokers in the pressroom—the pressroom!—right out the door. When Marlin wants a smoke he takes a walk on the ellipse.

He begins the ritual, biting and lighting. I fill time with small questions. So how's your love life? / Nothin', I'm still waiting for you. / Yeah but while you're waiting who're you seeing? / I met this new girl, woman, she's great. / So is it serious? / I don't know, what's serious? / Well, are you, like, doing it? / Peggy, I am shocked! You know I'm saving myself for you. You meeting anybody? / Yeah, I met an interesting guy. / Is it serious? / How dare you ask me such a—

He is laughing softly, his head against the top of the chair. He is a survivor, he keeps a list and never forgets; he is patient. He is funny, and more often than not a straight shooter. He gives me advice. Often it is, Be quiet.

"Tell me what to expect. Tell me about Regan's aides." He had worked with them at Treasury.

"Whatta ya wanna know?"

"Are they smart?"

He follows the smoke rings.

"They're not stupid. They're not first-rate."

Silence.

"Well, if that's as bad as it is it won't be bad."

"That may be."

I watched *Nightline* last night (Don Regan's book revealing the first lady's reliance on astrology has come out), and who should pop up in one of the little windows on the screen but a former White House colleague who was having a heck of a time telling Sam, who was sitting in for Ted, what an inept and disloyal chief Regan had been. He spoke with conviction, with an angry passion, even. His eyes said, I've had enough of that fellow, the sight of him hurting people has finally forced me to put my natural reticence aside and give him the national denunciation he deserves!

When Regan was on top, in the White House, the man in the little window felt differently. When he saw Regan in the halls it was all big hellos and just between you and me, and he argued, in private, that a tough guy like Regan is exactly what we need around here.

What happened to change my old colleague's mind? Regan fell. That's all. That's how simple and direct it can be in Washington. But what interests me is that he believes what he says. His eyes are wet with remembered pain.

Has he hypnotized himself? Has he forgotten how he felt? Did he always oppose Regan inside, and now he feels it serves a higher truth to declare his public opposition retroactive? Or is he just another hustler, just another guy who wants to be on the side that's winning? I don't know. What I resent is funny: It's not his expediency or his current fictions, it's that he believes he was brave.

Ben's office on a sunny, cold day.
"We have a new boss. Hold on to your hat."
"Who?"
"Pat Buchanan."
"The Pat Buchanan? Pat Buchanan ideological war-horse, peerless polemicist, battler for the right as God gives him to see the right?"
"That may be the one."
"Who picked him, the president?"
"Don Regan."
"I guess I don't get this."
"Protect his right flank."
"The president's?"
"Regan's."
Of course. I love politics.

This was the book on Buchanan: He sounds tough because he is tough, and trouble follows him. The wife of a network correspondent who had covered Washington during Watergate told me, "He is bad, he is just a bad, bad man, and you watch out."

I certainly hoped he'd like me.

I'd never met him, but now, as the new director of communications, he was my boss. We didn't hear from him for a while, but in time it got back to us that Buchanan said one of the things that worked in the White House was the Great Communicator's speechwriting shop, and he didn't intend to fix it.

I started getting calls.

"I talked to Pat today," a colleague would say. "Listen, he seems like a nice guy. And don't worry, I talked you up."

Well thanks.

Two days later, someone else: "I met up with Buchanan. I don't think you should take his worries about you too much to heart. Anyway, I told him you're great."

Thanks. What worries?

"You know, CBS and Rather."

Another call. "Uh, how is it with you and Buchanan? Then go meet him, go over and introduce yourself and show him you don't have fangs."

I called his office and asked if I could discuss a speech with him. Sure, come on over late this afternoon.

Well, I was ready. If this big jerk is going to assume I'm a bad guy because I worked for CBS, then he's stupid, and if this is the way you people are no wonder you always lose.

There he was at his desk, sitting straight as a marine, reading some papers. His white shirt was crisp as a cadet's, the cuffs thick and smooth; over a chair hung the jacket of a creaseless blue pinstripe. He is handsomer than on TV, with quick, bright eyes and perfectly trimmed brown hair, a big, slim, Brylcreemed man.

He motioned to a chair. The office didn't have any good furniture. It was obvious from the bare walls with the empty picture hooks that he hadn't given much thought to how it looked. I wonder if he knows what I've learned, that in the White House people judge the importance of your ideas by your personal importance in the hierarchy, and they judge that by certain indicators, one of which is a well-situated office with handsome furniture. Maybe I should tell him. Wait a minute, this guy survived Watergate. And he thinks I'm a commie, to hell with him. (Later I would find that Pat is among the tidiest of men, so fastidious that when he underlined particularly striking sections of speeches or memos the lines, jotted at his desk, were as perfectly straight and sure as if he'd done them with a ruler.)

He put the paper down.

So, he said.

Hi.

Hi.

I knew the thing to do was chat him up, show him I was okay, and if he had any questions, he could put them to me and I'd answer them coolly and frankly, and that would take care of his little problem.

We stared. He had a yellow legal pad; he was holding it like a shield. I had a legal pad too. I held it like a shield. His face was expressionless, not like someone who's bored but like someone who's made his face lax so nothing shows.

Things were certainly going well so far.

"So. Working on a speech." His voice was soft.

"Yeah, and I wanted to talk about it."

He nodded.

"So you know what I'm working on and what I'm doing."

"Uh-huh."

Silence.

I told him about it. I don't know what I said, but it was boring. Silence.

"So that's what I'm up to."

"Good."

"Well. I guess I'll go now."

Silence.

"So you used to work for my old friend Mr. Rather."

"Yeah. You know, he's very anti-Communist—"

AAAaaaaggghhhh.

"—I mean he used to be a marine—"

Shut up, fool.

"—He's your basic patriot it's just that in domestic affairs, of course, he's pretty liberal—"

Someone take a sock and put it in her mouth.

"—but in international affairs he's much more anti-Communist, as anyway my show certainly is, or actually was—"

Put the sock in deep.

"—but at any rate . . ."

Silence. Oh frick it.

"Actually I worked with him for years, and it was very interesting. I liked him. I liked CBS too, it was quite a place."

Uh-huh.

"And anyway, as for former bosses, I understand you used to work for Dick Nixon."

And frick him too.

He threw back his head and laughed.

"I sure did," he said. "I sure did."

He and Dan had never managed to make friends—"never quite made it to the altar"—bad blood from Watergate. Dan had been the embodiment of big media's anti-Nixon spirit. I told him of what I saw as Dan's almost compulsive skepticism, he had suspicions about everyone in public life and every decision, every form of government. Pat asked what it was like to be a conservative at CBS. I told him. Then I told him what a disappointment it was that people in the White House were just as disapproving of someone who worked at CBS as the dumber CBS people were of someone who was a conservative, and frankly I'd hoped for more.

He smiled and nodded, and there were no more phone calls from friends telling me of my problems with Pat. (Weeks later Rather called: "Are you having any troubles with your boss? Would it help if I denounced you?")

I grew to like Buchanan the way I liked Darman, with the same wary affection and real regard. They were not similar men, but they were more alike than they would have guessed, or perhaps liked. Each was the smartest man in his White House, the quickest mind, each was unusually literate, each had enemies. A difference was that Dick's reputation, while exaggerated, was at least near the mark, while in Pat's case I had never seen such a gap between public persona and private personality.

He is neither bombastic nor especially combative. He tends to speak softly. The public might guess that a hard-guy conservative like Pat would be no friend to women, but he was the most energetic promoter of women in the White House. His morning staff meeting with the people who ran his departments—Elizabeth Board in media relations, Agnes Waldren in research, me sometimes sitting in for Ben, Mari Maseng in public liaison—was known as Pat's All-Girl Band. He relied on all of us to run the show while he gave interviews to Lesley Stahl explaining what's wrong with the Equal Rights Amendment.

He loved poetry. Once, in one of the first speeches I ever wrote with him in charge, I used the phrase "show an affirming flame," and he underlined it and asked me later, "That's Auden, isn't it?" I was delighted. Yes, Auden's "September 1, 1939."

"Yeah. 'As the clever hopes expire/Of a low dishonest decade.' Great."

Buchanan summed up his disastrous three-week candidacy for president with a breezy, "We peaked too soon!" and said it was too bad, because we missed out on a great campaign slogan, "Why Not the Beast?" He was a climber (everyone is a climber) but not a snob (unusual in our society, I think; certainly unusual in that White House). He was effortlessly egalitarian. There's something in good conservatives that makes them happy to sit for an hour with a janitor and talk about life and the world in a way that one suspects a Ralph Nader or a Ralph Neas never could (for they seem to love Ralph Kramden only in the abstract—and Ralph Kramden knows).

He was, finally, much like Ronald Reagan, the man he adored. Like the president, he occasionally seemed naive about people and confused by bad motives. He could talk for half an hour and not pause once as he made the case against the Communist party of the Soviet Union and its propensity for lying and cheating, but he was surprised when people around him lied and cheated, and seemed disoriented by malice. It was as if he could accept the big concept, the abstraction, but not its common human application. Evil, yeah, I get evil, but why's Joe so mean? There was nothing small about him, no pettiness, no nastiness. Members of the press who knew him cherished him. (It is not true that reporters hate conservatives. Reporters respect earnestness when it's accompanied by good nature, and they like anyone who's good copy, who's bright and witty and who, above all, will tell them the truth.)

Hyperbole was in his nature; if he sounded fierce too bad you couldn't hear the happy snorts at the typewriter. He was moved by both deeply held political views and the joy of invective, which would have been an apt title for his memoirs if he had not already called them *Right from the Beginning*. (A book that beautifully captures a time and an ethos, but which also reduces Pat to a cartoon, with incident after incident of I-threw-the-roundhouse-right-after-he-threw-the-whiskey-bottle.)

Pat spent half his time in the Regan White House trying to dodge fights, which wasn't easy. In a way he was a dead duck the day he walked in, though he did not know it. So many people who did not know him hated him! And they gave him the full treatment, leaking against him in the press and forming tongs. The first lady's people didn't like him because the first lady didn't like him because his reputation was Nixonian pugilist and that was bad press, which was bad for the president. (People like Buchanan always made her suspicious because they believed in things, which meant, to her, that they were *ipso facto* disloyal. She didn't like people whose first loyalty was to abstractions and not to Ronnie.)

Larry Speakes saw Pat as a bureaucratic threat (he feared he would eventually have to report to him); Bud McFarlane saw him as a threat to his control of foreign affairs; George Shultz didn't want him anywhere near the foreign-policy apparatus.

A few years later Shultz told me presidential speechwriting worked fine until Pat came along and ruined it because he was such a rightwinger. The odd thing is that in the more than a year that I worked with him, Pat had very little day-to-day involvement in speechwriting. Sometimes we didn't hear from him for weeks at a time, and when one of the writers was having trouble with one of Regan's aides, Pat's attitude was, "I feel for you," not "I'll fight for you." As the White House, in 1986 and '87, made a series of mistakes in election strategy and in Iran-*contra*, Pat shook his head and wrote his memos but didn't, as they say in both gangland and our nation's capital, go to the mattresses with Regan or his aides.

Recently a reporter who has been covering the White House since 1985 asked me, Why did someone as tendentious as Pat give up so easily? I told him the question had preoccupied Pat's friends, and that a number of us used to meet in Ben Elliott's office to discuss Pat Theories. Ben thought it was that Pat had grown up in a big Irish-Catholic family where he'd absorbed a sense of hierarchy and learned it's wrong to buck Dad. My Pat Theory was that he was traumatized in the Nixon White House by one H.R. Bob Haldeman. Pat probably used to write ol' H.R. Bob and R.N. colorful memos with passionate ideas and H.R. Bob would read them and send them back with one word written on the top: No. Pat got used to frustration, associated it with the White House, and when he came into this one, the first thing Regan did when he met him was put up his hand and say, "No!," and Pat thought, I'm home!

The writer told me, "During the [1987] State of the Union preparations Pat and Ken Khachigian [who had flown in from his home in California to write the address] went to a meeting of Regan's fellows in the Roosevelt Room. They were all arrayed on one side of the table, and Pat and Ken were on the other."

"That's the way they used to do it," I interrupted.

"Regan's aides were saying the kind of things for which they became famous, 'agenda for the future' and such, and Khachigian after a while paled, and Pat sat back, and then he just got up and walked out! He didn't fight them at all!"

I said, "He later said he couldn't stand listening to their Constructive Republican Alternative Proposals, which is an acronym."

I guess my Pat Theory now is: He knew that after six or seven years of a Reagan presidency it didn't really matter what words Reagan was saying, because no matter what he said, people were hearing the same thing. And fights with Regan's aides were pointless; they had Regan. So Pat turned his attention from writing to doing—to arguing that Scalia should be picked before Bork, that the president should hold to SDI at Reykjavik—and in this he was probably right.

The first administration was rocky and successful, the second rocky and less so. Why? I thought a good part of the answer came from Michael Horowitz, counsel to the Office of Management and Budget from 1981 to 1985, who met me in his law office one day in the late eighties and told me what he knew.

"It was a presidency cut in half, with two very different administrations. The first term was an inefficient, yeasty, fractious administration of high-quality people with a passion for policy and ideas. These were serious people who produced for the president on a continual basis ideas and initiatives, and who provided him with real options on tough questions.

"In the first White House you had people of real substance who had access and who could therefore afford access to the various interest and policy groups they were comfortable with. So a lot of groups felt they had play.

"Deaver covered the institution of the presidency—the media side. Meese covered the president's ideological base with his connection to the ideological communities and perspectives. Baker was running things, long-term planning and outreach to the business community, among other things.

"That was the mix. It was a real mess and it really worked and it served the president well.

"But after four years the best people were tired, and they started to bail out. And Regan came along, and he was temperamentally unsuited and unsuited in terms of experience. And he had second-rate people around him and a Cabinet older than the Politburo.

"I'll never forget [a Regan aide] told me one day, 'We're appalled at how many assistants and deputy assistants can get to the president—and no doesn't mean no, it just means you lost for now, everyone wants a second bite of the apple—and damned if they don't get it!'

"Well, he was right. But what he and the other mice did was they created a hierarchical bottleneck—and all movement stopped. And so a Bitburg could come along, and it paralyzed the entire process because it totally consumed the few people who could do anything. They didn't create order—they created paralysis."

* ★ ★ ★ ★ ★ ★ ★ ★ ★ ★ ★

ELEVEN

Ich Bin ein Pain
in the Neck

How to explain the Strasbourg speech. I wanted it to be great. It failed, utterly. I was trying to get a speech that mattered through the system. It didn't work. It wasn't a scandal, just a disappointment. And an education.

You know how boring most speeches are? Everybody dresses up nice and sits as close up front as they can, and they're excited about seeing the president or the senator or the governor. And the speaker comes in and makes a joke, and everyone laughs, and then he starts to speak from a text. And you mean to keep your mind on it, to think along with him about foreign affairs or the homeless, to see what this guy has to say . . . and after a few minutes you're thinking about lunch, what's for lunch? I wonder if he wears boxers or jockeys, I bet boxers. Meaghan's birthday's coming, is she out of toddler sizes yet?

And you're not bored, you're entertaining yourself. You knew it would be boring. They're all boring. You're not listening. Why should you? Sometimes democracy asks too much.

For Strasbourg I wanted to try for a speech that wasn't boring, that was full of a lovely sweeping candor, and energy, and spirit.

In the spring of 1985 Ronald Reagan went to Europe to attend the annual economic summit of the major industrial democracies, which was held that year in Bonn. He would also mark the fortieth anniversary of VE Day with a speech to the European Parliament at Strasbourg, France. It was the big speech of the trip.

You know what I wanted. Reagan, Reagan, Reagan, the one American poet who could sing outdoors, and torchlights down the street to the end of the world.

The opening is obvious and lovely. Go to research and tell them you want to know how the West celebrated. Keep in your mind the great photo of the sailor kissing the girl in Times Square. Get old *Life* and *Look* magazines. In Paris they swarmed onto the boulevards, rallied under the Arc de Triomphe and sang the "Marseillaise." In Rome the church bells filled St. Peter's Square and echoed throughout the city. Winston Churchill walked out onto a balcony in Whitehall and said, "This is your victory"—and the crowd roared back, "No, it is yours!" Londoners tore the blackout curtains from the windows and put floodlights on the symbols of British history, and for the first time in six years Big Ben, Buckingham Palace, and St. Paul's Cathedral were illuminated against the sky. In New York, Times Square erupted. In Washington the new president said, "The flags of freedom fly all over Europe . . . And it's my birthday too!"

Then the meaning of the war, the meaning of our alliance, some history. Then break away from full throat sentiment into hard Reaganesque arguments. Europaralysis? Young Europe's blues? Tired old socialism and its heavy hand?

Now is the time, in the eighties, to break with the past. Now is the time to get the dead hand of the state off the necks of your people, to strengthen incentives and remove the impediments to economic growth—to lower tax rates on the people and let them enjoy more of the fruits of their labor, to restrain government demands, eliminate regulatory burdens, reduce tariff barriers. . . .

"My friends, pro-growth policies in one country enhance the economic well-being of *all* the world's citizens, for when we increase the supply and the demand for goods and services in one country, all the markets of the world are enhanced. And I believe we must realize that if our young people feel powerless, part of the solution is returning to them a chance at economic power . . ."

• • •

Talk about what works, acknowledge what doesn't. Talk about democracy:

"If reality is on the side of capitalism, morality is surely on the side of democracy. But I wonder, too, if all of us still have complete faith in this fact. It seems to me the dilemma is both political and perceptual. Forty years ago we in the West knew who our adversaries were and why. But some in the West today seem confused about what is right and what is wrong . . . This terrible moral confusion is reflected even in our language. Some speak of 'East-West' tensions as if the West and East were equally responsible for the threat to world peace today. Some speak of 'the superpowers' as if they are moral equals—two huge predators composed in equal parts of virtue and of vice. . . . Some speak as if the world were morally neutral, when in our hearts most of us know it is not.

"Let us look at the world as it is. There *is* a destabilizing force in the world—and it is not the democracies of the West. There *is* a political entity which, through its enormous military power, means to spread its rule—and it is not the democracies of the West . . .

"It is the Communist system, and especially the Soviet Union, which is the principal destabilizing influence in the world today. . . ."

And take this interesting argument from John Lenczowski of the NSC:

"All of us in this room want to preserve and protect our *own* democratic liberties—but don't we have a responsibility to encourage democracy throughout the world? And not because democracy is "our" form of government but because we have learned that democracy is, in the last analysis, the most *peaceful* form of government. . . . Democracy is the institutionalization of restraint on the possibility of irresponsible behavior by governments. Democracy is the forced submission of rulers to the peaceful desires of the people. . . ."

I was trying for a draft that says some things a lot of Western leaders and thinkers and foreign-affairs specialists say when the mikes aren't on. It was all unauthorized. But it was administration policy in that it was what the president thought. Having followed his statements and career for years, having seen him in speeches and give-and-take in the EOB, I was clear about what he thought. Send it out this way; it will get changed, but the essential character may remain. Take a chance, it's worth a gamble.

I had read the State draft, of course, and chafed at its formalism, at the soul-deadening predictability of all our international communications. One odd thing about foreign-policy professionals is that for all their sophistication, they tend to think the way to communicate with allies and potential allies is to compliment and soothe, compliment and soothe. But that isn't polite, it's patronizing, and to patronize is to insult. Candor is a compliment, it implies equality; it's how true friends talk.

I crossed my fingers and sent the speech to Ben, who crossed his fingers and sent it to staffing.

Two good things happened right away. Nancy Risque, a congressional liaison person and so an expert in not giving offense to hostile powers, called and said, "Peggy, I just want you to know we always criticize speeches and we ought to say when we think something's good—and the Strasbourg speech is really great." She lowered her voice. "It's even kind of brave. I guess you'll have some problems and you'll work them out, but it's a great speech and it's courageous." My heart leaped.

Then Sandy Muir, a teacher who had taken leave to write speeches for the vice president, wrote a note that said, *This speech says things that should be said.*

Otherwise, silence. For three days. And then:

A great breaking of crockery on the West Wing walls.

George Shultz had lunch with the president and told him the speechwriters are making policy again and this has got to stop!

There was a blowup at the morning NSC staff meeting with McFarlane being told they're tired of speechwriters doing their own thing and ignoring NSC-approved State drafts and it's just time to end this garbage!

And then someone told us the NSC was rewriting the speech.

And then someone told us State was rewriting the speech.

Then people who used to say hello to me in the halls stopped saying hello.

We got a copy of a memo to Bud McFarlane written by an important NSC staffer. "The draft which has been circulated of the president's speech in Strasbourg will be an unmitigated disaster in Europe if it is delivered in this form . . . The appeal for entrepreneurship and the implicit condemnation of European state-sponsored social welfare will be seen as an attempt to inject the president into internal political struggles in Europe. . . . The attacks on the Soviet Union are too strident for European tastes."

Well, I'll tell you how I feel about European tastes. I love Europe, we all love Europe. But there's that European attitude, the snide superior smirk you get sometimes in Paris or Bonn. I have only once seen it properly responded to, by the writer P. J. O'Rourke in a 1986 essay for *Rolling Stone* about his vacation in Europe. It was the end of the trip and he was having an argument about America with a "Limey poofter" and he finally blew his stack. "We're three-quarters grizzly bear and two-thirds car wreck and descended from a stock-market crash on our mother's side. You take your Germany, France and Spain, roll them all together, and it wouldn't give us room to park our cars. We're the big boys, Jack, the original giant economy-size new and improved butt kickers of all time. When we snort coke in Houston, people lose their hats in Cap d'Antibes. . . . We drink napalm to get our hearts started in the morning. A rape and a mugging is our way of saying cheerio. Hell can't hold our sock hops. We walk taller, talk louder, spit further . . . and buy more things than you know the names of. I'd rather be a junkie in a New York jail than king, queen and jack of all you Europeans. We eat little countries like this for breakfast and shit them out before lunch."

My feeling is: They should get O'Rourke in the diplomatic corps.

A courier from NSC, a thin boy with big glasses, began shuttling across West Exec from the NSC to the EOB, bringing me pieces of rewrites. At first he was friendly.

He brought a new State/NSC draft that had been heavily rewritten. I rewrote the rewrites overnight and sent them back. They rewrote sections and sent them to me.

I was trying, but they still hated the speech. They called it shrill, they said it used the word "Communist" too many times, they said this will really turn off Parliament members who see Reagan as an idealogue. You forget, they said, that a number of them are Communists. (I didn't forget. We should talk to them too, why make believe they aren't there?) The State/NSC people were difficult. In fact, they were shrill. And one of the biggest things they amused themselves doing was changing the way things were said, as opposed to what was said. This is when I started to realize that the problem wasn't so much the speech itself as the fact that State and NSC felt control of it had been seized from them. It was also when I realized there were more bureaucratic elements at play than I'd known.

There was a meeting between the State/NSC drafters, Buchanan, and Ben, who emerged to tell me it had gone well, we'd only lost 40 percent of the speech, it could have been worse. Ben had notes on sections that had to be dropped and rewritten and sections that had to be added.

The NSC writing was done by a committee of McFarlane aides. I rewrote Friday night and Saturday and sent the speech back to them in the afternoon.

I sent it with a cover memo that soon became famous in house. They were still making photocopies months later. This is parts of it. It's long, so I've omitted sections dealing with parts of the speech I haven't mentioned.

MEMORANDUM   FOR STRASBOURG SPEECH
                       COMMITTEE
FROM: NOONAN, WRITER OF THE SPEECH
SUBJECT: Strasbourg Address

Gentlemen, this is the latest and as you read it I believe you should keep this in mind:

1) State/NSC directives on the economic section have been included. State/NSC directives on S.D.I. have been included. State/NSC directives on treaty compliance, on the suffering of a divided Europe, on Nicaragua, on the new democratic forum, and on the people of the communist countries have been included. In addition, we no longer use the "F" phrase; we no longer say Free Enterprise. We have cut down on use of the "C" word also.

2) [Your] memorandum of 11:00 a.m. this date contends that we should not call the communist system and the Soviet Union the most destabilizing force in the world. This was argued out back and forth at the 4:30 meeting Friday, and it was decided that we WOULD so characterize the Soviet Union provided we also include a section on the human suffering caused by the division of Europe. This section has been included. . . .

3) I ask you all to remember that this is a speech that attempts to communicate a sense of history, a sense of the flow of time. Just as it is appropriate that the President begin by remembering the happiness of VE Day, the horror of Europe after the war, and the triumph that

followed, it is appropriate that the President address the realities of TODAY—Europessimism, etc. This is bold—it is the kind of thing great leaders are not afraid to do. And, as most of you have noted, Europessimism is a subject among Europeans themselves.

We cannot bolster Europe and inspire her at the end of the speech if we do not paint her predicament somewhere within. My position here is dictated not only by a concern for the content of the speech but also a concern for what is known, in the field of drama, as "the unities." Drama may seem to you an odd thing to mention here, but a speech is a form of theatre.

Similarly, it is important that we be frank regarding the Soviet Union. You will note there are no empires that happen to be evil in this speech, but there is, to an extent, a clearness and candor about who and what the Soviets are. Some of Young Europe's blues is traceable to a confusion, as we note in the speech, about what threatens us and what we can do about it. The speech attempts to state who threatens us and what, together, we can do about it. I believe this is necessary to the political logic of the speech.

4) [As for] the section on a reunited Europe . . . I do not think it in the interests of the President that you dull this passage and render it insipid. I am sure this is not your intention but it will likely be the result of your endeavors, because that's what happens to rhetoric when committees vote on it.

If Ted Sorensen had had to deal with your Committee in the writing of the 1961 Berlin speech, he would have submitted for your consideration the phrase "Ich bin ein Berliner." [It] would have been edited out by the Committee and replaced with "We in the United States feel our bilateral relations with West Germany reflect a unity that allows us to declare at this time that further concessions to the Soviet Union are inappropriate."

You would not have been serving your President well with this edit. But you would have made it because a) "Ich bin . . ." was an inherently dramatic statement, and dramatic personal declaration serve as red flags to Committees (sorry I said "red," that must be the 11th communist reference in this memo); b) The Official Worrier on your Committee would have pointed out, "A statement that strong really paints us in a corner when it comes to negotiations down the road. The press'll pick up on it and use it against us in the trade talks"; and c) the Literal Mind on your Committee would have pointed out, "The President isn't from Berlin and everyone knows it. He's from Massachusetts." . . .

8) The speech has already been weakened somewhat in various ways and to varying degrees. But it still has enough spring, I think, to make

an impression. If you make serious changes now I think you will find, in time, that you have produced an address that does indeed make history but perhaps not the kind of history you intend. It will be the famous Strasbourg Hammock Speech of 1985. The speech that had a nice strong tree holding it up at one end, at the beginning, and a nice strong tree holding it up a the other end, at the coda, and in the middle there was this nice soft section where we all fell asleep.

Thank you all, and God bless you, and your children, and your children's children."

Another great breaking of crockery on the West Wing walls.

In government you don't write memos like that. It's an affront to everything, to committees, to collegiality. But there was precious little collegiality going around. And you know, I wanted them to know how I felt.

The NSC courier stopped being friendly.

I sound jaunty now, but I was afraid of those guys. It was an anxious time.

That night I had a dream. It was a hot, bright day and I was careening down a highway in a rickety old car. I couldn't control it, couldn't tell the brakes from the gas pedal; I'd put my foot down to slow down, and the car would accelerate instead. The steering wheel shook. I was hurtling toward an underpass; it was dark within; I knew I'd be sun-blinded and that as soon as I emerged from the darkness the highway would veer sharply right and left, and I didn't know which turn to take to get where I wanted to be, didn't even know if I could make the turn because it might come too soon. There were no other cars on the highway, and I felt a panicky loneliness. Suddenly I was in the backseat and it was a taxicab with an old cabdriver—and *he* was the one who couldn't control the car. There is another passenger now, a big man with steel-colored hair sitting in front, and he doesn't seem worried. I can't see his face. He is a businessman. I feel fear, but also relief that I'm not driving, and the accident is going to be someone else's fault. But I'm still going to be in it. We hurtle incompetently toward the darkness.

I awake in a sweat. Feet on the floor. Look at the time. Put on the light.

The dream is about the speech and the staffing process, and perhaps about Ronald Reagan and his administration. But it hangs like a cloud of gloom for days, and I realize it's also about something else. That I have always attached myself to big institutions where I have done good work and succeeded, but where I am always frustrated. And yet I avoid leaving—getting my own car, driving myself—and going off to do books or a column or fiction, because I am afraid of being lonely, afraid of being without the institution and its limits. I'd miss the limits: They're what I blame for not doing great work.

When things should have been calming down they heated up. There was a blowup at a morning senior staff meeting at which Bud McFarlane accused Buchanan of tricking NSC staffers—"You rolled us!"— into thinking the speech had been changed when it hadn't. "Yes it was!" said Buchanan. "No it wasn't!" said Bud.

He went off and rewrote the speech on his own.

McFarlane's minions leaked a story to *The Washington Post* using direct quotes from the meeting, which is unusual. The story painted Buchanan as a troublemaker who oversaw a combative anti-Communist speech that was more fitting for a VFW meeting in Philadelphia than the European Parliament, and who goaded McFarlane into angry words at the staff meeting.

I saw Pat that morning. He was genuinely confused.

I don't know who Bud McFarlane was. I couldn't read him at all. He has friends I respect and enemies I respect, and I never knew what to think and don't to this day. But how he talked and how he thought made a strong impression.

Here's an example. Once, in a briefing at the Geneva Summit, a reporter asked McFarlane to react to the British writer Peregrine Worthshorne's contention that deployment of an American SDI might force the Soviets into actions that would ultimately result in less freedom for the people of Eastern Europe.

Before answering it, McFarlane paraphrased the question. "The question is, a recent article by a British conservative has asserted that U.S.-SDI could lead to inducing a massive investment by the Soviet Union which implicitly deprives other accounts from receiving those investments, and in particular would place a burden on the countries of Eastern Europe whose welfare would decline."

The reporter said no, Worthshorne said their *freedom* would decline.

McFarlane seemed to ignore the correction.

"I think that first of all [Worthshorne's contention] ignores the criteria that have been set for any ultimate development of the SDI program, and that is it wouldn't be pursued at all unless it met the criterion of being cost-effective at the margin, that is, cheaper than the marginal unit of offense required to overcome it. In addition, second criteria, that it would be invulnerable; consequently, that it would be fruitless to go to an extreme to develop a system to overcome it because it would be by definition unfeasible. Now, against those two criteria, it is reasonable to assume that if we meet those, the Soviet Union would have no incentive to develop offense and to make this massive investment you imply. So if you examine how we are going to conduct this, if indeed it is conducted, the Soviet point that it will invoke this massive offensive investment simply wouldn't be sensible."

Now there are a number of things you could say about that statement. One is that it would be impossible to jump into that muddy stream of words and emerge with the fish of a thought between your teeth.

But that is its science, for the reporter who asked the question was struck dumb. He stood and stared wordlessly, like a little boy who'd lifted a heavy iron lid with a stick and is overcome by fumes of gas.

I thought, That's why Bud talks like that. He silences them with incomprehensibility. They cannot challenge him because they cannot understand him. They fall back on form and nod sagely: Ah yes, I take your point.

Later I came to see it differently. I had a hunch McFarlane decided long ago, as young people sometimes do, that intelligent people speak in an incomprehensible manner. He adopted the style. In time he was no more capable of a simple public utterance than of a private one, that when dining with his wife, he would not say, "Pass the butter" but 'The stationary oleaginous object which is now not within my grasp or the grasp of others within this administration would be desirable, though not necessary, within my sphere and on my muffin," and that this was all part of the special high of power, which makes us—all of us—blind to our buffoonery.

McFarlane's version of the speech was like McFarlane's version of conversation:

"During the 1970s we went to great lengths to restrain unilaterally our strategic weapons programs out of the conviction that the Soviet

Union would adhere to certain rules in its conduct, rules such as neither side seeking to gain unilateral advantage at the expense of the other."

Foreign-policy professionals forget that presidential speeches are not aimed only at the foreign-policy specialists on the other side. They write to the kind of people they go to dinner parties with. They forget presidential speeches are aimed at least in part at normal people with a radio or TV. That's where public opinion begins to percolate, in the living room, not Whitehall. Foreign-policy specialists forget no normal human knows what unilateral means. (A clue that a foreign-policy specialist wrote a speech: They always take time to laud the historic contribution of diplomats.)

The Strasbourg speech was a flop—not a scandal or a story, just something that didn't register. Even the TelePrompTer broke down.

I went on the trip though.

There was this:

We were driving through the streets of Strasbourg on our way to the European Parliament. It was the fortieth anniversary of VE Day, an overcast spring morning. Thin crowds line the route as the motorcade slides by. Once again: They do not know what to do. They stand and stare. We stare back through smoked windows. Sometimes they smile the embarrassed smile of the eighties.

You would hardly know it is the fortieth anniversary of us liberating them. Until, until: We turn onto the drive that will lead us to a place where we will have lunch, and the crowd thickens two or three deep, and suddenly there is a woman, an old woman who has stepped off the sidewalk. She is laughing and waving a handkerchief in the air. I lean forward. She is in her sixties; she is unselfconscious, waving gaily, welcoming the Americans. She reminds me of something—what is it? The newsreels, the young girls in the newsreels who waved their handkerchiefs and laughed as the American tanks drove through. She was one of those girls! She is remembering her joy. She is saying thank you.

She is the only person that day who seems to know what it is about.

And there was this:

It is our last night in Lisbon, which is the last city on the trip, and I have just attended the state dinner the Portuguese threw for the president. It was held in a musty old palace the socialists had attempted to make regal again. They succeeded. Tapestries on the wall, lovely paintings. This is the Portuguese: They closed the palace years ago and didn't reopen it till recently, at which time they went through room by room to see what was there, and only then did they find the crown jewels, which no one had noticed were missing.

This too is the Portuguese: At this very formal dinner where very formal waiters are serving very formal food, the waiters cannot resist the impulse to informality. They bend beside me to proffer the trays from which I will take a slice of beef, lean close and whisper, "There, take the end, oh it is good!" When they bring the wine they whisper, "You will like, wonderful Portugal sherry."

It is after eleven, and I have returned to the Ritz. In the lobby, near the elevators, I see Mike Deaver. I nod. "How did it go?" he says.

"Good, relaxed. I think good of its kind."

He nods and turns away in a hunched, hands-in-pockets way. The elevator doors open. I get in; he gets in, the doors are beginning to close . . . when a hand reaches in and forces them open. In comes Bud McFarlane with the Strasbourg Speech Committee.

From the corner of his eye he sees a blonde in black and turns to me expectantly. I smile hello. He realizes who I am and turns away, stone face. He turns to an aide and says in a voice louder than it has to be, "Remember we have to rewrite the arrival statement."

"We'll get right on it."

Then: nothing. Silence to the eighth floor. Doors open. I'm the only one getting off. I say excuse me, struggle my way from the back of the elevator thinking, *What if no one says good night?* As if that small politeness mattered, as if its absence would have significance.

And: how to walk? What's a good go-to-hell walk when a rivulet of sweat is teasing down your shoulder blades? Back straight, head straight. No, they'll think they got your back up. Slouch a little, long strides, a go-to-hell sway. As I passed through the doors and moved down the hall, I heard a faint "Good night!," and laughter.

A week later I received a letter in my office from a McFarlane aide who had been a member of the speech committee.

"Just a quick note to lay a little valedictory offering on you. No Proustian remembrance-of-things-past number this; just a modest *mise au point . . .*"

Hey, do you think he was trying to prove he is, like, literate?

"The NSC is a collegial enterprise, which prides itself on C3— clearance, coordination, co-authorship—and maybe our two floors simply had a cultural conflict: see, we couldn't even assimilate, let alone accept, a concept that seemed to posit solo performers at the center of what is pre-eminently a corporate enterprise, i.e. the formulation and dissemination of national security/foreign policy . . .

"But maybe we're wrong. Problem is, whether we are or aren't, the collegial nature of the NSC (not to say its amorphousness) is not likely to change. Nor will that of our *âme soeur* in the policy fudging business, State. But by recognizing this, you can put your own spin on the ball simply by checking with us (co-opting if you prefer) early on in the game whoever happens to be the point person and/or persons whenever texts involving foreign policy substance are at issue. . . ."

Well, you know what? He was right to a degree; there was something to what he said. But you know what doesn't fit in to "what is pre-eminently a corporate enterprise"? The only American poet who can sing outdoors.

Another thing I learned: If you are a woman and you get the boys mad they will act like baaaaaad boys and send, as a member of the speech committee did, memos that begin "You're cute when you're angry!"

They had given me a new office, a big, tall, dark office on the southeast corner of the EOB. Sig gave me some new furniture. Now, I had a big couch and a conference table and bookcases and two end tables. Outside my window I could see the West Wing entrance to the White House, and the part where the NSC offices were. I shared a balcony.

Sometimes I would be sitting there and some old man would stick his head in, shyly, and I always knew what he was going to say: "I worked here once." They always come back. Once a man in an old rumpled suit came in and shook my hand and said, "I was here for a while for Eisenhower. Do you know who had this office before us? A young secretary of the navy who liked to sit outside on the balcony on a pretty day and stare at that old white house in a manner that struck some as longingly. His name was Franklin Roosevelt."

Once a Nixon hand came by and said, "This office was Jim St. Clair's. He planned the Watergate defense at that desk. Hope you have better luck!"

They all return, they all come back, they take my hand and say good luck. They touch a table or a chair and pat it unconsciously, wave good-bye and disappear through the door. (You know what I do when I visit the White House now? I go to my old office and tell them the history, pass on the lore.)

I was getting to know Washington better, starting to realize that the true tone of the city is not, as I had thought, Aaron Copland and *Appalachian Spring,* though it had and has its *Appalachian Spring* moments. The true tone of Washington is nearer to Jefferson Starship and "They Built this City on Rock and Roll." Someday perhaps a local TV station, when it signs off at night, will use the usual Washington stills—the Iwo Jima monument, the Lincoln Memorial—but it will add, say, a clip from a rude and raucous press briefing and another from an uninhibited moment on the Hill. Something should capture the inchoate energy of the reckless, feckless, worryless Washington, the Washington of the congressman with his hand on the girl's knee at the Monocle, the Washington of the PR guy giving interviews about his dialectic to the Style section of the *Post,* of the somber, serious senators getting happily tight under a crystal chandelier. . . .

Buchanan passed to me a copy of a memo from one of the mice on his plans to revamp the speechwriting system. It said that major presidential speeches would now be prepared from an outline approved by the chief of staff "and other senior staff as appropriate."

Outlines? Outlines!

The memo said, "At the Chief of Staff's discretion he may want to review the outline with the President in advance."

That's very nice of the chief of staff.

"One of the pitfalls of getting the President his remarks earlier will mean there may be more last-minute changes when he gets his half sheets the night before the event." I underlined this sentence and sent it to Buchanan: Why is this person allowed to edit our work?

But this was the key section:

". . . the staff officer with [responsibility for the event] ought to have primary control over the content of the remarks subject to the approval of the Chief of Staff. The speechwriters should incorporate the comments of the action officer as well as other staff with expertise in specific areas. For example, comments from senior NSC or Congressional staff should have primary [say] in foreign affairs or Congressional matters when the final remarks are being prepared."

This is perfect. We lose all control, they don't know the difference between good writing and bad, the president is going to sound bad, and when someone tells the first lady he sounds bad she'll go to Regan and the mice and they'll say it's the speechwriters, there they go again.

"They do that anyway," Ben said.

A CONVERSATION WITH ONE OF THE MICE

Hi, Peggy, how are you?

Fine, thanks, David. You well?

Yes I am. Ah, the speech to the Shriners.

Yes.

Ah, have a minute to go over it?

Go over it?

Yes, for changes.

I've already received everyone's comments, but I'm not done with it. . . .

Well, I've received comments too, and why don't we take a look at it?

All right.

Good. On page one, take out paragraphs three and four.

Why?

It's our feeling that the joke in graph three isn't funny. We don't think a witticism is necessary at that point.

Who is "we"?

"We" is those who've made the decision.

What does that mean?

Can we go to page two?

No, who is we and how did they make their decision? They have a staff meeting on the president's jokes now? You all vote or what? Anyone make a joke defense or was it all joke attack?

Silence.

David, I've been doing this for a while now, for two years, and I know a little about this.

Silence.

Can we go now to page two, please, he says, in a monotone.

I began to hate the staffing process, hate the comments, the additions and deletions and questions. I wrote and circulated this:

WHAT THE STAFFING PROCESS WOULD DO
TO THE GETTYSBURG ADDRESS

~~SOMETIME AGO~~
~~LONG AGO~~
~~EIGHTY-SEVEN YEARS AGO.~~
~~Fourscore and seven years ago,~~ our fathers ~~brought~~ CREATED *and mothers*

~~forth, upon this continent,~~ **here** a new nation, (conceived in) *too much sexual imagery— sounds like we're talking about teen pregnancy*

liberty, and dedicated to the ~~proposition~~ IDEA that all men

are created equal. *by* Now we are ~~engaged~~ *fighting* in a (great) civil

war, testing whether (that nation,) or any nation so *and women*

(conceived) and so dedicated, can long endure.

what's so great about it? delete!

We are met on a great battlefield of that war. We have

come to dedicate a portion of that field, as a final

resting place for those who here gave their lives that *sounds defensive— this isn't just a photo op (is it?)*

that nation might live. It is altogether fitting and

proper that we do so. But in a larger sense, we cannot

dedicate—we cannot consecrate—we cannot hallow this

ground. The brave men, living and dead, who struggled *AND WOMEN*

here, have consecrated it far above our poor power to *this is unpresidential— Reagan doesn't have poor power*

add or detract. The world will little note nor long

remember what we say here, but it can never forget

what they did here. It is for us, the living, rather to be

dedicated here to the unfinished work which they . . .

what nation?

too negative! let's talk about what we can do!

Why highlight our troubles?

Another thing that used to get edited out was the word happy. An aide to the president hated when I'd write "I'm happy to . . ." He'd say to Ben, "Why does she always use happy, What is it with her?"

Ben told me. So I started using gay.

That was taken out too. The ban on "gay" was taken to such absurd lengths that once in a little speech congratulating the US Olympic Team a worried advance man called me up and said, "You have him use the word gaiety. I think you better strike that."

"Why?"

"It sounds like he's calling them gay."

"Listen, I want to tell you something from deep in my heart: *No it doesn't.* No one will think, *no one would ever think,* that the president of the United States would hail our Olympic heroes by accusing them of being homosexual. I promise you this."

The advance man relented. On the phone. And had the word gaiety removed from the final draft.

At this point, this is how I felt about sending a speech out into the staffing process to be commented on by presidential aides, and their secretaries and their secretaries' cousins:

I felt like a mother who was sending her children to a day-care center where they'd be abused and where the head of the center—a huge, pale-faced, stringy-haired, toothless old woman with arms like thighs and a chin like a belly—would knead their little shoulders with a mad look, with crude, gross, and grubby fingers. Crude, Gross & Grubby— the law firm that was vetting my speeches.

Sometimes we would have meetings, and the president's aides would surround the speech and stare at it. They'd poke at it with sticks. And there I'd be, speed-breathing at the conference table, hyperventilating in the Roosevelt Room.

I saw on the schedule a speech about John Kennedy to be given at a fund-raiser for the JFK Library. Typically generous of Reagan to show up at the competition's blood drive. And what a chance to speak about the Kennedy who captured the country, to try and talk about who he was. I forgot to ask for the speech, but Ben gave it to me anyway.

The president worked on the remarks and waved his speech cards at Pat Buchanan as he left that night. "I bet you love my speech, Pat!" he said, and laughed as he bounded out of the West Wing.

Minutes later he was standing in the middle of a floodlighted garden at Ted Kennedy's house, talking of his brother.

"It always seemed to me that he was a man of the most interesting contradictions, very American contradictions. We know from his many friends and colleagues, we know in part from the testimony available at the library, that he was both self-deprecating and proud, ironic and easily moved, highly literate yet utterly at home with the common speech of the working man. He was a writer who could expound with ease on the moral forces that shaped John Calhoun's political philosophy; on the other hand, he betrayed a most delicate and refined appreciation for Boston's political wards and the characters who inhabited them. He could cuss a blue streak—but then, he'd been a sailor.

"He loved history and approached it as both romantic and realist. He could quote Stephen Vincent Benét on General Lee's army—"The aide de camp knew certain lines of Greek/and other things quite fitting for peace but not so suitable for war . . ." And he could sum up a current 'statesman' with an earthy epithet that would leave his audience weak with laughter. One sensed that he loved mankind as it was, in spite of itself, and that he had little patience with those who would perfect what was really not meant to be perfect.

"As a leader, as a president, he seemed to have a good, hard, unillusioned understanding of man and his political choices. He had written a book as a very young man about why the world slept as Hitler marched on; and he understood the tension between good and evil in the history of man—understood, indeed, that much of the history of man can be seen in the constant working out of that tension. . . .

"He was a patriot who summoned patriotism from the heart of a sated country. It is a matter of pride to me that so many young men and women who were inspired by his bracing vision and moved by his call to 'Ask not . . .' serve now in the White House doing the business of government.

"Which is not to say I supported John Kennedy when he ran for president, because I didn't. I was for the other fellow. But you know, it's true: When the battle's over and the ground is cooled, well, it's then that you see the opposing general's valor.

"He would have understood. He was fiercely, happily partisan, and his political fights were tough—no quarter asked and none given. But he gave as good as he got, and you could see that he loved the battle.

"Everything we saw him do seemed to show a huge enjoyment of life; he seemed to grasp from the beginning that life is one fast-moving train, and you have to jump aboard and hold on to your hat and relish the sweep of the wind as it rushes by. You have to enjoy the journey, it's unthankful not to. I think that's how his country remembers him, in his joy.

"And when he died, when that comet disappeared over the continent, a whole nation grieved and would not forget. A tailor in New York put a sign on the door—CLOSED DUE TO A DEATH IN THE FAMILY. The sadness was not confined to us. 'They cried the rain down that night,' said a journalist in Europe. They put his picture up in huts in Brazil and tents in the Congo, in offices in Dublin and Danzig. That was one of the things he did for his country, for when they honored him they were honoring someone essentially, quintessentially, completely American. . . .

"Many men are great, but few capture the imagination and the spirit of the times. The ones who do are unforgettable. Four administrations have passed since John Kennedy's death, five presidents have occupied the Oval Office, and I feel sure that each of them thought of John Kennedy now and then, and his thousand days in the White House.

"And sometimes I want to say to those who are still in school, and who sometimes think that history is a dry thing that lives in a book: Nothing is ever lost in that house; some music plays on.

"I have been told that late at night when the clouds are still and the moon is high you can just about hear the sound of certain memories brushing by. You can almost hear, if you listen close, the whir of a wheelchair rolling by and the sound of a voice calling out, 'And another thing, Eleanor!' Turn down a hall and you hear the brisk strut of a fellow saying, 'Bully! Absolutely ripping!' Walk softly now and you're drawn to the soft notes of a piano and a brilliant gathering in the East Room, where a crowd surrounds a bright young president who is full of hope and laughter.

"I don't know if this is true, but it's a story I've been told. And it's not a bad one, because it reminds us that history is a living thing that never dies. . . . History is not only made by people, it *is* people. And so history is, as young John Kennedy demonstrated, as heroic as you want it to be, as heroic as you are."

The president was flawless, graceful and warm. Everyone told me it was a wonderful evening. It was one of the times I wished I'd been there. But the next day the president called me. After the speech Jacqueline Kennedy Onassis had walked up to him "just glowing" and said in her breathy voice, "Mr. President, nobody ever captured him like that. That was Jack."

A few days later the president received a handwritten letter. "I only wish Jack could have been there too last night," Ted Kennedy wrote. "Your presence itself was such a magnificent tribute to my brother . . . The country is well served by your eloquent graceful leadership Mr. President." He signed it, "With my prayers and thanks for you as you lead us through these difficult times." Grace meets grace.

The speech was hardly edited at all. NSC was busy with the hijacking and hostage crisis of TWA flight 847 in Beirut, and informed me only that there were too many references to JFK swearing. "Delete, not necessary."

TWELVE

"That's Not off My Disk"

By the summer of '85 I had been through the Three Phases of the White House.

The first is, "Gee these people are gonna be so smart," and you keep quiet so no one knows how dumb you are.

The second is, "Hey, I'm as bright as the other guys," and the affirmation makes you generous, the happy pride makes you nicer to the lady in the cafeteria. But you're also a little disappointed, because you wanted to learn.

The third is, "Oh my God, we're in charge?" And you start having mild anxiety attacks and talking too much.

At this point you redefine things, rearrange your concept of competence, knowing that this White House couldn't be worse than any of the others; it has it share of fools, but that's not new, and we always survive.

And you realize there isn't, as you'd thought when you were young and in school, a place full of excellence and truly superior people. There is no safe place of high merit. Because if it isn't here, it isn't.

* * *

I am at a meeting upstairs in the military situation room in the Old Executive Office Building. It is a big room, the kind a Hollywood producer would want to see before meeting with the production designer on what the *Strangelove* set should look like. The table that dominates the room is about thirty feet long and five feet wide. On the side, at each point where there is a chair, is a telephone and a little locked drawer. There is a sophisticated speaker system, a lectern with a microphone, a blank space above where maps or screens can be pulled down and displayed. Above are clocks giving the time in Washington, Moscow, and Greenwich Mean Time.

A dozen of us ring the table: Constantine Menges from the NSC, Bob Reilly from the Office of Public Liaison, Otto Reich from the State Department, a few more from State and from NSC, Ben Elliott, Pat Buchanan, me. It is a weekly meeting of midlevel administration officials on how to drum up public support for the anti-Sandinista resistance in Nicaragua.

In the spring of '85 the *contras* were as usual out in the field and going broke, and their supporters in America were as usual scrambling to think up new ways to capture the nation's interest and support. Thus the meetings, which were chaired by Pat Buchanan, though there was another who attempted to dominate, a dark-haired fellow in a crisp suit with bright eyes and a certain boyish quality.

He talked like no one I had ever heard. When he wanted to say he was not responsible for a specific memo, he snapped, "That's not off my disk." A suggested idea was a "notional," and getting something going was "ginning up." Someone suggested getting the leaders of the *contras* to go on a two-week tour of local news and talk shows in America, and he warned, "You'll never get Triple A to go along with it." I wondered what the American Automobile Association had to do with it. Later I realized he was referring to Adolfo Calero, Alfonso Robelo, and Arturo Cruz.

I leaned over and whispered to Ben, "Who's Peck's bad boy?"

"Don't you know Ollie?"

He was standing now, talking about a memo, saying things like, "And don't forget this is in accord conversation Casey-North approximately fifteen hundred this date."

Someone said something about the rebel leader Edén Pastora.

"Don't talk to me about Pastora, I'm not speaking to Pastora," he snapped.

I started to laugh. He looked at me like I was a girl.

Ollie had the sunny, undimmed confidence of a man who lacks insight into his own weaknesses. It is true you would want him in a foxhole with you because he would be brave and resourceful, and true you'd want him in the field, where he wouldn't run when the firing got heavy. But in an office, at the conference table, you just knew: That's where he'd get snookered. Metternich said it was no trick to outmaneuver those who think themselves clever, but it's hard to fool a completely honest man.

I went to the first meeting uninvited. Ollie had made it plain to Ben that he didn't want me there, Ben insisted and there I was.

I did not feel welcome; I was not supposed to. When a sensitive document was distributed, handed from one fellow to another along the table, I half stood to reach for my copy when the man next to me seemed to forget to pass it on. He looked at the paper, looked at Ollie, and said, "There is some obviously sensitive material here which, if it fell into the wrong hands, could be embarrassing or misleading. This is a whole formal-looking schedule of presidential activities that hasn't even been okayed, but if someone got a hold of it . . ."

There was silence. I sat down. Someone said, "Why don't we hand them in at the end of the meeting?" I was given a copy. Which I did not hand back in. Nor did anyone else. But the message had been delivered.

I barely said a word at the meetings. There was some I'm Tougher than You, mostly from Ollie to Otto, the man from State. Otto is a solid, low-key type, and Ollie seems to take low-key for weak: he acts at moments as if he thinks Otto's one of those cookie-pushing faggots from Foggy Bottom who don't know diddlysquat about what's happening on the ground.

He ignores me in a way that is hard to ignore, looking past me when he speaks, at the man to my right when I do. I make believe I don't notice. I am unfailingly pleasant. I am probably too pleasant. He probably thinks I'm another cookie-pushing faggot.

Ollie told a story: Recently at a big Democratic gathering a congressman with a few too many drinks in him approached Tip O'Neill and told him—Ollie stops. And looks at me. "I can't repeat what he said in front of a lady."

The men around me are embarrassed. "Come on Ollie, tell."

"Tell," I say.

Ollie, with a blank face, says, "The congressman supposedly told O'Neill, 'You're gonna lose Central America for us and they'll blame our party you fat old . . . SOB!' "

"What did the fat son of a bitch say?" I ask pleasantly.

Everyone laughs. Except Ollie, who does not answer.

I always used to wonder when I was in the White House when I would finally pass in the hall a meeting, or have a short conversation that turned out, in retrospect, to be touched by dark history—like the secretary in the office next to John Dean hearing, "Mr. Liddy is here to see you, John," or overhearing in the hall, "Don Segretti, how are you, going to see Mr. Colson?" I guess the *contra* meetings were my moment, but I wound up taking notes on how people talked.

We made a list of our assets and someone said the biggest asset was obviously President Reagan. We talked about having the president make a speech in the Orange Bowl in Miami on the anniversary of JFK's famous speech after the Bay of Pigs. There was hopeful talk that we might inspire a commitment on the part of the American people.

We were full of ideas. Getting more congressional delegations to tour the refugee camps in Honduras, getting the editor of *La Prensa* to speak before editorial boards of American newspapers and TV and radio stations. Gather together famous Democrats who supported the U.S. position on the *contras*—Ed Koch, Bob Strauss, members of the bipartisan Kissinger Commission, the CIA and NSC directors since Nixon—to meet with the president in the Oval Office and then march with him into the Rose Garden, do a quick photo, and then have a brief, pungent statement by the president reading off the names of his guests and arguing that support of the *contras* is bipartisan and necessary, then asking the Democrats to mix with reporters.

Someone suggested having the president go down to House Speaker Jim Wright's district and argue the case for the democratic resistance, ending his comments, according to my notes, with something like 'Blank miles from here is the Alamo, where brave heroes blank, and where the commander of the garrison wrote during those terrible last days blank. It is accepted wisdom to say we are less than they were and that the issues that face us are less clear, but we're not and they're not. The issues are still clear; and we are still great."

Then, on the upcoming vote to offer military assistance to the *contras:* "This is more than a vote, more than an appropriation of money. This is a sign, a declaration, a commitment. We have drawn a line in the sand: this far and no farther. The Communists and communism must be expunged from the clean, free lands of the Americas."

It is odd to see that rhetoric now, to remember my conviction only five years ago that the problem of Central America was not only of the most profound but of the most *immediate* implications, that it was the place where communism would either tragically advance north, toppling little government after little government and creating a wave of foot people, or be stopped. Perhaps that was—and is—true. But now, at the beginning of the nineties, the Sandinistas seem weak and beset, their Soviet instructors distracted, the *contras* are almost gone, the Ortegas of the world seem antique, as old-fashioned as Fidel, the Beijing spring has inspired both right and left in the West to declare communism profoundly reactionary, the rhetoric of the day is the rhetoric of peace and the theater of the day is Europe, and NATO. Or so it seems.

What we most hoped for was a live presidential address on prime-time television in the days before the congressional vote. The Senate would vote first, and if the president could speak before then, who knows? What was needed was something different, not bellicose, not "rhetoric"—a thoughtful speech addressing real questions, including, I hoped, one we had never addressed: If Cuba has been Communist for a quarter-century now and everything's pretty much okay, why are you making such a big deal about Nicaragua? What's the difference? This is the kind of question normal people have.

All we had to do was get Deaver to okay it.

The meetings proceeded twice a week for a few weeks when, suddenly, trouble: Someone has leaked information regarding disagreements between State and the NSC on the *contras.* I am anxious; I am the person from CBS. Do they suspect me? Buchanan and the man from State are looking at me. I feel guilty.

I am one of those people who always feel guilty when something bad is done. When I was a child in school and someone stole candy, I was the one who couldn't keep eye contact with the teacher. I am convinced that if I ever had to take a lie-detector test, I would fail because when asked the critical question—Did you in fact pick up a knife and attempt to kill John Smith?—all the electrical impulses in my body would jump the jump of the guilty. I don't know why this is, but let me take a stab, as it were: People talk of Jewish guilt, but it is nothing compared to Irish-Catholic shame.

I stare back. Pause. Meeting resumes. Until a few weeks later when there is a front-page exclusive by Jeremiah O'Leary in the *Washington Times:* Administration heating up *contra* support, big Orange Bowl date set, major presidential address likely, etc.

Don Regan blew up at the morning staff meeting. He is proud of his leak-proof administration and can't stand it when things like this happen. Buchanan is rattled; somehow he is always in trouble.

Mike Deaver, who did not hide his political and personal aversion for Buchanan, was said to be leaking against him most energetically in the press. (Pat later retaliated by calling Deaver "Lord of the Chamber Pot.") Now Deaver was said to be spreading word that whether the president backs Pat on his Central America stuff is a crucial test of Pat's importance. Then Deaver could perhaps see to it that Pat failed and encourage press stories on Buchanan's fall from grace. So much of it came down to personalities; so much of history comes down to who likes who.

We never found who leaked to the *Washington Times.* It could have been a fool on our side who thought he could force the White House to take action; it could have been someone who knew Regan would be infuriated by the leak and scuttle the project; it could have been someone who merely wanted to ingratiate himself with a reporter. Whatever, the leak changed the realities. There were no more meetings of the Buchanan group. Deaver rejected the idea of a speech, no doubt buttressed by polling data that said the *contras* weren't popular. We lost that vote in Congress. And Ollie, it turns out, had other ideas.

The question of the *contras* was yet another expression of the conservative/pragmatist split, the division that cleaved the administration from its first day. The ideologues versus the Republicans, the young guys versus the old guys—whatever you called it, what it all came down to was a continuing disagreement over which issues should be pursued and what actions taken.

No one wanted the *contras* to lose, no one wanted the Sandinistas to flourish, but there was plenty of disagreement on whether to devote a great deal of time and effort to the issue.

"We have to pick easy issues so he can keep rolling up victories, and maintain the air of invincibility!"

"No, pick the hard ones that count, they're what we're here for, and dammit, political capital can't be hoarded—use it or lose it!"

I usually lined up with the latter view, though not always. I understood the importance in a fiercely political town of maintaining the aura. But if a president doesn't use his popularity, if he just keeps it in a safe-deposit box and takes it out at night to marvel at how it reflects the light, he loses his power to make good change.

The pragmatists thought you couldn't win on an issue when you'd lost *The Washington Post* and the networks. The conservatives thought you could win without them—by going over the heads of the media, as it were, to the people.

All you have to do is a speech in which you clearly and frankly present your side of the argument and then anticipate what your critics will say. As a matter of fact, say it for them, state their reservations fairly and answer them. If you do it honestly and with respect—and if you're right—the people will follow.

You don't have to be afraid of the media. John Chancellor has the right to think and say what he likes, the White House has the right to disagree, and the country has the right to referee, to call a TKO or order them back to their corners.

There were real issues disagreements. The pragmatists were generally moderate liberals in the area of what is clumsily called "values." They thought, Downplay that social-issues stuff; it makes us lose more ground with baby boomers and opinion leaders. The conservatives thought no, pursue those issues, with the right arguments we can convince the majority—when we don't have it already.

The pragmatists said, That's just your agenda.

The conservatives said, That's Ronald Reagan's agenda, and he won!

Complicating the conservative-pragmatist split was Ronald Reagan himself, who seemed to allow his top aides to forget what and who he'd long been. Once at a senior staff meeting during the second administration, someone mentioned a decision and mused, typically, "I wonder what the conservatives will think?" An aide leaned forward and said, "Gee, I don't know, let's go ask the president!"

Religion was another dividing issue, a quiet one. This is a small story that highlights it. It happened after I left.

THE CONSERVATIVE AND THE
PRAGMATISTS AT THE ISSUES LUNCH

Talk about your different views of reality!

Talk about your two completely different and irreconcilable views of what the facts of America are!

Talk about Gary Bauer at the issues lunch.

It is late in the second administration, and Gary Bauer, conservative activist and domestic-policy aide to the president, is raring to go. It is Monday in the Cabinet Room, and the president is meeting with top staff for the weekly issues lunch, at which important questions and events of the previous and coming weeks will be discussed.

The preceeding Friday at 2:00 P.M. each aide had submitted, according to form, a one-page preview of the issue he wished to discuss. These were reviewed by an aide to the chief of staff, who put them in a blue binder, which was forwarded to the president for weekend review. Sometimes an aide would be asked to rewrite his submission— "I really think it would be better for you, Joe, if you remove that one sentence, because Bob might really take offense." Sometimes a submission wasn't included. Sometimes you weren't told why.

In this meeting Gary Bauer wanted to discuss a topic he thought might not be too popular with his colleagues. In order not to raise alarms he refrained from asking in his submission for any presidential action ("Please meet with," "Please send letter to"). Recently he had taken to writing out his discussion point on an issue he thought would be accepted. Then, when called on, he would ease his way into talking about the unscheduled topic he really wanted to discuss.

Today, when called upon to discuss his issue (once he had been fourth or fifth on line, but now that it was known he was not always predictable he was next to last; they often didn't get to him), he burrowed in. A child in a public school down South had been chosen as valedictorian of her class and wished, at graduation, to do a speech on the importance of God in her life. School authorities, perceiving in this a breach of the separation of church and state, said no.

"Mr. President, this is exactly the sort of issue we should be discussing . . . the right of a child in our public schools to make a simple reference to her faith and to the Lord."

As Bauer spoke, he became aware of a silence. He looked around the table. His colleagues were embarrassed for him. Here they were assembled in the White House, ready to talk about serious things like the Soviets, and here's poor Gary telling him about some little kid in East Jesus.

They started to look at each other and laugh. The tittering spread. The president looked at them. They quieted.

Sometimes at these luncheons the president did not seem to be paying all that much attention. Sometimes he pushed the food on his plate. "It's understandable," said an aide. "These meetings are usually boring." The president no longer felt free to make his views known because in the first years of the administration he would find reports of what he'd said in the next day's newspapers. The leaks had dismayed him. Now friends such as Ed Meese would help him out when someone finished with an issue. "The president will take that under advisement, thank you."

"Mr. President," said Bauer, "there's something terribly wrong when an American child is silenced for trying to say what the president says in speeches every day."

Reagan was not bored; he was listening closely. "I want to do something about this," he said. "Is there anything I can do?"

"Of course."

"Gee, I'd like to help her."

"To meet with her would be fantasic. Or you could send her a letter."

"Let's do that."

The final letter said:

Dear Angela,

I read of the events surrounding your proposed commencement address with considerable interest. Like you, I have long believed in the paramount importance of faith in God.

Angela, your actions on behalf of your religious convictions demonstrate not only the strength and passion of those convictions, but your admirable personal courage in facing those who have challenged you. I know that it is often difficult to stand up for one's beliefs when they are being harshly challenged. But as one who has seen many challenges over a long lifetime, I can assure you that personal faith and conviction are strengthened, not weakened, in adversity.

Nancy and I wish you well throughout your life. God bless you.

It was signed "Ronald Reagan."

. . .

Why the laughter at the issues lunch? And why did Gary Bauer continue when it made him look foolish in the eyes of his peers?

The men who laughed had no hostility to religion. They made sure their children went to Sunday school or mass, and if not intensely spiritual themselves, you could bet that each had along the way "had a few talks with the fellow upstairs." But they felt this issue had been settled once and for all by the Supreme Court, and there was nothing to be gained by refighting it.

There was also, I believe, a bit of ye olde class antagonism at work: These nice men in their blue suits from Brooks would be embarrassed to acknowledge it but there was something distressingly trailer park about these fundamentalists and their ferocity and their I VISITED HERITAGE VILLAGE T-shirts. Such—bumptuous credulity, such smugness. To be on their side was to play the role Fredric March played in *Inherit the Wind*, when the hero of that movie, as we all know, was Spencer Tracy.

But Bauer saw an America in which the habit of religion has been removed from public life, in which the innocent expression of religious sentiment is banned by lawyers wielding documents the way Carry Nation waved her ax, to separate daily life from the grip of . . . spirits!

He thought that a seemly tolerance is in order, that religion after all tends to be a civilizing force, that those who worship intellectual achievement and man-made systems had been allowed to push their "fastidious disdain" down the nation's weary throat. He thought the administration was insufficiently alive not only to a legitimate issue of fairness and justice but a significant political reality: Show some identification with this sector of the electorate, and you'll awaken a lion.

But what was the nature of that lion? The men around the table who laughed feared the unleashing of the John Browns with all their crazed certitude, the unleashing of the profoundly illiberal impulses of—well, after all, this *is* the nation where Elmer Gantry was drawn from real life!

They didn't want to once again have to defend their administration to Elizabeth Drew and have that intelligent woman look at them with a sniff, didn't want to have to get on the shuttle to make a speech and see some guy from *Nightline* who'd say, "Well you guys lost New York this week!," didn't want to go to the barbecue with the neighbor who's a lawyer who stands poking the hot dogs and asking, "Why you people have to make appeals to those—those narrow-minded little people with a rather impressive history of anti-Semitism and racism, I'm really surprised you're on their side," and so on.

But when Bauer looked at those who would like to use a public schoolroom for Bible study after school hours, or put a crèche on the public square, he saw America, the America we've always been until things went crazy, an America of decent, undemanding people who'd been stunned and disoriented by the Carry Nations and *their* crazed certitude.

In a way it was a disagreement about what kind of behavior is narrow-minded, and who is narrow-minded, and what narrow-minded is.

The conservatives were sometimes embarrassed by their own constituency. The pragmatists were embarrassed by the funny feeling they got sometimes at 3:00 A.M.: If I'm on the side of liberality and openness, why am I on the side that's doing the not allowing?

You could see the conservative/pragmatist split here too, in a meeting Ronald Reagan held with members of the conservative community during the second administration.

The meeting, in the Roosevelt Room, followed an angry telephone conversation between the presidential aide Ken Duberstein and Paul Weyrich of the Free Congress Foundation. Duberstein, an affable and highly regarded Republican political operative, had been brought back to the White House after the departure of Donald Regan. He had run the White House congressional liaison operation in the first administration, where he had enjoyed considerable success.

Now, after a string of recent White House failures—Daniloff, Iran-*contra*, the failure to capitalize on the public support of Oliver North following his testimony, the Bork debacle—conservative frustration had reached such a pitch that the Weyrich-Duberstein phone call had ended with the former hanging up on the latter.

Duberstein reported to the president on the phone call and the president decided to call Weyrich and hear his criticisms firsthand.

Weyrich had given it to him both barrels. (Weyrich is a man not undone by presidents and princes; his commitment quite defeats any impulse he might have to defer.) He told friends after the call, "I have good news and bad news. The good news: The president is not senile. He was vigorous and sounded fully engaged by the topics discussed. The bad news is that he is almost completely misinformed; the worst news is that he does not know this and appears to doubt it."

The president agreed to Weyrich's request for a meeting with conservative activists, who decided to devote the hour to three topics; the *contras*, SDI, and Mozambique.

The mood: the conservatives were both feisty and hopeful. They had never got over their love for Ronald Reagan, and would never forget that when no one in the country would go against the current wisdom it was he alone of national politicians who'd held true. On the other hand they'd known him for years and shrugged: You know how he is.

The presidential aides with whom they'd meet were also conservative. But they had spent a lifetime on the Hill. The small *c* conservatives believed that action must follow consensus. The big *C* Conservatives said consensus follows action. (Moreover, they said, You guys don't even try to build consensus, you just hope to find it in the polls!)

The small *c* conservatives had been doing yeomans' work on the Hill when conservative ideas there didn't have a chance. Their way of operating had been forged in defeat; Republicans come of age during Vietnam and Watergate, they were used to losing, and saw part of their job as limiting the loss. Dammit, they thought, I was doing the hard work of politics when you guys were sitting around writing think pieces for Dysentary! You guys were playing with theory while I was up to my ass in the art of the possible with Bobby Byrd!

Each side felt unappreciated by the other. Each side was right. Thus the epithets, spoken in private: Reactionary! Unprincipled hack! Dammit, if it weren't for us you never would have gotten your precious tax cuts through Congress! Dammit, if it weren't for you we would have had a realignment!

Howard Baker and his men approached the Roosevelt Room in one long sigh. First we get beat up by Jim Wright, now we get beat up by Jim Right!

The Conservatives had fielded a worthy crew: the scientist Robert Jastrow, with his quick Columbia University brightness; the activist Grover Norquist; the philanthropist Bob Krieble, a man with a genuinely serious mind who could discourse with sureness on anything from Adam Smith to the history of helium; William Kennedy, publisher of the *Conservative Digest;* and Huck Walther of a conservative defense committee.

Into the room marched the president, accompanied by Duberstein, Howard Baker, Frank Carlucci, Paul Laxalt (the president's unofficial liaison to the right; if the meeting degenerated, it would be Laxalt, respected on both sides, who could say as no one else, "Now boys . . ."), and Caspar Weinberger.

The president opened the meeting without three by five cards. "This is your meeting. We wanted to get together and discuss some of your concerns."

Two Conservatives talked about the *contras*: The White House had missed an opportunity to get *contra* aid when it refused to move after the public ground swell of support after Ollie North's testimony.

The president answered, But public opinion wasn't behind more *contra* aid even after Ollie's testimony. "Dick Wirthlin's polls—and he's the best, most accurate pollster in the country—showed that we didn't have the popular support even after Ollie."

When the president had made just this point to Weyrich a week before, Weyrich had answered, "If public opinion was the decider in this country you'd have gun control and prayer in the schools. In fact, public policy is driven by small, concentrated, highly motivated groups of activists who focus their political energies on these questions. If you had moved, we would have moved—and we would have won."

Now someone answered the president saying the popularity of Ollie North's position was better illustrated by the football stadiums full of people who were stopping the game and cheering when planes came overhead with banners saying OLLIE FOR PRESIDENT—that a point had been reached at which every marginal vote, every swing vote, would have swung our way, where every senator with his finger in the wind would have felt a hurricane!

We had the votes, we could have won, said a participant.

Your vote-counters don't know what they're doing, they've been historically bad, said another.

The back and forth was vigorous. The president promised to keep in touch on strategy.

On SDI, a participant said, Mr. President, you ought to announce you're going for immediate deployment of SDI. If JFK had said, "We're going to research going to the moon," he never would have gotten funding, not to mention support. You ought to say we're going to have a defensive shield that will stop incoming missiles before this decade is out.

The president shook his head. Again, he said, I have to note that we just lack public support for SDI.

Jastrow leaned forward: *No one goes to the barricades for research funding!* Tell the people over and over what SDI can do, how it can protect us, and tell them we're going to deploy at least some parts before the decade is out.

The secretary of defense turned to the president. "There is of course the argument that the Soviets are simply trying to slow us down long enough to get their SDI in place. I don't mean to suggest they're doing it consciously, but by holding up strategic defense, the Democrats in Congress are doing the work of the Soviet Union for them. I don't mean to say they're doing it consciously, but—"

"Well, I will," said Reagan. Everyone laughed. (Reagan the paradox, cautious in strategy and incautious in his comments. Why does he say these things? If he really feels the Democrats are helping the Soviets, why doesn't that add a sense of urgency to his position on SDI? And if he doesn't think it, why does he say it?)

Now the presentation of the youngest person there, Grover Norquist, thirtyish, Harvard-educated, a free-lance Conservative operative.

With ten minutes to brief his first president, Grover had called around to friends who had worked in the White House and asked, How do I keep his attention on a subject he may not find naturally interesting? The day of the meeting he gave a presentation in which the president was forced to look at a picture, read a short letter or respond to a question. All this not so much so Grover would keep his attention, but so the president's staff would notice he'd kept his attention. "I wanted them to know the president had heard my arguments and would remember them, so they'd have to take that into account when they discussed Mozambique with him."

He captivated the president with a kind of show-and-tell on Mozambique—that the governing party is Marxist-Leninist; President Chissano is a Communist. You may have been given the impression by the State Department, which tends in its worldview to assume a black African is too dumb to be a Communist, to think that's only for white Europeans—you may have been given the impression that the people of the Mozambique government are not serious. But they are.

But there is a strong opposition, he said, a guerrilla army with twenty-two thousand men under arms, the fastest-growing anti-Communist insurgency in the world. It is pro-democratic and pro-Western in its outlook.

"Sir, this is a picture I took of one section of a very large official government mural that is placed very prominently on the highway between the airport and Maputo, the capital. The mural is placed alongside the Plaza of Heroes, which every person who enters Mozambique must pass as he leaves the airport. As you can see, this part of the mural shows a white man with a Star of David very prominent on his military cap. He is strangling and manacling a young black man. The message is obvious: Zionism is the enemy."

He handed the photo to the president.

"Mr. President, the government of Mozambique has picked up all the Soviet Union's bad habits, from concentration camps to secret police to anti-Semitism. These are decisions and positions the Soviets tell them to take. By the way, I asked a high official of the government why anti-Semitic art is part of an official government poster. He said, 'Oh, the artist did that.' "

Reagan was studying the eight-by-ten color glossy.

"Mr. President, did anyone ever tell you of this mural?"

"No."

"Well, Mr. President, you can't miss it."

The president asked if he could keep the photo. At that point, for the first time in the meeting, Weinberger, Carlucci and Howard Baker picked up their pencils and wrote on their white White House pads.

"Mr. President, they have East Germans running the secret police, and you know and I know who East Germans are: They're Nazis without the charm."

The president laughed. Howard Baker wrote on his pad, "Nazis without the charm." He underlined it.

The president said, "Well, I fought the Communists years ago in the Screen Actors Guild, and I understand them." He told a story of how he had to carry a gun for a year. He said there was a plan by some of the Communists in the union to throw acid in his face so he'd never be able to work in pictures again.

"Well, they were successful," Weyrich said dryly. "You haven't made a picture in years."

Everyone laughed, and stood to leave. Norquist walked around the table to the president.

"Sir, when you meet with President Chissano in October, keep one thing in mind: Chissano used to be the head of security in Mozambique, and in that capacity he once had one of his lieutenants murder his own father in front of a thousand government troops to teach them what revolutionary discipline really means. Do you know how the man killed his father?"

Reagan shook his head. Norquist drew an imaginary dagger from his belt, pointed it toward the president's abdomen and traced up and over.

The president winced and stepped back.

"So remember," said Norquist, "when you meet with Chissano: plastic cutlery."

You've noticed that in some of the stories in this book there are three little words that pop up, "Dick Wirthlin's polls."

I am going to break into "seriousness" here, and I'm afraid this may seem dull because it starts with things you know. But it may end with things you don't, so stay with me.

Polls are the obsession of every modern White House and every political professional, Republican and Democratic, I know. In every political meeting I have ever been to, if there was a pollster there his words carried the most weight because he is the only one with hard data, with actual numbers on actual paper.

Everyone else has an opinion; the pollster has a fact.

Every modern president has kept an eye on his approval ratings, but in the eighties it reached critical mass. When I left the Reagan White House I felt that polls are now driving more than politics, they are driving history.

There is nothing wrong with taking the temperature of the electorate in order to know how the people of a vast nation feel about an issue. Lincoln himself said, "Public opinion is everything," and he might have appreciated having such a sophisticated tool to help guide him in how to achieve an objective.

But we would like to think—in fact, we know—that he would not have used polls to tell him whether to pursue the objective, or whether it was worth pursuing.

In our time leaders throughout the government are advised by their aides to fight for something or not fight for it depending on the chances of victory as suggested by the polls.

This is not so bad, you say—at least it means leaders are tied directly to the will of the people, which is what pure democracy is. But no it's not. Pure democracy is a constant argument, an unending tug of war over what is right and how and whether to achieve it.

One of the reasons Lincoln was great is that he would have looked at the data presented by his pollster and said something like, "I see they're against the war, so I guess I'll have to communicate the argument for keeping the Union together better than I have." He would not have said "Gee, they're against it—guess I better not spend my capital on a losing game just to help the Negroes!"

The chief tool of the pollster looking for an in-depth sense of the views of the people is the focus group. A modern focus group is, simply, a group of a dozen or so citizens invited to attend a meeting at which they are asked to answer questions regarding their feelings on public issues as honestly as they can, and for which they're often paid a nominal fee.

There is a focus-group leader who asks questions—Do you know who the *contras* are and what country they're in? How do you feel about them? Does Michael Dukakis seem to you to be an honest person? Does it seem that he knows what he's talking about?

As the people answer and comment, the proceedings are quietly videotaped, so political professionals back in Washington can view the people at their leisure. They put a great deal of store in what they see. It's one of the few times they get to see "the people." They live Washington lives, they're not out there.

All this may sound benign, and in some ways it is.

But it also means: Do you know who's in charge now in America? The guys who sat around in Paddy Chayefsky's *Marty* saying, "I don't know, Marty, whatta you wanna do?"

The pollsters, conveying the words and will of Marty and the guys, seem like populists—Hear the voice of the people!—when in fact they are missing a few essential elements.

Marty and the guys *themselves* know you can't find out from the people what to do about, say, the drug problem, because they don't know. That's what they pick leaders for, to come up with answers. Do they have opinions? Sure, and they'll share them. They'll also tell you, "But I haven't spent my life studying this."

The fact is, if you stopped time and pulled them out of the dialogue in the luncheonette and told them the impact of what they're saying, they'd say, "Ya mean we're in charge? Then something's screwed up!"

And if perchance, oh, Edmund Burke happened to stroll in and say,

"Your representative owes you not his industry only, but his judgment; and he betrays you instead of serving you if he sacrifices it to your opinion," Marty and his friends would most likely say, "You got that right, Bubba."

There's more. A focus group in 1863 would have backed a negotiated peace with the Confederates. A focus group in 1963 would have frowned on Martin Luther King, Jr., taking to the streets of Birmingham. Focus groups can communicate opinion, but they cannot tell you what is right.

And is even the opinion they convey "right"? The dynamic of a focus group is like that of any group: People sometimes act as if they have an opinion when they really don't but think maybe they should, or get pulled along a little by the fellow who speaks with sureness. A lot of what gets said reflects momentary swirls of culture and style and what they overheard on TV.

It is not only the men around modern leaders who are in the thrall of polls and popularity ratings. The press too trumpet these ratings; they are believed by everyone in Washington to mean something. When asked if a public figure is doing well, it is not unusual for a Strobe Talbot to say on a *Washington Week*, "Yes, he has very high approval ratings." The media's approval buttresses the pollster's standing.

The aides are like this because they know their principals want to be liked, and it's always nice to be able to offer proof—hard data!—of the electorate's ardor. But they also do it for history: They do it so history will say their presidents were popular, because they think popularity equals success.

And here's the funny thing: History won't be fooled. If Lincoln had ended a war to please the people, history would not call him a giant— though yes, his popularity ratings in the spring of '63 would have been considerably higher, and Mrs. Lincoln might have been in a better mood more of the time.

Here's the final funny thing: Being led by the polls isn't practical. Because when you rule by the polls, the people can finally tell. The fact is it's practical to do what you think is right and keep talking to the people honestly about it. It's practical to believe in something. Because the people can tell. They're distracted but they're smart, and they can tell as time passes when you're sincere and led by principle.

And they honor these things even if they can't always articulate their approval at focus-group meetings.

THIRTEEN

Challenger

The Irish have a certain affinity for death, an interest in talking about it and thinking about it. I mean of course the real Irish, not these big, beefy blonds of no known ethnic origin, but Irish-Americans who still bear the mark of their ancestral pains and habits. They used to say the Irish like wakes because they serve whisky, but I think they liked them because the blunt finality of death jolted them out of their normal everyday depression. Life is for some of them so serious that it cheers them up to remember it will end. Also, the Irish are often nervous about having the appropriate face for the occasion. They have to be happy at weddings, which is a strain, so they get depressed; they have to be sad at funerals, which is easy, so they get happy.

My generation has suffered a lot of abstract deaths, the deaths of leaders and singers and soldiers, but most of us still have our parents and brothers and sisters. In the most personal way death hasn't become real for us yet. When it does, in the nineties, it will affect our art and culture and the themes of our plays, and I suspect it will be another force that turns us toward religion, and belief. (No one has lived for and been immersed in the ephemera of the entertainment era like my generation; when that energy is channeled into other, more interesting things, it may well be dazzling.)

I love eulogies. They are the most moving kind of speech because they attempt to pluck meaning from the fog, and on short order, when the emotions are still ragged and raw and susceptible to leaps. It is a challenge to look at a life and organize our thoughts about it and try to explain to ourselves what it meant, and the most moving part is the element of implicit celebration. Most people aren't appreciated enough, and the bravest things we do in our lives are usually known only to ourselves. No one throws ticker tape on the man who chose to be faithful to his wife, on the lawyer who didn't take the drug money, or the daughter who held her tongue again and again. All this anonymous heroism. A eulogy gives us a chance to celebrate it.

It was a pretty morning. It was relaxed. There was no big work pressing on me. The biggest recent personal drama for me was giving up smoking. I had for years been afraid that if I couldn't smoke I couldn't write, so intertwined were they. (I told a friend who is a writer, "But I need it at the typewriter." She said, "Maybe it's a good thing to need something while you write.") I'd stopped three months before, had written nothing worthwhile since, and hoped to snap out of it.

Ben had brought his daughter, Meredith, to work. She ran from office to office, tripping gaily as some children do. She was seven years old and happy and sensitive. She looked like girlhood pictures of Grace Kelly.

I was on the phone with a friend. The TV a few feet away was, as always, on, at the moment tuned to CNN, which was covering a space shot live. The shuttle was going up. I was laughing at something the person on the other end was saying when Nancy Roberts, Ben's assistant, came rushing in.

"Something happened to the shuttle. They think it blew up."

"What?"

The TV screen is blue with a trail of white smoke. Pieces of something are falling through the sky.

"What? What happened?"

"They think it blew up!"

Meredith walked in softly. "The teacher is on it," she said. "Is the teacher all right?"

The silence on TV is broken by a newscaster who knows as much as we do. You know it's bad when they don't know more. It's clear from the broken trail of smoke and the debris falling through the air that something terrible has happened. You know from the sound and look of things that everyone is gone.

Meredith walks over and puts her hands on my armrest. She watches, fascinated. Her face says; This isn't bad, is it? I am breathing as I did when the pope was shot, and Reagan. It is like the sixties, and This is a Special Report. I do what CBS trained me to do: handle the horror by writing the show.

"Tell your father I'm writing the president's remarks."

I press a plastic button on the IBM word processor; the screen lights up, the buzz begins.

Things to cover: update on the situation—are they dead, search continues? I need a cigarette.

Dick Darman's on the line from Treasury.

Dick.

Is he going to speak? Are you writing it?

Don't know but assume so, and yes.

Good. Every grade-school child in America was watching, and older students too, did you know that?

No, but Ben's daughter was here upset.

Well, my sons were watching. The president has to speak to the children and reassure them that the world isn't ending and that there is both inherent purpose and danger in scientific exploration.

I know.

It's very important.

I got it, Dick, thanks.

Karna Small, Bud McFarlane's assistant from the NSC, calls.

I was with the president at the meeting with network anchors for the State of the Union, she says, and I took notes on what he said.

Oh God, thanks. Send 'em over.

"What can you say," her notes quote him, "it's a horrible thing. I can't rid myself of the thought of the sacrifice of the families of the people on board. I'm sure all of America is more than saddened. . . ."

Q: Do you think it was right to have a citizen on board?

"They're all citizens—all volunteers. That is the last frontier, the most important, the space program has been most successful. We've become so confident that this comes as such a shock. . . ."

Q: Who brought the news to you?

"We were all sitting there [Oval] preparing for your questions when the Vice President and Admiral Poindexter came in and said they had received a flash that the space shuttle had exploded—we then went to see the TV [to the study] saw the replay—it was just a very traumatic experience.

Q: Do you take comfort in the fact that we have not lost as many as the Soviets?

"We all have pride in that, but it doesn't lessen our grief."

Q: What can you say to the children to help them understand?

"Pioneers have always given their lives on the frontier. The problem is that it's more of a shock to all as we see it happening, not just hear about something miles away—but we must make it clear [to the children] that life goes on.

Q: But how do you feel about the teacher?

"I can't put out of my mind—her husband and children—the others [other astronauts] knew they were in a hazardous occupation . . . but here, your heart goes out to them."

A call from the West Wing—the president can't go on until the search is suspended, but we need the remarks as soon as possible, keep it short, five minutes. . . .

I'm done. Type it up. Three copies, quick. And tell Buchanan we're coming.

A meeting with Buchanan and the mice. Pat reads quickly, nods. "Terrific, let's go." Dennis shakes his head. (Pat said later, "Did you see how he held it? Like a dog had relieved himself on it!") I need a cigarette.

Into a larger meeting in Mr. Regan's office, all of us plus the chief plus Larry Speakes. Speakes reads and looks at me; his face is sensuous and dumb.

"Ah don't know if you get across that the space program continues."

Mmmmm, I say, nodding. "Uh, well, actually we do have here 'We'll continue our quest in space. There will be more shuttle flights and more shuttle crews . . . Nothing ends here—our hopes and our journeys continue.' "

"Well ah read it and ahm not sure you made it clear to me."

Well I didn't have crayons. "Maybe we can ask the president to punch up that graph."

"Ah guess."

No one is pleased, but there is no time to rewrite. I am depressed. I failed when the whole country needed something and we actually could have helped. Buchanan kept saying, "This is really good," but he was always odd man out.

They got the speech to the Oval Office. The president came on the air looking . . . unsure.

"Ladies and gentlemen, I had planned to speak to you tonight to report on the State of the Union, but the events of earlier today have led me to change those plans. Today is a day for mourning and remembering.

"Nancy and I are pained to the core by the tragedy of the shuttle *Challenger.* We know we share this pain with all of the people of our country. This is truly a national loss.

"Nineteen years ago almost to the day, we lost three astronauts in a terrible accident on the ground. But we have never lost an astronaut in flight. We have never had a tragedy like this. And perhaps we have forgotten the courage it took for the crew of the shuttle. But they, the *Challenger* Seven, were aware of the dangers—and overcame them, and did their jobs brilliantly.

"We mourn seven heroes—Michael Smith, Dick Scobee, Judith Resnik, Ronald McNair, Ellison Onizuka, Gregory Jarvis, and Christa McAuliffe. We mourn their loss as a nation, together.

"To the families of the Seven: We cannot bear, as you do, the full impact of this tragedy—but we feel the loss, and we are thinking about you so very much. Your loved ones were daring and brave and they had that special grace, that special spirit that says Give me a challenge and I'll meet it with joy. They had a hunger to explore the universe and discover its truths. They wished to serve and they did—they served us all.

"And I want to say something to the schoolchildren of America who were watching the live coverage of the shuttle's takeoff. I know it's hard to understand, but sometimes painful things like this happen—it's all part of the process of exploration and discovery—it's all part of taking a chance and expanding man's horizons. The future doesn't belong to the fainthearted, it belongs to the brave. The *Challenger* crew was pulling us into the future—and we'll continue to follow them.

"I've always had great faith in and respect for our space program— and what happened today does nothing to diminish it. We don't hide our space program, we don't keep secrets and cover things up, we do it all up front and in public. That's the way freedom is, and we wouldn't change it for a minute.

"We'll continue our quest in space. There will be more shuttle flights and more shuttle crews and, yes, more volunteers, more civilians, more teachers in space. Nothing ends here—our hopes and our journeys continue.

"I want to add that I wish I could talk to every man and woman who works for NASA or who worked on this mission and tell them: Your dedication and professionalism have moved and impressed us for decades, and we know of your anguish. We share it.

"There's a coincidence today. On this day 390 years ago the great explorer Sir Francis Drake died aboard ship off the coast of Panama. In his lifetime the great frontiers were the oceans. And a historian later said, "He lived by the sea, died on it, and was buried in it." Today we can say of the *Challenger* Crew: Their dedication was, like Drake's, complete.

"The crew of the space shuttle *Challenger* honored us by the manner in which they lived their lives. We will never forget them, nor the last time we saw them—this morning, as they prepared for their journey, and waved good-bye, and "slipped the surly bonds of earth" to "touch the face of God."

It went almost as written. The staffing process had no time to make it bad. The worst edit, which Ben fought off—in fact it was the worst edit I received in all my time in the White House—was from a pudgy young NSC mover who told me to change the quote at the end from "touch the face of God" to "reach out and touch someone—touch the face of God." He felt this was eloquent. He'd heard it in a commercial. I took it to Ben and said, I'll kill, I'll kill, I'll kill him if this gets through. Ben, alarmed, assured me he would explain if pressed that you don't really change a quotation from a poem in this manner.

When the president finished, he looked lost. I knew: He didn't like what he was given.

Darman called. "Perfect."

The next morning there was a deluge. Secretary Shultz called me, Admiral Poindexter, Senator Chafee. Ann Higgins sent up telegrams. A man sent words for a song, "They left us looking heavenward." Charles Jones, the manager of the White House mail section, wrote, "I have worked in the mail section for 31 years. This is the first time that I have written to a staff member. Please excuse the intrusion, but I want to congratulate you on a great speech."

"Operator One, is this Miss Noonan? Please hold for the president." They always sound so happy, as if they're giving you a gift.

"Peggy? Well, I just wanted to say thank you for your wonderful remarks yesterday."

"Oh, Mr. President, thank you."

"Well, they were just wonderful."

"Well, it was from you. They sent me notes from what you said."

"You know, the funniest thing. I did the remarks, I read them and then at the end I just had this feeling that I'd failed. I thought that I'd done badly and I hadn't done justice. And of course I was so sad about what had happened. And I got off the air and I thought, Well, not so good. But then I got these calls and telegrams. . . ."

"I heard."

"An avalanche. And I guess, you know, it did work, and I didn't know it."

"I did something that may have put you off your stride. I forgot to write God bless you, as you always say at the end. And you were on the air and maybe sensed something was missing and couldn't think exactly what."

"That little poem, that Magee. I hadn't heard that in years, but of course I knew it from years back, the war. And I think it was written on a sort of tablet or plaque outside Patti's school that I took her to when she was a young girl."

My secret: I *knew* he knew that poem. It was precisely the kind of poem he would have known, from the days when everyone knew poems and poets were famous, everyone knew Robert Frost and Carl Sandburg. It had been popular during the war. Flyers could recite it.

"Could you send me a copy? And maybe I could read the whole poem at the prayer breakfast next week."

"Good, I'm doing those remarks. Thanks for calling, and don't worry about your delivery yesterday. If you felt sad maybe that was the right way to look. It was a sad day. And you comforted everybody."

I wanted to say: You know, I didn't have a cigarette.

That afternoon I got a call from a Hollywood press agent who said, "It's funny the president used that poem in the speech, because it was read the other night from beginning to end by Claire Trevor, you remember her, at a little party for Tyrone Power, Jr. 'High Flight' was one of his father's favorite poems—in fact, the day Ty Senior came home from the war, that night Gary and Rocky Cooper had a little party for him and they invited Ronnie, the president, and Jane, who was his wife, of course. And Ty Senior recited from memory 'High Flight.' He carried it with him all through the war—he was an air-force flyer you know—and he could recite it by heart. When he died Laurence Olivier recited it over his grave. Anyway, the president reading it brought back so many memories of the old days. Would you say hi to him and remind him of Ty reading it?"

Sure, I said, and wrote a memo.

A few hours later I got a call from a gossip columnist for the *New York Post.* He'd just had a call from an agent and wanted to know if it was true the president quoted "High Flight" because Ty Power read it to him years ago and he never forgot it? And then Claire Trevor read it at a party the other night and the president heard about it?

Not really, I said, not really.

December 16, 1985

He stands alone at the lectern in the front of the hangar and looks at the families. A stricken look crosses his face. It rattles him to see pain that cannot be helped. If he had been a *Titanic* survivor he would have rowed his lifeboat straight for the men flailing in the water, but he would have turned away and refused to look when the great ship went down.

He doesn't go to the funerals of his friends. But now, forced by duty to look anguish in the face, he does so, and the effect on his pale features is more eloquent than words.

He clears his throat and stumbles. "We are here in the name of the American people—the passing of American soldiers killed as they returned from difficult duty abroad. . . ."

Days before, a transport plane loaded with 248 soldiers of the 101st Airborne coming home for the holidays had crashed on takeoff in

Gander, Newfoundland. They'd been on a peacekeeping tour in the Mideast, and when they left Cairo they were singing raucous Christmas carols. Now all were dead. This was their memorial service.

Reagan wanted to comfort, but what could he say? There is no comfort, and there was so little time. But I knew Reagan was thinking what America was thinking: *God, all those young men. And their families getting the news at Christmastime.*

There are no words that can cut such grief, but words can convey meaning, and meaning lessens horror. A death in battle derives its meaning from big things—duty, honor, country, personal bravery and sacrifice. But at Gander they died in an accident. The plane malfunctioned; it was just one of those things. And so many of the boys were young, nineteen, twenty years old, old enough to fight but not old enough, many of them, to have become fully enmeshed in life, to have a wife and a baby and the wallet with the picture from Sears.

Most soldiers still are working-class boys and middle-class boys, and their parents had them when they were young. The affluent wait till their thirties, but the nonrich have kids at seventeen and twenty-four. So the parents would be in their forties and early fifties, and this would be for some of them the first great loss of their lives, the first great trauma.

Another thing about class and the death of children: The rich grieve for what they didn't say, the poor for what they said. A generalization, I know, but it's what I've seen, I think. Imagine a small apartment in Knoxville where two parents sit, concussed, and sob over all that unfinished love: What was the point of those twenty years, what was the point of that life, those Christmases, those angry words?

But there was a point. There was a reason for all those awkward embraces, that baby's laugh. That wasn't something wasted, that was a gift. And gifts don't go for nothing to nobody.

Reagan believes in God. He says it so often—"Well, I don't mind saying I had a little talk with the fellow upstairs"—that you think it's a line, but it's not. God is real to him, part of the picture. Or the picture. "Or the artist."

And to believe in God is to receive a kind of coherence. God gives us his children to take care of, but when he takes them back it is to a place that is huge and comforting and full of love, love that goes through you like an X ray, an X ray you can feel. Those fleeting moments when we feel in life a pure happiness: they are a kind of unconscious apprehension of heaven.

Reagan doesn't see it all as pointless; Reagan sees meaning, but a meaning we do not and cannot fully understand.

And so he said:

"Tragedy is nothing new to mankind, but somehow it's always a surprise, [it] never loses its power to astonish. Those of us who did not lose a brother or son or daughter or friends are shaken nonetheless. . . . We cannot fully share the depth of your sadness, but we pray that the special power of this season will make its way into your sad hearts and remind you of some old joys.

"Remind you of the joy it was to know these fine young men and women, the joy it was to witness the things they said and the jokes they played, the kindnesses they did and how they laughed.

"You were part of that, you who mourn: You were part of them. And just as you think today of the joy they gave you, think for a moment of the joy you gave them, and be glad. For love is never wasted, love is never lost; love lives on and sees us through sorrow. From the moment love is born it is always with us, keeping us aloft in the time of flooding and strong in the time of trial. . . .

"And so we pray: Receive, O Lord, into your heavenly kingdom the men and women of the 101st Airborne, the men and women of the great and fabled Screaming Eagles:

"They must be singing now, in their joy, flying higher than mere man can fly, as flights of angels take them to their rest."

"Flights of angels . . ." of course, from *Hamlet.* "In their joy," like "in his joy" from the JFK speech, is from James Agee's *A Death in the Family.* They're the words the mother wanted put on her husband's tombstone because it was how he was taken and how he would be remembered.

After the speech, the president and Mrs. Reagan did the remarkable thing they began that was so comforting for the families. They walked from the lectern down to the audience, and one by one they embraced each mourner. They had a word for everyone. A pregnant woman sobbed; another showed a picture of her son. The president came face-to-face with an old black man who had been standing shakily as the president neared him. For a moment they looked at each other. The president moved toward him, and the old man leaned against him and put his head on the president's shoulder. The president held him, as if he were trying to absorb the old man's pain.

The mourners were not afraid. They didn't doubt that they deserved a president's attention. They knew Reagan in their hearts. They knew he was happy to help them. They knew it doesn't matter if he goofs off sometimes, hell, I goof off too, it matters that he knows how I feel about my son who died in the army of our country. And he knows.

Reagan embodied; he became the nation holding you, he was the nation hugging you back, and there was nothing phony about it, nothing careless.

Those mournings in the hangar in the eighties did more than comfort the families of the dead. They released the nation from a style of mourning that had dominated since the sixties—the stoicism mania, begun by the Kennedys as they buried their husbands and fathers blank-faced, dry-eyed, and dignified. It set a style the middle class adopted. (The effects of the repression still reverberate, I think, in some families.) Only blacks rebelled: Dr. King's children cried, those churches rocked with grief.

Now, in the eighties, it righted itself. People were allowed to show pain again, allowed to act out their grief.

★　★　★　★　★　★　★　★　★　★　★

FOURTEEN

Come Walk with Me

My search for Reagan continued over the years. I'd talk to anyone who knew him, bore or jar people at social occasions with what seemed obvious questions, or personal ones, occasionally see their faces go blank—what is her agenda, why does she want to know? — and wonder if I seemed in the grip of something. Don't look back, a nice woman told me, look forward.

It wasn't that he was the whale and I was Ahab, I didn't want to catch him. I wanted to find him, though, stand close and see his shape, look in those eyes, understand that hugeness, perhaps gain insight into history, and my own fascination, and love.

I would turn to politics, the ocean in which he most successfully swam.

One day in 1987, a few months after I had left the White House, I visited Dick Darman. We had lunch in his spacious sunny Treasury Department office and talked about the man who absorbed us both.

To understand Reagan, said Darman, you have to realize he is not a Republican and not a conservative. To understand him you must realize he is a populist, an expression of the American populist movement and spirit of this century and the previous century.

"The populists were people who were not poor but who were often lower-middle class or working class. They were people with just enough money to stick their heads up, look around, and feel certain feelings. They were people who always thought someone or something was keeping them from getting ahead, from achieving in some way. They were resentful. It is partly a resentful movement. But they were also hopeful. They believed in America and the American dream; they came from people who packed up in Europe or wherever and took a dangerous journey across the ocean, often alone, in search of a better life. That is not the action of someone who is demoralized or driven into helplessness by circumstances. It is a profoundly hopeful act."

I interrupt, "This hope, it's almost in the gene pool by now, part of the national genetic makeup."

He nods. The immigrants who came here were fleeing the state or the church or the landlord, an authority figure or institution that was inhibiting them or making them unhappy in some way.

"The bully of the drama."

"The bully of the drama. In the past decade, since at least the seventies and for many years before that, the bully has been the state. Before that it was the railroads, or the monopolies, the malefactors of great wealth, Wall Street—"

"In its ugly expression it was the Catholic Church, the Jews, blacks—"

"Yes, and I'll get to that. Reagan's genius was in seeing and reacting to the fact that in the modern era it was the state that was the bully, the eastern intellectuals, the establishment, the bureaucrats who 'can't park their bicycles straight.'"

"And the second part of his genius is that he made it benign." He never allowed a racial or ethnic group to be identified as the bully, the devil. Reagan was an inclusive figure: He wanted to include, to take into his embrace the disparate groups. The pope isn't the enemy, the state is the enemy, Catholics are welcome in this movement.

Why, with all his intuitive understanding of the populist impulse in the American nature, wasn't Ronald Reagan's presidency an obvious realigning presidency?

"There are a number of reasons. One is that Reagan was surrounded by three kinds of people who had different agendas and different methods of operation. There were Mrs. Reagan and her friends, and the California crowd, and the corporate types."

The California crowd—Meese, Nofziger, Judge Clark—had been with the president since his early days, and they judged people by "Where were you in '72?" "Actually it was often, 'Were you with us in '68?' They had loyalty tests—are you ideologically correct, are your credentials in order, how far do you go back in the movement? They were conservatives who were exclusive, they excluded. But when you exclude you don't make a majority."

I picked up. "That's one of the great sins of the right, isn't it, that they make converts feel unwelcome. The magic part of the New Deal was that everybody was invited, that ol' party rocked with different music and different dancers, everyone's invited, y'all come."

"Yes," he says. "Remember the end of the stump speech in the 1984 campaign, 'Come walk with me'. But they didn't really want you in their parade."

"It is partly generational," I say. I know almost no Republicans beyond middle age who understand this, but the younger ones get it. Someone could really galvanize the party by making a passionate speech that says, "This is the future—you're a working-class party, the party of the people who are learning to speak English for the first time." Redefine why we're Republicans—freedom and opportunity, connect with the desires of the poor and just-barely-making-it, which are the same as those of the middle and upper-middle. We blame it on the blacks that they allowed themselves to be bought by the Democratic party, but at least the Democrats wanted them, at least they cared. They not only invited them to the party, they gave them a door prize!"

(When you walked into a big conservative dinner, you might see the economist Walter Williams at this table, the writer Tom Sowell at another, Clarence Thomas over here. Otherwise, mostly whites. I asked Walter Williams once what it's like to be a black in the conservative movement. He said it was fine, no problem, except now and then when he walked in a big room and realized he was the only black. "You feel like a housefly in a bowl of buttermilk."

(How did the party of Lincoln lose the blacks of America? You know the reasons, some the GOP's fault and some not. I would add here another: The conservatives, in the sixties and seventies, didn't go to the churches, to the neighborhood gathering places, and make their case with fire. And when they went, they didn't stay. Reagan went to Bed-Stuy in 1980, but I don't think he ever returned.) (Jack Kemp is there, in the projects. Watch him. What he is doing is the future of the Republican party.)

Darman nods but is not engaged. He does not, as a rule, find the ideas of others to be as compelling as his own.

He continues:

"Then there are Mrs. Reagan and her friends, and their interests would generally not be described as populist. They were interested in wealth and position and such.

"The final group surrounding the president is the corporate types. The millionaires, self-made or inherited, the Wall Street Republicans. This type is epitomized by Don Regan—"

Who, as we know, was brought stock-market averages on the hour by his aides, who got the information from a special computer Mr. Regan had installed in his office.

"The corporate types represent the kind of official Republican that Ronald Reagan never was, the Wall Street executive in the gray flannel suit. Regan is also a perfect example of this type because he forgot his working-class roots. He was too busy tugging on his gold cuff links. Everyone knows Tip O'Neill had contempt for Don Regan, and it's because Tip sensed that Don was ashamed of his background. Both working-class boys from Cambridge, from the same neighborhood. Tip loved to go back home and then go to breakfast at the White House and say, 'Don, I saw your aunt Agnes back home, she says hello.' And Regan pulls on his cuff links. Diamond Don could never admit his background, and it's sad, because he had so much to be proud of."

A few months earlier Darman had gone to Harvard's 350th anniversary. Tip O'Neill was asked to open the festivities the morning it began. They all dressed in morning coats and tails, and Tip came in, walked down the center of the aisle, and got a standing ovation. They stood and cheered. And he opened with some brief remarks. He said, I grew up in Cambridge. I grew up only eighteen blocks away from here, but it was another world. I wanted to get a good education but when it came time this great university was out of the question. I didn't have any money, and so I had to work while I was in school. But I didn't miss out on Harvard completely. See those lawns?

He pointed at the soft rolling grass of the Yard.

I used to mow those lawns. I mowed them every day in the summer. So happy birthday, Harvard. Happy birthday.

Imagine if Republicans talked like that. Or thought like that.

"But the Regans don't," said Darman. "Diamond Don is ashamed, and Tip sees it."

And nobody has contempt for an Irishman who's ashamed of where he came from like an Irishman who isn't.

We never quite finished our talk; my notes show no Darman summation. But now I think: There *was* a realignment, but it was quiet, and it has only just begun. The FDR realignment was total and complete by the end of the war, thirteen years after he assumed the presidency. The effects of the Reagan realignment will reach their fruition in the nineties.

What were Reagan's convictions?

He was a conservative who truly believed that a government big enough to give you everything you want is big enough to take everything you've got. He believed that government out of control is the main threat to individual freedom in the modern world. And he believed (experience had taught him) that where man was, evil was possible; that there is good and bad in man and that while the better angels are there, so is the thing that makes the death camps and the boat people. He believed that when men too filled with evil organize the Reich results, and the Soviet revolution.

But there was even at the heart of all this hard thought—and these are hard thoughts—the glow of an innocence. He believed in the redemption of man, of every man. He thought he could change Castro's mind, and Gorbachev's. He said that if he could only take Gorbachev up for a ride in a helicopter and they could go over America, over Iowa and its bursting silos, California and its swimming pools, that Gorbachev would be dazzled by the abundance of the free market. "See?" Reagan would say. "All our workers in America have a home and a car! See those aerials? Color TV, everyone has one!" As if Gorbachev would look up, surprised, and shout over the whir of the blades, "Gee, Ron, you're right, capitalism *is* better!"

The innocence—it's part of what made him so moving. And it's what frustrated the young of his administration, who thought (as a younger Ronald Reagan had) that what divided us was more than mere misunderstanding. And anyway, who would think freedom's bounty is a swimming pool? Couldn't you show him a book? Or a Bible? And what is this implicit suggestion that our desires or motives are similar? Had he forgotten his history, and a certain disappointed death in Warm Springs?

There were times when I would see the earnest young people in the middle levels of the administration trying to get someone to listen to their thoughts, fighting to advance ideas that were not country club but human, and compassionate, and see the sunny president who did not seem to know or notice, and I would think to myself (if I was tired enough, frustrated enough) that the battle for the mind of Ronald Reagan was like the trench warfare of World War I: Never have so many fought so hard for such barren terrain.

We didn't know, I didn't know: He wasn't a revolutionary, he wasn't a missile drawn to the heat of a new idea. He didn't really care for new ideas; he was pretty content with the old ones. The timeless ones. He was conservative in part because he was old-fashioned.

He was a man who got upset because the feds were taking all his money back in the fifties when he was working for GE. There he was, finally making the big money regularly, and he's looking at the check and seeing the bite Washington's taking and he had a wife and four kids and two marriages and private-school bills and a mortgage—and he got mad. He got mad! And he figured the Soviets, the biggest confiscators of all, were the exact expression of how bad it could get. He wasn't an innovator and he didn't really mean, as he used to say in quoting Tom Paine, to remake the world. He was, in many ways, a pragmatist in full-throated pursuit of that least romantic of goals, the practical solution.

He was temperamentally unsuited to a revolution. He believed in negotiation and compromise; he was inclined to split the difference.

He was unused to the rough folk who lead revolts. He liked and respected the rough-and-ready type, but somehow he always wound up with the establishment. He enjoyed people with money and a certain amount of glamour—the Annenbergs, Kay Graham, Francis Albert— and when he delegated, he delegated to people who were upscale.

The press, the media, unintentionally obscured who Reagan was because they really thought he was way out there on the wild-eyed revolutionary right. Why? Partly because of things he said—killer trees, "We begin bombing in five minutes." (The media heard that and thought, Aha, the real Reagan. And it was. But not Reagan the leader,

Reagan the comic who couldn't not go for a laugh.) And partly because by the time he arrived on the national scene there hadn't been a viable national conservative in so long that his views seemed outlandish to the sophisticated boomer ears of young reporters and editors. In the sixteen years between the Goldwater candidacy and the Reagan inaugural the left had become the middle, the middle was to the right, and the right was way out there.

An example: By early 1974, when Reagan was first being taken seriously as a presidential candidate, it was the common wisdom of the opinion class that Vietnam was not just a mistake but an evil blunder caused by hubris. Reagan never veered "right" on this issue; he just stayed in what had been, ten years before, the middle. (In the mid-1960s Gallup reported the majority of Americans supported the U.S. presence in Vietnam.) But the young coming-to-power members of the media tilted left, and the farther they tilted, the more they pointed at the man standing straight and said, "See how far he leans!"

The press perceived him as far right, the left encouraged the perception, and so in a way did Reagan—whose attitude seemed to be, If this is far right then far right's a good thing to be!

It was all there in the Speech, the one he gave for Barry Goldwater in 1964 on the eve of the election, the one that made the guys in the kitchen Cabinet look at each other and say, This fella could be governor, Hell, Justin, he could be president! I read it over and over in '86. I'd never read it when I was in the White House.

On one level it's a speech about freedom, about the relationship of the individual to the state. On another it's a speech about what works in government. But it's primarily a speech about money.

It's a speech that reminds you he was a child of the Depression. He knew what it was not to have anything. The young conservatives around him had never seen people sell apples on the corner, had never gone to bed hungry. It didn't all come down to money for us. It didn't have to.

But for him, when he looked at government, the bottom line shone through:

". . . the three-fourths of farming unregulated and unsubsidized has seen a 21 percent increase in the per-capita consumption of all its produce. Since 1955 the cost of the farm program has nearly doubled. Direct payment to farmers is eight times as great as it was nine years ago, but farm income remains unchanged while farm surplus is bigger."

This is the essential Reagan, picking the facts he loved and offering them to a public he assumed would find them as compelling as he did. ("Specificity is the soul of credibility.")

And this, after saying that federal, state, and local welfare combined spend $45 billion a year, and still more than 9 million families live in poverty:

"If this present welfare spending was prorated equally among these poverty-stricken families, we could give each family more than forty-five hundred dollars a year. Actually, direct aid to the poor averages less than six hundred dollars per family. There must be some administrative overhead somewhere. Now, are we to believe that another billion-dollar program added to the half a hundred programs and the $45 billion, will, through some magic, end poverty?"

Listen, he is saying, you're wasting our money, and gaining nothing.

". . . we find that today a young man in his early twenties, going to work at less than an average salary, will, with his employer, pay into Social Security an amount which could provide the young man with a retirement insurance policy guaranteeing $220 a month at age sixty-five—and the government promises him $127."

Listen, he is saying, if we're defining justice through money then it's time to admit we've become unjust.

It is a speech that warns, a speech that defines and points to problems. It wasn't a speech that offered remedies—beyond "Go back!"— or a new way to look at things.

I used to think that for modern conservatism, Reagan was the big strong elephant that trampled down the high grass and flattened the bushes to ease the way for the younger, quicker animals. If he was slow he was also strong, and without him the gazelles and leopards wouldn't have had a path that had been broken, and made safe.

There was no Reagan without Carter. Only four years of steady decline and lack of clarity could have lurched the country over to this—this *actor*. We forget how radical it was to pick a former Hollywood movie star as president of the United States. And a divorced man, the first. And a Goldwater-type conservative. What a lurch. We wouldn't have gone from Nixon to Reagan, from Ford. Only Carter and his unluck and confusion could have done it. And by the time he did, Reagan's old-time conservatism seemed new again. Which, in power, it was. He brought a whole generation of young activists into government; they never would have been there if he hadn't opened the doors; they are creating the new conservatism that may well shape our politics through the turn of the century.

He was up to the challenge. By the time he came to power, the American people wanted so much from a president. They wanted him to be witty, decent, and kind—and shrewd, unillusioned, and tough. They wanted every little tyrant to shake in his boots at the mention of his name, and they wanted the squirrels to eat from his hand. We treat our presidents like kings and then to prove we're not mere subjects we tear them down. Then some fellow who wants to make a name for himself kicks him in the teeth and instead of censuring him we applaud and say, Isn't democracy wonderful?

We wanted so much. And what did we get?

In political terms maybe the most important thing was this: that back in the sixties and seventies some of us began to fear for our country, and its skepticism, cynicism, and drift. And the thing Ronald Reagan did was to represent in his person the views, the commonly held views of the American people and remind us they still had legitimacy.

Someone once said the most important word in "We the people" is "We." Reagan knew this in his bones. He represented the idea that all of us together, the American people, "hold these truths"—that all men are created equal, that democracy is better than dictatorship, that justice is a standard we must each seek to meet. He brought back the "We."

FIFTEEN

Summits

Richard kept saying when we're married. When we're married we're going to live at my house, so you'll have to get up early to get in. When we're married we'll visit these friends when I make speeches in Europe. I was irritated by his assumption; I was impressed the way he was taking charge. I feared he was courting disappointment; I wondered what our children would look like. He pressed and pressed; my resistance and desire lacked conviction.

Sometimes this is how I felt: You're on a raft and the river forks and you do not know: which way? The waters are turbulent, rushing. He says, This way!, and you think, Does he know more, or is it only a need to command? You will run aground on the land—decide! Both routes lead to the unknown, and contain the possibility of joy—decide! You drop the rough, crude rudder and let the river choose. It does. The route by the trees, and the farmland, and unknown rocks.

I talk to friends. He is a good man and it's time. Do you love him? I love many things in him. Are you in a swoon? I don't know, I'm thirty-five—is a swoon a good idea for marriage, or do other things matter more?

He's been married twice. Does that mean he's had enough experience so he knows how to do it now, or is it a warning sign, Do Not Stop Here? Why the hurry? He says he knows his mind. I am struck by Michael Caine's remark to the analyst in *Hannah and Her Sisters:* "I am an intelligent and experienced man, and yet I cannot fathom my own heart."

I am chosen to go to Geneva, to the first Reagan-Gorbachev summit, and I cannot believe my luck. I have been assigned the speech to the joint session of Congress that the president will give when he returns. It had to be written and staffed before we left. Ben said, Assume the meetings will be cordial and frank. Whatever happens we'll be rewriting every day, and the final draft probably won't look much like the first. But we can't go over there with nothing, so get cracking.

What I did to get cracking was get a copy of JFK's speech to the nation after his first meeting with Khrushchev and attempt to adopt the same tone of confident, searching strength. I tried, did all right but no better.

Before the trip there was a big security meeting in a small theater in the EOB. We were told the KGB had done psychological profiles on every one of us in the presidential party, and they were good. "They know you." Be discreet, stay away from discos, don't hang out at the bar in the hotel: Whatever vulnerabilities you think you have they think so too, and they're precisely the vulnerabilities they might exploit.

Later I was told by a high Regan aide that the KGB research on Regan was brilliant, because they knew exactly what his soft spot was. At the first U.S.-Soviet reception the Soviet foreign minister, Eduard Shevardnadze, made a beeline for Regan, and the first thing he said was, "You know, Gorbachev likes you. He really admires you. He says you are tough man just like him!"

"Regan's chest went out to here," said the aide. "He was elated. And ever after he saw Gorbo as another Regan. It was mirror imaging. I asked him once if we could trust Gorbachev. He thought for a minute, and said, 'Yeah, we can trust him, he's a man who'll keep his word.'"

(A digression on mirror imaging:

(A year after the Geneva summit, just before the December Washington summit, I talked to George Shultz at a dinner. Shultz is a charming and accessible man in private, more so than one might guess if one knew only his public self.

(He told me of how Gorbachev is trying to make change and having a hard time. "Russia isn't a country that has a lot of people who say, 'Oh freedom, how nice!' There's no tradition of freedom from the czars to communism. Now Gorbachev is trying to get an entire country full of these people to accept some measure of economic liberty and be eager for it. And there are many people who don't want this."

(Is his biggest opposition coming from other and perhaps older members of the Politburo, or the KGB?

(It's the bureaucracy, he said. "I would say that the bureaucracy there is something we can't even fathom, it's so huge and entrenched. And naturally trying to get this huge almost grid of people to move, he has made some enemies. Their civil service alone, their government workers—it's really impossible to make them move, or may prove impossible. . . ."

(Which made him think of Congress. "This town has changed since I've been here almost completely. The Hill now is anarchy. There hasn't been a budget passed in years. A freshman member can get on television and tell us about his foreign policy, and that beats slogging it out as a committee chairman any day. The leadership can't control them with money, as LBJ and Wilbur Mills did. . . ."

(A woman listening said, "When you go around the country, you find people are anxious about this, and crying out for leadership."

("Leadership isn't the problem," said Shultz, "it's followership! No one is willing to defer anymore. . . ." He puts a State Department appropriation into Congress, and everyone and his brother is tagging on amendments. They're holding up ambassadors, refusing confirmation until they get their chance to micromanage policy. It's really impossible to make them move, this huge almost grid of people!

(I thought, He identifies with Gorbachev. Both of them modern, sophisticated men trying to get good policy through an entrenched bureaucracy.

(I imagine Gorbachev sitting at a long brown table, his hands one over the other, watching things with his keen, bright eyes, a light smile playing on his lips. A junior aide spills some water as he pours from the pitcher and Gorbachev looks at Shultz with a wry look that says, See what we have to put up with, you and I, from our well-meaning young "handlers"! And Shultz looks in his eyes and sees—quickly, just for a moment—a narrowing that is almost a wink. And he thinks, He comprehends! He has his problems too, his own goddammed Jesse Helmsoviches, his own bureaucracy of egoists, his own . . . hidebound conservatives! And Shultz will remember this as the moment of communion, two good and modern men trying to tug the world by inches into a safer, better mooring for all mankind.

(Could Shultz be right? Is that light of comprehension a real light, the light that brings clarity where shadows were? Shultz is sophisticated, experienced; he's seen men make decisions I've read about in books.

(But mirror imaging must be the great temptation of diplomats. It must make you feel better, more secure, to think your adversaries are pretty much like you. And it's a short leap from "Never judge a man till you've walked a mile in his moccasins" to "He wears the same moccasins I do, they're just as tight!" Which may be true and may be not.

(Perhaps it comes down to this. The writer Charles Krauthammer says for conservatives the paradigm is Munich [evil appeased and thereby inspired] and for liberals Sarajevo [cataclysms happen by accident, explode into a vacuum where wisdom was supposed to be]. I think often of Chamberlain and Churchill. I look into Shultz's eyes and see anxiety for the archduke.)

The KGB had done a profile on me too, and it must have said something like "Longs to be treated with respect," because at the same reception at which Regan was embraced by Shevardnadze, a Soviet official whose important work had been described to me walked over, introduced himself, and chatted in a way that suggested I was his equal or more. He said with a sad shrug that it is too bad the United States has to be involved in militarizing the heavens and putting weapons in space.

I told him yes, it's too bad we're forced to try and catch up with your marvelous SDI research and development, which has been going on for at least a decade now, not to mention your civil-defense program which includes massive fallout shelters, which we, as you know, do not have, and—

He said, The Soviets do not have an SDI program!

I said, You ought to know the Soviets have it, because you are the head of it!

He said, No, other science research we do!

He turned to talk to someone else, and never turned back. Which allowed me to look around and see that the room was full of similar knots of people, Americans leaning forward and jabbing the air, and Soviets leaning forward, looking surprised. This wasn't what they got when they met with Carter's people. This wasn't what they got when they met with Ford. They are surprised by conviction. It has been a long time since they have seen Americans like this.

It was an exciting trip, Reagan meeting a Soviet leader for the first time in his presidency ("Wasn't my fault, they kept dying on me!"). On TV in my room as I worked, I watched the first handshake, with Reagan bounding down the steps in his suit jacket and Gorbachev muffled up in a heavy topcoat and scarf. It looked like Reagan versus Carter in the 1980 debate. I met Ron Reagan, Jr., who was taking notes in the kitchen of a villa near where his father was meeting. He was writing an article for a magazine and wearing the first Reeboks I ever saw.

I was to meet the Gorbachevs.

All I could think of was Nancy Astor, and her greeting the day she met Stalin: "So when are you going to stop killing people?" I wanted to say something pleasant and appropriate too, like, "So when are you going to let the innocent people out of the gulag?" But that would have caused difficulties and, more to the point, got me fired.

Ben was excited. As we waited on the slowly moving line in a glittering diplomatic hall, he turned to Jack Matlock, one of the NSC experts on the Soviet Union.

"How do you say 'I hope communism dies' in Russian?"

Matlock sputtered. "You're not really going to say that!"

"How about, 'Your system is cruel and indecent'?"

"You're not!"

"No. I'm not."

Matlock sighed. Soon after he became our ambassador to the USSR.

It was Ben's turn. He walked quickly to the Gorbachevs, put out his hand, nodded, and moved on. A man took a picture. When Ben got it, he filed it with his unimportant papers.

I framed mine and am looking at it now. You notice two things: Gorbachev's amused and attractive smile, and a gold crucifix I wore on the front of my dress. To make his face fall off. He is smiling just like a guy who is thinking, "Thees ees the one who wants to quote the fascist, wait til I answer about the negroes in Attica."

"Hi," I said. Our hands touched and held. I puffed out my chest so he wouldn't miss the cross. He nodded and said something in Russian.

I turned to Mrs. Gorbachev. She pumped my arm like a cistern. "Hello," I said.

"Hellaw!"

People say, What did they look like? I say, the way they look on TV. She like the manager of the Elizabeth Arden in Romania, he like a retired hockey goalie.

Later an aide to the first lady and precisely the kind of person you'd trust on these things sniffed, when I asked him what he thought. "They are simply the most ambitious couple I have ever in my life met! They never thought they'd come so high, and now look. I am telling you: *She wants to run the world!*"

The night before the summit ended, a group of us—Jack Matlock, Pat Buchanan, Ben, some NSC aides, some mice, met around a hastily set-up table in a hotel room and went over the joint-session speech. It was a desultory affair. The summit had gone fine, but I got the impression they didn't think that was a big enough thing to say.

What I remember most from the speech is the phrase "We went to Geneva with peace as our goal and freedom as our guide." A fine and meaningless sentence, precisely the kind of thing a mouse would find eloquent. A mouse did, and for weeks insisted on getting it in. Who cares? It takes three seconds and won't take away from anything, right?

But it became for me a symbol. You know what I did to be mean? Just to be low and snively I went to great lengths not to put it in. I'd take out whole paragraphs if I found the sentence in the third line. He'd resurrect it and put it in the next page. He finally got it included on the plane on the way back. At least I made him work for it.

Later I received the president's letter to all the members of the official party, thanking us for taking part. The letter had been prepared and written before we'd left for Geneva. It was standard *pro forma.* But one sentence caught my eye. "We went to Geneva with peace as our goal and freedom as our guide."

The speech went fine, I was told. I wasn't there. I was in Rome getting married.

This is what finally decided it: We had another fight and I missed him, and we reconciled, and talked, and I said yes.

I would join life. I'd been a lone cowboy riding by and observing long enough. Now I would stop by the campfire, pass the coffee, and watch the flames against the fellas' faces. Do my chores, take part: Be part.

This is what settled it: We had dinner with Millicent Fenwick, who knew Richard from old Republican days.

She was now U.S. ambassador to a U.N. agency in Rome. She is beautiful. The planes of her face make you think of what someone said of Hepburn—those cheekbones are the largest natural calcium deposits since the white cliffs of Dover. A strong, tall woman, the kind a man of her era might have captured with, "Now *that's* one terrific dame!"

To meet her is to feel nostalgia for the disappearing Protestant ascendancy, for the members of a society that had rules every bit as demanding and rigorous as the rules of the Old West, the first of which—answer the cards, sit with the elderly, draw out the dull bachelor, invite the homely cousin—was an awesome self-discipline. (Mrs. Bush is one of these.)

We went to a small Roman restaurant where they snapped to attention—a great flapping of napkins and drawing out of chairs, a proffering of matches as she drew a small pipe from an elegant purse and began to meditatively puff.

Well, you ducks look just marvelous! Puff puff. Tell me about what's happening in the great capitals of the world!

We're going to get married, Richard said. Will you be our best man?

You bet! Be honored!

And that was that. Because one simply wouldn't let Millicent down.

We would marry at 11:00 A.M. in the Campidòglio, where foreigners in Rome marry. That morning there was a frantic call from Millicent: there was a surprise vote she couldn't possibly get out of, terribly terribly sorry, but I'll still send my *wonduhful* assistant who is just *enormously* excited about meeting you and helping out, and she's got my car and driver and you'll have time to get another witness when you're there. They'll pick you up within the hour!

They got caught in a big demonstration. Richard paced in front of the hotel. I sat upstairs wondering if a civil ceremony in a foreign country is really a wedding. The pope's down the street, I could always ask him.

I went downstairs. Erin, Millicent's beautiful blond assistant, ran up, breathless. We're sorry we're late, she said in the most perfect and impeccable Brooklyn accent. A landsman.

The limousine got caught in the tail end of the demonstration. We could not move. Surrounded by shouting workers and red flags. A Communist demonstration. What a great story. A bus driver gets out, lights up, and leans against the fender. It's going to be a long one. We look at each other. And bolt.

We ran down the block and the next, ran up the long, broad, endless stairs past the statue of Marcus Aurelius, the ribbons of my bouquet flapping in the wind, and arrived, breathless, at the Renaissance palace that is the Campidòglio.

The ceremony was quick, in a cavernous room, conducted by a big round man in a brown suit with a big sash around his stomach. Music like the score for the Italian pastoral scenes in *The Godfather* comes from a little Sony. We are called forward. The big man is talking, looking at us one and then the other.

"What is he saying?" I ask Richard, who is listening to a translator.

"He appears to be saying, if I understand him correctly, that you have no rights as the wife, and I have no rights as the husband, but the marriage itself as a collective has rights."

"And now you may kiss."

Outside we pose for pictures and are surrounded by a group of schoolgirls who are visiting the museum next door. *"Auguri"* they chirp like little birds. *"Auguri."*

What does it mean?

"Best wishes," I am told. "Good omens."

SIXTEEN

Leaving

I could tell I was leaving that spring. Nothing had happened, at least nothing new, but every time I took a guest to the mess, I'd think, I wonder if this is the last time, and when the president waved up to us from below the balcony when he came to the EOB, I'd wonder, Is this wave the one I'll remember as the last.

In two years I had learned the White House is a wonderful place for a writer, and a terrible place. Wonderful because what you wrote mattered, made an impact, sometimes made things better. Terrible because what I did was so removed from any ongoing reality that it seemed, sometimes, bizarre. This was when I started to think, I am on the periphery of a void. And: This White House is like a beautiful clock that makes all the right sounds, but when you open it up, there is nothing inside.

And Reagan? I knew he'd done more good for our country in six years than any president since Roosevelt, but it is not without meaning for me that when I thought of him in those days, it was as a gigantic heroic balloon floating in the Macy's Thanksgiving Day parade, right up there between Superman and Big Bird. I felt like the kids in the apartments on Central Park West, watching the giant heads bob by.

I had made friends in the White House whom I admired and looked up to—Fred Khedouri and Mike Horowitz, Craig Fuller, Ben, Mari Maseng. People of great talent like Darman and Buchanan. I had met my husband there, and become somewhat known as a writer. I owed the White House a great deal, had grown attached to it, dependent on it. I knew I should be looking around. An OPL aide, as she was leaving, stuck her head in my office one day and said, "The average White House stay for a special assistant is eighteen months. There are reasons for that." I'd been there twenty-four.

And yet I could not leave. I felt like a detective who was being taken off the case too soon. I could do the work well and take it easy, get used to marriage, float. And what did I want to do next. Columnist? There are enough columnists already, don't you think, filling the air with their pungent little opinions? Does anyone need mine too? Then again I'd always had this fantasy about doing a column like FPA in the 1920s—literature, gossip, jokes, politics, criticism, doggerel—something that radiates a sense of this is America now. But the idea of summoning my energy and bringing it together to launch a creative endeavor left me . . . dozing. "Born to nap," a friend at CBS had offered to tattoo on my arm.

An odd thing happened after I quit smoking: I fell asleep. I'd get up in the morning at six, arrive at work by seven-thirty and nap till nine. I'd go to lunch, come back at two, and fall asleep. I'd go home at seven, eat dinner, and fall off at ten. In between I wrote speeches to which I now brought great personal authority on the waste of taxpayers' money. I went to the doctor and told him I felt fine except for the narcolepsy. He did some tests and told me that interestingly enough my thyroid had stopped working somewhere along the way, and heavy smoking had covered it up. But now that the stimulant of nicotine was gone, the problem was obvious, and had I been gaining weight? Yes.

He put me on a pill that had the unfortunate side effect of waking me up. And still I could not rouse myself.

There had been a fight over the State of the Union a few months before. I hadn't written it, Ben and the speechwriter Josh Gilder had, and it was good. The mice rewrote it. I weighed in with memos to Buchanan.

. . .

It's hard to stay serious when you're criticizing a piece that contains such gems as "We cannot perpetuate these problems no longer" and "Many of the programs that exist today were literally created in the 1930s to the 1960s, while others are oriented to the problems as they existed then" . . . "Be all that it can be" is a Madison Avenue crudity; "Our agenda for the future" is utterly trite; "Breaking free from the failed policies of the past" and "We must be aware of our past but cannot be bound by it" are known as clichés. You might call this speech "A Cavalcade of Clichés." It doesn't have a title, so let's. "Rather than looking to the past, we must look to the future"—well, what can a grown-up say? "I am confident of our future because so many of our young people have already shown that they are leaders for tomorrow"— the caboose of the cavalcade of clichés. This speech will make Ronald Reagan sound like a stupid fool.

Some of these comments were leaked to *Newsweek* by someone, a friend or enemy, who knows, and made famous the appellation the mice. Which did not win for me their gratitude.

Then there was this interesting meeting. (I'm getting ahead of myself in terms of the narrative, but why not?)

(I'm even going to do a digression. The sentence that begins the preceeding paragraph—"Then there was this interesting meeting"—is, and I really hate to admit this, a *thirtysomething* sentence. It's how my retarded generation talks. I was a special assistant to the president of the United States, this is my book about the political era I was fortunate to take part in, and the sentence should be, "I took luncheon with the undersecretary and his able assistant and afterward attended a fascinating meeting, which, in hindsight, spoke volumes about the inherent problems of the second administration." Instead, I sound like Michael talking to Elliot: "Then there was this feeling I just like . . . so, you know, I kissed her." A more affluent version of "I don't know, Marty, whatta you wanna do?" And we are the best-educated generation in the history of the world. [Actually we just had the most days in classrooms.])

It was after the State of the Union, and the speechwriters were called into Mr. Regan's office to meet with Dick Wirthlin, the president's pollster. He was to tell us about the response to the State of the Union according to his focus group. He felt he had a very good read on public response because he'd worked intensely with a group of a few dozen people the night of the address. He'd given them each a little plastic button to hold in their hands. (The networks do this too.) The buttons were connected through wires to a tabulator, and when a person heard something he had an emotional response to, he squeezed. (Hollywood does this too.) It provided a second-by-second response to the speech. Wirthlin charted which phrases got the most squeezes and then talked to the group about why they squeezed. Now he was here to tell us which phrases were the most popular so we could use them again. (The Democrats do this too.)

It was at this meeting that I began to have a recurrent vision of a woman throwing her apron over her head and running screaming from the kitchen.

For instance, Wirthlin said, early on in the speech where the president says, "Reach for the stars"—that got a very positive response. The word "free" is also a good word—"free mankind from the prison of nuclear terror." We got a very rapid and positive charge with the section that says the best way to judge our welfare system is the extent to which it frees people from welfare. Very good.

We looked at each other. *I'll give you a positive charge, you little—*

We also got a rapid and positive charge, he continued, when the president said to Tip O'Neill, "The system's broke, let's fix it." And we got a very good response when he said, "Let's not cut the family budget; let's cut the federal budget." That worked well.

Ben stared straight ahead. I looked at Buchanan. His body was tense and poised. He looked like an Indian hunter prowling the hills looking for buffalo and come upon a grotesque monster.

Wirthlin continued in his pleasant voice. He is a polite man, low-key, never insists.

Now the parts of the speech that didn't play, that just didn't work, were those sections that were not positive in some way. In these sections people feel that some of the things the president said were untrue. It wasn't really a negative response so much as more a question about the appropriateness of the issue.

For instance, the section where the president spoke of the freedom fighters in Afghanistan, Angola, Cambodia, and Nicaragua. First of all they didn't know where these countries are. Also, someone said, It sounds like we're launching a five-point war. . . . Part of the problem seems to be that the language was so powerful it put them on edge. It made them feel "down." It wasn't positive.

Aaaaaaaaagggggggghhhhhhh. They limit the amount of time we can give to anti-Communist insurgencies, so the speechwriters load the paragraph up to get your attention, and it doesn't work—and that becomes the excuse not to talk about the rebels. If they hadn't written it hot, it would have been brief and cool, which would have been boring, which would have been the other reason not to mention them.

The only sound was Don Regan taking notes. The only movement was Don Regan nodding.

Now when we talk about tax reform, Wirthlin says, drum it in. It's pro-family, pro-jobs, pro-future, pro-America. Pro is positive.

I was fingering my skirt as if it were an apron. This isn't what a speech is; this is what they do in Hollywood to judge what sitcom to buy. I write in my notes, *This doesn't allow us much room for a more intellectual, sophisticated, or elevated approach.* If Wirthlin were Churchill's pollster: "I won't ask for your blood, sweat, and tears, but we'll reach for the stars nonetheless." Squeeze.

This isn't writing; this is one small step for focus groups, one giant step for the Where's-the-beef-ization of mankind.

Thank you, Dick, said Regan. That was very helpful.

Ben was pale and still, Buchanan motionless. There was a clearing of throats and a shuffling of feet. Now we would turn to the real purpose of the meeting: our problems with the editing techniques of Regan's aides.

Ben took the lead. We just can't work with these guys the way they operate, the rewriting, the staffing system—

The staffing system doesn't work anymore, said another speechwriter. It's lost its integrity.

ARE YOU QUESTIONING MY INTEGRITY? Regan exploded.

No sir, I'm questioning—

MY INTEGRITY!

His voice was hot but his face was cool. This wasn't genuine anger it was manufactured, he was acting.

I'm not questioning your integrity, I'm—

WHAT ARE YOU QUESTIONING? He looks at Ben. Are you telling me you met with the president under Dickie Darman? He snorted.

In fact, more than we do now, Ben said.

Another speechwriter leans in. It's nonsense to say the other White House was better. This is a good White House, and we can all work with you, sir. (Albert Brooks in *Broadcast News:* "No, I think it's ass-kissing when you pucker up your lips and put 'em on the boss's butt and smooch!")

Regan sits back, mollified. A friend! (A break in the ranks!)

I clear my throat. Actually if I could meet with the president now and then, see him at a meeting maybe, I could listen to him and it would make my writing better.

You couldn't write better, says Regan.

Which to this day I insist on taking as a compliment.

The meeting broke up. Later Regan took Buchanan aside. He was honestly perplexed. What's the matter with them? he said. They write it, we edit it and send it in. That's all. That's how they do it on newspapers. I know, I was on the board of a newspaper.

The job of head of the Office of Public Liaison opened up when Faith Whittlesey left the White House to return as ambassador to Switzerland. OPL was, by long tradition, the highest staff position held by a woman in the White House. Elizabeth Dole headed it before she became secretary of transportation.

It was a job with significant political impact because it involved running the president's political outreach—his "liaison" with labor, business, Catholics, blacks. Now it was open, and once again they were rounding up the usual suspects.

Some backed Anne Dore McLaughlin, the smart and accomplished politico-bureautico Republican, some Connie Marshner, a talented longtime conservative activist. The decision was Buchanan's, and apparently he found it difficult. Everyone was weighing in, and so did I. I told him to choose Ann Higgins, the assistant to the president who handled his correspondence office. The next day Pat asked me to come by.

"I read your memo. Shelley read it too, and she said something interesting. She said why not Peggy Noonan?"

I was surprised. It hadn't occurred to me.

"Oh Pat, I don't know. I don't have enough clothes."

A pause.

"You could buy some."

A pause.

"I don't know if I'm temperamentally suited. You have to talk to all these people and I'm not good at that. I'd have to think. Are you offering it to me?"

"Yup. How much time?"

I asked for the weekend, but I knew going out. Another memo, this one nonincendiary and leak-proof. It isn't for me, I told him. Its rewards are rewards I don't desire; its demands are demands I would not enjoy. I'm realizing I don't want to carry the banner, I want to sit and think quietly in front of my word processor. I keep thinking of what Clare Boothe Luce told Gloria Steinem: If you really go into politics, you'll never be a writer. I don't want to be the official woman of Reagan Two and I don't want to ask my husband to make adjustments in his professional life—OPL deals with business, a conflict of interest would loom.

In the end he made a better choice in Mari Maseng, who was now, as they say, in the private sector—a vice president at Beatrice.

We had a meeting with the president. We were all excited. The president was polite and pleasant and bored. I see from my notes he said, "FDR ran for a third term boasting he'd gotten unemployment down to 14 percent," and "From 1790 to 1875, when we were becoming a giant, every year we had a deficit," and, interestingly, "We don't realize how uncivil we've become. In World War I the rules of warfare were you don't make war on civilians. Now the [arsenal] is aimed at millions of civilians, to me SDI is a lot more civilized."

There is a metronomic quality—question, answer, bup bup bup.

Suddenly there was an unguarded moment with those unguarded eyes. Someone said something the president liked and his head snapped up. The look on his face was like the look on the old men at the nursing home when someone walks in the front door and they look up expectantly, hope unselfconsciously spread across their faces. And then it's not a visitor for them, and they keep the conversation going and lapse for a minute and look at the shine on their shoes.

The person he'd looked at was me. When I looked up from my notes and met his eyes, I lost my train of thought. He looked down at the shine on his shoes.

Suddenly he jumps forward in his chair. His face is animated. "There he is!"

We look through the paneled glass doors facing the Rose Garden as a blur races by.

"That's him, the rat!" He looks at Don Regan. "I told you!"

Regan shakes his head. Apparently there is a wee rodent problem in the Rose Garden. Regan says, We'll take care of it for good. The president sits back, deflated. Real life had intruded, and fled.

Oooooh if I told just one reporter there's a rat in the Rose Garden, there'd be some great cartoons. But . . . they'll be pinning a tail and sharp little teeth on Deaver-the-lobbyist-who's-cashing-in rat, and Meese-the-subject-of-ethical questions rat. . . . Nah. But it gives me a chance to say to myself, sitting on a couch in the Oval Office of our nation, "But it would be wrong, that's for sure."

MY BIG INSIGHT OF 1986

I would think of the happily wagging foot when he was told that day two years ago that the meeting with the speechwriters was off, and I wondered, finally, if this wasn't true:

That this enormously polite man wouldn't show it, but the thing was he thought writers were a big pain in the ass. I had read his autobiography, *Where's the Rest of Me?*, and he talked about actors and stars and producers and directors and designers, about Ty and Coop and Howard Hawks and Edith Head, but he had nothing to say about writers. They didn't even register.

And why not? What was his experience with them?

Writers become the Hollywood Ten, writers write obsessed letters of grievance to the president of SAG, writers get drunk at the dinner party, throw up, and slyly spoof the hostess with "It's all right, the white wine came up with the fish," writers make up funny nasty poems about actors and read them at parties, writers cry because no one pays attention to them and whine if you change a single word of their precious dialogue, writers like to tell the story of the German actor who was booed when he played Hamlet and stopped midsoliloquy to turn to the audience and say, "Don't blame me, I didn't write this shit!," writers keep diaries and writers write books showing the actors warts and all. Writers—writers think they wrote the script!

That was the thing: Writers were a constant reminder that the actor didn't make up the words! And this is hard on them because they're told so many times, "I loved when you said, You better smile when you say that, pardner'—and the actor nods with a most engaging modesty and thinks to himself, That *was* clever of me, wasn't it? And he turns the corner of Studio B and runs right into . . . the writer. And the actor feels a tad uncomfortable.

Whose side do you suppose Ronald Reagan was on when Bette Davis had the blowup with the playwright in *All About Eve*?

LLOYD: You better stick with Beaumont and Fletcher, they've been dead 300 years!

MARGO: *All* playwrights should be dead for 300 years. . . .

LLOYD: I shall never understand the weird process by which a body with a voice suddenly fancies itself as a mind! Just when exactly does an actress decide they're her words she's saying and her thoughts she's expressing?

MARGO: Usually at the point when she has to rewrite and rethink them to keep the audience from leaving the theatre!

LLOYD: It's about time the piano realized it has not written the concerto!

You see I have given the writer the last word. This is known as revenge.

I went to dinner with a reporter from New York, an old friend, and shared my insight. Oh yes, he said, this has already been boiled down to a joke. "D'ja hear about the Polish starlet who went to Hollywood and screwed a writer?"

I wrote an article for a magazine about the president's wit and got a call from him.

"I just wanted to thank you for collecting all those old jokes."

"It was fun."

"I was thinking . . . do you have a minute?"

"Sure I do." I laughed. Of course I do. He laughed too.

"Well, I just wanted to tell you a little story and give you a joke no one else has. It's a story that never appeared in print or anywhere else to my knowledge. Way back when I was [first] running against Pat Brown, I made my announcement and made it official I was running. Well, we had the speech, and then I took questions from the reporters, and someone said—these were the days when if one candidate appeared on TV, the other one had to have as much time on TV, and I, of course, had been doing *Death Valley Days,* so I'd been on TV a lot. And one of the reporters yelled to me at the end, 'Will you give Governor Brown equal time?' And I said, 'Well sure, our audience is accustomed to seeing both ends of the horse.' "

For the first time with him I laughed a natural laugh.

"Well, as soon as I said it, I just wanted to put my hand over my mouth. And I knew that would lead all the TV and the radio, that's what they'd report. And I knew the whole day was for nothing. And you know what? No one ever mentioned it. I was amazed, and all I could figure was they didn't quite hear it, and there was so much other news no one asked."

"That's a wonderful story."

"Well, I wanted to give it to you. Maybe someday you can use it when you're doing other things."

When he hung up, I thought, He knows something I don't know. He knows I'm going to write about these days.

I would walk the halls. I would nod at Tim McCarthy, the Secret Service agent who was shot with Reagan, as he stood like a sentinel near the Oval Office. Go by Buchanan's and see Karen Fuller, his secretary, and chat, stick my head in to say hello to Pat and feel the edgy affection I felt for him, go by the EOB, to Ben's office, say hello to Nancy and Donna, the secretaries, pick up my mail, stand on the balcony and stare out at the construction on the West Wing—they're building Regan an outdoor dining area, I was told—and settle into a big chair in my office where I'd read the papers, or copies of the president's mail, or Sherwood's biography of Hopkins. Sometimes I'd just listen. There were always birds; there was always a faint hammering, a phone ringing, a printer cl-cl-cl-clicking out a memo.

But this is the picture of that time that stays with me:

It is upstairs in the Roosevelt Room, and members of the senior staff are gathered. As usual, the Regan aide is doodling, sketching intensely at the meeting table. The light on his nose, the brightness of the flesh where the hair is receding.

It is part of the tradition of this house: JFK launched sailboats on legal pads, Ehrlichman sketched clever Nixons, Reagan draws winsome cartoon figures, cowboys and prizefighters. It is the tradition of the brilliant: Tom Wolfe is a fine sketcher, as is Updike.

And here is our Regan aide sketching with absorption, all the while holding his own in a discussion on strategy, as if his talents are so—protean!—that no single task can exhaust them.

For a year, a solid year, another aide watched, fascinated. And finally got a peek. They were stick figures.

"Even his drawings weren't good," she said with wonder. "It's not that he had no talent, it's that he had no idea!"

I came in early one day that spring and saw Ben standing reading the newspapers near his conference table.

"I've been fired," he said.

"You're kidding."

The sun streamed in prettily, past the cream curtains and onto the rich rug.

"By who?"

"Regan. Buchanan had to do it."

"Why? What did he say?"

He shrugged. "He was upset. Tried to change Regan's mind. He doesn't know. Too many battles."

"Does the president know?"

He shrugged.

"Oh, Ben." I put my hand on his back. "Oh, Ben."

He walked away and did not let me see his face.

What a sadness. How could it be? He got into battles, but that was his job. If the man who led the creativity department was fired for independence then Reagan's rhetoric was over, finished. Ben didn't fit into the corporate style, but who would? What writer worth his salt would flourish here, now?

And who would head speechwriting? They'd never accept me, I was just more Ben. But, I wondered, don't they want to keep me? They'll offer it to me, and then I can turn it down.

But for weeks Buchanan said not a word. I wrote him a note saying I was just wondering, since a few months ago you offered me a job I wasn't suited for, why you're not considering me for one I am. He laughed, and a few weeks later offered me the job. I turned him down.

This time he pressed, hard. Finally I told him I'd take it and do my best, but only if I could talk to Mr. Regan first and see if we could reach some agreement on how speechwriting was to be run, work out a peace.

Otherwise I'd fight like Ben and be fired like Ben, so what was the point?

For weeks Buchanan went into Regan saying, She's my choice. Will you talk to her? Regan would say nothing or change the subject and then say, Keep looking, we don't have to decide now.

Ben said, "Regan calls you the girl who does the poetry. I'm not sure if that's good or bad. The mice tell him you're difficult to work with."

"I wish they'd write it, so I could cut it out and pin it on my blouse."

I talked to Darman. "You should go for the job, you deserve it. But you have to go to the mice and tell them you can work with them and look forward to being on their team."

"Oh Dick, I can't do that."

"I know it's demeaning, but grit your teeth."

"Oh, I'll try."

But I never did. It would be like Maggio telling Fatso Judson he runs a good brig.

I met Jeane Dixon at a big party, introduced myself, and, on impulse, told her what was happening. She put her hand on my arm. "I know," she said. What should I do? "Your time with Reagan is not over," she said. "Your work is not done. But you have a problem. You have enemies around the president. Donald Regan does not like you."

"Why?"

"The president thinks well of you. Regan is jealous."

You gotta be kidding. "Jealous of me? He runs the world."

"He feels jealousy."

The next day I told Buchanan, who laughed. "Either she's an excellent reporter or—she's psychic!"

I don't know what to think about jealousy. I couldn't believe Regan was jealous, but others? Yes. I got a lot of attention, and praise.

When a woman at work in a male environment draws jealousy, there's little she can do. For all our sophistication and symposia, she has problems men don't. You can't go down to the gym, which is where the middle-level guys work out their truces, and snap towels, raise little welts of laughter and identification, lean back, scratch, and talk work, wine, and women. When you go out for a drink with the boys you change the dynamic just by being there. Remember those consultants who ran around in the seventies telling women they'd fit in if they'd just learn how to follow football and talk about Sunday's game at the water cooler? This is what I've learned: Boys don't want to talk football with girls. They want to talk football with the guy down the hall who played guard for Ohio State.

All a woman has to protect her is her work; you do your best and slug on and hope the quality will accumulate. Darman once told me, "The only way to take the slings and arrows is to work hard for thirty years, and at the end they'll look back at a body of work and judge you from that. That's the only way to think of it. Try not to worry about the day-by-day."

Ben had a big good-bye party. Most people didn't know he'd been fired; they thought he'd decided to help Jack Kemp in his presidential bid, and Kemp in fact was glad to have him. But there was a sadness. Ben was affectionate and bitter. I'm not sure he even knew who'd done him in. He was a good judge of policy, but of people? No. He was lost there, lacking the insight he could apply with ease to an economic argument. Darman made a speech. It was in speechwriting, he said, that the political and philosophical tensions of the Reagan administration were worked out day by day, and never with more dignity and good humor than by Ben. We applauded.

My internal debate continued. Each day I awoke afraid I'd get the job and afraid I wouldn't. I knew I wasn't suited to the bureaucratic end, to the endless wrangling over sentences and semicolons. And I had a sense of coming disaster. I told my mother, "I just think with all the kind of dumb and aggressive people here that something will happen, and if I take the job a year from now I'll be testifying before a committee." She still reminds me of this. "Listen to your instincts," she said. When Iran-*contra* broke, she called and said, "This is what you were talking about."

Yet I wanted to be given the job, wanted the statement to be made. It wasn't the desire to shape Reagan's rhetoric, because the next person who had Ben's job would shape nothing but his or her response to the diminution of the office's power. And I didn't want to assign the speeches and do the paper work and tell the researcher why she couldn't get a raise. It was ego, only ego. And bad motives bring bad ends.

Finally one day Regan told Buchanan, No, not her.

Pat called me at home. "He turned you down. He wouldn't say why."

"Who got it?"

"No one, he hasn't decided."

"Then I'm leaving, Pat, I'm out, it's not fun anymore. And speech-writing here is finished."

"I know," he said. "Good luck."

I wrote a letter of resignation to the president, and signed it with x's for kisses. My secretary said no, they won't like it, so I sent a plain one, got mad and sent the kisses. I don't know if it ever reached him.

Regan said nothing when Buchanan told him. I never heard from the president. Two weeks later I got a form letter thanking me for my contribution to the administration. It was signed by the autograph pen.

The day Ben left, he had a last meeting with the president. For weeks he'd been debating whether to tell him what happened. At the end he decided he had to know if the president knew. As they stood together, he said, "Mr. President, I hope you know I was fired."

Reagan stepped back as if he'd seen a weapon. "Oh," he said, softly. They shook hands. The photographer clicked.

The day I left, weeks after, I didn't get a good-bye moment. Regan said it wasn't necessary.

I spent the rest of the summer floating in the pool and reading Edith Wharton—*The Age of Innocence, The House of Mirth,* the R.W.B. Lewis biography. A friend asked why. Because I want to understand people in society, I never have, and because she left everything, an entire world, when she left her husband and went to Europe.

You mean she burned her bridges.

None she didn't wish in cinders.

My aunt Peggy used to tell me, "Sometimes you must sit and wait for the future to reveal itself." I was a writer and there were a million things to write, job offers, senators calling for speeches. But none of it was right.

I met with Ted Kennedy about a book he wanted to do, a memoir of the late thirties and early forties, when his brothers were young and in the navy and his father was ambassador. But he couldn't seem to say what he wanted to say, and referred me to his friends for his memories. I met with his staff, who seemed to control the operation, and with no great respect. That's civilization, and, as Huck said, I been there before.

It was a luxury to indulge my confusion, but it seemed prudent to indulge. One day as the leaves were falling and the woods of northern

Virginia turning gray, I heard on the radio a first report of what they were calling the Iran-*contra* affair. I thought, It's over. I'd better write about it before it fully recedes. I needed to work at home anyway; in seven months I would have a child.

I visited the White House for atmosphere. In the first weeks after I left, people would glide past me with a quick hello and never stop. After Regan left, the same people kissed me and said how much they missed me. "I hate to say it, but I never liked those guys, they were just—well, you know." They all wanted to be on the record.

It was the dynamic by which people in an institution protect it, and themselves. You leave unhappily and abruptly, and you soon find that people are running you down, because if you were good then your absence means the office is diminished and if the office is diminished then their stature is diminished. So they denigrate your work. You hear about it and feel bad. And you're surprised a month later when you see them at a party and they give you a big hello as if nothing's happened. And you realize two things. One is that even their enmity isn't authentic. The other is that it's not personal, it's only business, like the Mafia.

The day Regan stormed out of the White House, I got a call on my answering machine: "Hey Peggy, Don Regan didn't get his good-bye moment."

A year later I went to a small dinner for Beryl Sprinkel, the chairman of the Council of Economic Advisers, at the Chevy Chase Club. In walked Don Regan. We sat across from each other. He was responsible for my leaving the White House, but the mess he made contributed to his downfall: The way I figured it, we were even. We had a drink and a nice time.

Later a friend laughed. "The Irish," she said.

"No, that wasn't Irish, that was Washington. As Sam Donaldson said, 'Only the amateurs stay mad.' "

Regan's fall was savage and hurt him to the quick. But there was something moving in how he dealt with it. So much of life is what you admit, and Regan wouldn't admit he was finished, so he wasn't. He got the advance, wrote the book, signed on with a network, gave the speeches, went to the club. He survived, and this is what I learned from watching: All defeat is a collaboration. And as usual, Don Regan wouldn't cooperate.

.   .   .

A few months later, in the early winter of '88, I was in the car with my mother in Virginia. She was visiting from New Jersey. We were on our way to get the weekly food order and listening to the radio. There was a soundbite of George Bush, who'd just arrived in New Hampshire after losing the previous night to Bob Dole in Iowa. He sounded lost. "I am one of you," he said, echoing Dole's effective line to the farmers outside Des Moines.

I had quietly rooted for Kemp, but he was finished. It was going to be Bush or Dole, either/or. Now it was a contest, when I'd always thought Bush would win in a walk. Dole's fine, I told my mother, but he's not the Reagan revolution, he's not the continuance, he's a guy on the Hill who does deals.

I had been on the sidelines for a year and a half, living a very un-Washington life, nursing a baby and going sometimes to the Safeway at night, seeing women push carts up and down the aisles. Why do you shop at nine at night? I asked a woman who lived down the road. "Are you kidding? I do this for fun. I leave him with the kids, and get out of the house!" I was far from the White House, from that world.

And now here was Bush, a good man who was losing. He now was the continuance of Reaganism; he was the next step, the most likely guy to continue what drew me from journalism to politics. And he was misunderstood.

I turned to my mother. "If I went away for a week, could you stay down and take care of the baby?" Sure, what're you thinking of? "New Hampshire."

I turned the car around, called Craig Fuller, Bush's chief of staff, who said, Come up! And so I was in politics again.

The light is white as cotton outside the cool windows. The overnights are bad. They're doing daily polling and we're losing, we're losing—two, three, four points a night. Wirthlin, we hear, has called Dole Mr. President. The snow becomes a blizzard. We sit in a hotel—it's all hotels in a campaign, and when you get home you dial nine for an outside line. Fuller, a full man, is calm; Teeter does not totter; Atwater's aggression keeps depression at bay, except for one moment three days before the voting when he ruffles his hands through his hair, elbows on knees, and says, "We're gonna lose this thing, we're gonna lose it, I can feel it." No one replies. He shakes his head as if to shake it out, and does. The next day he is his fighting self. He lives on the balls of his feet.

Bush had been placid but frustrated. I had joined him on Air Force Two, kissed him hello and said How are you? I'm okay, he says, but we gotta get me out there, we gotta sort of get me out there, they don't know me.

He is right. He is famous but unknown. I had worked with him on his announcement speech, spent time with him, listened, probed. I am not as shy with him as with Reagan; I am older now. I go to the back of the plane. "He's got to tell them who he is," says Teeter. "We've got to get him to talk about himself and show what's inside him," says Pete Teeley. He's Irish and lives on wit and coffee. "Make it clear what the differences between him and Dole are," says Atwater.

I went to my room with my typewriter and set up business. A speechwriter asked me later, "Were you like Dick Goodwin when he went up to New Hampshire in '68, threw his typewriter on the bed, and said 'I'm going to take down a president'?"

No. I forgot to be romantic. But it was the dream of every speechwriter to come in at a crucial time and make a difference. This time I was going to get it right, no staffing process to mess it up, no suits. I'm going to do it the way it should be.

I wrote from memory. The things he had told me about the war, and going to Texas to start a business and worrying about the payroll, being a father. In the speech he would tell who he was and say—for this, I think, is what he thinks—"I feel like Lincoln, here I stand, warts and all." Which I also wrote from memory, and was caught by the catcher in the wry, William Safire, who told me, Lincoln never said that. I run to Bartlett's. It was Cromwell, in a letter to an artist about his portrait. And "here I stand" is an echo of: Luther. Well, anyway, Lincoln had warts.

We travel by day, in a caravan through the state. I write by night. I have never been away from the baby, and when I see a child at a rally, I lactate, which is embarrassing, and difficult in a male environment to explain.

I go to dinner with Bush and ask him questions. We sit in the back of a restaurant; Bob Teeter is with us. It is late, we are tired, we have a drink. People come by and say hello, and it's so unlike being with Reagan. With him the aura kept people away. With Bush no one is shy; they come up and touch him and pat his back, whisper, This

Tuesday I'm voting for you, give him a little punch on the shoulder. He is conversational, curious.

The knock is that he is not Reagan. He's not. Why should he be? He is a quiet man. Don't try to make him sound like something he's not. Can the high rhetoric. Listen to what he says about the war. *I am a quiet man, but there's nothing quiet about my love of country.*

We talk about the Rather-Bush bout. I tell him that I used to work for Rather, I love him, I was maybe the only person in America that night seeing two people she personally cared about tearing each other apart on live TV. It was like being a child at the top of the stairs hearing her parents in a terrible fight. He laughs, is philosophical—I've always liked Dan too—seems to carry no anger. As we walk out, the people in the kitchen come out to wave.

We are in a van, careening along a highway. We beep at Pat Robertson's motorcade, which is going to where we just left, and Kemp's. Maybe Ben is there. All the combined expertise of the most sophisticated men and machines is working to tell us what will happen in just two days, what the voters will do, but only one person knows. She is sitting in the back, quiet and unassuming. I think she is a secretary's mother. No no, I am told, she's Nancy Sununu, the governor's wife. Oh.

"Mrs. Sununu, you know New Hampshire, and you know these people. Is Bush going to win?"

"Oh shawuh, he's gonna win fine."

Everyone turns and looks at her.

"By how much?"

"Five to ten points. Don't worry, five to ten points."

Which was in fact correct.

* * * * * * * * * * *

SEVENTEEN

A Thousand Points
of Light

"**G**ot the terminal jits." "Wearin' a raincoat called fear." "Fine 'cept for the family of squirrels that's living in my intestines chasing a walnut up and down." I always expressed my anxiety in a southern accent. I think it made me feel distanced, as if it were someone else waking up at 3:00 A.M. with dysrhythmia.

I was working on the vice president's acceptance speech, which was to be delivered in two weeks to the Republican National Convention in New Orleans. I had spent two days with him on the road, trailing him from plane to limo to holding room to limo to plane. Where he went I went, peppering him with questions.

In June we hadn't known it would all be so important, but then Dukakis gave his speech, and the Democrats came out of their convention fourteen points ahead, and suddenly the acceptance speech was crucial. Ten days before the Bush speech, the papers were saying if he failed in New Orleans, his campaign would be all uphill. Then came Quayle, and the controversy surrounding his choice. The speech clamor reached a crescendo: "If the speech doesn't vault him over the debris Thursday night, he will have lost his own convention; and he will never recover."

I am looking at a memo I sent to the vice president in July. It is annotated in his handwriting and shows some of the confidence he felt.

"This is arguably the most important speech of your life. More people will see you than have ever seen you before; some of them will be making their first judgment about you." In the margin a simple "Yes."

"This is an opportunity to talk about why you went into public service and what it means to you . . . This is an opportunity to talk also about the philosophy that guides you. I suspect you think, I am in basic agreement with basic conservative principles—small government is better than big, low taxes better than high, strong defense better than weak . . . if this is what you think then let's say it." To which he wrote, "Yes, but more passion."

"It might be good if somewhere along the line you could talk a bit about how you see yourself in this race . . . What I mean is: Hubert Humphrey used to tell his aides that maybe he wasn't dramatic like Bobby and a big intellectual like Gene, but he was a good solid man with long experience and he could do the job. He understood his own unflashy superiority. If he'd been able to communicate that in a way that didn't criticize anyone else, he might have won by a point instead of losing." The vice president wrote, again on the margin: "à la N.H'shire OK (see attached notes)."

Bringing up the combination of excitement, competitiveness, and tension that would hit anyone on the night of such a speech, I wrote, "Think of this: You're going to walk out there into the lights and face a cheering, frenzied mob . . ." On the margin he wrote, "I have no fear of that."

The "attached note" was the first of many, six handwritten pages containing his thoughts on what he wanted to communicate.

"[I] know where I want to go—have the experience to get there— jobs, peace, education.

"My background is one thing . . . I've worked, I've fought for my country, I've served, I've built—I want to lead.

On foreign policy: "Let others propose turning our decisions and our leadership over to a multilateral body—We have a special obligation to lead—we must not forsake our responsibility . . . We owe it to the free nations of the world—to lead to stay strong, to care."

On arms control/defense issues: "No unilateral cuts in the essential military strength of this country . . . Pride in staying firm until we accomplish what had *never* been done in nuclear age—ban an entire generation of weapons." And, "Chemical-Biological—The image of mother shielding her child from invisible death—horror—I want to lead[,] would find way to ban chemical, biological weapons."

On the national character: "We are just plain the kindest nation in the world so that when a baby is starving in Ethiopia we reach out." On domestic issues: "Probably need a reference to sanctity of human life," and "Yes, I do feel kids should say the Pledge of Allegiance," etc.

More: "What hurts? an abused child a scared child an unloved child." And: "I do not fear the future . . . Opportunity—Experience—Jobs—Private lives—Faith in God."

Even a list of words that have special meaning for him: "Family, kids, grandkids, love, decency, honor, pride, tolerance, hope, kindness, loyalty, freedom, caring, heart, faith, service to country, fair (fair play), strength, healing, excellence."

And about George Bush himself: "Others may speak better, look better, be smoother, more creative but I must be myself. I want you to know my heartbeat—this is where I'd lead" and "I'm proud of USA I'm experienced I know good honest people when I see em," more on his feelings on ethics and education and the disabled and children. Finally, of the speech itself: "Let's aim for the right or left field seats—just inside the foul line—top deck though -"—and signed "GB."

More notes would come. I'd be sitting at the word processor in my living room when suddenly a long black White House car would ease down the driveway, and soon Mr. Kim, the vice president's driver, would be calling from the car phone three feet from the front door. "You come out, please—you big dog, move on!" I'd grab our too-friendly German shepherd; Mr. Kim would hand me an envelope all taped up by the vice president with more directions.

One day it was a two-page typed letter headed "WHO I AM." The vice president had, simply and without rhetoric, set down where he and Dukakis differ on current and longstanding issues. It later became a well-known and highly effective part of the speech.

"I am one who is *not* a card carrying member of the ACLU.

"I am one who feels it is *wrong* to release from prison murderers who have not served enough time to be eligible for parole.

"I am one who believes it is *right* for teachers to say the 'Pledge of Allegiance' to the flag of our country.

"I am one who opposes federal gun control—but who favors judges who will have a little less sympathy for the criminals and a little more for the victims of crime.

"I am one who would not cut the inside from our strategic defense—one who, based on experience, would build on our record of banning for the first time in this nuclear age an entire generation of missiles.

"I am one who does not believe that every Governor should have the right to veto a decision by the Commander-in-Chief to dispatch the National Guard to wherever required.

"I am one who respects the sanctity of human life and is deeply concerned about the 20 million abortions that have happened . . ."

On it went, as he drew the line between himself and Dukakis.

"I am one who knows that it is only the United States that can strongly stand up for freedom and democracy around the world.

"I am one who understands the limits of Federal Government and understands the power of the private sector—churches, families, local governments—one who understands the power of the individual to help his fellow man.

"I am the one who believes in public service and aspires to the highest possible standards. People should come to Washington to serve—not to profit.

"I am one who will work with Congress but understands that one party domination of Congress by big spenders there resulted in huge deficits. It is Congress that appropriates every dime and tells the Executive Branch how to spend every dime. I will cooperate but I will not be intimidated."

The line-item veto. Balanced-budget amendment. Support for voluntary prayer in the schools. And, "I will put a freeze on spending and I will not raise taxes."

One thing the list did was break the "I" barrier. George Bush hated to say "I." The speculation among his friends and staff was that it was due to his doughty old mom, who used to rap his knuckles for bragging, a brag apparently being defined as any sentence with the first-person singular as its subject. It was a problem for me because when I wrote "I" in a speech, rather than change the pronoun, he'd sometimes kill the whole sentence or thought.

I became adept at pronounless sentences, I did. Instead of "I moved to Texas and soon we joined the Republican party," it was, "Moved to Texas, joined the Republican party, raised a family." Had the benefit of sounding natural and relaxed, the drawback of sometimes being hard to pull off. Imagined him raising his hand on the Capitol steps—"Do solemnly swear, will preserve and protect . . ."

During the campaign, I don't know why, the I-ectomies ended. But we were both so used to the "I"-less style that I tended to keep writing it, and he tended to keep saying it.

In the two days I spent with Bush that June I saw more of him than I had since New Hampshire, which in turn was the most I'd been exposed to him since the White House. I had known him slightly there, worked on a few speeches with him, thought he was the next president. When, in the fall of 1987, I worked with him on his announcement speech, my interest quickened.

He would be at his desk, casual, legs stretched out, head cocked. I sense his diffidence and his determination. None of the great-man manner, self-deprecating, modest. And yet: He will have this thing.

I find that it is easiest to engage him on the plane; the fact that it is speeding through the air seems to relieve his need for movement. The car is good too.

Once during the trip I was trying to push Bush to be more personal and reflective on the subject of the family—its role in society, what it means to him. He was distracted, elliptic. We were on our way from the airport into New York City, the vice president sprawled on one side of the seat, Mrs. Bush, who was traveling with him for the day, next to him, I on the jump seat.

I asked about Texas, about what it was like moving there and being young and newly wed. Mrs. Bush told funny stories about the man down the street who still went around in a horse-drawn wagon, and the man who always used to come over to say hi to George at dinnertime, so after a while she just started putting three potatoes in the oven, three chops in the pan. The vice president was looking out the window, adding a word here and there.

Finally, exasperated, I said, "Well, what made you have a family anyhow? Why did you start having kids?"

Mrs. Bush's eyes went wide. "Why, Peggy!"

"Oh my!" I said, embarrassed. "That *was* personal, and I do apologize." The vice president began to laugh. I reddened. Mrs. Bush, having caught me, saved me.

"Don't apologize. That's a perfectly appropriate question for your generation, because, of course, for all of you the decision to have a baby is truly a decision. But in our time it was different, you married and had children, it was what you did. And we did too."

The conversation gave me something: What she remembered about Texas was that it was so hot in the summer you could hardly bear it, but even with the discomfort, even though they were apart from their families, they weren't lonely or anxious. They thought it was an adventure, in part because there was a certain Eleanor-and-Franklin component to the move. Mrs. Bush told me, "George's mother was a formidable and strong woman, and so was my mother, and we wanted to get out from under the parental gaze, be on our own!" Forty years later her eyes blazed with the memory of her hunger.

She is a strong woman, not ego-driven but protective of kith and kin. Those merry eyes, the warmth, the ability to get the help cracking in a jolly way, and then not so jolly. A lack of pretension, a breeziness, but underneath she is Greenwich granite, one of the women who settled the hard gray shores of the East and summoned roses from the rocks.

They say that she had been hurt by Mrs. Reagan, patronized or ignored. I do not know if it is true. There are always such stories. But if it was, she would not take revenge, or would take it so subtly, so much the slight absence of a warmth than the presence of a coolness, that Mrs. Reagan would barely see it, and only feel later, in bed, a slight discomfort at . . . what? An undigested bit of beef, a crumb of cheese, a fragment of an underdone potato?

Resolute with an air of flexibility. A good match: a team.

One afternoon on the plane I asked the vice president when he first became aware, as an adult, of the reality of poverty. He told me of getting to know the barrios and border towns of Texas, when he was a young man first running for Congress. He was walking in a barrio when he saw coming along the street a little boy who was wearing ragged clothing, an old undershirt, no shoes. With him was his mother. They were holding hands. Bush saw the poverty, but was struck by something else. He said, This little boy had nothing in terms of physical things, but here he is with his mother, and they're together and he's happy, there's love, and it was a feeling of how much we have in common. He was like my kids.

He talked about children, how he worries about the kids in the cities who have nothing, and he doesn't know what we can do to help them,

"But that doesn't mean you give up." He spoke of going to Africa and holding in his arms children who were victims of famine. "The one I feel in my heart was when we held the seven-year-old kid in our arms in Somalia." He made a cradling motion. "Seven years, seventeen pounds. It haunted me."

I asked Bush about a note he'd sent that said, "I know what drives me . . . Everyone matters." He talked about how America has challenged the world to solve the problem of poverty. "You have to put something back in, put something back. It's caring about others."

I had already received his list of words that had special meaning for him—"kindness," "caring," "decency," "heart." I thought of what he had told me. He spoke with a gentleness that was striking. This was the genesis of "I want a kinder, gentler nation."

(People ask me if I knew it would become the phrase that people thought of when they thought of Bush and his presidency. The answer is no. I knew it was striking because it marked a break with what had been perceived, often rightly, as the careless effulgence of the Reagan era; and because it was Bush; and because it reflected the future of conservatism and the yearnings of the young of the Reagan administration. But such phrases only work if they're genuine to the man and part of the warp and woof of the text, and for that reason they don't jump out at you as you go over the speech. But I keep as a prized memento an early draft in which after "I want a kinder nation" there is a scribbled little caret with the word "gentler.")

Bush spoke of the sanctity of human life, of his son's newly adopted daughter, how he and Mrs. Bush had wept at the christening. "Try to touch on this delicately."

On public service and ethics: Government isn't supposed to be personally profitable. "I was worth four times as much in 1960 as I am today . . . But it doesn't matter. We don't want to do fancy things or own stuff."

He told me that in his speech he wanted to take issue with the idea that America is in decline, "all that doom and gloom." He spoke of how he and Mrs. Bush had lived in forty-three houses in twenty-one cities since he'd left the service, which made him a uniquely national candidate. "When you do that, you understand this country. Its patriotism, strength, love. 'And so I come to you a national candidate.' "

There was another conversation on Friday morning, the day after Dukakis's convention speech. I had left Air Force Two as the speech began and listened to it in the car as I drove home from Andrews. It was workmanlike but undistinguished. I was relieved. We can take this guy, I thought.

I stand by that judgment of the speech as literature, but I missed the impact of the presentation—the darkened hall, the booming rendition of "Coming to America," the dramatic entrance through the crowd, the almost glimmer Dukakis had as he seized his moment and squeezed it like a diamond. Stagecraft can make a so-so speech a fine speech, as I had well learned in the Reagan White House, and that is what happened to Dukakis that night.

But I didn't know it then. Friday morning I arrived early at Andrews, and as soon as we were in the air, the vice president called me to his cabin. I told him Dukakis was okay, no big deal. He shook his head: He was good.

But, he said, "Dukakis said, 'The Reagan era is over.' Well: Really? The era of prosperity, an era of unprecedented opportunity, an era of pride in our country?" He went through the policy differences that divided him and Dukakis and directed me again to include them in clear, blunt language. "Dukakis never mentioned freedom, democracy, liberty—what about these?," and "Our peace today is less fragile, more guaranteed. [The foreign-policy] credential is totally lacking." And, "This is no time to get someone with no experience into the ball game—with the Communist world tremors—this is a time for tested men. This is no time to gamble."

I left that night with a final instruction from Bush: "No personal attack on Dukakis. Nothing personal. Just the issues."

I went home that weekend, gathered my notes, and began to write. "Ladies and gentlemen, thank you very much . . ."

Dukakis had spoken for almost an hour, including applause, so he probably walked in with a forty-, forty-five-minute speech. About twenty, twenty-five pages, double-spaced. We'd go as long.

I wrote every morning from nine to noon. My son was just over a year old and had recently learned to walk. He would come into the living room, drawn by the sound of TV or the stereo, see me at the computer, laugh, and run to me in a kind of dance—he was so proud of his new ability that sometimes in his excitement he'd throw both legs into the air and fall backward with a great whoosh from his diapers—climb onto me and get down to business, which is the keyboard, which he slaps palms down. He thinks the word processor is a form of TV with a black screen and squiggly green letters; he likes to make the cursor dance.

The baby-sitter would gather him up, take him down to the kitchen to play; I'd hear him gurgling and trying to speak. (Oh lucky to be a writer and not a surgeon—"Mees Noon," Carmen would say when she comes to clean on Thursdays, "You makin a big mess with all this blood, and last week we found a leg in the pantry!"—or a trial lawyer— "Ladies and gentlemen of the jury: Do you want more coffee? Watch that chair, there's a screw loose in the back"—or a waitress. Lucky to lose neither profession nor propinquity.)

I'd break for lunch, go back to work, break at four. Every day I'd hear on the phone from a friend these words: You must be nervous, kiddo, 'cause if he's great he could win, but if he blows it he's ghost-he's-toast-he's gone.

Thanks.

"Ladies and gentlemen, thank you very much. I have many friends to thank tonight. I thank the voters who supported me. I thank the gallant men who entered the contest for the presidency this year, and who have honored me with their support." Acknowledge the keynoter, and former president Ford. Then, get to the point: "I accept your nomination for president." And show your resolve: "I mean to run hard, to fight hard, to stand on the issues—and I mean to win."

Refer to Reagan with love and respect and get him off the stage. Then:

"But now you must see me for what I am: the Republican candidate for president of the United States." ("But now you must see me . . ." an echo of the duke of Windsor's "You must believe me when I tell you . . ." Utterly earnest, yet conversational.)

"And now I turn to the American people to share my hopes and intentions and why—and where—I wish to lead." (Lean forward, I'm going to tell you who I am and what I mean to do.)

Where to after that? To Bush's last words to me when I left the plane: no personal attacks, no personal references.

"I reject the temptation to engage in personal references. My approach this evening is, as Sergeant Joe Friday used to say, 'Just the facts, ma'am.' [Everyone in America over age thirty-five—which is to say most voters—would understand the reference to the old detective series *Dragnet.*] After all, the facts are on our side."

And after that—what?

After that came the laying on of hands. You could call what follows "Now is the time for all good men and women to come to the aid of their party." Because they did.

The speech was a success because it reflected some of the best ideas of the Republican party of the past twenty years, the very ideas that were peeling voters from the Democratic party in the quiet realignment of the eighties. And some of the best minds in the Republican party collaborated on it, though they did not know. It was spontaneous, unplanned. They thought Bush was in trouble, and they wanted to help.

Every day calls and letters would come to my home from people with advice and ideas. I'd be writing upstairs, and my mother would be answering the phone and taking notes in the bedroom, and the fax would be spitting out memos in the kitchen, and the baby would be running to catch them and throw them in the air.

Peter Wallison, President Reagan's former lawyer, sent a letter saying, Dukakis talks about competence but what measure of anything is that? Competence makes the trains go on time but doesn't even know where they're going!

Senator Bob Kasten called to say Bush would be most effective if he almost took the stance of a military officer outlining the mission to the party faithful. Roger Ailes wrote a memo noting that Bush tended to see life in terms of missions assigned and completed, and perhaps good use could be made of this.

Jack Kemp told me, Hit hard on taxes, Bush will be pressured to raise them as soon as he's elected, and he has to make clear he won't budge. (This became, "The Congress will push me to raise taxes, and I'll say no, and they'll push, and I'll say no, and they'll push again. And all I can say to them is read my lips: No New Taxes." Aides to the vice president later took out "read my lips" on the grounds, I believe, that lips are organs, there is no history of presidential candidates making personal-organ references in acceptance speeches, therefore . . . Anyway, I kept putting it back in. Why? Because it's definite. It's not subject to misinterpretation. It means, I mean this.)

Mike Horowitz, counsel to the OMB in Reagan's first term and an old White House friend, sent me a book of memoirs of pioneer women in late nineteenth-century Kansas, which contributed to the education section. He urged that Bush make clear he's spent a lifetime rejecting privilege, that the America that appeals to him is the pioneer spirit, that's what Texas was about.

Congressman Newt Gingrich of Georgia called to say the speech must delineate the differences between Bush and Dukakis in the area of traditional values; do not forget the old strengths and the differences between them on such elementary and cutting issues as crime and punishment, gun control, right to life.

Craig Fuller, the vice president's chief of staff, wrote out rhetorical advice: Set up the idea that the campaign hasn't really begun, but now is the moment it has—"Tonight's the night!"

I asked a gifted humor writer in Los Angeles named Doug Gamble to do some jokes in which Bush would poke fun of himself and his patrician background. Doug came up with what I think is the best and funniest joke of the '88 campaign—"There are actually those who claim that I don't always communicate in the clearest, most concise way. But I dare them to keep it up. Go ahead, make my twenty-four-hour time period."

He contributed wonderful witticisms, but his most important contribution was not a joke but a beautiful metaphor taken from FDR's 1940 campaign slogan: Don't change horses in midstream. "My friends, these days the world moves even more quickly, and now, after two great terms, a switch will be made. But when you have to change horses in midstream, doesn't it make sense to switch to the one who's going the same way?" Months later Ronald Reagan told me this was the single best statement of what was at issue in the 1988 campaign.

For two weeks I stayed home and wrote and threw away and wrote; if you had seen those drafts, you would have seen clots of ideas on clean paper, globs of rhetoric awkwardly phrased. Write, comb it out, rewrite, keep combing. You love that little phrase and you keep keeping it in, but it doesn't connect with anything anymore and it doesn't matter if it has a kind of half-eloquence. "We must kill our little darlings," said Mary McCarthy.

Staticky calls from the vice president.

"This is White House Signal, Air Force Two for Peggy Noonan."

"This is her, she."

"The vice president calling Miss Noonan."

"Fine."

"This is not a secure line."

"Fine."

"Please hold."

You hear the seas and the oceans.

"Peg? How the heck are ya?"

"Fine."

"Going okay?"

"Yup. Fine."

"Can I get you anything? You okay with enough ideas and thoughts and all?"

The baby screaming, hitting the floor with a salad spoon.

"How are you doing, really?"

"Well, I'm in the part of creativity where you realize you have no talent."

Silence.

"Uh, actually I'm fine, I just have the jits but it's going great."

"Don't let the gurus get on your nerves. If they bother you, tell me."

"Thanks."

"Okay. Over and out."

Bob Teeter called to say that it was crucial that the speech communicate the fact that George Bush has been around the presidency for twenty years and understands what being president is. A writer named Ray Siller sent to the vice president a stinging rejoinder to a Dukakis jibe about Reagan: "The other day, in referring to the Reagan administration, Michael Dukakis said that there's an old Greek expression, 'The fish rots from the head down.' I'd like to make the governor aware of an old American expression, 'A small man never got taller by chopping the legs off a giant.' " The fact that Bush sent it to me meant he was in a certain mood; I put it in, thinking he'd take it out. He did.

I went to a meeting with young members of the campaign staff—the domestic-affairs adviser Deborah Steelman, foreign-affairs adviser Dennis Ross, political affairs adviser Jim Pinkerton—and somebody said (in quotes in my notes with no name attached), "The thing to get across is, you've never had it so good—don't let 'em take it away."

"You've never had it so good" is, of course, a boastful and unpersuasive LBJ-ism and was being used as shorthand, but 'don't let 'em take it away' became a highly effective refrain, with Bush as protector: The good economy has helped empower women and give hope to young people, "and I'm not going to let them take it away from you."

But it was Bill Gavin, one of the stars of Richard Nixon's murderer's row of Safire, Buchanan, Price, Gavin, and Stein, the 1928 Yankees of speechwriting staffs, who provided the fist of the speech, the center of intellectual energy from which all else flowed.

Gavin is a bluff, gruff Irishman, generous and quick-talking, who wrote in the early 1970s something that had a strong impact on young incipient conservatives: *Street Corner Conservative,* a memoir of how a working-class kid from a Democratic home made it over to the other side, and why. It was the first time anyone in national politics spoke directly to the up-and-coming constituency of young ethnic Catholics who were, in the early seventies, forming political views and trying to figure out where they fit in.

Gavin called to say he wanted to fax some material he felt would be helpful. What he sent was a little mini-essay on the idea of community, an idea he'd touched on before but that became clearer and more concrete for him when he read the work of William Shambra in the magazine *Catholicism in Crisis* in 1984.

Shambra argued that the old New Deal idea of a national community—the vision of the country as one big family or town with a powerful central government to express and reinforce that vision—was over, for a number of reasons, and what had taken its place was something of a synthesis of New Left and New Right impulses: a nation of many different communities, formal and informal, living and working together.

Shambra drew on the work of Michael Novak, who had written in *The Rise of the Unmeltable Ethnics* of a growing self-awareness and self-assertiveness among various American ethnic groups who did not wish to accept the imposed values of a single homogeneous national community. The descendants of the immigrants of Eastern and Southern Europe possessed, he wrote, a strong sense of family, custom, neighborhood. Novak argued that this could lead to a new kind of politics for America.

Gavin noted that George Bush's views on local control, local involvement, and where the real wellsprings of American energy are (you guessed it—they're local) were perfectly reflected in Shambra's and Novak's work.

And he was right, it was all there, I read and thought, This is Bush; this is what he means. (Gavin said, This is also the perfect answer to Cuomo and his wagon-train metaphor, where the nation is a wagon train and he's the wagon master. The nation isn't a wagon train it's many, many wagon trains, and many different kinds of wagons, and destinations, and ways of getting to the destination.)

It became the center of the speech. To lead into it, a restating of the conservative credo:

"An election that is about ideas and values is also about philosophy. And I have one.

"At the bright center is the individual. And radiating out from him or her is the family, the essential unit of closeness and of love. For it is the family that communicates to our children—to the twenty-first century—our culture, our religious faith, our traditions and history.

"From the individual to the family to the community, and on out to the town, to the church and school, and, still echoing out, to the country, the state, the nation—each doing only what it does well, and no more. And I believe that power must always be kept close to the individual—close to the hands that raise the family and run the home.

"I am guided by certain traditions. One is that there is a God and He is good, and His love, while free, has a self-imposed cost: We must be good to one another. . . .

"And there is another tradition. And that is the idea of community—a beautiful word with a big meaning, though liberal Democrats have an odd view of it. They see community as a limited cluster of interest groups, locked in odd conformity. In this view the country waits passive while Washington sets the rules.

"But that's not what community means—not to me.

"For we are a nation of communities, of thousands and tens of thousands of ethnic, religious, social, business, labor union, neighborhood, regional and other organizations, all of them varied, voluntary, and unique.

"This is America: the Knights of Columbus, the Grange, Hadassah, the Disabled American Veterans, the Order of Ahepa, the Business and Professional Women of America, the union hall, the Bible study group, LULAC, Holy Name—a brilliant diversity spread like stars, like a thousand points of light in a broad and peaceful sky.

"Does government have a place? Yes. Government is part of the nation of communities—not the whole, just a part."

That litany of organizations—reading it still gives me a chill. That's the America I know, maybe the America you know. Holy Name and the Knights of Columbus, that's what they went to on Wednesday night in Brooklyn and Massapequa. The Order of Ahepa was my own small joke: It's the Greek fraternal organization.

No one knew what an impact "a thousand points of light" would have. It became Bush's shorthand way of referring to the network of helping organizations throughout the country, and it became in some circles the object of derision, or at least good-natured spoofing. The cartoonist Herblock had a neighborhood drunk asking for "a thousand pints of Lite," and a character on *Murphy Brown* wound up getting invited to the inauguration because "I'm the guy who gave him 'a thousand points of light.' I thought it was a joke—I didn't know it would win the election for him!"

It was my favorite phrase in the speech because its power is born of the fact that it sounds like what it is describing: an expanse of separate yet connected entities sprinkled across a broad and peaceful sky, which is America, the stretched continent. Why stars for communities? I don't know, it was right. Separate, bright and shining, each part of a whole and yet discrete. Why a thousand? I don't know. A thousand clowns, a thousand days—a hundred wasn't enough and a million is too many.

The phrase later caused some problems. First, someone in Pennsylvania apparently called a radio talk show a few weeks after the speech and said the phrase a thousand points of light is from a Nazi hymnbook, or was a famous Nazi phrase. This sent the campaign into a tizzy; I started getting calls from young campaign aides asking, "Could you tell us which Nazi hymnbook the lights thing came from?"

I'd sigh and say, "Look, in the age of Joe Biden you don't plagiarize, and if you do, you don't plagiarize from Nazis, do you? 'Cause that could really hurt the ol' career!" They believed this: It was practical.

I worried for weeks. Was it possible a Nazi had used the same phrase? A number of media outlets went on a search and found nothing. Weeks later, one morning in bed, it hit me: the thousand-year Reich! Some old guy who's losing his hearing or was drunk misheard it.

Then part two: "A thousand points of light" is from the Bible. Oh no, it is? Nah. Then: It's from an old English poem, from the time of *Beowulf.* Oh no, it is? But it was just a rumor. Five months after the speech, in January, the "Inside the Beltway" section of the *Washington Times* said that Van Gogh in his letters described stars as "points of light," which didn't surprise me—that *is* what stars look like—but also that the great C. S. Lewis had used the phrase "a thousand points of light" in one of his science-fiction books, which did surprise me. I haven't read it, but I assume the *Times* was right because it cited the page number of a specific edition, a show of confidence that suggests the writer had the book in his hands as he wrote. People ask me now if that's where it came from. I say no and think of Joseph Brodsky at his trial: "I thought that it came from God." (Thousand-points update: Mike Royko just said the phrase "a thousand points of friendly light" is in Thomas Wolfe's *The Web and the Rock.* Which I read as a teenager. Is it possible it was on file in my unconscious and bubbled up when I needed the right phrase? Yes.) (POL update, summer '89: The president's researchers in June of '89 found a letter in which Alexander Hamilton, urging General Washington to seek the presidency, wrote, "The point of light in which you stand . . . will make an infinite difference. . . .") (POL update, autumn '89: William Safire sends on a copy of a speech given by an engineer at the turn of the century. He urges the city fathers of Venice to electrify the city and fill it with "a thousand points of light.")

When I had finished the draft, I brought it into an informal speech committee of Dick Darman, Bob Teeter, and Bob Zoellick, a former aide to James Baker when he was secretary of the treasury, and in the campaign an aide to Teeter. We met in Teeter's small and cramped office in the campaign, going over every word and phrase, having disagreements, usually minor.

Teeter—tidy, fastidious, Zenlike in his approach to management (let it unfold!), full of sound judgment but perhaps not fully alive to the fact that some things cannot be quantified—Teeter felt that we hadn't given enough attention to those who have been left out of the recovery. Zoellick contributed the emotional language that punched up this section: "I've seen the urban children who play amidst the shattered glass and shattered lives. . . . They're there. We have to help them."

But it was Darman who was the key to the process, Darman who'd bore in and find the weakness in the word, the soft point in the sentence; Darman the inimitable, whom I admire and respect and would sometimes like to punch in the nose. I hadn't seen him much since I'd left the White House, and felt a surge of relief when he first walked in. He has never touched failure.

He saved me from much trouble, and saved things others didn't understand. "Points of light," he said: Make sure that's always in. He understood "kinder, gentler" on all levels. (Not everyone did. A young aide told the vice president, at the end, when I was in the room, "Uh, sir, all this gentle this and gentle that—could it lead to a resurgence of the wimp stuff?" It was the end of the process, and I was in my Ethel-Barrymore-with-a-baseball-bat phase. "Listen," I snapped, "only a man utterly comfortable in his own strength can talk like that, only a strong man can say this!" He blinked. Bush continued reading.)

Darman was, I thought, sometimes too neat, too unknowing of the value of vagueness, and mystery. (Mario Cuomo in his 1984 convention speech talked about how hard his immigrant father worked and how they knew the value of work then, and added, almost as an aside, "and they didn't need psychiatrists to tell them." Which meant nothing— and everything. A Republican vetting that speech would have said, What does psychiatry have to do with it? This is irrelevant, delete!) But my only real complaint was that Darman is a millionaire of the Eastern Establishment, and they always think they know the working class and Reagan Democrats and say things like, "Don't use 'excellent', they think that's an elitist term."

I grunt and sigh. "They" like the word "excellent" just fine; in fact, the highest compliment being paid these days by gentlemen such as my brother Jim, a former teamster who is now a limousine driver and whom perhaps you've bumped into the odd Friday night at La Guardia holding a little sign saying DARMAN, is that something is "fucking excellent."

It's fun pulling class rank with Republicans, cheap but fun: They get so mad. I always talked bad around Darman and Teeter so they'd believe my opinion on regular people had weight. That's how Protestants who went to Harvard think the working class talks.

"Don't use the word 'boutique,' it's elitist."

"It isn't elitist, Dick, it's a mall word, get with the culture."

Nine days before the convention I walked into the vice president's office with Bob Teeter and gave the speech to him and Jim Baker. They read it, seemed to like it, had suggestions for changes and additions.

Baker wanted me to punch up the good economic news; I hadn't put the terms of the expansion forcefully enough. Teeter wanted the speech to communicate the idea that what we're talking about in this election is change—but will it be change as in risk, which is what

Dukakis represents, or change as in improvement, which is what Bush stands for?

Bush worried over the section on contrasts and figured out what was bothering him. He changed the ending on the questions—"Should public school teachers be required to lead our children in the Pledge of Allegiance? I say yes—though my opponent says no," to "My opponent says no, but I say *yes!*" Make it affirmative, he said, not an attack on his views but an affirmation of ours.

He took out a line I loved. It was the end of the section in which he refers to himself and his admitted lack of charisma: "I guess I am plain as a post, but a post can be a pretty sturdy thing."

He read it dryly, then looked up, his glasses perched like a professor's halfway down his nose. "I'd say this if I were plain, but as you can see, I'm not." He looks at me, expressionless. "Can't offend Mother." And wiggles his eyebrows.

The biggest frustration for me was the ending. At first I'd wanted an ending inspired by a quotation from Thornton Wilder's play *Our Town*. There were concrete metaphors in the speech—one in the section that began "at the center is the individual"—that featured a kind of opening up, a flowering or growing of words from a central idea into other ideas. I kept thinking of a part in the play where the Stage Manager/narrator simply and movingly, after all the stories about Emily and George and the rest, places the town of Grover's Corners in the universal scheme of things. I bought a copy and found it wasn't at the end but the beginning, and it wasn't the stage manager but Rebecca Gibbs talking to brother George:

REBECCA: I never told you about that letter Jane Crofut got from her minister when she was sick. He wrote Jane a letter and on the envelope the address was like this: It said: Jane Crofut; The Crofut Farm; Grover's Corners; Sutton County; New Hampshire; United States of America.
GEORGE: What's funny about that?
REBECCA: But listen, it's not finished: the United States of America; Continent of North America; Western Hemisphere; the Earth; the Solar System; the Universe; the Mind of God . . .

It kept moving me, and I kept doing an end that rippled out to "the mind of God" but I couldn't make it work. Just thinking about

Wilder's words though, having them there in my mind, made me jump when Bob Teeter mentioned in passing that the Caterpillar Tractor Company, which only a few years ago had been on the ropes, had just put a third shift on in one of their factories and—

That was the end of the speech! And the moonlight was "the mind of God":

"A few days ago I was told of a factory out in the heartland. Eight years ago they were in big trouble, and it looked like they might go under. But the new economy allowed them to turn it around—and now they've added a third shift. It starts at midnight, goes to eight.

"That's where I'm going to begin this campaign. I'm going to stand there in the moonlight and put out my hand to the men and women who did the work of the expansion. I'm going to tell them thanks. And I'm going to talk to them about a mission.

"And so it begins, with joy and resolve, for what is in the hands of man is in the hands of God—

"an epic campaign for a better America, for an endless dream, and a thousand points of light."

Only Bush didn't really like it. And Baker didn't really like it. And Teeter didn't really like it. And there were problems. Highlighting an individual company is looking for trouble of all kinds; it would mean last-minute scheduling changes, and telling the other side where you're going gives them time to plan a demonstration and arrange a spontaneous and embarrassing exchange with a worker. . . .

The final ending was one Bush was more comfortable with—a quick summation and a resummoning of imagery.

I still like that speech; I reread it the other day. I felt as if I'd pulled together the strings of the highest, strongest kites, tied them together, and handed it off to a man who used it to lift him up high—ten points and fourteen points, and higher.

I watched the speech on the floor of the convention. The networks, I was told, had spotters looking for me. I hid behind placards near the Delaware delegation with a congressman who to this day tells people I mouthed the words along with Bush. I don't remember that, but maybe I did. I was in a kind of shock at the beginning, like a soldier approaching shore who knows he's up to the battle but who also is, in some way, suspended.

But I remember an old woman who got up on a chair and began to chant, "Read my lips." I remember the kids who began to sing "Three

Blind Mice." I remember the faces of the people in the hall as they heard the Republican credo—community, dignity, a moral generosity, the statement not only of a man but of a party. And I remember, when it was over, walking by the VIP box in the stands and seeing Mosbacher, who was calling to me and moving his arms. "Out of the park," he was yelling, "Out of the damned damn park!"

There was a big party later where Lee Atwater would play his guitar, but instead I walked through the streets of New Orleans, burned off the excitement, went back to my room and to bed.

The next morning as we left New Orleans, the vice president called me up to his cabin. The Quayles were there, and Mrs. Bush. Quayle was funny and friendly. He looked like a midlevel executive who'd been plucked from the bowels of the corporation and, to his astonishment, been appointed CEO; he gripped the armrests to keep from floating.

Bush asked how I felt. I said relieved—this morning for the first time in weeks I didn't have the tic in my right eye.

You had a tic?

Yeah, the first time I ever got one. Didn't you notice at meetings, my eye jumping?

No, I thought you were winking at me.

He squinches up his face and winks like an uncoordinated person, laughs, snaps his napkin, and digs into breakfast: yogurt, with a sprinkling of granola. Next stop, Huntington, Indiana, and the beginning of the campaign.

EIGHTEEN

Hydroplaning

Garrrruuuuuuuuuuuuuuuuummmmmmmmmmmmmmmmmmm.
Garrrruuuuuuuuuuuuuuuuummmmmmmmmmmmmmmmmmm.
Garrrruuuuuuuuuuuuuuuuummmmmmmmmmmmmmmmmmm.

The engines weaving in and out; the air-conditioned hum; the soft murmurings of power: I'm flying.

I look down at the tiny houses and tiny pools, see a toy car make its way down a toy road and wonder, again: What does it do to your perspective to spend so much time looking out a window where everything that is real is small and you and your friends, the men up here above the clouds—are big? What does it do to your judgment to spend so much time where even the mountains are small? America gets lost in the shuffle, lost in the flow; no one ever says "America."

I turn to the others on the banquette. We are in the senior staff cabin of Air Force Two, nicknamed by the secretaries the power cabin, which is next to the vice president's cabin, which is today full of friends and family. It is the day after the election and around me are the wizards of '88, the managers of the Bush campaign. Bob Teeter sits across from me; next to him the secretary of the treasury, long and lanky Nicholas

Brady; nearby is Dick Darman, who will soon head the Office of
Management and Budget; Roger Ailes, the media manager; Jennifer
Fitzgerald, who runs the vice president's Hill office; Margaret Tutweiler, aide to James Baker; and John Sununu, governor of New Hampshire, friend to the vice president and soon to be a president's chief of
staff.

Bluff, gruff and hearty we are as, triumphant, we make our way
north, to Washington, where the vice president will be met for the first
time as president-elect by a crowd that has gathered in his honor at a
hangar at Andrews.

The heady brrrrrr, the heady hummmmmmm.

Garrrruuuuuuuuuuuuuuuummmmmmmmmmmm.

I'm flying; I daydream.

I had worked at home through most of the campaign, to be near my
son. The campaign ran a line to my house and put in a fax. They'd fax
me directions, I'd fax back a speech, but I wanted to be here for the
end, for the last ten days, to experience a national campaign and be
there for Bush's victory. Now it is over, and already I miss the sleeplessness and fear.

"I wake up every hour and lie there saucer-eyed," I told Kathy Smith,
Craig Fuller's secretary, a few days ago, and Jim Baker's eyes flashed
as he walked by. "I wake up every hour on the hour like all-news
radio—bong!" It's not that we think we will lose, or really fear it,
though the pollster has his moments. It's that it's history. It sits there
like a gargoyle on your shoulder and stares at you with agitated eyes.

I keep wondering if people grow addicted to anxiety, physically
addicted to the adrenaline pumped out by fear, if we need it, need the
high.

The alarm pierces the night. In my exhaustion it breaks through, a
howling whine. I sit up, startled, spring out of bed, and scramble toward
the air vent in the corner of the ceiling. I stand at attention and come
awake. There are sounds in the hall, but they are not the sounds of
panic and running. I return to my bed and am falling asleep when a
voice barks from the vent, "We're sorry! The fire alarm was activated
by mistake! There is no fire! Repeat, there is no fire!"

Where am I. I am in California. No, New Mexico. The one after
that. Colorado. A tall hotel in Colorado. This could be a dream.

The next morning we are riding in a staff van behind the vice president's limousine on the way to a rally, when I remember. "Hey, did you all hear an alarm last night?"

Heads shoot up. "Yeah, I forgot." An advance woman says, "I lunged for the phone 'cause I thought it was the wake-up call." The accountant from the campaign says pleasantly, "I just got up and ran around in my underwear like a nut."

We tell sleep stories. Kathy came off the road after eight straight days and had just fallen asleep in her bed at home when she heard something and realized it was an interloper. She screamed. It was her sister. She thought it was the maid.

I forget right now what a campaign looks like from the outside, from the living room, but from the inside it's one long motorcade, a highway in the sun and a long line of limos, cars and vans with flashing lights accompanied by a detail of motorcycle cops moving their arms in graceful arcs. Hurry up. Slow down. Get into this lane. Yesterday and today blend together and you don't know where you've been or where you're going. Disorientation is constant. I come to think of the campaign as a long tube of blue time that is bent here and there by rallies and arrival speeches, all of which go under the name "event," as in, That was a good event, good balloons.

Your friends and family take you seriously and think you talk about issues and policy, but what you talk about is food. First thing they say in the motorcade in the morning after the breakfast speech is, Do we get breakfast on the plane? Second question: Do we get lunch? Third: Where are we going? Fourth: How long a ride to the airport? This is to ascertain if it's worth it to fall asleep.

We take an unspoken pleasure in the mundaneness. It is one of our secrets.

The day before the election at an airfield outside Mansfield, Ohio, we wait aboard Air Force Two for the vice president to return from a rally. Half the top staff is here. They are tired, nervous, up and down. They replay their greatest hits. "We ran a much tougher campaign than '84, much more uphill," and "You know, the longest day of the campaign for me was Iowa, and rewriting that fucking statement in the back of the convertible." An aide says, "Listen, if we hadn't gone in hard back then, we wouldn't win this thing—if we win this thing.

Where do you think we woulda been today if we hadn't gone in hard?"
Silence. "Fourteen points ahead," says another.

Tate on the telephone as the clouds go by. She sits at a table in the
cabin behind the power cabin, her fist rolled around a shiny white
phone. Signal, this is Sheila Tate, can you get me the campaign?
Thanks. Yeah. Hi. Okay. Get to *USA Today* and find out why they
want Bush's statement on why he should be president to be handwritten. Maybe. And maybe they're gonna have somebody analyze his
handwriting. A guy from CNN is getting married, and they want the
vice president to go on camera for an in-house tape congratulating;
we'll do it. And I wanna get him with Meyers of NBC, we told her.
Well, we've got to. Good. Click.

Steve, the head advance man walks by.

"One of your deputies lit up a cigarette near the platform as we
waited for the vice president at the last event."

"So?"

"It is not professional and it is not proper for our people to stand
around smoking in public, and if she worked for me I'd fire her."

"And I'd rehire her." Their eyes lock. He looks away.

We are in the air from there to there and Arnold Schwarzenegger
barrels by. What a wide man. It's hard for men who work out like that
to look elegant in suits. I want to feel his arm and see how hard it is
when it's relaxed. But one can't, can one. I am next to Tate, tapping
notes on a Toshiba.

"And what do yooo girls dooo?"

Beat beat. His big teeth. Poor man's from Europe, how would he
know. "I'm a speechwriter."

"Goot! And you?"

Tate looks at him and turns with a pleasant smile. "I have to go
now," she says.

It's all lie around and sprint, lie around and sprint. You're in the back
of the van with your head thrown back and your mouth open snoring
at the roof, and then you get to where we're going and you scramble
to get out, run to the event, watch the speech, and run back to the van.
The vice president's limo is always in front and always leaves first and

the motorcade follows immediately, and if you're not in, you're out; they wait for no one. Everyone has stories of being left somewhere.

Baggage call is at five or six in the morning, so you have to put out your bags before you go to sleep, first separating everything you will wear or need the coming day. Mistakes are made. That's why the woman over there with the beautifully cut soft wool suit is wearing dirty sneakers and the advance guy has a hair dryer poking out of his trench coat. Once a girl packed her skirt and had to keep her coat on all day.

The people who travel with the vice president call themselves the road warriors. They make up words and have their own language.
"What time you get up?"
"O:dark:30."
"Velcroid at two o'clock with heavy limo bait."
"Roger. We're talking major face time."
A velcroid is a guy on the airport reception line who attaches himself to the candidate and won't let go. Limo bait is what he says to get invited into the vice president's limousine. "I've got the latest on the Iowa poll, but I don't want to bother you." "No no, come on in." Face time is what you get when you're alone with the candidate, right there in his face.

In the back of the plane the press is playing Nose Wheel Bingo. They draw lines on the nose wheel of Air Force Two before it takes off, initial sections, and see which section comes up at the top when the plane lands. The pot gets up in the hundreds of dollars.

People think there is tension or antagonism between the press pool in the back and the operatives up front, but there isn't. A happy skepticism abounds. A few nights before the election a reporter takes the plane's public-address system and reads a spoof of the acceptance speech. "I am that man / Green eggs and ham." Bush offers a sentimental good-bye. "It's been such a long journey, so many twenty-hour days, and there were so many times I'd see you scrambling for a bus in the darkness or shivering in your parkas on a tarmac somewhere at dawn, and I'd think: That's tough. Too bad. It's not my problem. Get a real job. Get a haircut."

This is what we have in common: We are propelled at high speed through each day, propelled by caffeine, sleeplessness, and the push of big events. We are standing in the aisle talking to the network correspondent or we are the network correspondent, our faces are famous or our names, and we are gracious with each other. We are doing things; there is movement in our lives, and a lack of coherence; we are hydroplaning.

Garrrruuuuuuuummmmmmmmmmmmmm.

Why hasn't it changed? Why do the men who do the business of politics always become mice? In New Hampshire and for the acceptance speech I was a visitor. Now I am staff, the old rules pertain, and we are back to form.

Yesterday at the Houstonian I had come upon the wizards rewriting a speech without my knowledge. I walked into a room by accident and saw, immediately, their worst collective look: pugnacious guilt. Like boys caught smoking behind the barn. They size me up as they cough smoke rings in the air. Can Miss Brown really get us in trouble? Or can we tie her to a tree!

The usual argument, this time with the pollster. The media adviser shuffles by. "What are you complaining about" he says. "I have to show my work to focus groups."

"Well that hasn't exactly made things better, has it?" It hasn't exactly ennobled the process. He shrugs and walks on.

Even the last barricade, the speechwriters themselves, has begun to fall. One, a long-haired young man with an Ivy League background, had rushed up to me nights before, a thick wad of paper in his hands. "I've got the verbatims from the latest polling. We can write a new stump off it!"

I look at Darman and say, on impulse, "Individually I find most of you to be likable, poignant, even, sometimes. But in the aggregate I find you to be deplorable." What I mean is, when men in politics are together, testosterone poisoning makes them insane.

He smiles and shakes his head. He has heard me before. Margaret Tutweiler laughs. As I walk into the nonpower cabin, she motions to me. "You call 'em the cabal, but when ah see 'em all together, I just call 'em the baaaaad boys."

I think again of a conversation I'd had weeks ago. I am talking to a friend and wringing my hands: I've been in politics at a significant level for almost five years, I have beliefs that whether right or wrong are truly held, and I'm in the midst of a great campaign, and yet somehow my battles are always with my own side.

And he said, You don't get it, do you? You don't have a side, you're a writer. *You're on the side of your work.* You ought to think about

Orwell: A writer can do anything for his side but write for it. You either take whatever talent you have and let it lead you where it leads you, or you harness it to a political viewpoint and let political considerations decide what you do and do not write, do and do not see. In which case you are a partisan and a polemicist, but not a writer. You have to decide what you are.

NINETEEN

Hail and Farewell

Y ou have to decide. But I knew, really, finally, in my heart. And there was one last thing to do.

Shortly after the acceptance speech the White House called. It is Mr. Duberstein, the president's chief of staff. Can I come and see him? We sit in his office, Don Regan's old office. The last time I was here there was yelling. Now birds chirp, and how do you take your coffee? He asks if I will work this coming January on President Reagan's farewell to the nation. He is pleased at the honor he is offering.

Does the president want me to? It was his idea! Come on. I'm serious, he asked for you personally. I am surprised but yes, of course. And it will be my farewell too, to speechwriting and this time. I will be given something we rarely receive in life, in the world: closure. And I am grateful because yes, it is an honor.

I would work once more with Reagan, my Reagan, and this time I would know him. My mind raced as I drove from West Exec. Reagan was a gift to the country, his farewell should be glorious. Three things will stay in my mind. The beautiful letter Thomas Wolfe wrote to Max Perkins from a hospital bed in Seattle, where he lay dying—"I've made a long voyage and been to a strange country. . . . and I don't think I was too much afraid . . ."—a last letter in that pained and endless friendship. And the scene from John Huston's movie about Toulouse-Lautrec, *Moulin Rouge,* the end, where the showgirls and dandies of the Parisian scene come and dance for him, twirling through the room. And the last words would be Tom's final words to his world, to memories of Laura and the gentleman caller in *The Glass Menagerie*—"And so good-bye. . . ."

I met with Reagan five times that December and January, the two of us and Duberstein and Mari Maseng, the White House director of communications. When I came to the White House, it was to take Mari's speechwriting job; she took OPL when I declined. Now she was running the communications shop and overseeing all the speechwriters. She is quiet, smart, loyal and watchful. I think those times when I am with her that we get along in part because of an interesting dynamic: I am her id. "It was a great campaign," I tell her. "I only threatened to stab Bob Teeter once." Her eyes widen in fear for me, and narrow with delight.

Duberstein is like a character from Dickens, broadly drawn: grinning, winking, snapping out one-liners, a man who lives on energy and cunning, who wants to be liked and not rock the boat and get the job done. He did not come at you like an arrow but enveloped you like a cloud, surrounding you, sometimes making it hard for you to see.

The four of us on five mellow winter afternoons. You know the chairs Reagan used to sit on when you saw him on the news chatting with a visiting head of state? The two white chairs and the fire in the background? That's where we sat. I wasn't down on the couch but up on a chair. So he could hear me, easily.

I am treated like a person of accomplishment. I'd worked for him and worked for the vice president and the work hadn't changed, but the acceptance speech was now famous, and they had read the reviews. And there is something different in me: In two years my curiosity has grown bigger than my awe.

He was at his desk. He came toward us warm as ever; he hardly seemed aged. Does he remember me? I think so but am not sure. He is Reagan: the polite, surprised eyes, the air of sweetness.

I had prepared long lists of questions. I would start with big things and then, as he got used to me, be more personal, elicit a truth, be surprised.

I was to ask, How should Americans think about the Soviet Union in the future, when you're gone? But as we seated ourselves and he made small talk, I thought of Lenin, of a story told by his enemies. His wife's father was dying in their home and one night as she retired, she asked to be awakened if he needed her. In the morning she awoke; her father was dead. "Why didn't you wake me?" she asked Lenin, who had been up reading. "You said to call if he needed you. He died, he didn't need you." It was the kind of story Reagan would have told once, would have embraced as true.

"Mr. President, someone, I think a westerner, once said of Lenin, 'When I looked into his eyes, I could see the gallows, I could see the noose.' You look in Gorbachev's eyes and you don't see that, do you?"

"Why, no." He leans away quickly, shifts in his seat. "After all, he's different. He has a different attitude, different approach, different from Stalin and the others and so forth." Gorbachev is the first Soviet leader who has not restated the idea of one-world Soviet domination, both of us have a frustration with the bureaucracy.

"What of those who say you got soft? You're not sentimental about Communists—"

No. "My views have not changed." He was, remember, "blooded" in the fight against communism, "when I was president of a union, not a country." A story about fighting Communist infiltration in Hollywood. I know it by heart; I can recite it with him.

Other meetings, other talk.

"Mr. President," said Duberstein at the second meeting, "I have been wondering what was the most difficult day you ever had in this office."

He cocks his head and looks at the eyeglasses in his hands. I watch and know: There weren't any difficult days for him.

"Oh well, I don't know. I—" He shakes his head and looks at his hands.

"I have a feeling it may have been the day the marines died in the barracks in Lebanon," offers Duberstein.

"Oh yes." His face is impassive, or sad.

"And the shuttle explosion."

"Oh yes."

"And Grenada."

"Yes."

"The marines in Lebanon and the Grenada invasion happened the same week," says Duberstein.

"Oh yes." Nodding.

I say, "Didn't you have to call the families of the marines the day they died?"

"I met with so many. . . ."

"How does a day like that make you feel? How is that when you're president?"

Silence.

"Well, you feel you are in charge, and they are dead. . . ."

The ticking of the grandfather clock in the corner. I can hear him breathe.

Someone mentions Qaddafi. Reagan comes alive, remembering the Gulf of Sidra. There had been a meeting at which it was discussed what American fighter pilots should do if they're shot at while on maneuvers. "That was the first time I said that if and when our men ever come in any danger, they are going to shoot back. And then someone, a navy captain, I believe, asked, 'What about hot pursuit?' And there was silence for a moment. And then I said, 'All the way into the hangars!' "

Another memory:

"In 1982, in the depths of the recession, I was being urged to include more federal spending and a jobs-service program. Tip O'Neill was here. And there was a sharp exchange right here where we're sitting, and someone on the couch said, 'Ronald Reagan has set a course of disaster,' and 'Let go, Mr. President!'

"And I said, 'But the tax cuts just went into effect last week! We're gonna hang in there and wring out some of these problems we inherited.' " And he did.

When asked about policy, about great events, the answers seem rote. At the third meeting I go to the personal, hoping to get something of outward events from the telling of inward ones.

"Do you ever feel like the boy in the bubble?"

"Who was that?"

"The boy who had no immune system, so he had to live in a plastic bubble where he could see everyone and they could see him, but there was something between him and the people, the plastic. He couldn't touch them."

"Well, no."

"Oh."

Silence.

"I used to wonder, seeing you here and outside, surrounded by the Secret Service, by a human barricade, always something between you and the people . . ."

"No, but there are times when you stand upstairs and look out at Pennsylvania Avenue and see the people there walking by. And if I wanted to run out and get a newspaper or magazine, or just to walk down to the park and back. But, and you miss that, and how long since I could do it. And you miss that, of course."

More on looking out of windows in the residence and the limousine, and seeing the people. What I think I perceive is not a feeling of estrangement but a wistfulness about connection.

"I was born over a bank in Tampico. Then we moved into a house, and then we moved around, Chicago, Galesburg, Monmouth."

"And your father was a shoe salesman."

"Yes, he was for some time. And you know, people think a shoe salesman, but he'd talk to people and they'd come to him and say, 'I'm having this pain here and this problem right over there,' and he would diagnose it and get them the right shoes, and their aches would go away."

I said, "Do you ever remember some people who didn't have money, mothers for instance coming in to get shoes for the kids for school, and they didn't really have the money?"

"Oh yes. And when we could help, we did. We were so poor we ate oatmeal meat. Do you know what that is?"

"No."

"Hamburger and oatmeal. You mix it up and fry it like pancakes. I loved it. I didn't know it meant we were poor, I just loved it."

The thing the old always want to communicate to the young: America was hungrier once, and happier.

"Is it true," I ask, "that throughout your childhood or young adulthood you had a dream that kept coming back, a dream that you lived in a big white house?

"Well, it was like that. The dream was a repetitive dream as an adult that I had. It just kept coming back. And it was that I was going to live in a sort of mansion with big rooms like this one—high ceilings, white walls. And I'd have it over and over. And it was clear to me in the dream that it was a house that was available at a price I could afford. And then I came here to Washington to live in this house, and I haven't had the dream since. Not once."

A house that was available at a price I could afford.

"Mr. President, since we're on 'Irish topics,' I've wanted to ask you: How do you feel about being the first president to break the jinx on presidents elected in a year ending in zero?"

"I'm not sure I understand."

"The jinx that has seemed to follow presidents elected since early last century, that a president elected in a year ending in a zero has a mortal illness or—"

"Well, I think we took our part of that back in '81."

"When Mr. Hinckley . . ."

"Yes."

"Maybe that used up all your bad luck?"

"Well, you know, those chains—everything like that has to be broken at some time. That's what they're there for."

He will not reflect. So many politicians resist introspection, as if they fear that looking back will catch them in webs, their arms pinned to their sides; only look forward! But Reagan takes it farther than most. I want to shake him; I want the long tape of triumph. Where is the anguish that usually comes with greatness?

I'd go into the White House for meetings, sit on a little couch outside Maseng's office, take my notes, and think, Down here, eight yards down the hall, is one president, doing his work at his desk; and right over here, five yards down the hall, is the soon-to-be president, doing his work at his desk. As if it were FDR right down here and Truman down here, Lincoln down here and Johnson here. I would sit straight, and listen. The sounds of an office—a laugh, an overheard hello. History never sounds like history unless it is a war.

As the day of the inauguration approached, there seemed a shifting of gravity. Down the hall toward the Oval Office it seemed darker, and quieter. Down toward Bush it was movement and action and a great whoosh of doors as delegations came and left. A breeziness, a new energy.

When I agreed to work with Reagan, I knew I could not work with Bush. There would be no time; you cannot hear two such different voices in so short a space and do them justice. But when I told Bush he would not take no, made me laugh—"How can I do another speech without you in the corner looking nervous? Just one more and you're free"—and, when I told him I had given my word to Duberstein, Bush bounded into the Oval Office, asked the president if he would mind— "Why, no, George, not at all"—and told me there was no problem.

I had lunch with Bush downstairs in the small senior staff mess. Presidents and vice presidents don't dine in the mess, but Bush likes to. He likes to see everyone and say hello. We sit at the table closest to the door. People would walk in bored, suddenly start at the sight of him, and bound over with hearty hellos. Kathleen Kennedy Townsend, at lunch with the speechwriter Tony Dolan, hands a camera to a friend, comes over, and stands with Bush to have her picture taken. She is as excited as a tourist.

Bush is humorous and hungry. It is the first I've seen him since the election.

What does it feel like to be the next president? Does it feel different?

Oddly enough, no. He is mildly disappointed. "You find other people treating you a little different when you get out of a car or something. And some friends you don't know all that well. But otherwise, no. You know with me it's all friends and family, and we've got enough of 'em, we're all so close, that it's hard to feel different."

He pauses. "You know, it *is* something . . . only forty-one guys who've done it."

"Forty-one out of hundreds and hundreds of millions of Americans in our history."

"But you know, I haven't put myself among the forty-one yet. Maybe in part it's that I've been here eight years, I've been on the inside, I know what happens in there, so I'm not awed. . . ."

"Have you had any dreams that reflected the presidency coming? Any new anxiety in your dreams, or joy? Abe Lincoln putting his hand on your shoulder and saying, 'Do good, George'?"

He laughs but is interested, shakes his head. "Not at all, oddly enough."

He is what his staff calls the new George Bush: funny, lanky, comfortable with himself. This is not the tragedy of the man who got what he wanted, this is an affirmation of ambition: He was right to want it, and he's going to be good. He takes out notes on what he wants in his inaugural address and reads them to me.

The food comes—it is Thursday, Mexican Special day, and he has

ordered a big plate of nachos. He eats bent over the dish, holding the
napkin against his chest so he won't soil his tie. Like a big teenage boy,
unembarrassed by hunger.

I walk to my car on West Exec, see a man I'd dated long ago and
far away; home to my son, to dinner and television and books.

It is very unfeminist of me and perhaps I shouldn't say it, but perhaps
there is a wider truth here. People ask me, Do you ever get crushes on
the men you work with? And the truth, which I usually find ways not
to say, is yes, often, don't you? All these men and women running
around America in their gray suits in the boardroom, in the television
commercials where the woman in the meeting utters the topper: I
think they're all half in love with each other and have trouble recognizing it, never mind admitting it, because it is potentially dangerous, and
awkward, or painful, never mind politically incorrect. (The last time we
talked about this in America was when we debated whether male cops
should have female cops as their partners, to which it seems to me the
only answer is "Yes, if you want them to fall in love" because they will,
driving through a dangerous world in the darkness. They're just a more
obvious version of the rest of us who are relying on close colleagues of
the opposite sex to protect and support us as we pursue shared objectives, the first of which is: survival.) And the only thing to do, because
men and women are going to keep working side by side, is: take that
tension and turn it into creativity. Harness that electricity, turn it into
the TVA. Or, rather, tenant ownership of public housing. Thank you.
(And the language ought to catch up. "Crush," what a word for what
happens between men and women at work, in the eighties, in the new
world.)

Another meeting with Reagan. "So because you're so dazzling and
the president of the United States and you're Ronald Reagan—do you
ever have people come in here and when they shake your hand they
think, I'm touching *him!*, and they get so excited they forget to let go?"

He laughs. "Well yes, there is that sometimes. But you know, one
of the ways I deal with it is—here." He puts out his hand.

"I take it like this." He places his hand in mine, pressing close into
the groove of my thumb. He holds firmly, shaking up, down, up, down,
squeezes firmly once more before letting go and withdrawing.

"That way you get 'em nice and firm and they can't squeeze. But there's always someone, and usually it's a little old lady with gray hair, about four feet tall, who grabs your fingers and just squeezes for dear life!"

"I guess you can't lift your foot and push 'em away."

He laughs. "You can't shoo 'em away."

It was our last meeting. I had told Mari of an odd question I wanted to ask. It would take time to set up but it might lift a curtain. She listened and said, "Do it if you want, but I don't think it will give you what you're looking for."

But for once I knew she was wrong.

The fire crackled; our time was almost done, the conversation running down. I leaned forward.

"Mr. President, there was once a wonderful movie starring Jimmy Cagney that won the Academy Award in 1942 I think, *Yankee Doodle Dandy.* The story of George M. Cohan."

"Oh yes." His eyes are warm with interest.

"And in this movie at the very end you may remember a lovely scene in which Cagney-as-Cohan is called into the White House to receive their version of the Medal of Freedom. And it's a beautifully played scene, remember? The actor who played FDR is warm and so complimentary, and Cagney is so moved, and he says, 'My mother thanks you, my father thanks you,' and they shake hands and Cagney leaves—"

He nods, remembering. His eyes shine.

"—Cagney leaves FDR's office and gets to the big marble stairs over there in the residence, and he starts to dance down the stairs. Just out of joy he dances all the way down and goes out to Pennsylvania Avenue, where he joins some soldiers who are marching singing, 'Over There.' "

"Oh yes. I remember."

"Mr. President, I have always had a hunch that movie had a special resonance for you, that the fellow playing FDR had something to do with how you conducted yourself in the presidency—that people came in here and you put them at their ease and thank them for their country for their accomplishments. And I've seen it, by the time you were done with them, they wanted to dance down the stairs."

"Oh, well." He is modest and pleased.

"You were moved by the movie."

"Oh yes."

"And it made an impression, and—was it for you unforgettable?"

"Yes." He is eager.

I leaned in.

"Why, Mr. President?"

"Because no one knew Jimmy Cagney could dance."

From the couch a muffled choking sound. It is Mari, laughing. Duberstein too laughs.

I look at the president, who is remembering. "No one imagined him as a dancer, that was the surprise. Up till then in the movies, you know, he'd played convicts and criminals and so forth. But he started, you know, as a dancer."

"A Broadway hoofer."

"A hoofer, yes, on the boards."

The serious things he said wound up in the speech. The lighter things, the attempt to elicit some kernel of unknown information, yielded little. I would never know him, but now I thought I knew why. He did not need to be known. He did not need to ease his loneliness, if that is what he had.

Reagan had had strong feelings about the speech, and at the end there had been trouble. They'd put a "tight hold" on it. Only a handful would review it but one, the head of NSC—why is it always NSC, what is in the air conditioners there?—had read it and declared it "flighty." Flighty, my my, what an interesting word for a big man in epaulets to use about a speech written by a woman. I read it over. This is a serious document, what is he talking about? I told Mari maybe I should talk to him and tell him, Listen, I don't tell you how to invade Grenada and you don't tell me how to write speeches. Instead we had meetings, and the speech was cut and changed.

We had gone through many drafts, and at the end the president had the speech he wanted. I had been thinking of a majesty made of magnanimity. Your presidency was a gift, be big, and being big, in part, is talking about what you didn't do or couldn't do. Perhaps speak of the people in the cities whose intractable poverty we could not touch, talk about how to touch it in the future. He listens and nods, but when I write a regret he reworks it, and it becomes an assertion. His attitude: Claim your successes and call them what they are, proclaim.

We had a quick meeting in the Oval Office. Everyone knows your successes, I told him. If we recite them and insist on them, people will lean away—there's a tropism to a speech—but if you make your claims and then talk about the things you wish you'd gotten done, they'll lean toward you, and supply the encomiums on their own. The people are generous.

"I hope you don't mind that I'm blunt," I said.

"And I hope you don't mind that I'm stubborn," he replied.

"Well you are the president, sir, and this is your speech."

"That's right," he said, pleasantly.

He smiled. We shook hands and parted. I turned for a last look. He was walking toward the desk. He gave me a little wave. Like James Tyrone, only with Reagan the insistence wasn't anguished but sunny, no dark soliloquies. There was a childlike quality to his robust self-regard, an innocence even to his sin.

I watched the farewell in the Oval Office. The agent Tim McCarthy was there, and Edmund Morris, the president's biographer, leaning against the wall, taking notes in his small, careful hand. Mari and I sat near the president's desk, but I knew I couldn't sit still for twenty minutes, and moved to the back.

My heart is racing. Something is ending.

". . . I've spoken of the shining city all my political life, but I don't know if I ever quite communicated what I saw when I said it. But in my mind it was a tall, proud city built on rocks stronger than oceans, windswept, God-blessed, and teeming with people of all kinds living in harmony and peace—a city with free ports that hummed with commerce and creativity, and if there had to be city walls the walls had doors, and the doors were open to anyone with the will and the heart to get here. . . .

"And how stands the city on this winter night? More prosperous, more secure, and happier than it was eight years ago. But more than that: After two hundred years, two centuries, she still stands strong and true on the granite ridge, and her glow has held steady no matter what storm—

"And she's still a beacon, still a magnet for all who must have freedom, for all the pilgrims from all the lost places who are hurtling through the darkness, toward home. . . ."

"And so, good-bye."

The farewell was January 11. On the twelfth I gathered together the vice president's notes, spoke to him and his staff, and began work on the inaugural. Bush knew what he wanted: Begin with a prayer, maintain a gentle tone, a section on bipartisanship, a plea for unity—"The people did not send us here to bicker."

Quick work, in to Bush on Sunday the fifteenth. No dramatic or portentous statements, neither John Kennedy nor John Wayne. A man who does not choose to talk like that is here. He will be low-key, direct, domestic. More conferences, input from Sununu, Darman, and Teeter, late nights. I am, at the end, the kind of tired that makes you feel brittle as a stick. And I am not a speechwriter anymore.

I watched the inauguration from a spectators' gallery, surrounded by people I did not know and had never seen. On days like this people in politics bring everyone they know, as if to say, This is what I do.

The Capitol was arrayed in flags and bunting. Such magnificence and panoply! A chorus sang, two dozen men and women in white and red robes.

In time, as I listened to the songs, I was swept by a longing. It was the words, and the tug of the old songs that we never really hear anymore.

"*I have seen Him in the watchfires of a hundred circling camps . . .*"

And Dixie, which is not, as the chorus sings it, a martial song, but a gentle song of yearning:

"*Den I wish I was in Dixie, hooray, hooray! In Dixie Land I'll take my stand, To live and die in Dixie . . .*"

Such thick-lunged longing. Their voices are rich and deep. Some Cohan—"Grand Old Flag"—and then,

"*Oh Shenandoah, I long to hear you . . .*

I catch my breath.

"*Away you rolling river . . .*"

A love song whose object of desire is our beloved country. I look at my mother, who sits at my side. Such an odyssey. I am here in this wonderful place on this wonderful day. The happiness and lack of meaning make me cry.

I bow my head and look at my hands. It is the distance between the grandeur of old history and the thinness of the daily endeavor, the thinness of what we do as we do the business of history day by day.

The music becomes martial, the caissons go rolling along, I stare at the sky and imagine. A crack, a thump in the chest—my shoulders heave. The winter sky widened and revealed another panoply, and the caissons rolled, lumbering over the clouds, over the capital, over and back, and they were all there, all the old boys, Rough Riders, bonus marchers, doughboys and cowboys, caissons and covered wagons bumping and bouncing, motorcades gliding, eliding, ticker tape tumbling. General William Booth led a big brass band through a cumulus cloud, and Lee galloped through the wilderness surrounded by the boys of the Texas Division—"We won't go on unless you go back!"

The air filled and sang, jubilant, billowing. All the old boys—plutocrats, democrats, Indians and trappers, presidents, pollsters, and riverboat gamblers, preachers and teachers from flat-caked plains states, and children in from the fields. . . .

A Rough Rider stopped and looked back:

"Don't be sad, it's life! The heave and the haul, it's life, it just keeps rolling. You know what he said—'Hate on and love on for unrepining hours . . . our souls / Are love, and a continual farewell'!"

And he threw back his head, waved his sword, and moved on.

My mother is speaking. You're so quiet. What are you thinking? Nothing. A Rough Rider is quoting Yeats. We look at each other and laugh. I do what writers do, taking notes on what I'm seeing. And so it disappeared.

Bush gave the speech in a forceful voice, the shields of the Tele-PrompTer vibrating slightly in the wind. He reached the end:

"Some see leadership as high drama and the sound of trumpets calling; and sometimes it is that. But I see history as a book with many pages . . .

"The breeze blows, a page turns, the story unfolds—a small and stately story of unity, diversity, and generosity, shared and written together."

It was a quiet speech, and we left quietly, a big silent throng of us wafting from the Capitol and taking the broad avenues. Suddenly above us there was a great booming sound and a wind. It sounded like Vietnam.

We stopped and looked up. "It's Reagan's helicopter," said a woman. "It's Reagan leaving," I said to my mother, and we stood and waved and hoped that he saw.

EPILOGUE

Most of the people I knew in the Reagan administration have left government. They practice law, work for securities firms, went to the think tanks or into private consulting. Pat Buchanan writes his column and books with the same glee and passion. He holds a special place in the conservative community in Washington, respected for his integrity and turned to for advice: He's been through the wars. He would be surprised to know that when new kids come to town, young conservatives, when they see him across the room at a reception, their eyes go wide: He is, prematurely, one of the grand old men of the movement. Dick Darman is head of the Office of Management and Budget, where his work contributes daily to what will no doubt be said when they review his thirty years—brilliant, and important. Mr. Regan's still bouncing the globe, making deals and showing up on TV now and then; his friends really love him. Ronald Reagan is rich and happy in Bel Air; they say he doesn't miss the presidency. When people come to his home, he likes to answer the door himself and surprise them.

Ben removed himself from the scene. After Kemp's campaign folded he began writing speeches for conservative intellectuals, and Ollie. The trauma of the end of his Reagan years made him skeptical not only of politics and power but of his own ambition. The other day he gave a speech himself—on how you can lose your soul in Washington, and how you can try to get it back. His friends love him too. The mice went into lobbying, and insurance.

There were other changes. Richard and I separated and, after living in Georgetown for a while in a wonderful old Victorian that leaked from the ceilings (one block from the famous P Street House of Hiss-Chambers fame, next door to where Jack and Jackie lived when they first wed. My landlord there is in her eighties, a writer, a lovely liberal Democrat; when I open her books, tracts she wrote attacking Lyndon Johnson's conservative critics flutter to the floor), my son Will and I returned to New York, to family and old friends. I realize what I had not fully realized: In my five years in Washington I had kept, by phone, as my best friends my old New York crew who, like New Yorkers, responded to the news that I was returning, changing my life utterly, with, Of course you are. As if they had known all along. (My friend Terri came down from CBS after the breakup and said, "Are you going to stop wearing barrettes now?" I stopped the Jeep and threw them out the window.) At the end, when I traveled with the Bush campaign, I was so happy when we went to a New Jersey town or to Queens that the secretaries would call back in the van when the schedule came out, "Peggy, we're going to a neighborhood!" Richard and I had lived in quasi-rural Virginia, and oh I longed for places with more people than squirrels, for Jewish delis and diners, for yiz. I hungered for kin.

It is hard to write about the end of a marriage. The spirited arguments continued, and in time were not so spirited. There were things that were not right when we began, but I thought that with the propinquity and enforced intimacy of marriage, with the force of its ties, that they would get better, or not matter, or other satisfactions would take their place. I did not know that marriage doesn't make some essentials better; you'd better go in with them strong, because marriage will pull at them and tug. The Washington life didn't make it easier. I didn't want to do the room in tandem; I didn't want to do the room.

But from our disharmonious union came a son who was born happy. Children remind you that happiness is the natural state; we forget. He thinks grown-ups were put here to make him laugh, and runs to them with expectation. When he was an infant he rarely cried when strangers picked him up, and gurgled with delight at whoever came along. For a while we called him Reagan. The other night he made his first verbal tease. I was putting him to bed, and we went through the ritual—good night, ni' ni', I love you, ni'. As I walked away I threw back a final "Good night, Will." He answered with a soft and tender "Goodni', peepee!" When he was christened the priest, a man who knew his parish, said, "And now you can go on to become a senator or congressman," but I think it's clear from his attitude toward those in power that he has the makings of a journalist.

ANOTHER EPILOGUE

(Well, at least it's epiloguesque)

It is autumn 1989, and what is happening in the Soviet bloc is, simply, astonishing. Communism is crumbling and everyone—Dan Rather and Ronald Reagan, Ken Duberstein and Paul Weyrich, all the conservative activists and liberal news producers, all the columnists left and right—is dazzled, and happy, and moved. We have been taken aback by history. When the children rose up in Tienanmen Square, quoted Jefferson and sang, "We Shall Overcome," I called a former speechwriter, a Democrat who had put in his years writing about freedom. "How do you feel?" he said.

"Wordsworth. 'Bliss was it in that dawn to be alive / but to be young was very heaven.'"

"I know," he said. "It's been in my mind all day."

Now the Berlin Wall is falling and the poet is Yeats: "Surely some revelation is at hand / Surely the Second Coming is at hand." My mother watched as the young people attacked the wall with pickaxes, and said, "I never thought I would live to see this day in my life." Aunt Peggy came over to watch the news with us and said, "Do you think the Virgin Mary said this at Fatima?"

The last time I worked with Ronald Reagan I thought he was wrong to gamble on Gorbachev. They used to say in the Nixon White House when RN became captivated by an idea or a person, "The boss is in love." That's what I thought about Reagan and Gorbachev. But now, it seems, Reagan was right. His trust in the future, his sunny belief that change, big change, was possible—the very things that occasionally infuriated the young of his administration—turn out to have been appropriate to the times. Sometimes the shrewdest thing is to not be too skeptical, not be too "wise."

When historians write of these days, some will suggest Reagan had little to do with it. They will be wrong. It would not have happened this way without him. He was the strong man of the West who told the Soviets he would not stop talking, would not stop building, until they changed. When he faced down Gorbachev at Rejkjavik it may have been a turning point. And perhaps Reagan's resolve gave Gorbachev something to go home with to the Politburo. Now he could say, "The man is immovable, and the West will not change. Perhaps we'll have to find another way." Perhaps Reagan's toughness gave Gorbachev an out, the excuse he needed to do what he wanted to do. You have to wonder what they said to each other in all that private time they had together at their last summit in Washington. I wonder if it will ever get told. Reagan liked Gorbachev, you can see it all in that picture of the two of them in a hallway in the White House, both of them looking at their watches in mock exasperation as they waited for their wives. I think of them alone together; it's one of the few times you wish there were still tapes in the Oval Office.

We are entering, I think, an antirhetorical age. There seems a rhythm to such things. FDR's great oratory was followed by that of the more prosaic Truman, Churchill in time by the less rhetorically compelling Eden and MacMillan.

Ronald Reagan spent the eighties reminding us of things we used to know and had forgotten, and telling much of the world what it didn't quite know and might find useful. Across the ocean, Margaret Thatcher spent her first two terms talking about something that hadn't been talked about much in Britain: freedom. Now she manages the changes made possible by her early persuasiveness. Reagan found high rhetoric congenial. Bush does not. He is less inclined to move people through words, more inclined to change things, quietly, through deeds.

The eighties marked a revolution in thought, a re-finding of old truths. Ronald Reagan, like Franklin Roosevelt, led a domestic realignment. The attitude of the American people toward government (you don't want it too big) and taxes (you don't want them too big either) has changed. He changed them.

He was a giant; some of us left him disappointed. But then we wanted so much. We brought him our unfocused creativity, our yearning to break through, and wanted him to be like us when he wasn't. We wanted him to be young. We wanted him to be a new-style conservative, engaged by the poor and moved by those trying to belong. But he wasn't. He believed in old-style ideas—bow to a bully and you encourage him; love liberty, yes, but celebrate license and you'll make society worse, not better. He held to these views when they were not esteemed, and when, through the seventies, his ideological enemies failed, the public turned to him with trust. As he knew they would. And he went to live in the house that was available at the price he could afford, and proved the public right.

What did I learn in my time in government?

If you join government, calmly make your contribution and move on. Don't go along to get along; do your best and when you have to—and you will—leave, and be something else.

Don't fall in love with politicians, they're all a disappointment. They can't help it, they just are.

Beware the politically obsessed. They are often bright and interesting, but they have something missing in their natures; there is a hole, an empty place, and they use politics to fill it up. It leaves them somehow misshapen.

If you must be with them, consider this. There are, I think, two kinds of serious political activist: those who are impelled by love, and those who get their energy from hate. The ones moved by love—for America, for the poor, for freedom—often contribute to the debate. Those moved by hate—for liberals, for conservatives, for the rich, for America's sins—make the process ugly. They cannot engage in honorable debate because they cannot see the honor on the other side. They are like diggers who will never reach the treasure because they're too busy throwing the contents of their shovels at each other to get to the gold.

Beware the rich, who are overrepresented in politics. I know it's not polite, I know class antagonism is distressingly retro, but the problem with the rich in America is that they are often embarrassed by their affluence, ashamed they have more (ashamed they want more!). They believe, as the born-in-affluence director Oliver Stone had Gordon Gekko say in *Wall Street*, "It's a zero-sum game." Meaning if I have more, someone else has less. They do not know that wealth can be created. They think there is a set amount that doesn't change, and their ability to pay with ease for *escargots* means a working-class mother in Kearny, New Jersey, cannot buy Keds for the kids.

Those who have inherited their money—and these are the ones who have time to go into politics—are the most difficult cases of all, for they don't have a clue what you do to make money, but they're sure whatever it is it must be bad, because that's how the family fortune was born. (You know why I think Ted Kennedy has historically supported raising your taxes? Because old Joe was a bootlegger and a Hollywood buccaneer. He thinks all wealth is tainted and all rich men thieves, and he doesn't mind hurting them to help the poor. Unfortunately he didn't hurt them—or himself—he hurt the middle class.) (Well all right, maybe all rich men *are* thieves, but this is a problem better addressed by, say, the archbishop of Canterbury, the Lubavitcher rebbe and the pope than the senator from Massachusetts.)

The rich think people hate them. They're partly right, but not for the reason they think. I think people are more skeptical of them than anything else because they know the rich are totally out of touch with the real desire of the nonrich, which is to get rich. And the rich are in their way. Not because they have so much money but because they assuage their anxiety by creating costly programs for which the nonrich foot the bill; so they can't get ahead. The nonrich also notice that the rich man's tax hike was long accompanied by the rich man's tax shelter, which doesn't amuse them at all.

When you meet the rich in politics, tell them that when it comes to economic justice, growth is all, and growth doesn't come from noblesse oblige, thank you very much.

And: for all this, America is still wide open. You can come here from anywhere and do anything. This is the truest and most moving cliché in mankind's political history. One of those boat people rocking the hard seas of the seventies: one of their children will be president in the next century.

I often think of something a British writer said in the magazine *The Economist:* "In America they call waiters sir." Yes, we do. This is the fairest place there ever was, it's wide open, and no one has cause for bitterness.

INDEX

Agee, James, 261
Ailes, Roger, 307, 319
Allen, Fred, 158
Allen, Woody, 102
Anderson, Marty, 166
An Wang, 83
Arden, Elizabeth, 277
Astor, Nancy, 276
Atwater, Lee, 113, 295–96, 317
Auden, W. H., 211

Baker, Howard, 245, 246, 248
Baker, James, 34, 42, 43, 46, 50, 122,
    135, 150, 158, 168, 169, 171, 180,
    186, 187, 190, 195, 198, 202, 213,
    313, 314, 316, 319
Baldrige, Malcolm, 94
Baldrige, Margaret, 94
Barrymore, Ethel, 314
Bate, Walter Jackson, 73
Bauer, Gary, 175, 241–44
Beatty, Warren, 142
Beckwith, Charlie, 175

Belli, Terri, 32
Benét, Stephen Vincent, 73, 231
Bennett, William, 42, 58, 98, 182–83
Benny, Jack, 142
Berry, Chuck, 110
Biden, Joseph, 4, 312
Block, John, 174
Board, Elizabeth, 210
Booth, John Wilkes, 97
Booth, William, 337
Borges, Jorge Luis, 205
Bork, Robert H., 213, 244
Bradlee, Ben, 96
Bradlee, Sally, 96
Bradley, Omar, 22
Brady, James, 28, 29, 38
Brady, Nicholas, 318–19
Breslin, Jimmy, 11
Broder, David, 201, 202
Brodsky, Joseph, 313
Brokaw, Tom, 139
Brooks, Albert, 285
Brooks, Preston, 105

Brown, Edmund G. "Pat," 288–89
Bryan, William Jennings, 69
Buchanan, Pat, 91, 164, 174–75, 207–13, 220, 223, 228, 231, 235, 238, 239, 255, 256, 277, 281, 283, 285–86, 289, 290–91, 292–93, 310, 339
Buckalew, Judi, 53
Buckley, William F., Jr., 14, 164
Burdett, Winston, 18
Burke, Edmund, 250–51
Bush, Barbara, 278, 302–3, 304, 317
Bush, George, 25, 43, 55, 65, 109, 130, 143, 178, 183, 295, 296, 297, 298, 299, 300, 301, 302, 303–4, 305, 306, 307, 308–9, 310, 312, 315, 316, 319, 321, 322, 330–32, 335–36, 337
Byrd, Robert, 245

Cagney, James, 157, 203, 333–34
Caine, Michael, 273
Calero, Adolfo, 235
Calhoun, John, 231
Cannon, Jimmy, 11
Capote, Truman, 177
Capra, Frank, 116
Carlucci, Frank, 246, 248
Carson, Jack, 155
Carson, Johnny, 18, 142
Carter, Jimmy, 50, 54, 90, 91, 92, 124, 150, 170, 179, 187, 270, 276
Casey, William J., 3–4, 235
Castro, Fidel, 126, 127, 238, 267
Chafee, John H., 258
Chamberlain, Neville, 275
Chambers, Whittaker, 96
Chancellor, John, 140, 240
Chayefsky, Paddy, 250
Chissano, Joaquim, 247, 249
Church, Frank, 26
Churchill, Winston, 128, 216, 275, 284, 344
Clark, William P., 166, 169, 265
Clifford, Clark, 91
Clift, Eleanor, 90
Clines, Francis X., 128, 199
Cohan, George M., 157, 333

Collingwood, Charles, 22
Colson, Charles, 202, 237
Coolidge, Calvin, 187
Cooper, Gary, 259, 287
Cooper, Rocky, 259
Copland, Aaron, 228
Cosby, Bill, 137
Costello, Frank, 142
Crisp, Donald, 161
Cromwell, Thomas, 296
Cronkite, Walter, 21, 24, 26, 27, 28
Cruz, Arturo, 235
Cuomo, Mario, 66, 310–11, 314

Daniloff, Nicholas, 244
Darman, Richard, 33, 34–35, 60–61, 63–64, 65, 67, 76, 78, 90, 120–22, 131, 138–39, 144–48, 149–50, 166, 180, 186–87, 190, 191, 196, 197, 210, 254, 257, 263–67, 281, 284, 291, 292, 313–14, 319, 323, 336, 339
Darrow, Clarence, 29
Davis, Bette, 62, 288
Davis, Patti, 62, 164, 258
Dean, John, 202, 327
Deaver, Michael, 42, 58, 60, 84, 85, 86, 88, 89, 98, 110, 144, 149–50, 163, 164, 168, 169, 170, 177, 197, 198, 200, 213, 226, 238, 239, 287
Dickens, Charles, 70, 326
Dixon, Jeane, 291
Dolan, Tony, 87, 187, 331
Dole, Elizabeth, 285
Dole, Robert, 182, 295, 296
Donaldson, Sam, 181, 206, 294
Donovan, Ray, 119
Downs, Hugh, 137
Drake, Sir Francis, 257
Drew, Elizabeth, 243
Drury, Allen, 114–15
Duberstein, Kenneth, 244, 246, 325, 326, 327, 331, 334, 343
Dukakis, Michael, 71, 107, 250, 298, 300, 301, 304–5, 307, 308, 309, 315
Dunlop, Becky Norton, 175
Dunning, Bruce, 38

Eden, Anthony, 344
Edwards, Douglas, 22, 28
Ehrlichman, John, 289
Eisenhower, Dwight D., 21, 42, 92, 128, 205, 227
Elliott, Ben, 33–36, 38, 51, 57, 59–61, 65, 67, 70, 72–73, 75, 79, 83, 90, 124, 144–48, 186, 187, 189–92, 194, 195, 197, 198, 199, 207, 210, 212, 218, 220, 229, 230, 231, 235, 236, 253, 254, 257, 273, 276, 277, 281, 283, 284, 289, 290, 292, 293, 297, 339–40
Elliott, Meredith, 253–54

Fellini, Federico, 156
Fenwick, Millicent, 278
Ferber, Edna, 74
Ferraro, Geraldine, 130, 147
Fisher, Paul, 35
Fitzgerald, F. Scott, 11, 155
Fitzgerald, Jennifer, 319
Fitzwater, Marlin, 128, 206
Flynn, Errol, 62, 156
Flynn, Ray, 20–21
Fogelby, Elma, 172
Fonda, Henry, 156
Ford, Betty, 118
Ford, Gerald R., 179, 270, 276
Ford, John, 101
Fox, Michael J., 137
Frank, Barney, 105
Friedman, Milton, 92
Frost, Robert, 258
Fuller, Craig, 109–10, 122, 176, 281, 295, 308, 319
Fuller, Karen, 289

Galbraith, John Kenneth, 14
Gallup, George, 269
Gamble, Doug, 308
Gavin, Bill, 309–11
Gephardt, Richard A., 107
Gilder, George, 105
Gilder, Josh, 281
Gingrich, Newt, 105, 308
Ginsburg, Douglas, 203

Glenn, John, 9, 126
Goldsmith, Oliver, 174
Goldwater, Barry, 269, 270
Goodwin, Richard, 91, 296
Gorbachev, Mikhail, 181, 267, 273–74, 276, 327, 343, 344
Gorbachev, Raisa, 276, 277
Gore, Albert, Jr., 107
Graham, Donny, 113–14
Graham, Katharine, 113, 268
Grant, Ulysses S., 43, 161
Greenfield, Meg, 113–14
Guevara, Che, 126

Haddon, Hal, 142
Haig, Alexander, 158
Haldeman, H. R. "Bob," 212
Hale, Mother, 199
Hamill, Pete, 18
Hamilton, Alexander, 313
Hammett, Dashiell, 103
Hart, Gary, 36, 126, 140–41, 142
Hawks, Howard, 287
Hawthorne, Nathaniel, 53
Head, Edith, 287
Hellman, Lillian, 103
Helms, Jesse, 105, 274–75
Hemingway, Ernest, 11, 103, 116
Hepburn, Katharine, 96
Herblock, 212
Herman, George, 192
Hicks, Louise Day, 20
Higgins, Ann, 171–72, 173, 258, 285
Hinckley, John, 28–30, 330
Hiss, Alger, 96
Hitler, Adolf, 232
Hoffman, David, 166
Holladay, Doug, 53
Hollings, Fritz, 126
Hoover, Herbert, 146
Hopkins, Harry, 96, 289
Horowitz, Michael, 53–54, 122, 213, 281, 307
Hottelet, Richard C., 21
Hudson, Rock, 106–7
Humphrey, Hubert H., 299

Huston, John, 326
Hyde, Henry, 105

Jackson, Andrew, 167
Jackson, Jesse, 107, 126
Jackson, Michael, 34
James, Henry, 149
Jarvis, Gregory, 256
Jastrow, Robert, 245, 247
Jefferson, Thomas, 43, 99, 171, 187,
   343
Jenkins, Jim, 169
John Paul II, Pope, 254
Johnson, Lyndon B., 91, 92, 171, 179,
   182, 187, 309, 330, 340
Johnson, Paul, 99, 105
Johnson, Samuel, 73
Jones, Charles, 258
Jordan, Hamilton, 170
Jouett, Matthew, 43

Kahn, Roger, 87
Kasten, Bob, 307
Kearns, Doris, 91
Kefauver, Estes, 142
Kelly, Grace, 253
Kemp, Jack, 265–66, 292, 295, 297,
   307, 339
Kennedy, Caroline, 58, 141
Kennedy, Edward M. "Ted," 231, 233,
   293, 346
Kennedy, Jacqueline, see Onassis,
   Jacqueline Kennedy
Kennedy, John F., 6, 9, 11, 13, 42, 69,
   72, 91, 96, 114, 127, 133, 142, 171,
   179, 187, 231–33, 237, 246, 261,
   273, 289, 336, 340
Kennedy, Joseph P., 52, 346
Kennedy, Robert F., 9, 12, 299
Kennedy, William, 245
Keynes, John Maynard, 99, 152
Khachigian, Ken, 126, 132, 187,
   212–13
Khedouri, Fred, 54, 166, 281
Khrushchev, Nikita S., 13, 273
Kilgallen, Dorothy, 11
King, Martin Luther, Jr., 11, 69, 251,
   262

Kirkpatrick, Jeane, 4, 99, 127
Kissinger, Henry, 92
Koch, Edward I., 237
Kohl, Helmut, 171
Koppel, Ted, 206
Krauthammer, Charles, 275
Krieble, Bob, 245
Kuralt, Charles, 23

Laffer, Art, 57
Laxalt, Paul, 129, 130–31, 246
Lee, Robert E., 231, 337
Lehrman, Lou, 100
Lenczowski, John, 54, 217
Lenin, V. I., 327
Leon, Richard, 102
Lewis, C. S., 313
Lewis, R.W.B., 293
Liddy, G. Gordon, 237
Lincoln, Abraham, 11, 69, 70, 124,
   164, 171, 173, 177, 178, 179, 249,
   250, 251, 265, 296, 330, 331
Lincoln, Mary Todd, 251
Lindbergh, Charles, 152
Lindsay, Vachel, 136
Long, Russell, 180
Luce, Clare Boothe, 286
Lucky (dog), 177
Lugar, Richard, 146
Luther, Martin, 296
Lynch, Kevin, 33

MacArthur, Douglas, 92
McAuliffe, Christa, 256
McCarthy, Eugene, 299
McCarthy, Joseph, 24, 25, 26
McCarthy, Mary, 308
McCarthy, Tim, 289, 335
McFarlane, Robert C. "Bud," 90,
   115–17, 163, 175–76, 202, 212, 218,
   220, 223–25, 226, 254
McGovern, George, 16, 26, 142
McLaughlin, Anne Dore, 285
MacMillan, Harold, 344
McNair, Ronald, 256
Madison, Dolley, 47
Madonna, 119
Manes, Donald, 106–7

Marshner, Connie, 285
Marx, Karl, 82
Maseng, Mari, 183, 210, 281, 286, 326, 330, 333–34
Matthews, Christopher, 91
Matlock, Jack, 276, 277
Meese, Edwin, 109, 110, 144–46, 166, 168, 169, 171, 180, 213, 242, 265, 287
Menges, Constantine, 235
Merman, Ethel, 194
Metternich, Prince Klemens von, 236
Mondale, Walter, 36, 123, 125–27, 130, 131, 134, 140, 148
More, Sir Thomas, 58
Morris, Edmund, 164, 335
Morrow, Lance, 122
Mosedale, John, 35
Moyers, Bill, 35, 36, 121
Mudd, Roger, 26, 107
Muir, Sandy, 218
Murphy, Gerald, 77
Murrow, Edward R., 22, 24, 31–32

Nader, Ralph, 211
Nathan, Norm, 18
Nation, Carry, 242, 244
Neas, Ralph, 211
Neuhaus, Richard John, 105
Nguyen, Jean, 199
Nields, John W., Jr., 102
Nixon, Richard M., 6, 21, 57, 91, 92, 168, 169, 170, 171, 179, 187, 202, 210, 212, 227, 237, 270, 289, 309, 344
Nofziger, Lyn, 57, 169, 265
Noonan, Cookie, 6
Norquist, Grover, 103, 245, 247–49
North, Oliver, 102, 141–42, 175, 235, 236–37, 239, 244, 246, 339
Novak, Michael, 105, 310

O'Leary, Jeremiah, 239
Olivier, Laurence, 259
Onassis, Jacqueline Kennedy, 6, 96, 161, 233, 340
O'Neill, Dapper, 20

O'Neill, Thomas P. "Tip," 202–3, 236–37, 266, 283, 328
Onizuka, Ellison, 256
O'Rourke, P. J., 219
Ortega, Daniel, 238
Orwell, George, 324
Osgood, Charles, 18, 21
Osmond, Donny, 18
Osmond, Marie, 18

Paine, Tom, 268
Pallodino, Pixie, 20
Pansullo, Jim, 18
Pastora, Edén, 235–36
Pei, I. M., 83
Perkins, Max, 325
Pinkerton, Jim, 309
Plante, Bill, 35
Poindexter, John M., 255, 258
Potter, Deborah, 50
Pound, Ezra, 73–74
Power, Tyrone, 259, 287
Power, Tyrone, Jr., 259

Qaddafi, Muammar, 328
Quayle, Dan, 298, 317
Quayle, Marilyn, 317

Rahn, Will (Noonan's son), 305–6, 340–41
Rather, Dan, 3–4, 21, 27–29, 30–32, 35, 36–37, 38, 51, 139, 208, 209–10, 297, 343
Reagan, Jack, 153
Reagan, Maureen, 62–64, 160–61
Reagan, Nancy, 59–62, 142, 160, 161–65, 193, 198, 200, 202, 206, 212, 229, 256, 261, 264, 266, 303
Reagan, Neil "Moon," 153
Reagan, Nell, 153
Reagan, Ron, Jr., 276
Reagan, Ronald, 3, 4, 26–27, 30, 32, 33, 34–36, 49, 52, 58, 62, 64, 65–67, 69, 72, 81, 83, 89, 90, 92, 98, 99, 100, 104, 107, 112, 118, 120–21, 122, 123, 124, 126, 129, 132–36, 143, 144–48, 149–85, 186, 187, 189–92, 193, 195, 197, 198, 202,

Reagan, Ronald *(cont'd)*
203, 207, 211, 215–16, 222, 231,
237, 240, 241–42, 244, 245, 246,
247, 248, 249, 254, 255, 256–57,
258, 259, 260, 261, 262, 263–71,
273, 277, 280, 282, 286–93, 296,
297, 306, 307, 308, 309, 325,
326–30, 337, 339, 343–45
Regan, Donald, 76, 116–17, 169, 186,
187, 195, 197, 201–14, 229, 239,
244, 266–67, 273, 275, 282, 284–85,
287, 289, 290–91, 294, 325, 332–35
Reich, Otto, 235
Reilly, Bob, 235
Resnik, Judith, 256
Revel, Jean-François, 99, 105
Reynolds, Nancy, 153
Rich, Richard, 58
Ridgway, Matthew, 88
Risque, Nancy, 62, 218
Robelo, Alfonso, 235
Roberts, Nancy, 253
Robertson, Pat, 297
Rogers, Will, 192
Rohrabacher, Dana, 91
Rooney, Andy, 37, 192
Roosevelt, Alice, 97
Roosevelt, Eleanor, 233, 303
Roosevelt, Franklin D., 25, 42, 52, 69,
125, 157, 227, 267, 280, 286, 303,
308, 330, 333, 344
Roosevelt, Theodore, 47, 97, 124
Rosebush, Jim, 59–61
Ross, Dennis, 309
Rossow, Benjamin, 173
Rosten, Leo, 201
Royko, Mike, 313
Rubin, Jerry, 14
Rusk, Dean, 9
Rusthoven, Peter, 64–65
Ryan, Fred, 197

Safire, William, 63, 91, 296, 310, 313
St. Clair, Jim, 227
Salant, Richard, 56
Sandburg, Carl, 258
Savimbi, Jonas, 103
Savitch, Jessica, 107

Sawyer, Diane, 35, 36
Scalia, Antonin, 213
Schieffer, Bob, 26
Schlafly, Phyllis, 47
Schlesinger, Arthur, Jr., 91
Schwarzbaum, Lisa, 17, 18
Schwarzenegger, Arnold, 321
Scobee, Dick, 256
Sears, John, 164
Segretti, Don, 237
Sevareid, Eric, 16, 18, 96, 170
Shakespeare, William, 70
Shales, Tom, 30
Shambra, William, 310
Sharansky, Anatoly, 104
Sherwood, Robert E., 289
Shevardnadze, Eduard, 273, 275
Shultz, George, 89, 173, 174, 212, 218,
258, 273–75
Sidey, Hugh, 201
Siller, Ray, 309
Simon, Howard, 119
Simon, Paul, 107
Sinatra, Frank, 268
Skutnik, Lenny, 198
Small, Karna, 254
Smith, Adam, 99, 245
Smith, Al, 125
Smith, Edgar, 164
Smith, Kathy, 319, 320
Smith, Michael, 256
Sobran, Joe, 33
Solarz, Stephen, 105
Sorensen, Theodore, 72, 91, 187, 221
Sowell, Tom, 265
Speakes, Larry, 50, 66, 128, 129–31,
191, 206, 212, 255
Sprinkel, Beryl, 294
Stahl, Lesley, 35, 148, 166, 210
Stalin, Joseph, 276
Steelman, Deborah, 309
Steffens, Lincoln, 17
Steinem, Gloria, 96, 286
Stockman, David, 122, 166, 174, 176,
190
Stone, Oliver, 346
Strauss, Robert, 237
Sumner, Charles, 105

Sununu, John, 319, 336
Sununu, Nancy, 297
Swanson, Gloria, 162

Talese, Gay, 11
Tarbell, Ida M., 17
Tate, Sheila, 321
Taylor, Robert, 47
Teeley, Pete, 130, 296
Teeter, Robert, 295, 296, 309, 313, 314, 316, 318, 326, 336
Tennyson, Alfred, Lord, 53–54
Teresa, Mother, 150
Thatcher, Margaret, 171, 344
Thomas, Clarence, 265
Thurmond, Strom, 135
Toulouse-Lautrec, Henri de, 326
Townsend, Dallas, 22
Townsend, Kathleen Kennedy, 331
Townsend, Lee, 35
Tracy, Spencer, 243
Travolta, John, 155
Trevor, Claire, 259
Tribe, Laurence, 104
Truman, Harry S, 42, 92, 127, 330, 344
Tutweiler, Margaret, 135, 169, 319, 323
Twain, Mark, 152
Tyrone, James, 335

Updike, John, 289
Uris, Leon, 11

Valenti, Jack, 91, 92
Van Gogh, Vincent, 312–13
Vaughan, Lynn, 19
Vidal, Gore, 134
von Bülow, Claus, 107
von Damm, Helene, 169

Waldren, Agnes, 210
Wallison, Peter, 307
Walther, Huck, 246
Warhol, Andy, 136
Washington, George, 47, 313
Wayne, John, 336
Weinberger, Caspar, 246, 248
Welch, Joseph, 142
Welliver, Judson, 91
Weymouth, Lally, 113
Weyrich, Paul, 244–46, 248, 343
Wharton, Edith, 293
Wheeler, Jack, 103
White, Theodore, 115
Whitman, Walt, 97
Whitmore, Chip, 20
Whittlesey, Faith, 285
Wilder, Thornton, 315–16
Will, George, 164, 201
Williams, Walter, 265
Williams, William Carlos, 95
Windsor, Duke of, 306
Wirthlin, Richard, 123, 190, 246, 249, 282, 283, 284, 295
Woititz, Janet, 153
Wolfe, Thomas, 313, 325–26
Wolfe, Tom, 11, 289
Woodruff, Les, 18
Woods, Rose Mary, 18
Wordsworth, William, 343
Worthshorne, Peregrine, 223–24
Wright, Jim, 105, 237, 245
Wyman, Jane, 259

Yeats, William Butler, 337, 343

Zanata, Lisa, 87
Zirinsky, Susan, 35
Zoellick, Bob, 313

About the Author

PEGGY NOONAN wrote speeches for Ronald Reagan and George Bush from 1984 to 1989. She was previously a producer and writer at CBS News in New York. She lives in New York City.